HISSING

vol. 6

Kang EunYoung

Yen
Press

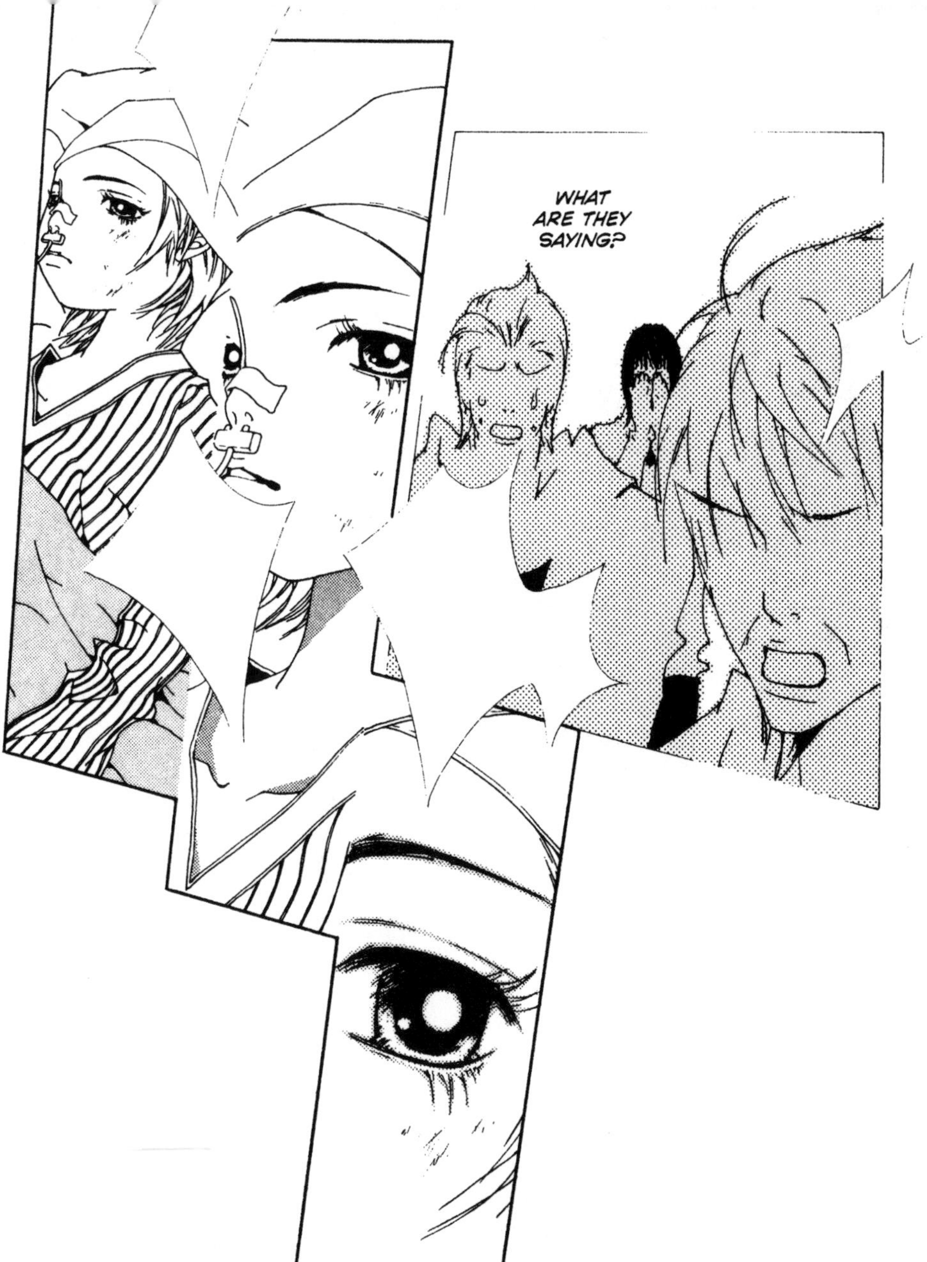
WHAT ARE THEY SAYING?
DAD, BROTHER, AND SISTER ...?

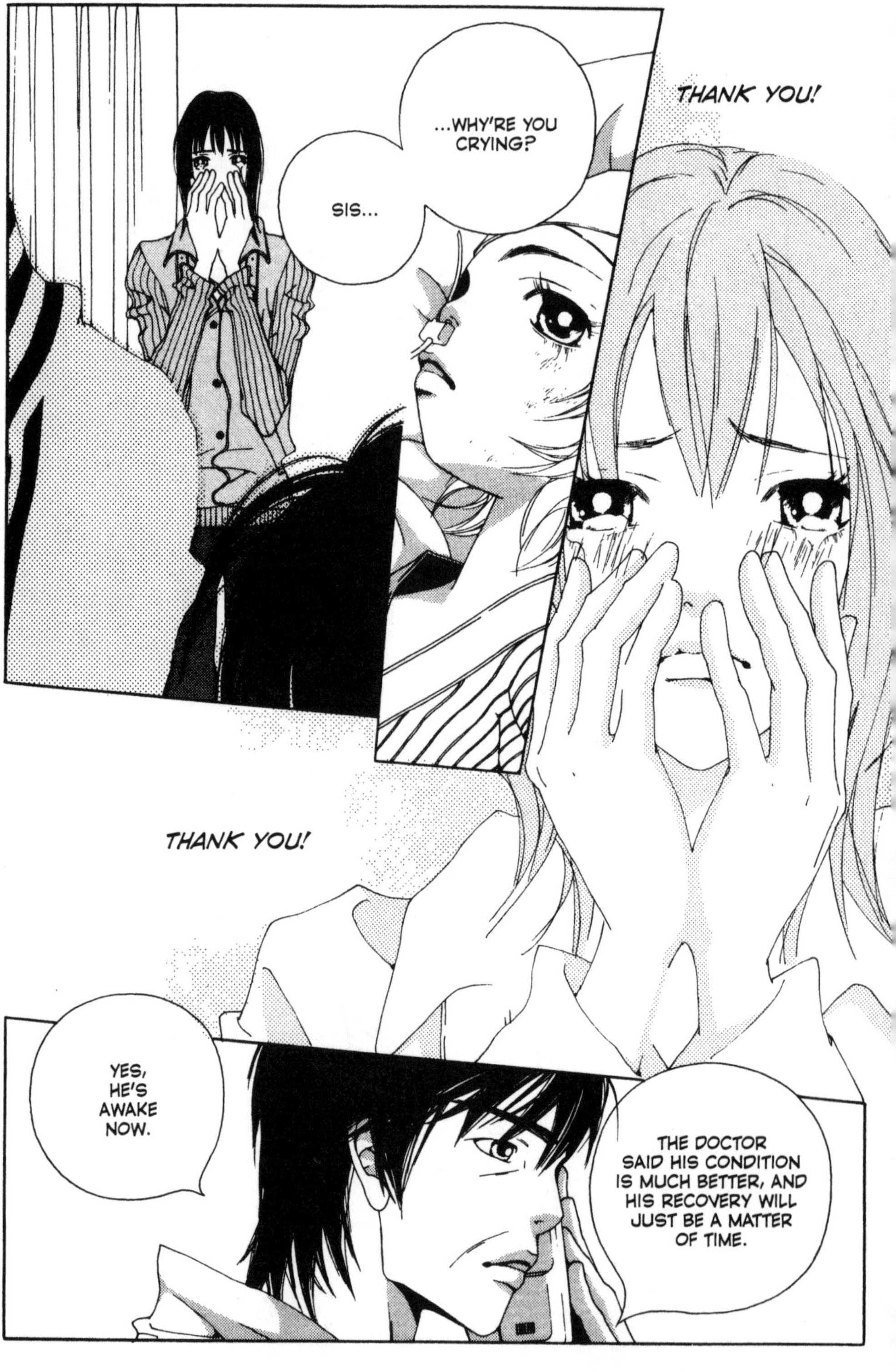
SIS...
...WHY'RE YOU CRYING?
THANK YOU!
THANK YOU!
YES, HE'S AWAKE NOW.
THE DOCTOR SAID HIS CONDITION IS MUCH BETTER, AND HIS RECOVERY WILL JUST BE A MATTER OF TIME.

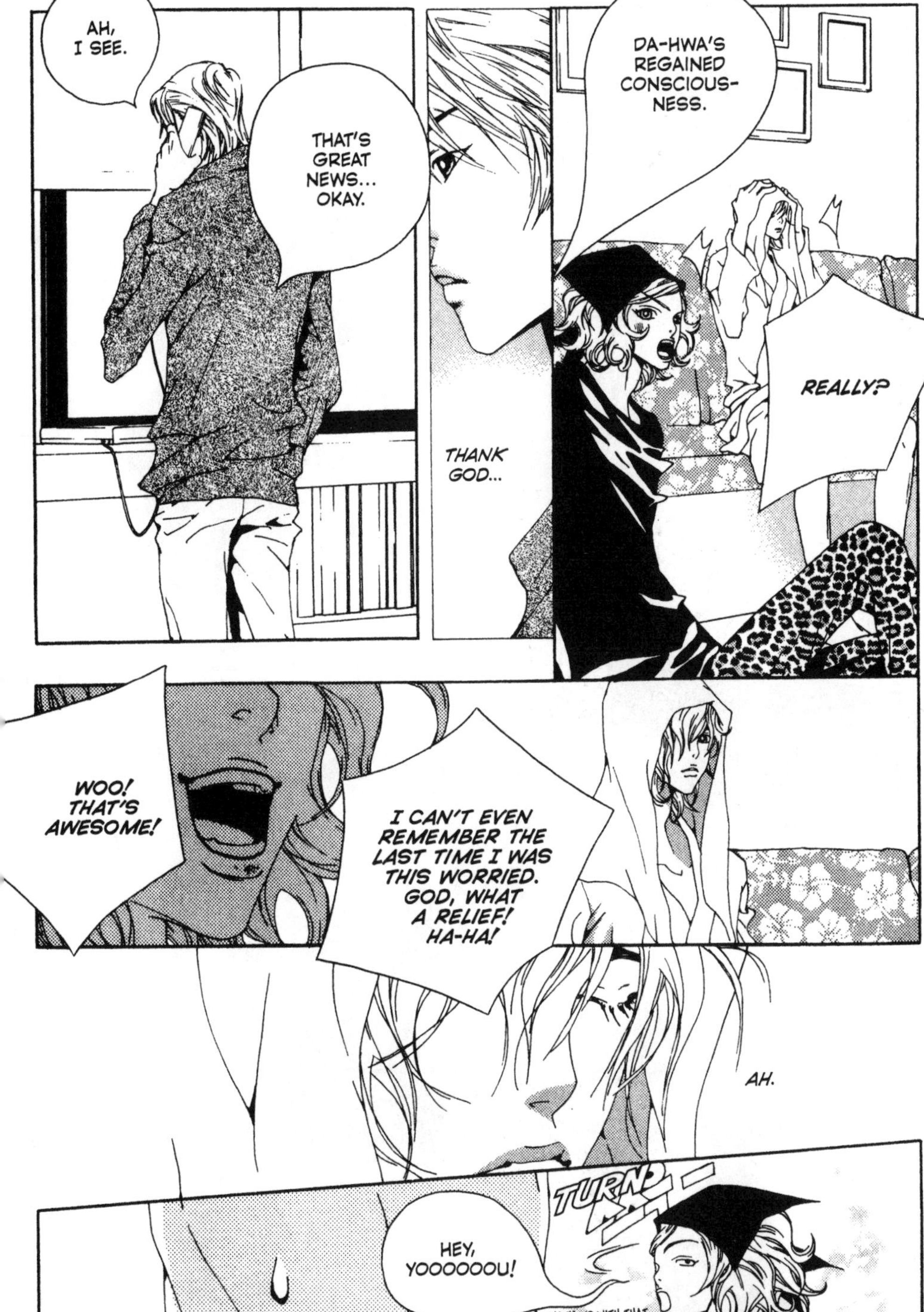
AH, I SEE.
THAT'S GREAT NEWS... OKAY.
THANK GOD...
DA-HWA'S REGAINED CONSCIOUS-NESS.
REALLY?
WOO! THAT'S AWESOME!
I CAN'T EVEN REMEMBER THE LAST TIME I WAS THIS WORRIED. GOD, WHAT A RELIEF! HA-HA!
AH.
HEY, YOOOOOOU!
TURN
WHAT'S UP WITH THAT LOOK AND THAT TONE OF VOICE? STOP IT, WOULDJA?

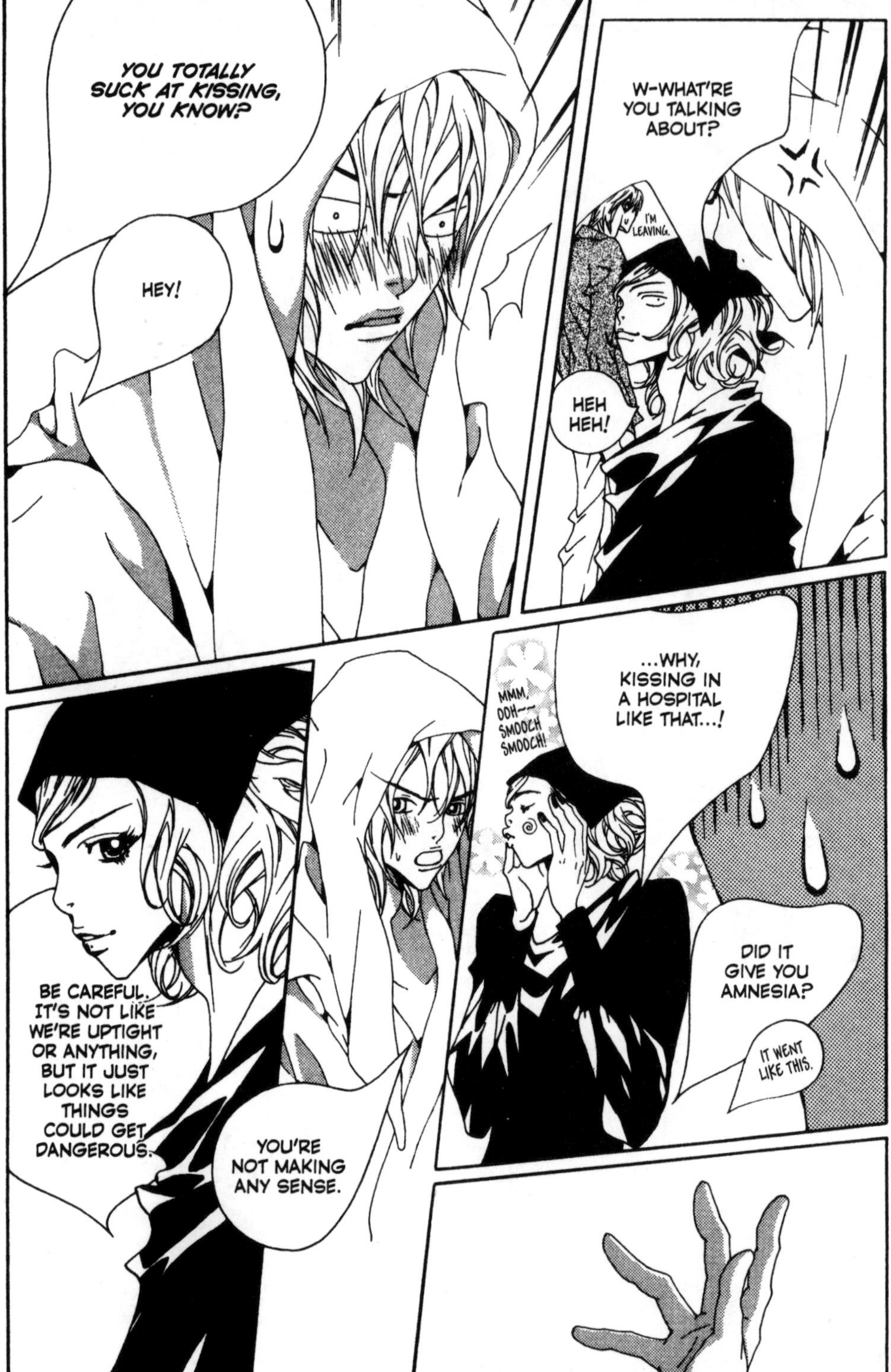
YOU TOTALLY SUCK AT KISSING, YOU KNOW?
HEY!
W-WHAT'RE YOU TALKING ABOUT?
I'M LEAVING.
HEH HEH!
BE CAREFUL. IT'S NOT LIKE WE'RE UPTIGHT OR ANYTHING, BUT IT JUST LOOKS LIKE THINGS COULD GET DANGEROUS.
YOU'RE NOT MAKING ANY SENSE.
...WHY, KISSING IN A HOSPITAL LIKE THAT...!
MMM, OOH-- SMOOCH SMOOCH!
DID IT GIVE YOU AMNESIA?
IT WENT LIKE THIS.

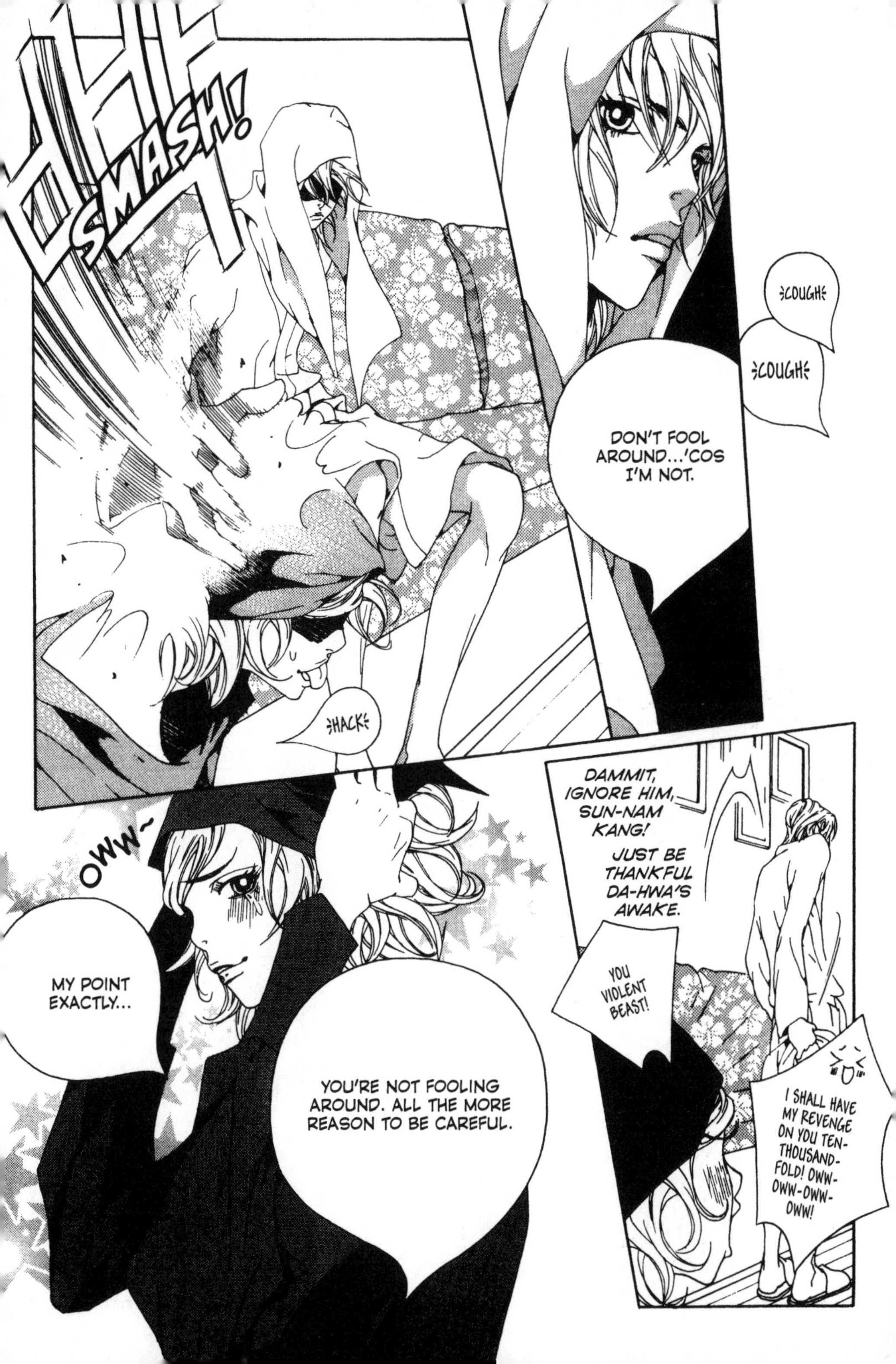
SMASH!
HACK
DON'T FOOL AROUND...'COS I'M NOT.
COUGH
COUGH
OWW~
MY POINT EXACTLY...
YOU'RE NOT FOOLING AROUND. ALL THE MORE REASON TO BE CAREFUL.
DAMMIT, IGNORE HIM, SUN-NAM KANG!
JUST BE THANKFUL DA-HWA'S AWAKE.
YOU VIOLENT BEAST!
I SHALL HAVE MY REVENGE ON YOU TEN-THOUSAND-FOLD! OWW-OWW-OWW-OWW!

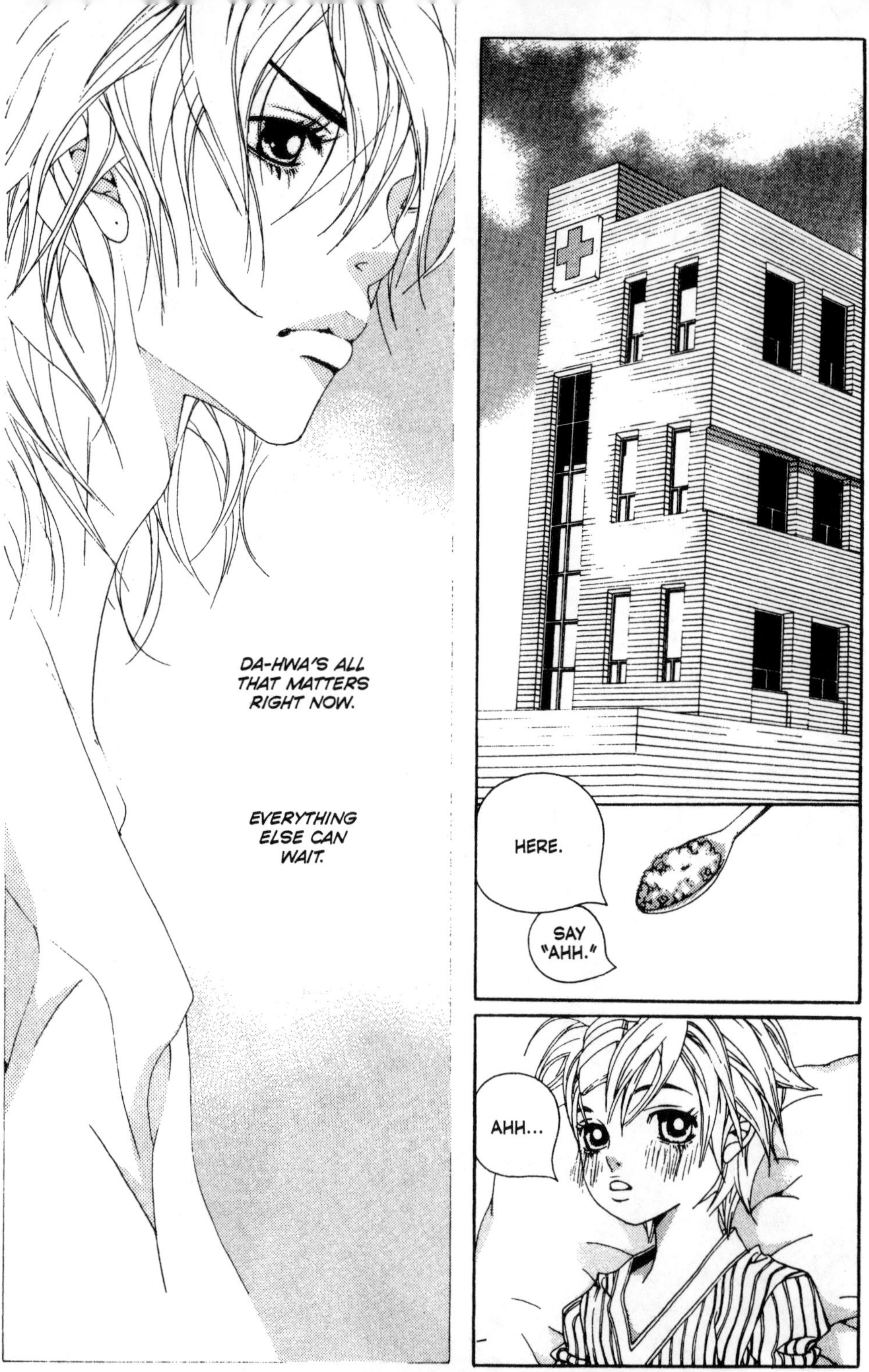
DA-HWA'S ALL THAT MATTERS RIGHT NOW.
EVERYTHING ELSE CAN WAIT.
HERE.
SAY "AHH."
AHH...

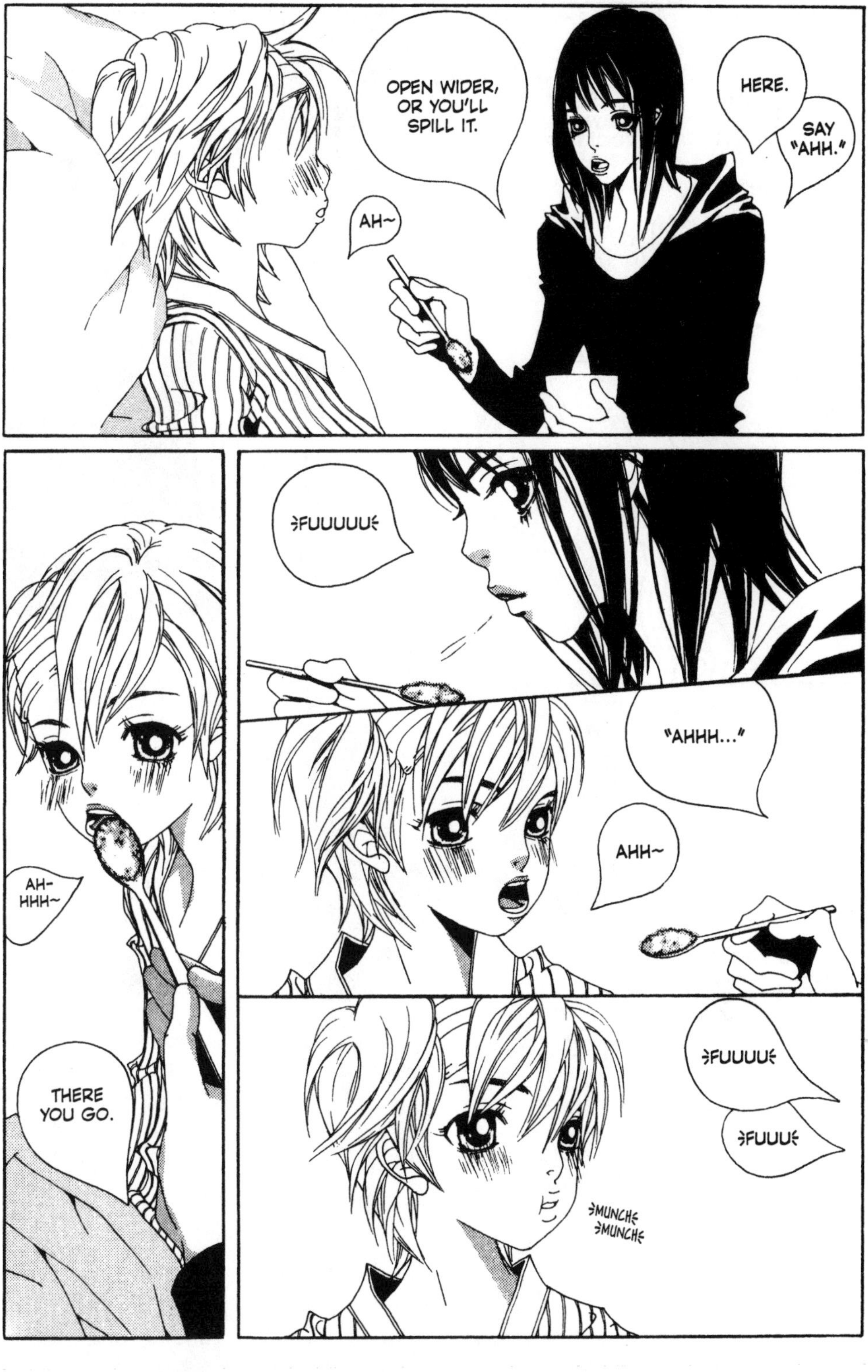
OPEN WIDER, OR YOU'LL SPILL IT.
HERE.
SAY "AHH."
AH~
AH-HHH~
THERE YOU GO.
FUUUUU
"AHHH..."
AHH~
FUUUU
FUUU
MUNCH MUNCH

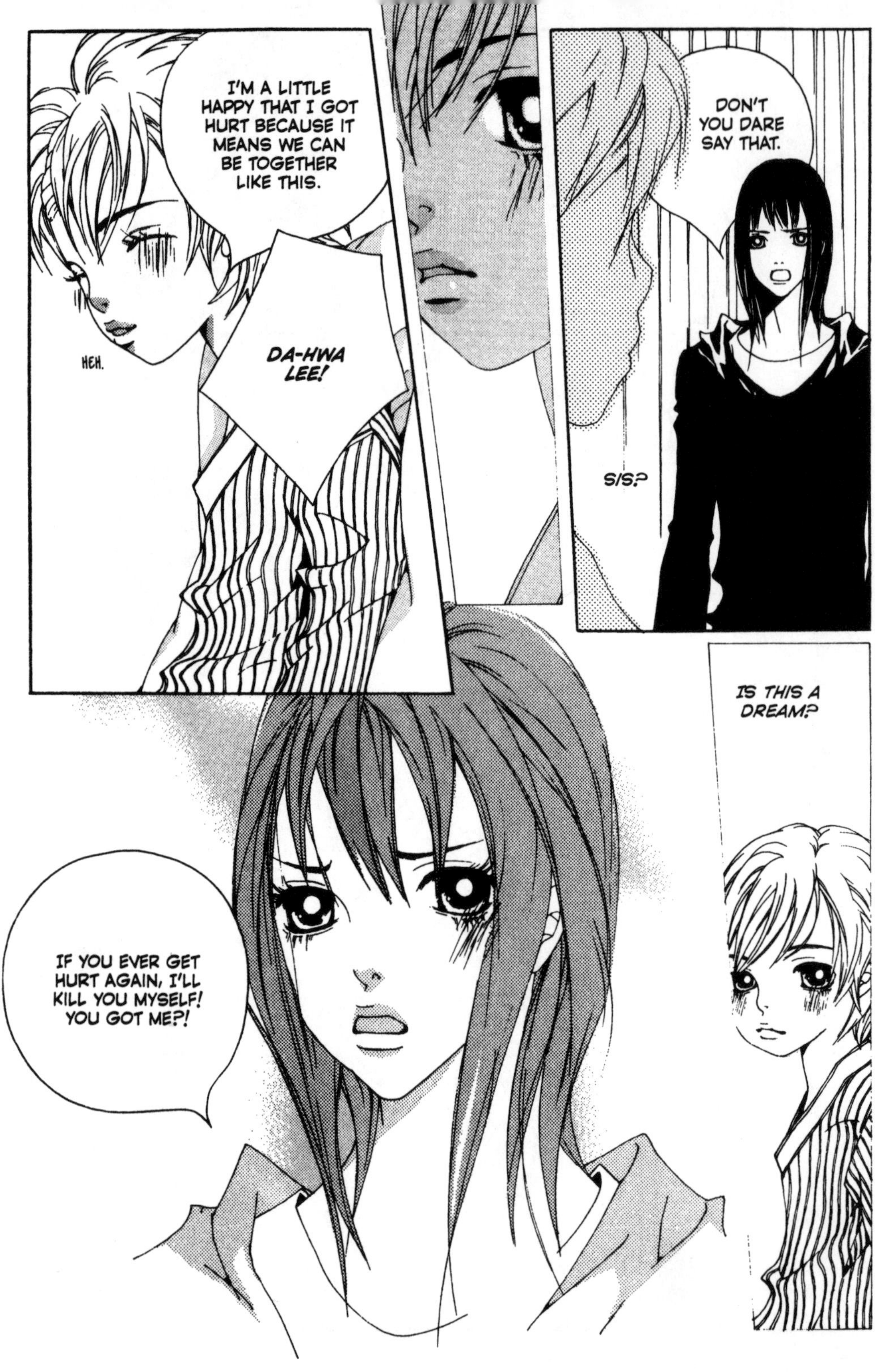
I'M A LITTLE HAPPY THAT I GOT HURT BECAUSE IT MEANS WE CAN BE TOGETHER LIKE THIS.
HEH.
DA-HWA LEE!
DON'T YOU DARE SAY THAT.
SIS?
IF YOU EVER GET HURT AGAIN, I'LL KILL YOU MYSELF! YOU GOT ME?!
IS THIS A DREAM?

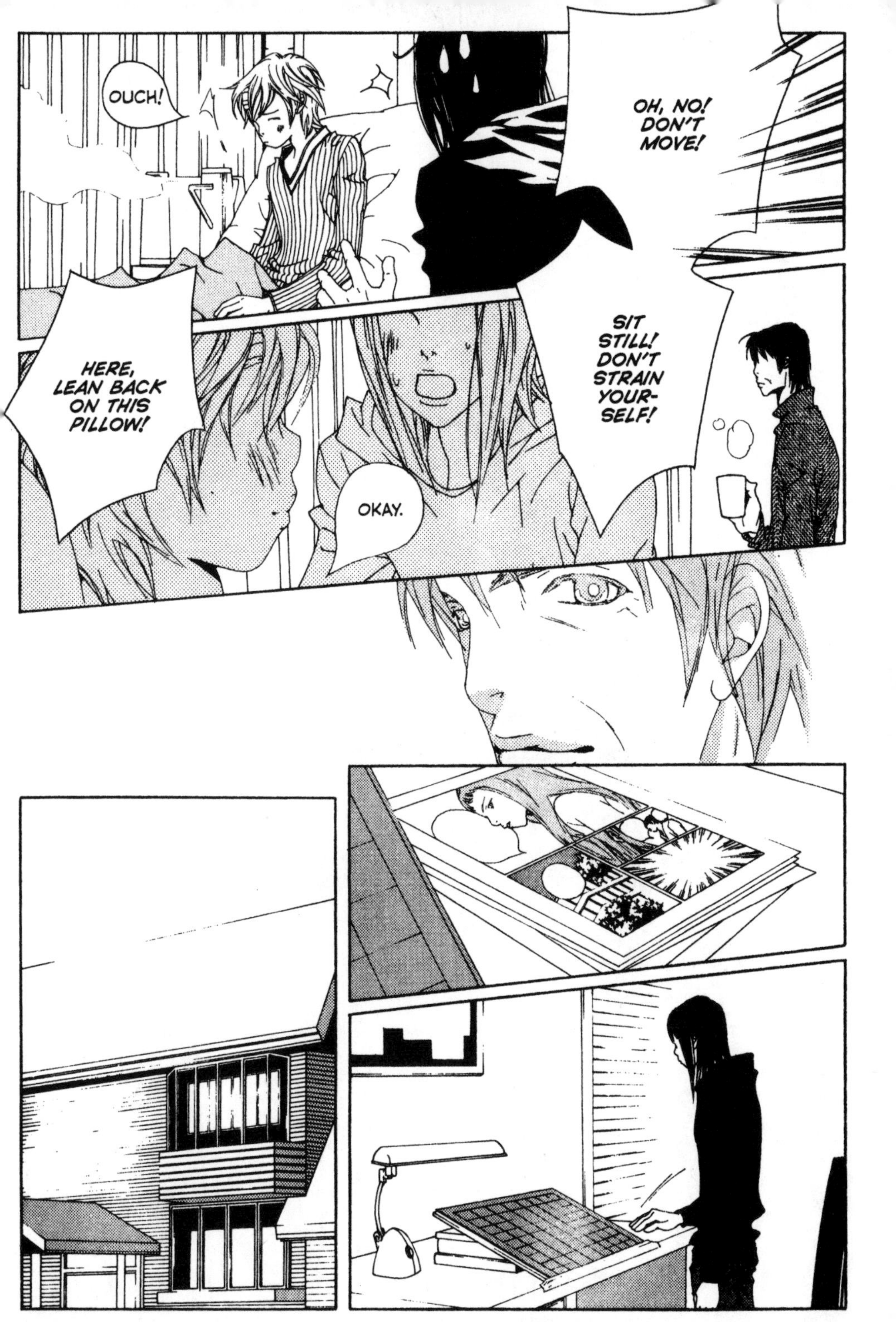
OUCH!
OH, NO! DON'T MOVE!
HERE, LEAN BACK ON THIS PILLOW!
OKAY.
SIT STILL! DON'T STRAIN YOUR-SELF!

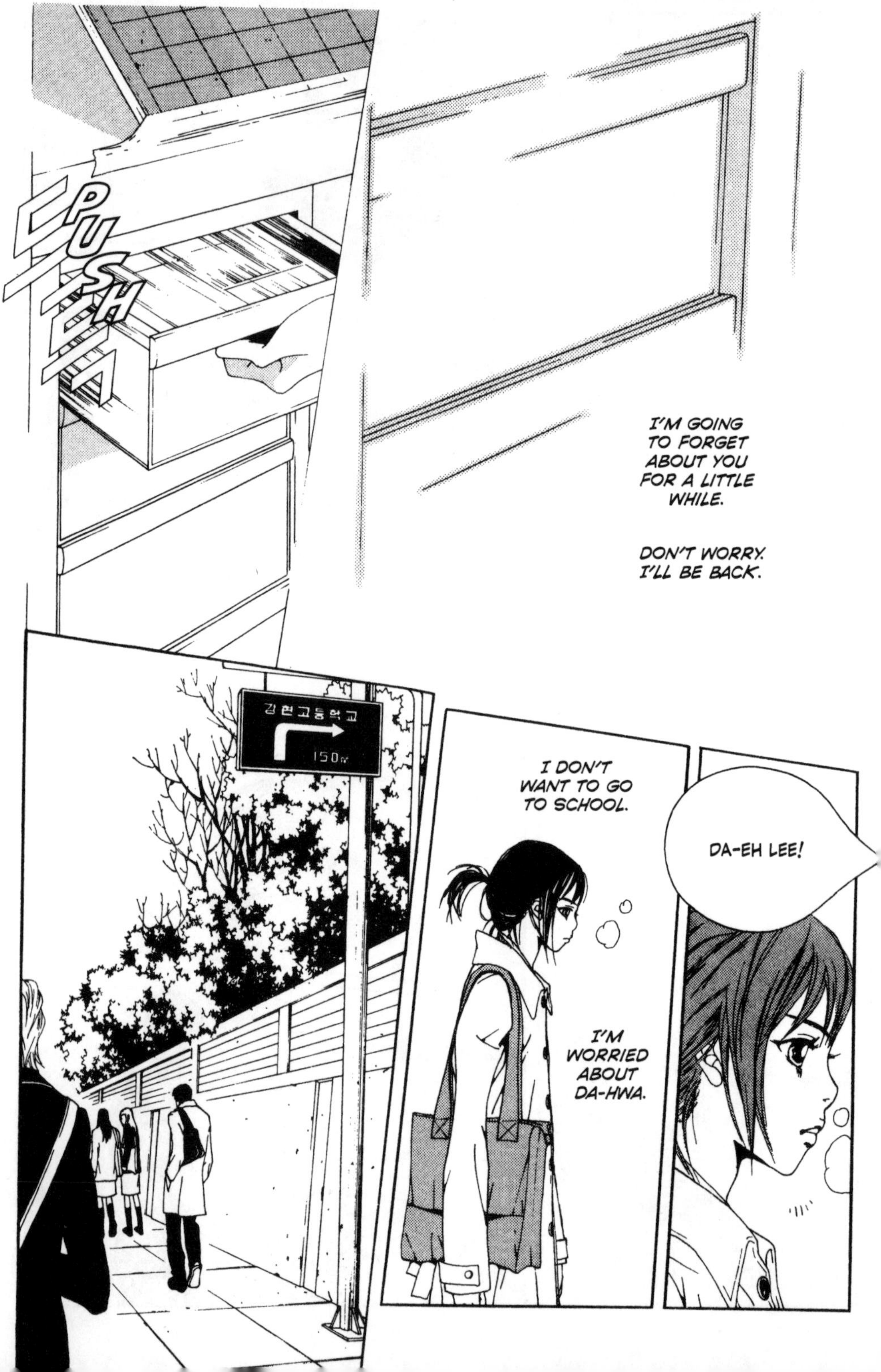
PUSH
I'M GOING TO FORGET ABOUT YOU FOR A LITTLE WHILE.
DON'T WORRY. I'LL BE BACK.
I DON'T WANT TO GO TO SCHOOL.
I'M WORRIED ABOUT DA-HWA.
DA-EH LEE!

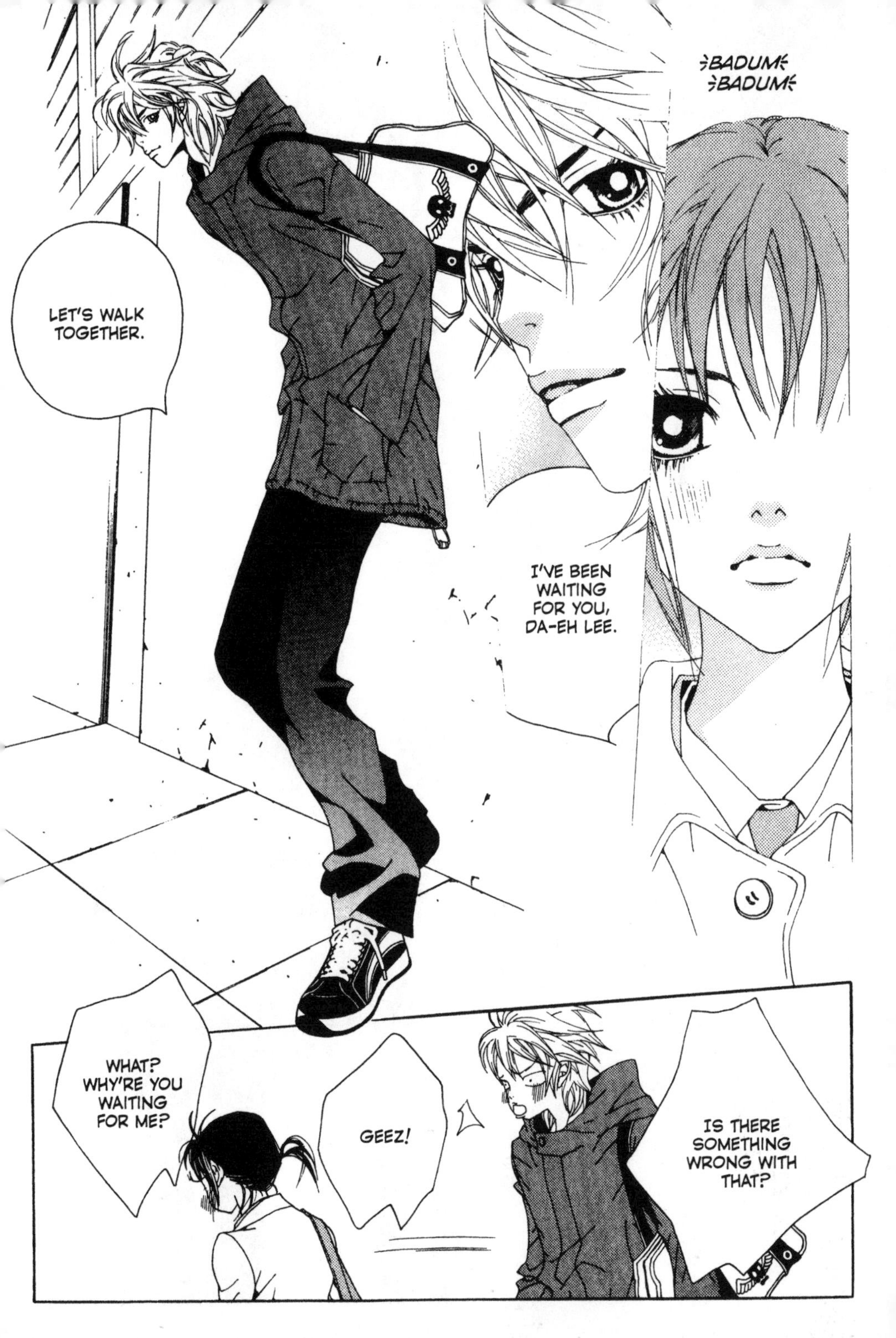
LET'S WALK TOGETHER.
BADUM BADUM
I'VE BEEN WAITING FOR YOU, DA-EH LEE.
WHAT? WHY'RE YOU WAITING FOR ME?
GEEZ!
IS THERE SOMETHING WRONG WITH THAT?

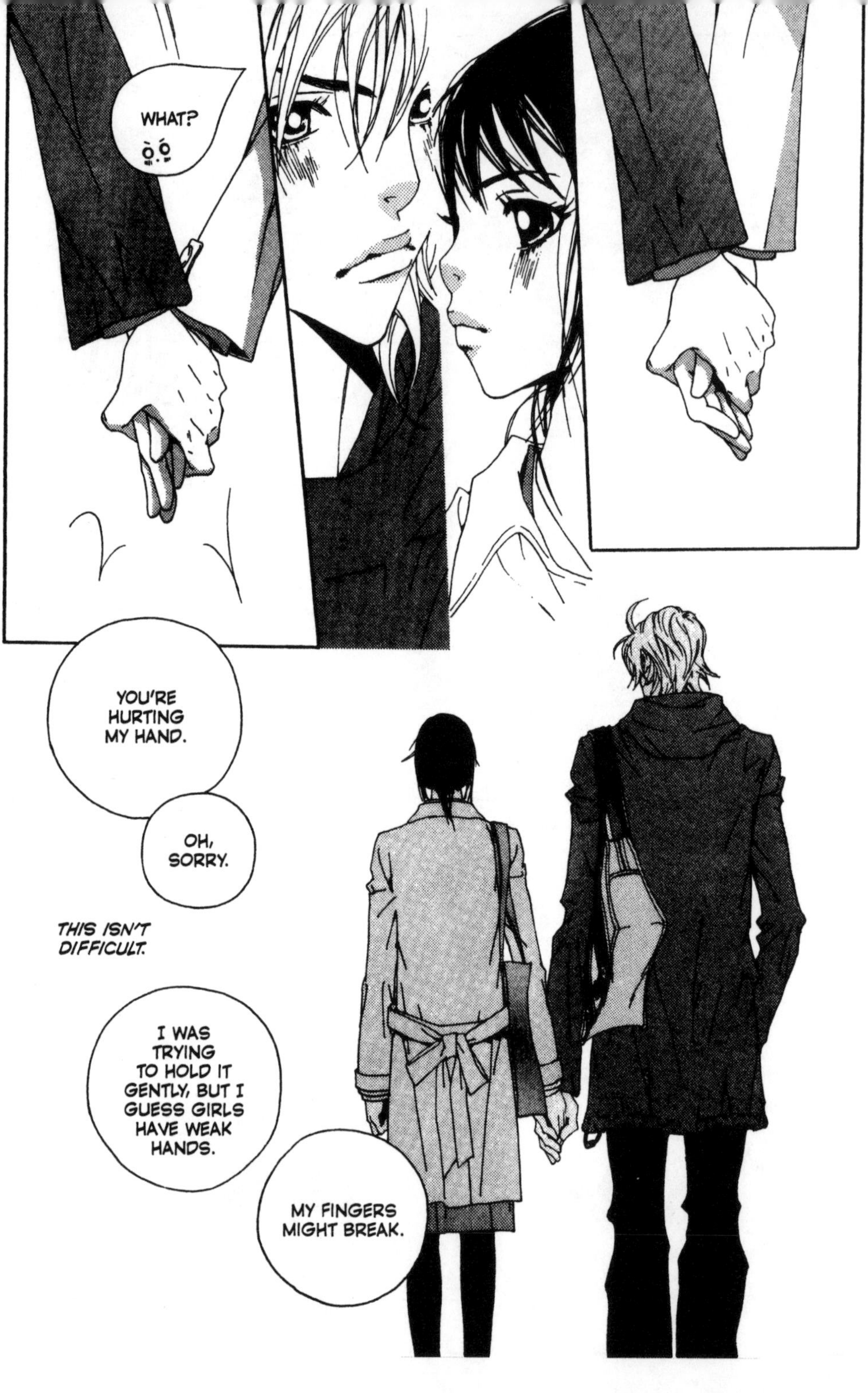
WHAT?
YOU'RE HURTING MY HAND.
OH, SORRY.
THIS ISN'T DIFFICULT.
I WAS TRYING TO HOLD IT GENTLY, BUT I GUESS GIRLS HAVE WEAK HANDS.
MY FINGERS MIGHT BREAK.

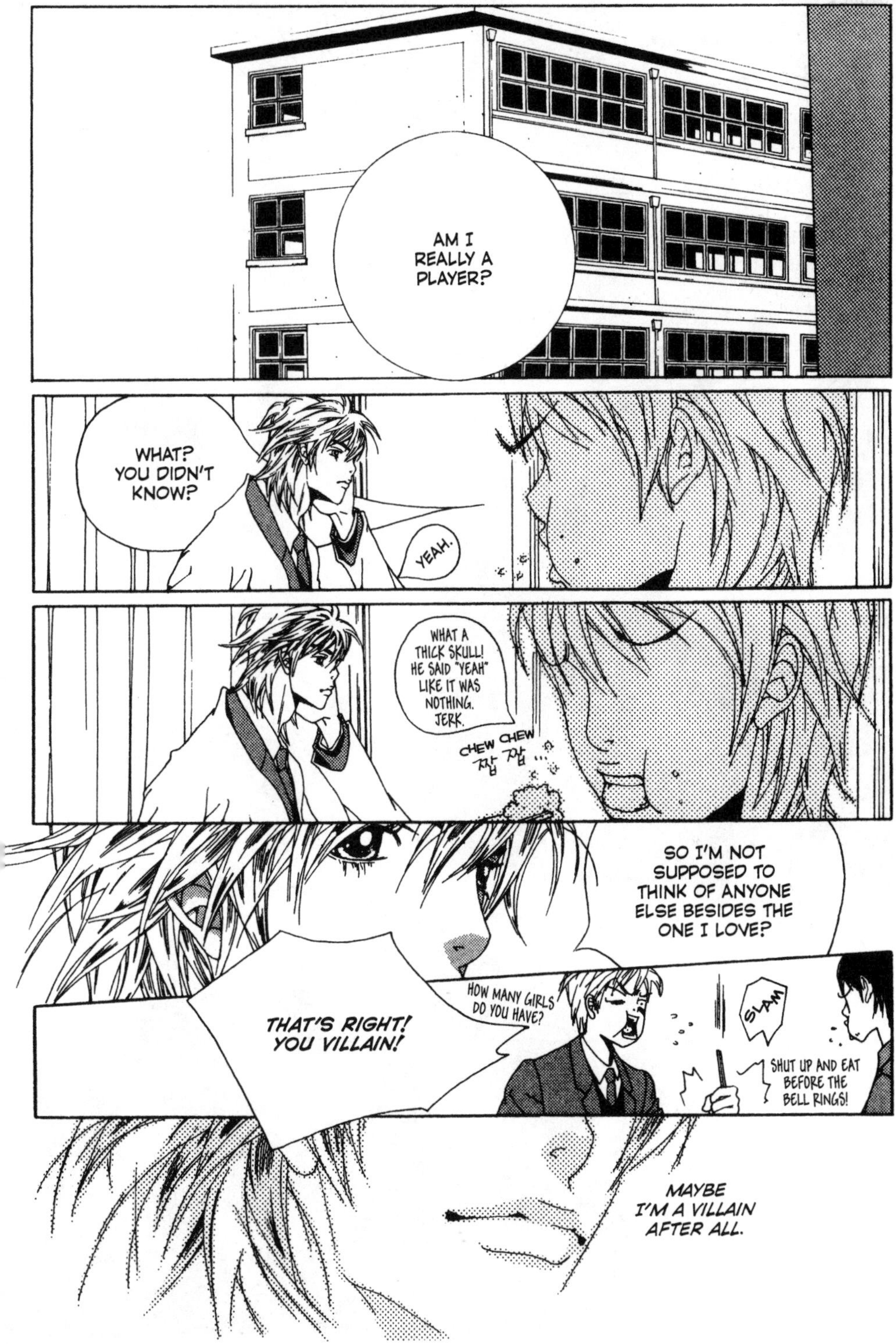
AM I REALLY A PLAYER?
WHAT? YOU DIDN'T KNOW?
YEAH.
WHAT A THICK SKULL! HE SAID "YEAH" LIKE IT WAS NOTHING. JERK.
CHEW CHEW
잡 잡...
SO I'M NOT SUPPOSED TO THINK OF ANYONE ELSE BESIDES THE ONE I LOVE?
THAT'S RIGHT! YOU VILLAIN!
HOW MANY GIRLS DO YOU HAVE?
SLAM
SHUT UP AND EAT BEFORE THE BELL RINGS!
MAYBE I'M A VILLAIN AFTER ALL.

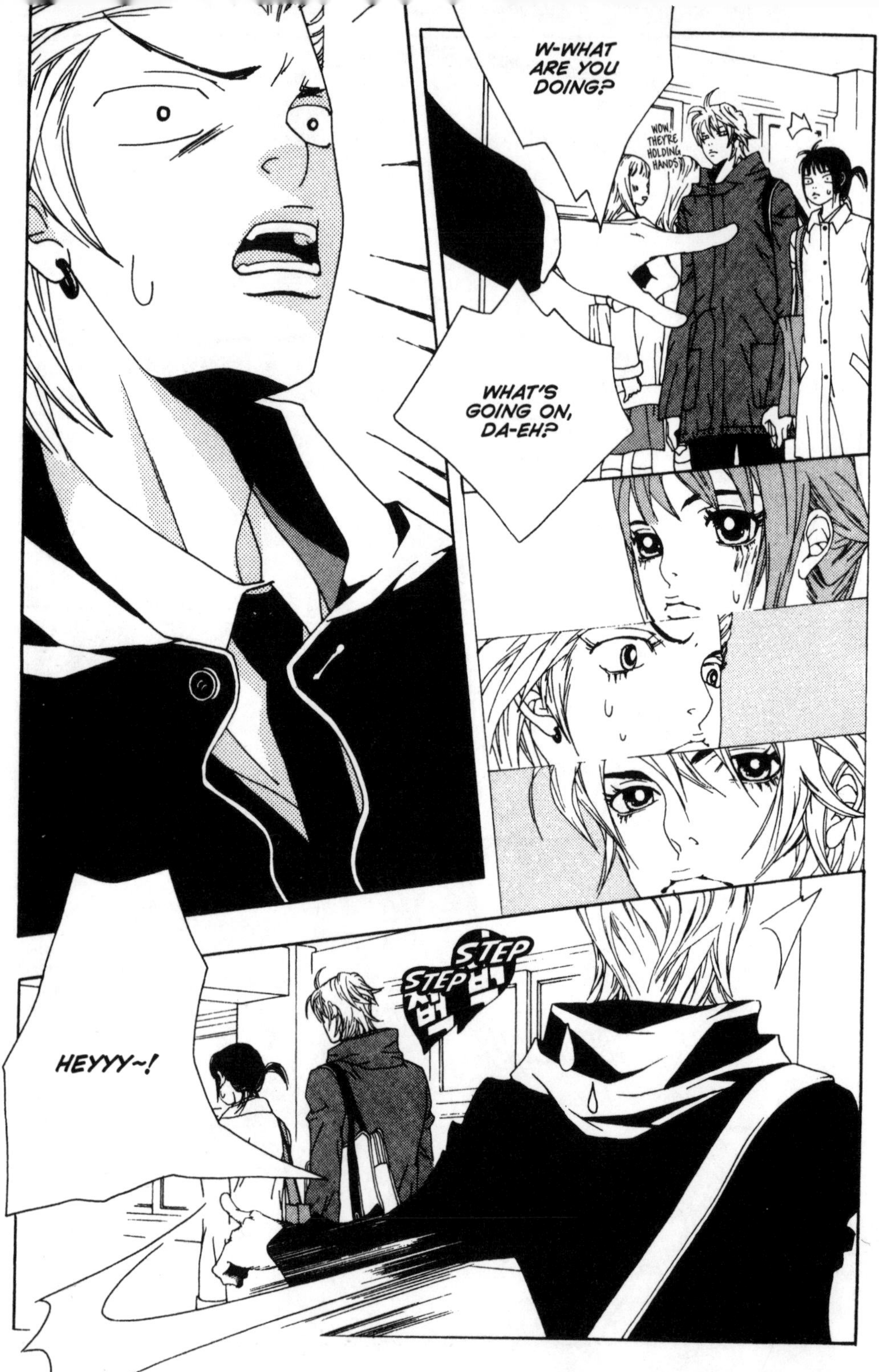
W-WHAT ARE YOU DOING?
WOW, THEY'RE HOLDING HANDS!
WHAT'S GOING ON, DA-EH?
HEYYY~!
STEP STEP

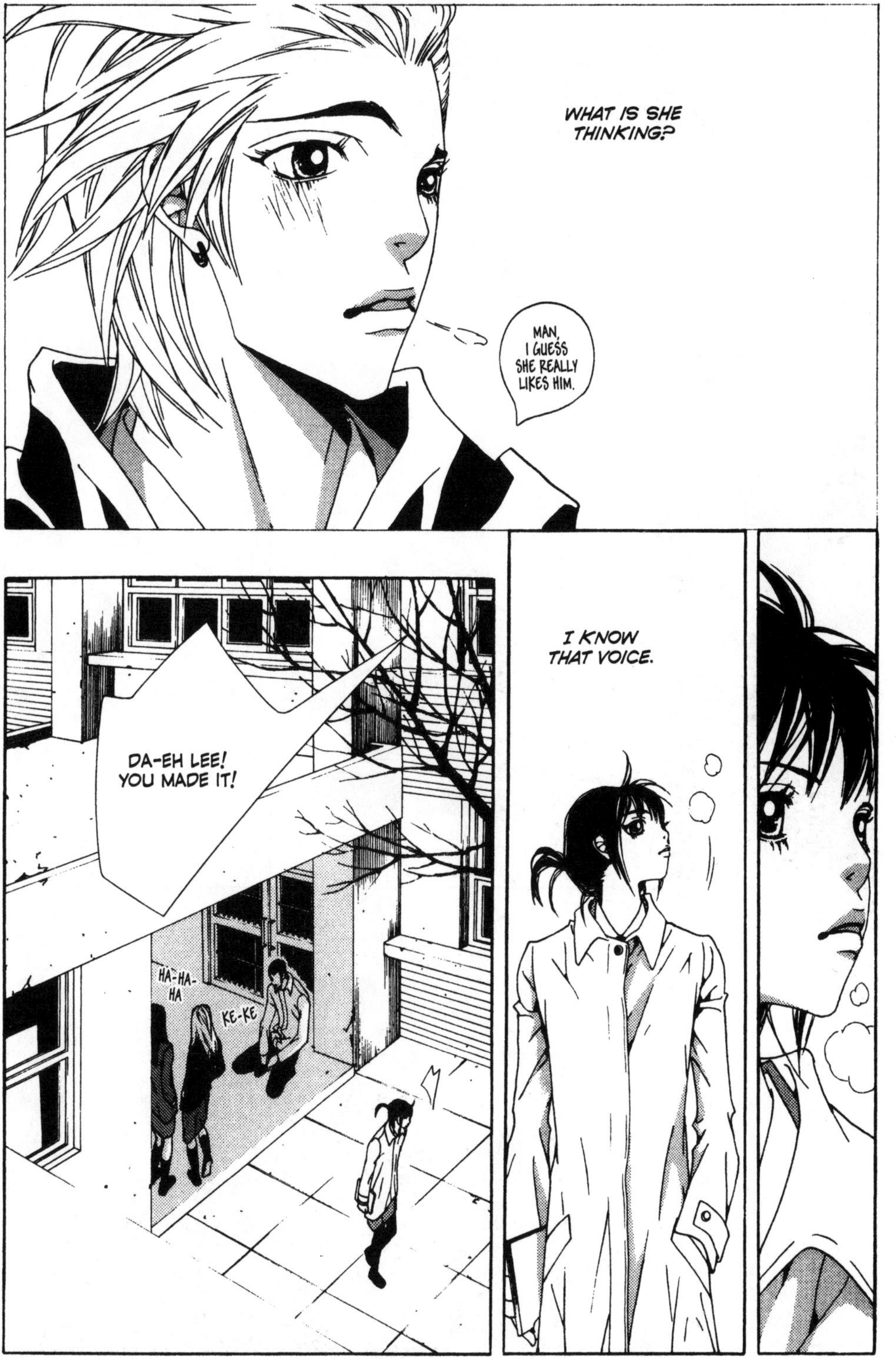

WHAT IS SHE THINKING?
MAN, I GUESS SHE REALLY LIKES HIM.
DA-EH LEE! YOU MADE IT!
HA-HA-HA
KE-KE
I KNOW THAT VOICE.

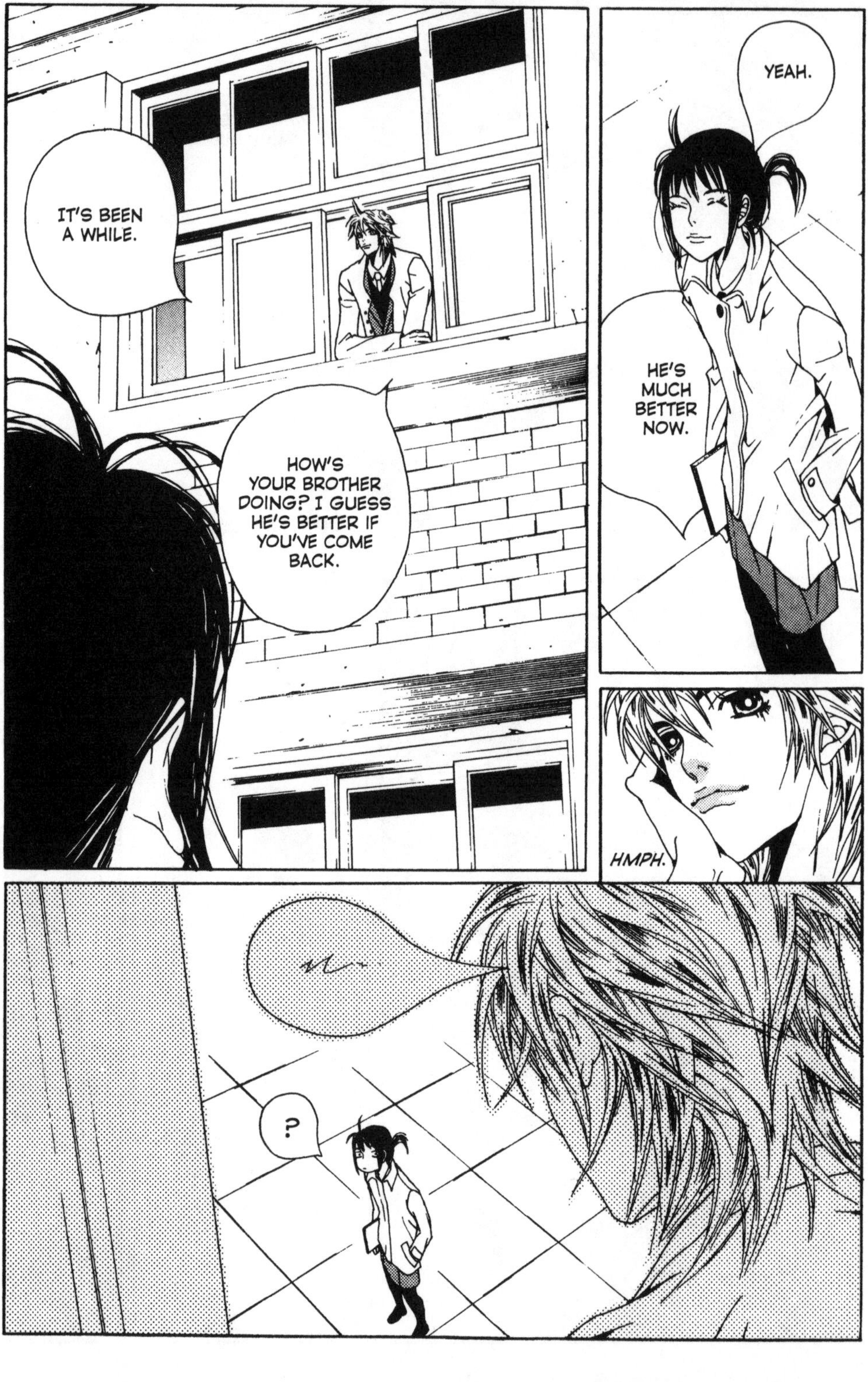
IT'S BEEN A WHILE.
HOW'S YOUR BROTHER DOING? I GUESS HE'S BETTER IF YOU'VE COME BACK.
YEAH.
HE'S MUCH BETTER NOW.
HMPH.
?

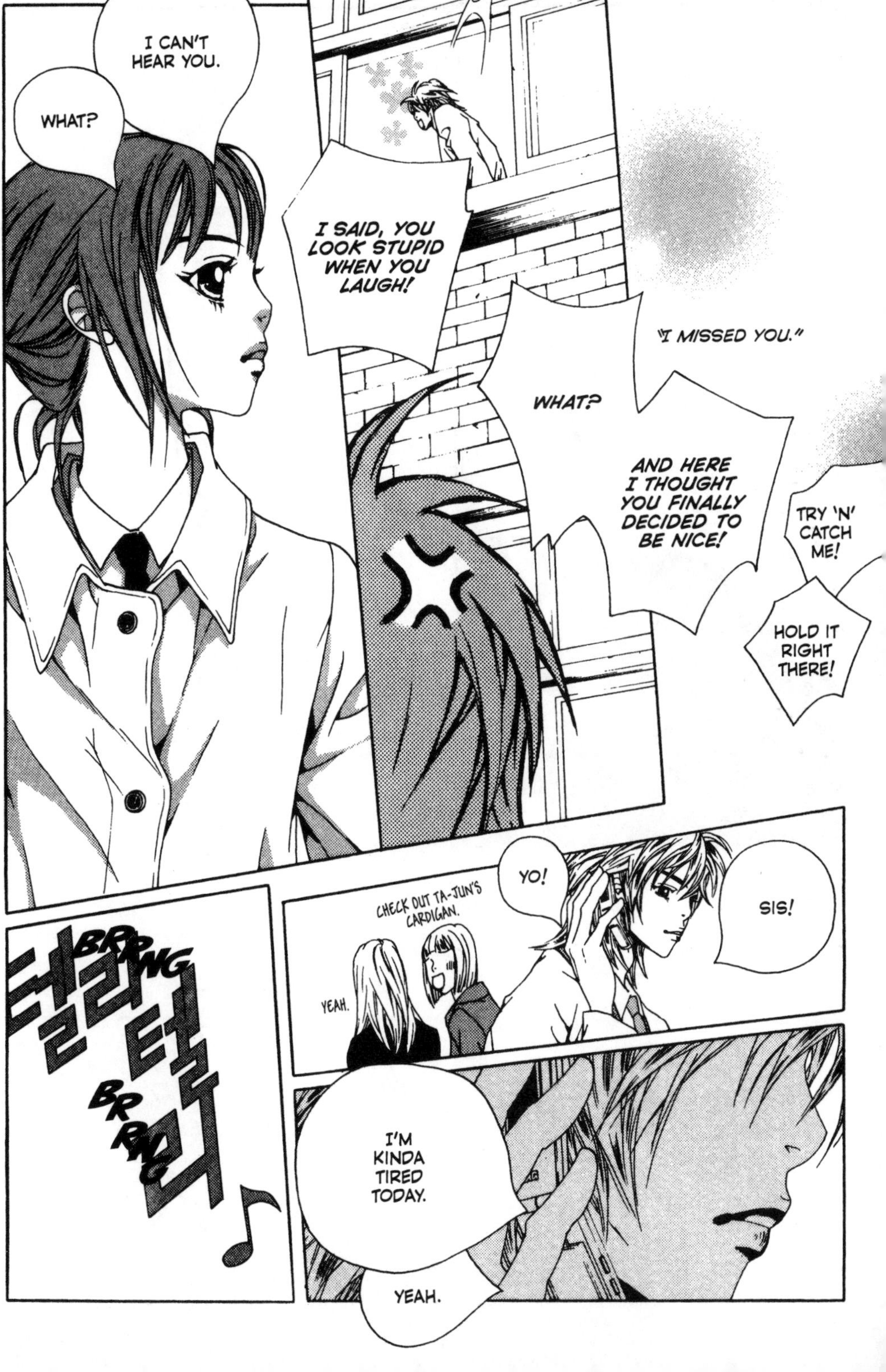
I CAN'T HEAR YOU.
WHAT?
I SAID, YOU LOOK STUPID WHEN YOU LAUGH!
WHAT?
"I MISSED YOU."
AND HERE I THOUGHT YOU FINALLY DECIDED TO BE NICE!
TRY 'N' CATCH ME!
HOLD IT RIGHT THERE!
BRRING
BRRING
CHECK OUT TA-JUN'S CARDIGAN.
YEAH.
YO!
SIS!
I'M KINDA TIRED TODAY.
YEAH.

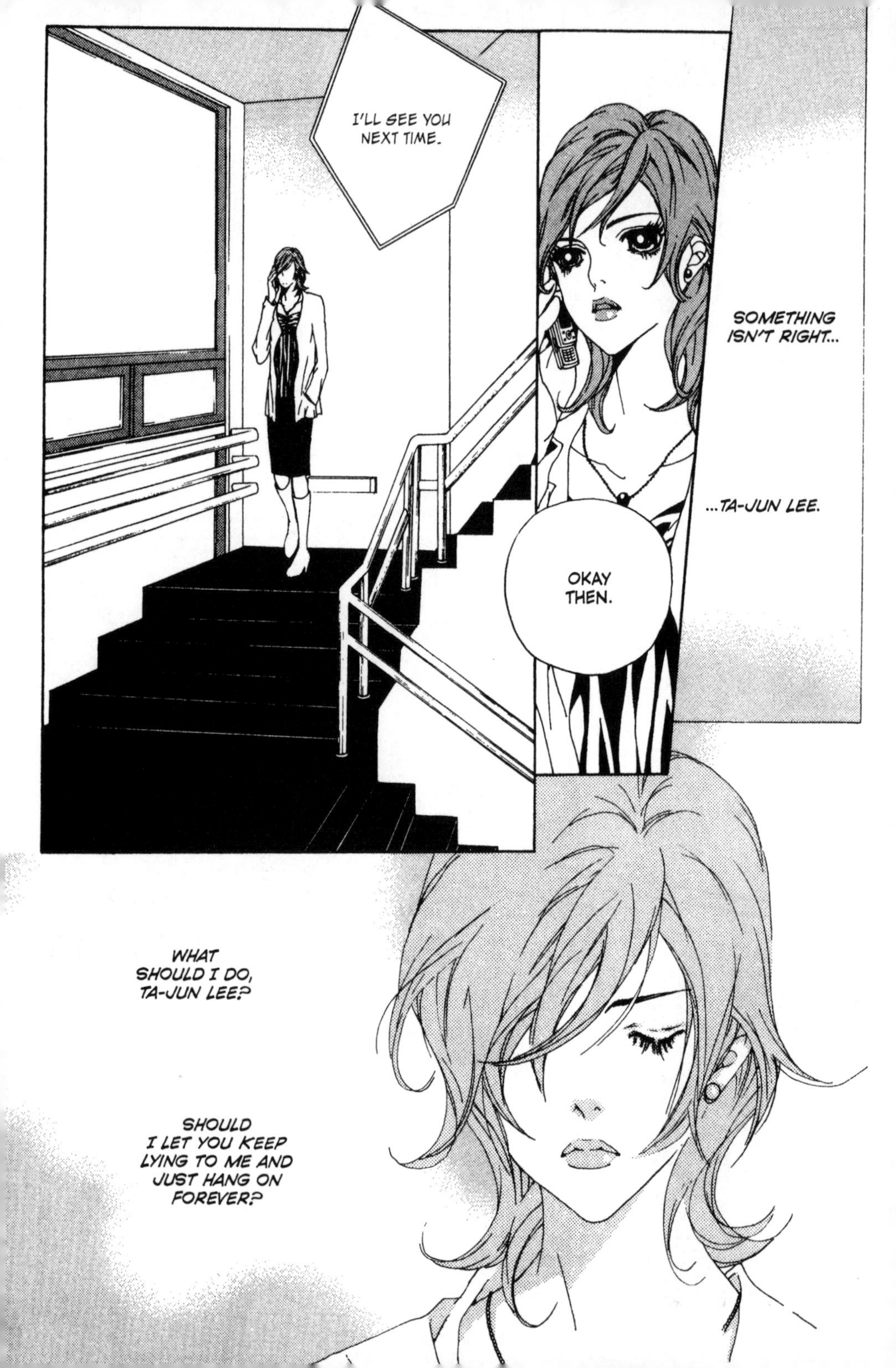
I'LL SEE YOU NEXT TIME.
SOMETHING ISN'T RIGHT...
...TA-JUN LEE.
OKAY THEN.
WHAT SHOULD I DO, TA-JUN LEE?
SHOULD I LET YOU KEEP LYING TO ME AND JUST HANG ON FOREVER?

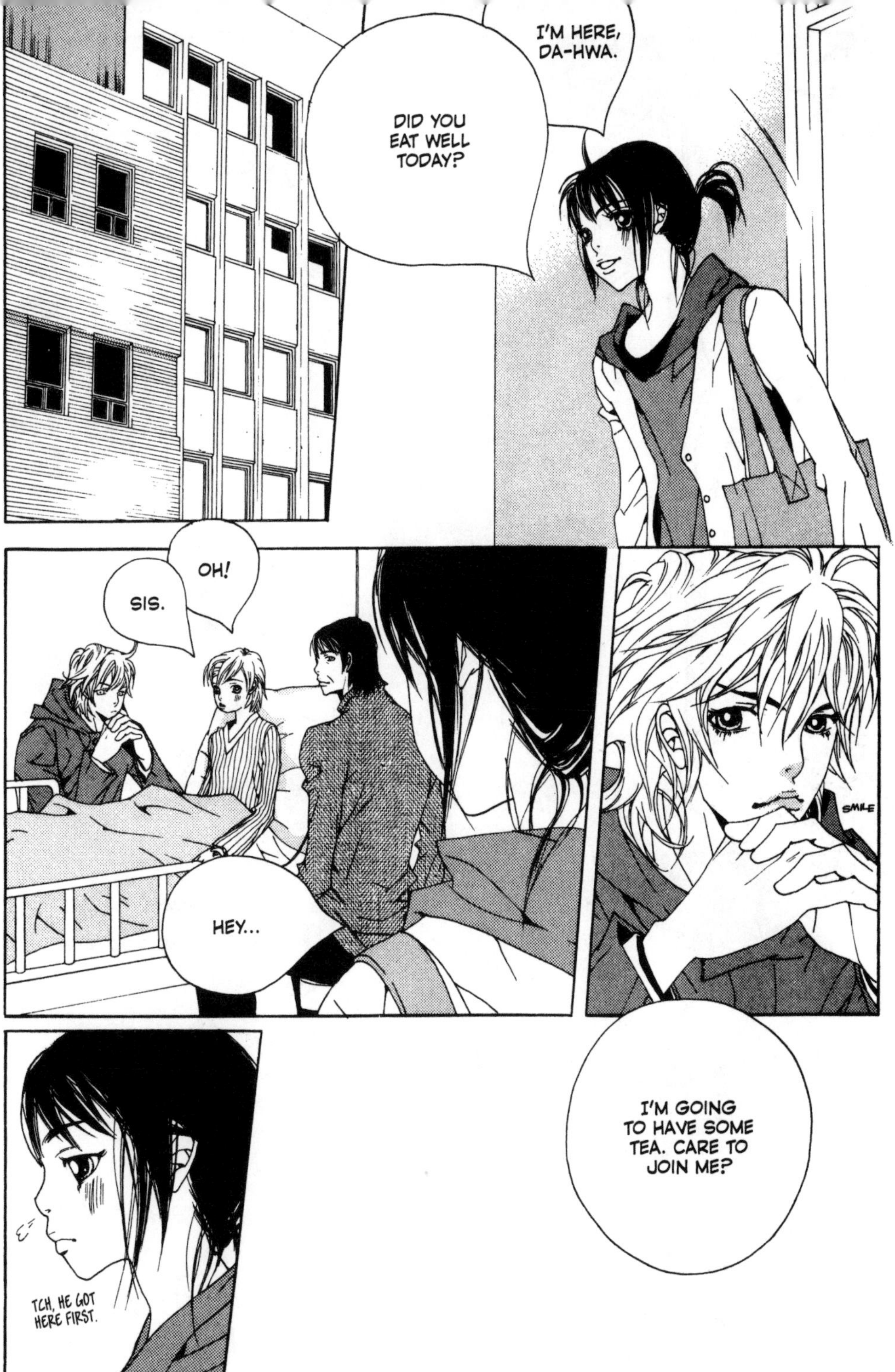
I'M HERE, DA-HWA.
DID YOU EAT WELL TODAY?
SIS.
OH!
HEY...
SMILE
TCH, HE GOT HERE FIRST.
I'M GOING TO HAVE SOME TEA. CARE TO JOIN ME?

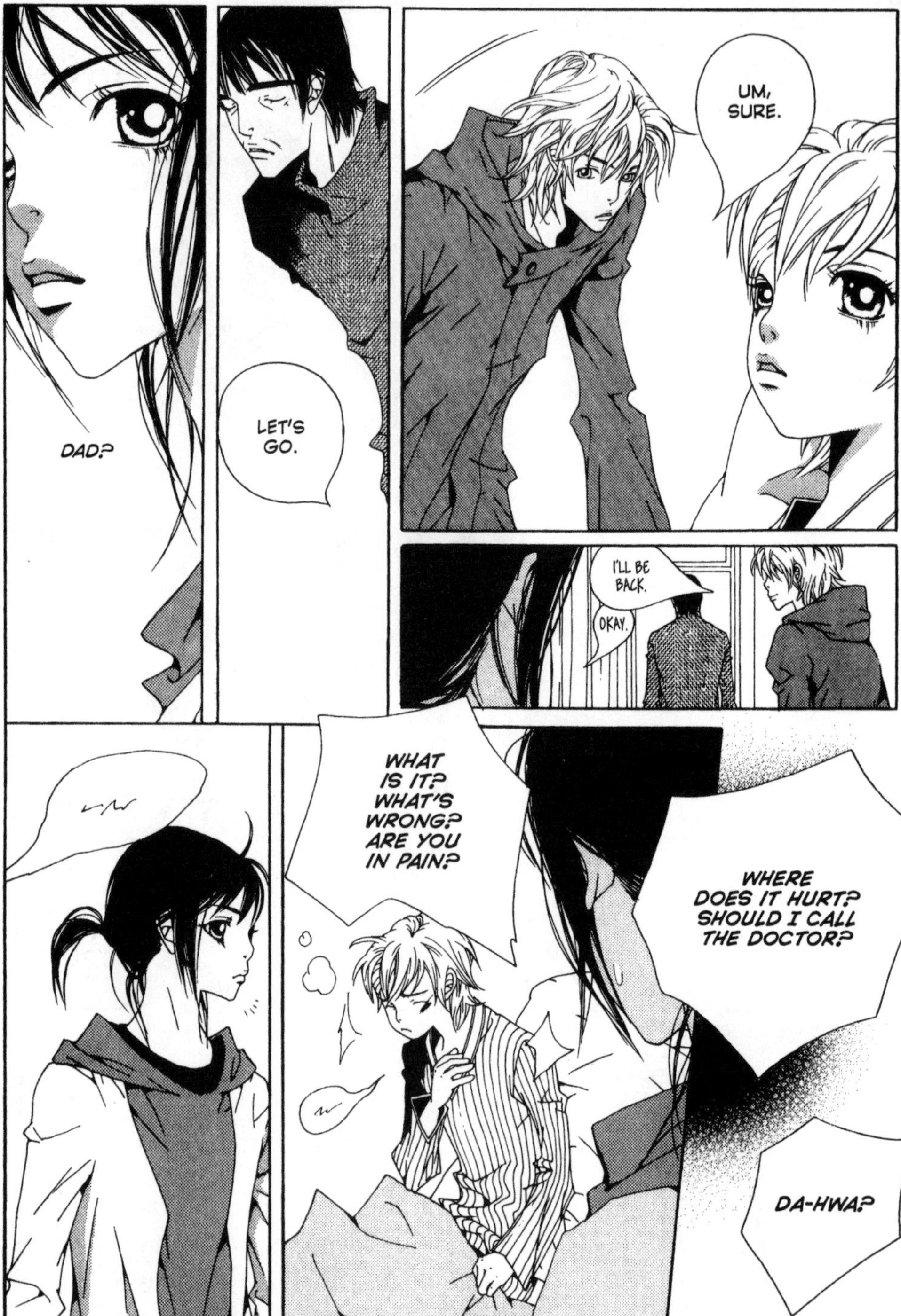
DAD?
LET'S GO.
UM, SURE.
I'LL BE BACK.
OKAY.
WHAT IS IT? WHAT'S WRONG? ARE YOU IN PAIN?
WHERE DOES IT HURT? SHOULD I CALL THE DOCTOR?
DA-HWA?

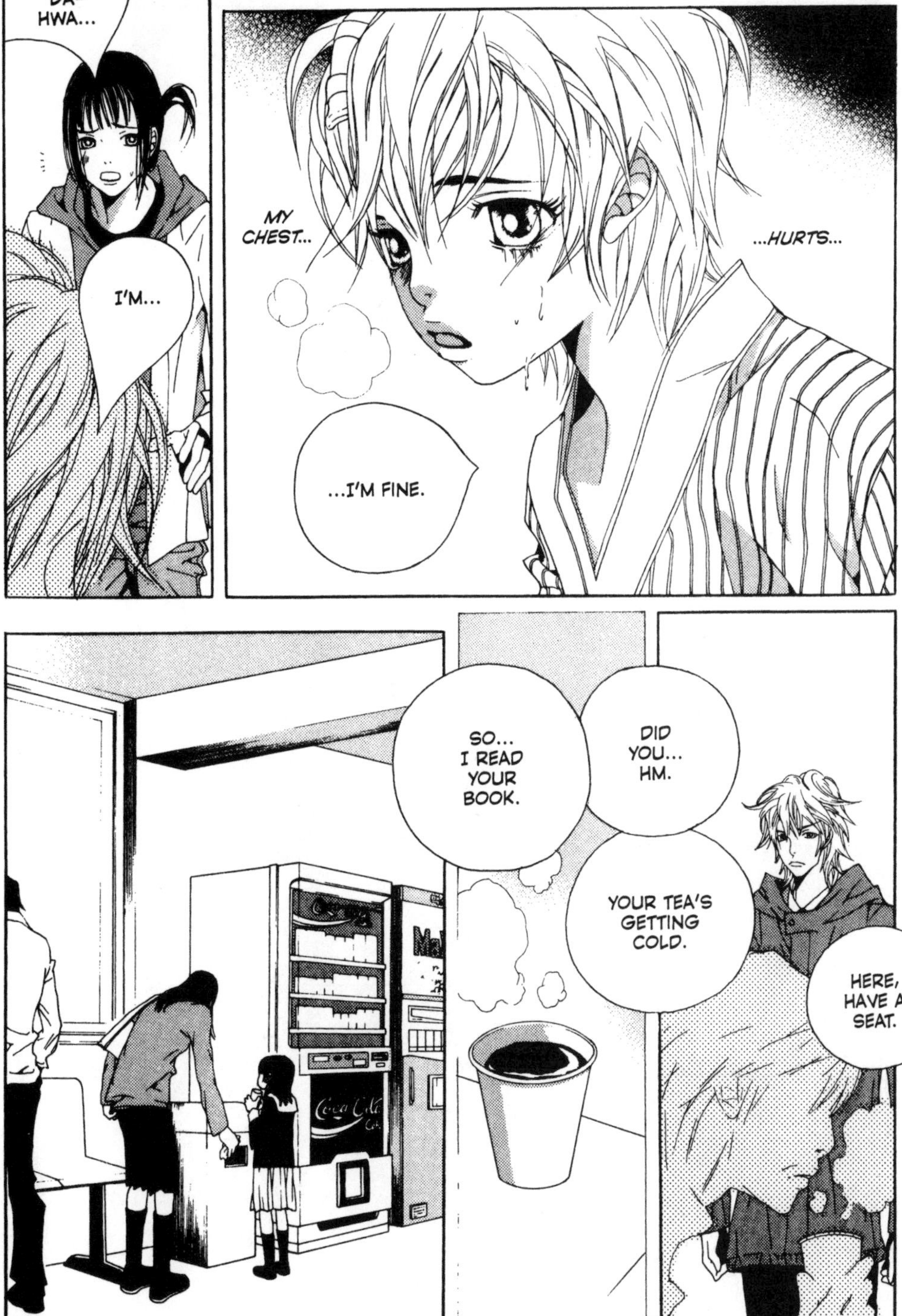
DA-HWA...
I'M...
MY CHEST...
...HURTS...
...I'M FINE.
SO... I READ YOUR BOOK.
DID YOU... HM.
YOUR TEA'S GETTING COLD.
HERE, HAVE A SEAT.

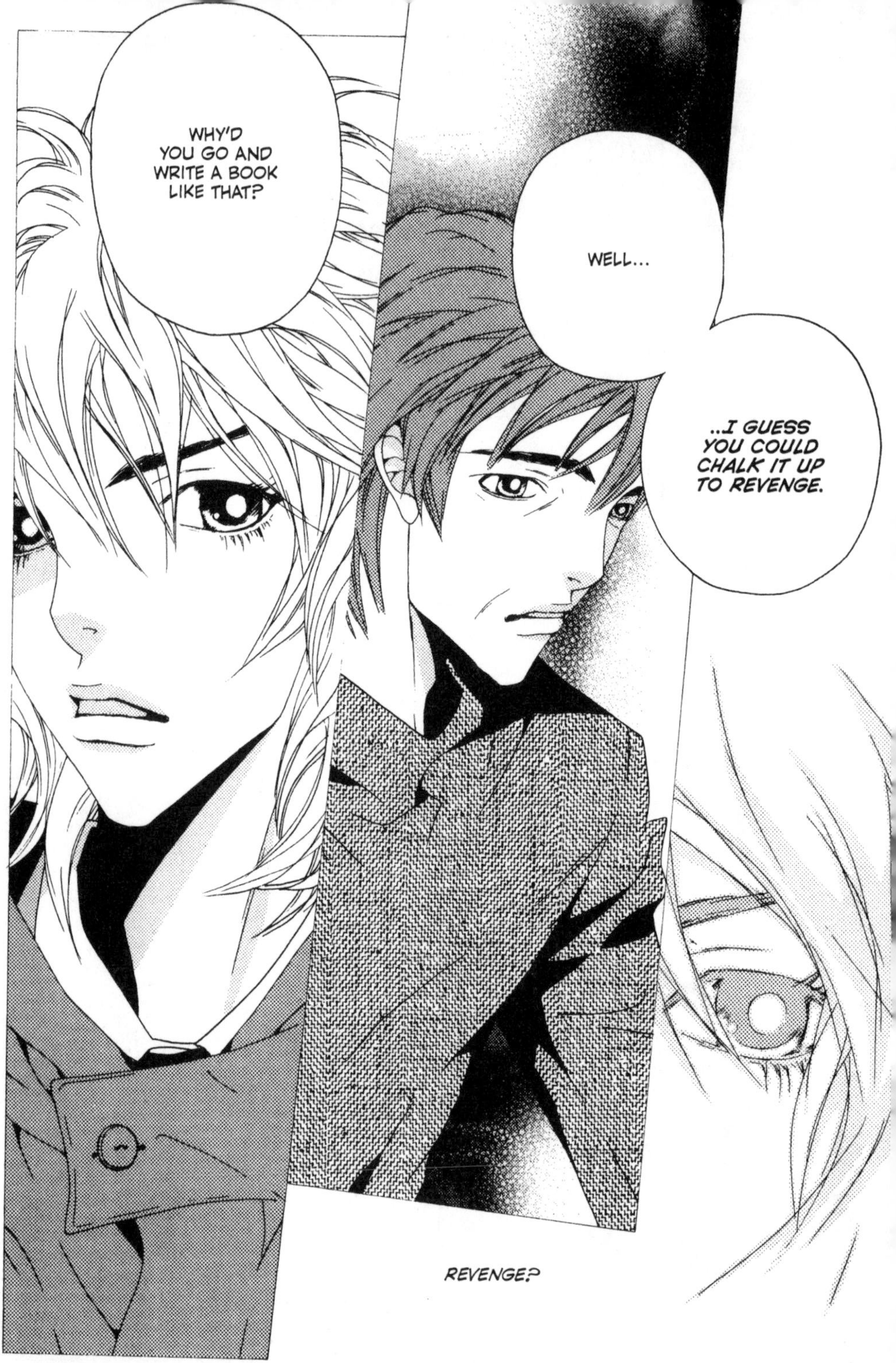
WHY'D YOU GO AND WRITE A BOOK LIKE THAT?
WELL...
...I GUESS YOU COULD CHALK IT UP TO REVENGE.
REVENGE?

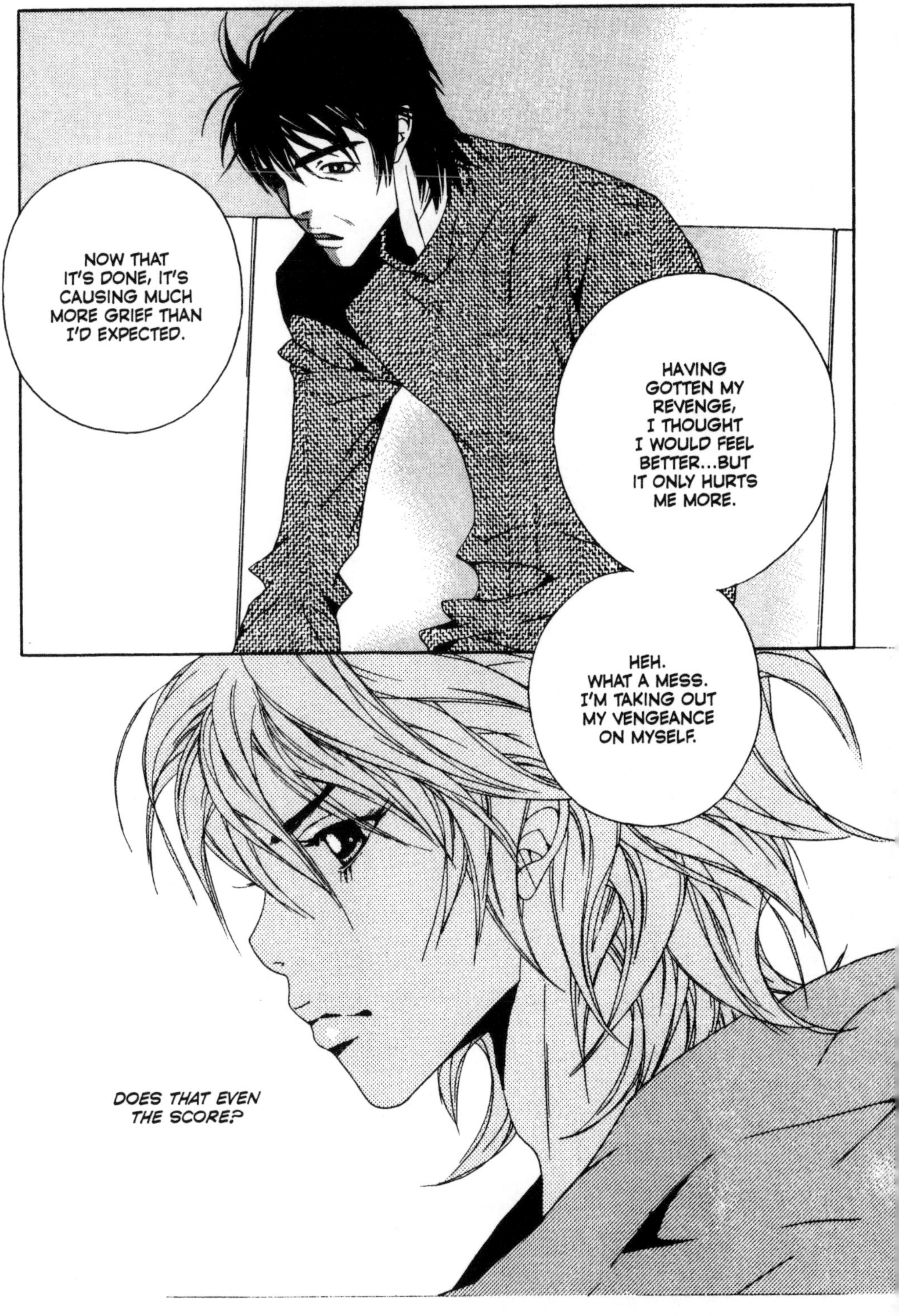
NOW THAT IT'S DONE, IT'S CAUSING MUCH MORE GRIEF THAN I'D EXPECTED.
HAVING GOTTEN MY REVENGE, I THOUGHT I WOULD FEEL BETTER...BUT IT ONLY HURTS ME MORE.
HEH. WHAT A MESS. I'M TAKING OUT MY VENGEANCE ON MYSELF.
DOES THAT EVEN THE SCORE?

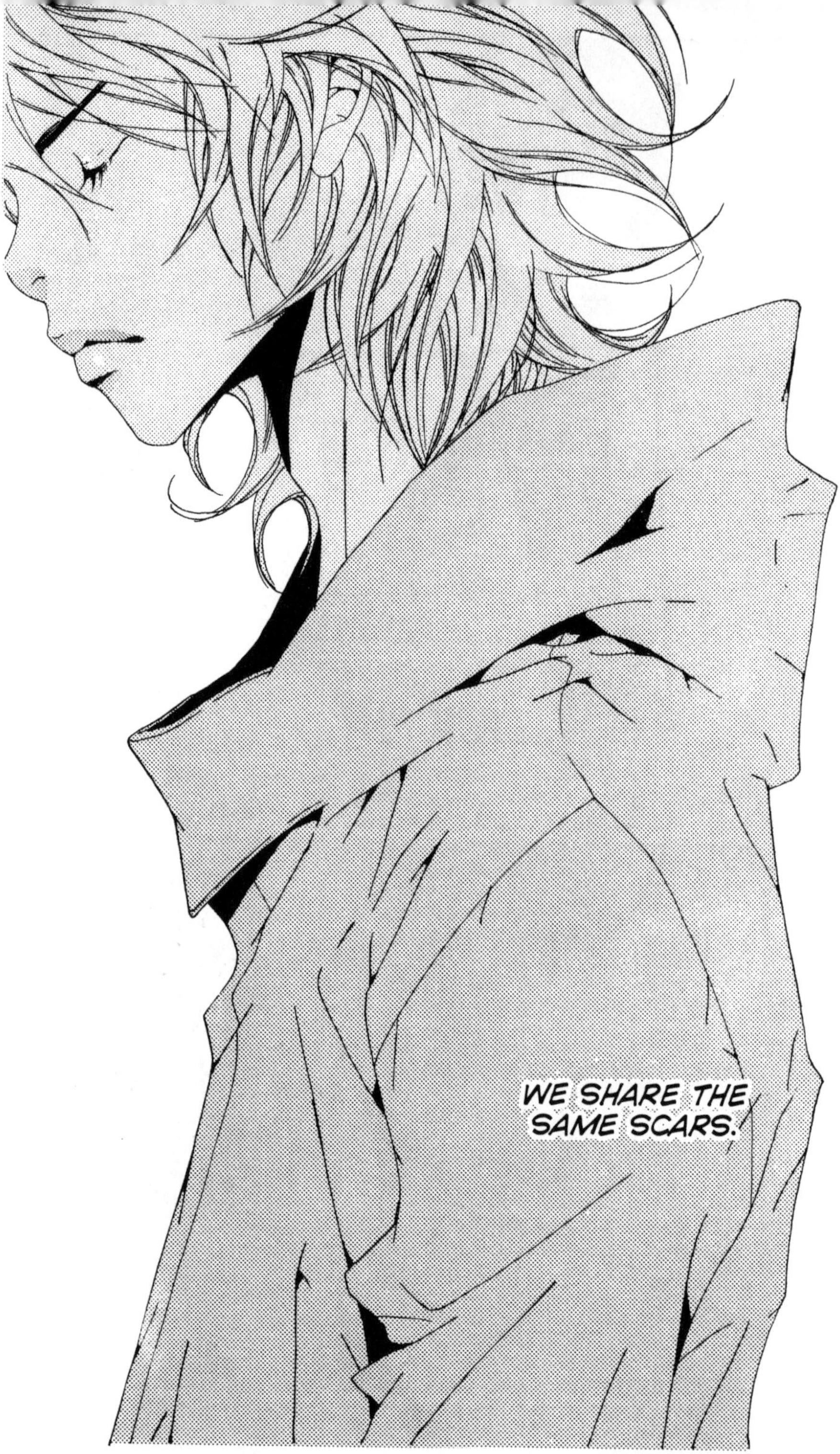
WE SHARE THE SAME SCARS.

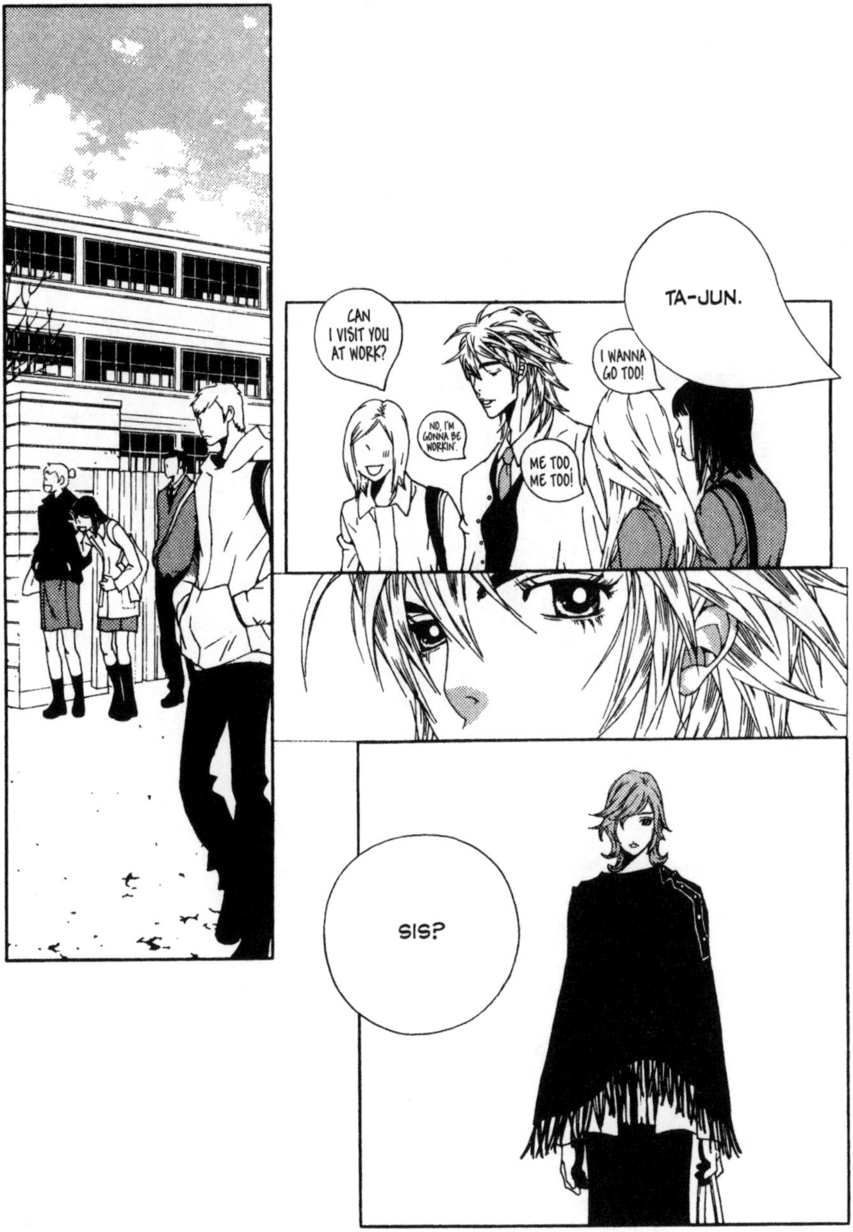
CAN I VISIT YOU AT WORK?
NO, I'M GONNA BE WORKIN'.
ME TOO, ME TOO!
I WANNA GO TOO!
TA-JUN.
SIS?

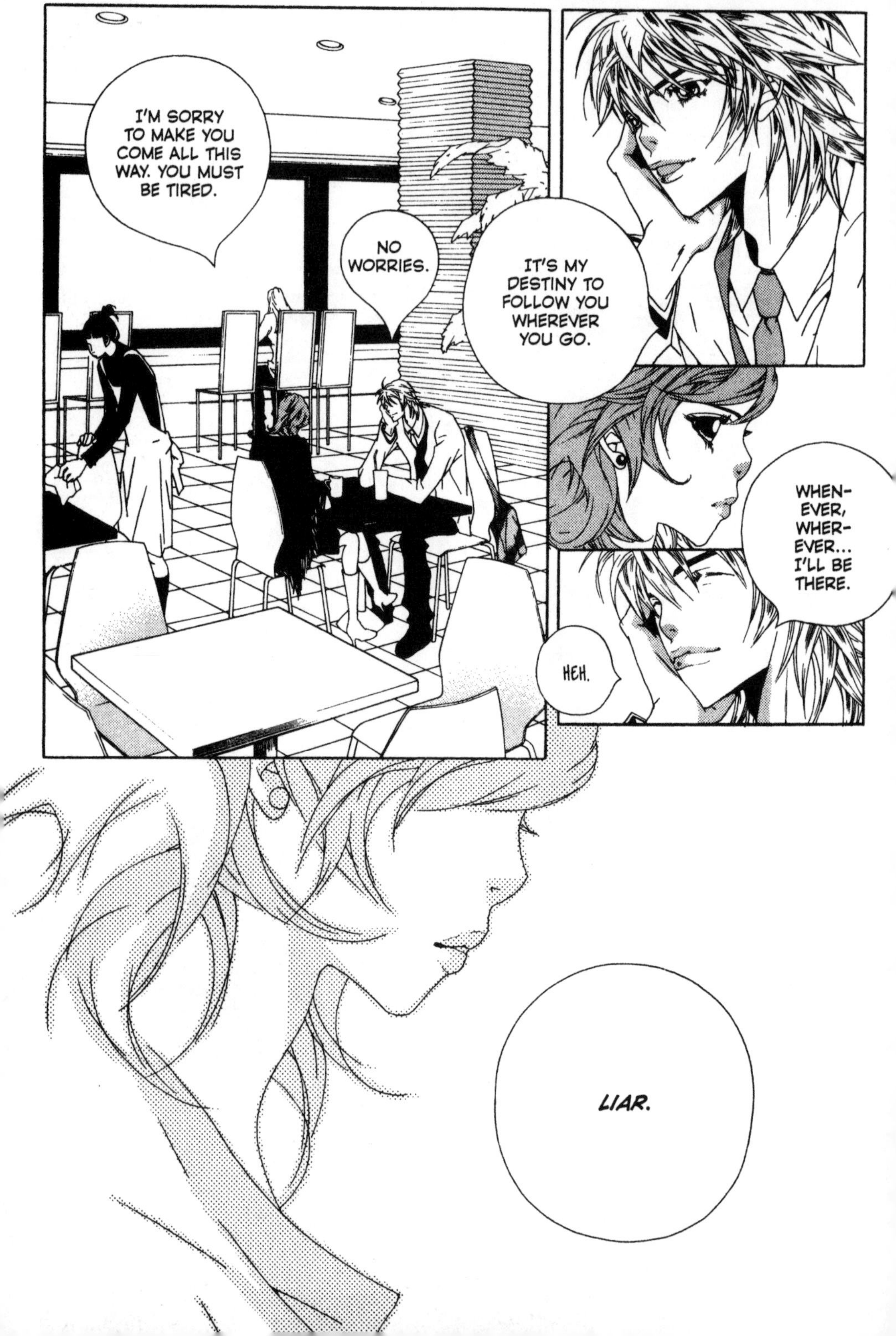
I'M SORRY TO MAKE YOU COME ALL THIS WAY. YOU MUST BE TIRED.
NO WORRIES.
IT'S MY DESTINY TO FOLLOW YOU WHEREVER YOU GO.
WHEN-EVER, WHER-EVER... I'LL BE THERE.
HEH.
LIAR.

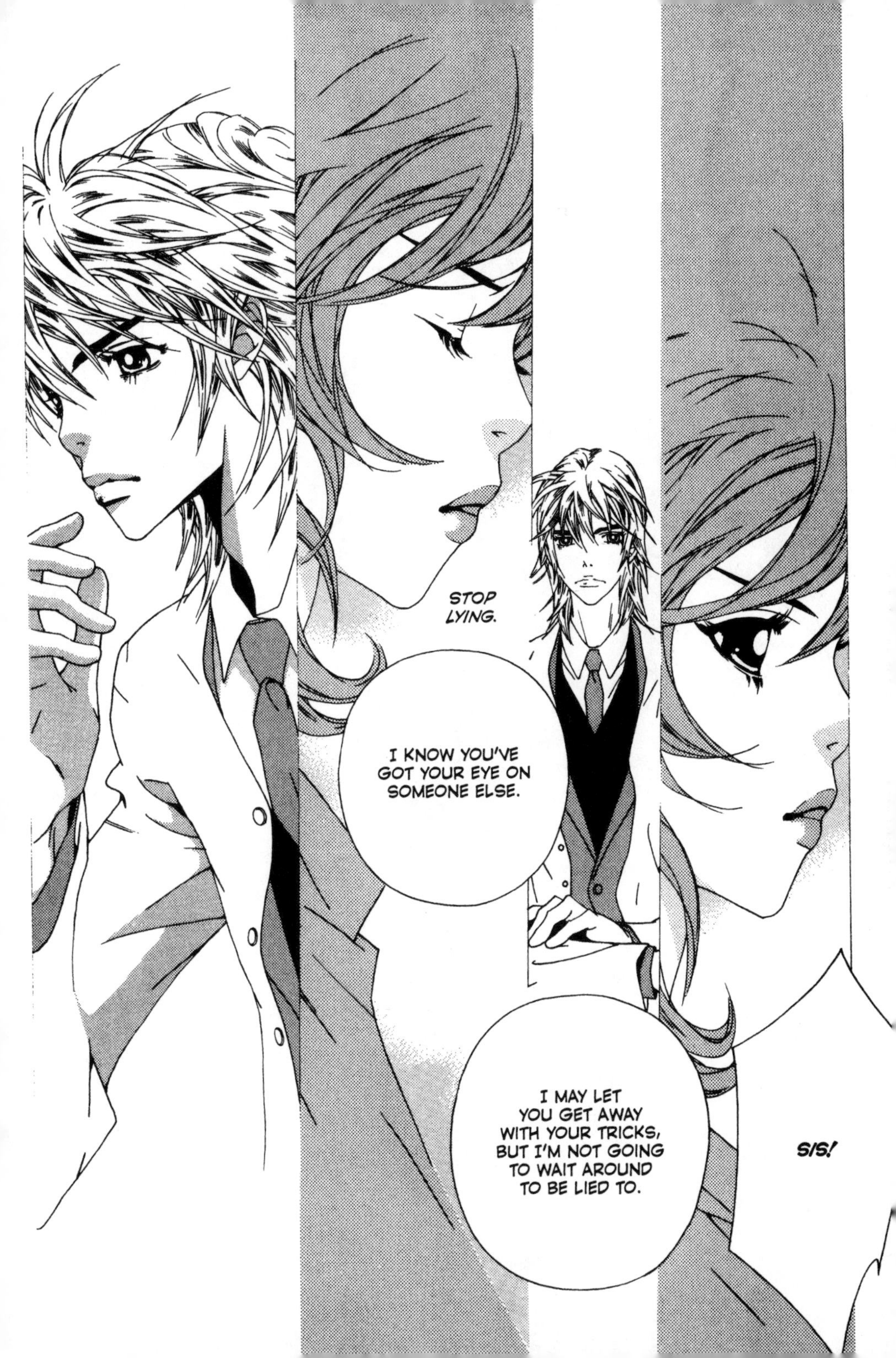
STOP LYING.
I KNOW YOU'VE GOT YOUR EYE ON SOMEONE ELSE.
I MAY LET YOU GET AWAY WITH YOUR TRICKS, BUT I'M NOT GOING TO WAIT AROUND TO BE LIED TO.
SIS!

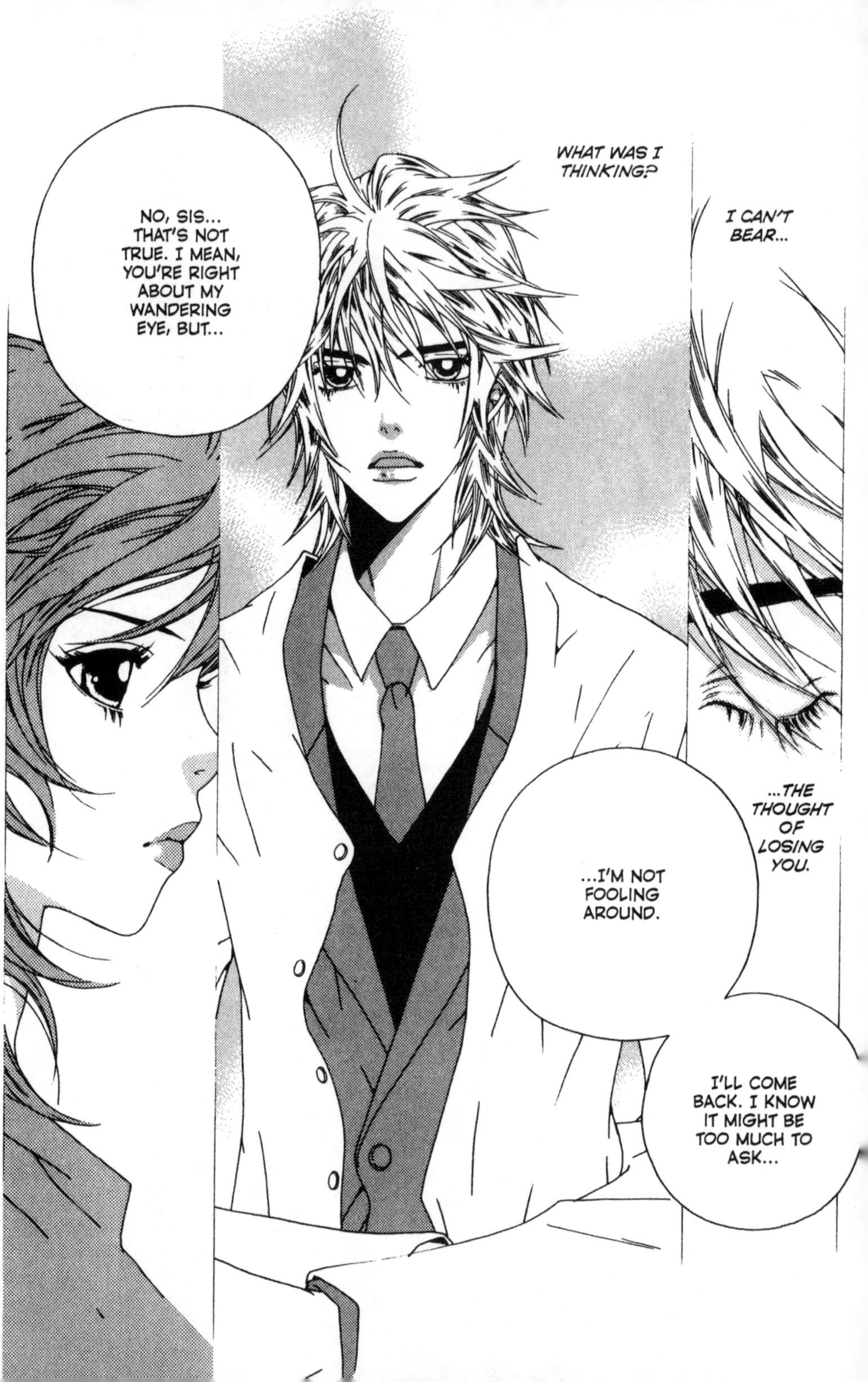
NO, SIS... THAT'S NOT TRUE. I MEAN, YOU'RE RIGHT ABOUT MY WANDERING EYE, BUT...
WHAT WAS I THINKING?
I CAN'T BEAR...
...THE THOUGHT OF LOSING YOU.
...I'M NOT FOOLING AROUND.
I'LL COME BACK. I KNOW IT MIGHT BE TOO MUCH TO ASK...

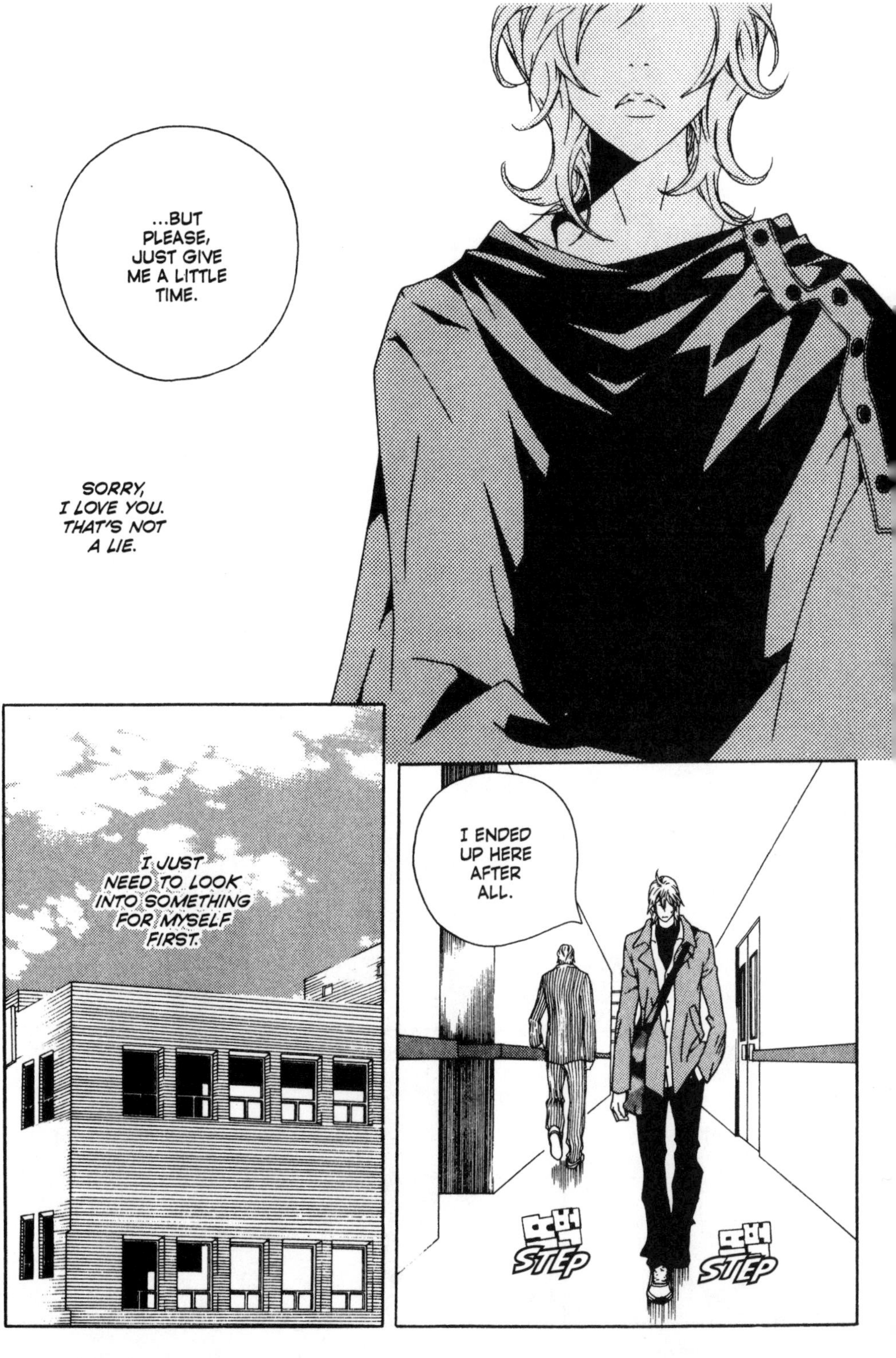
...BUT PLEASE, JUST GIVE ME A LITTLE TIME.
SORRY, I LOVE YOU. THAT'S NOT A LIE.
I JUST NEED TO LOOK INTO SOMETHING FOR MYSELF FIRST.
I ENDED UP HERE AFTER ALL.
또박
STEP
또박
STEP

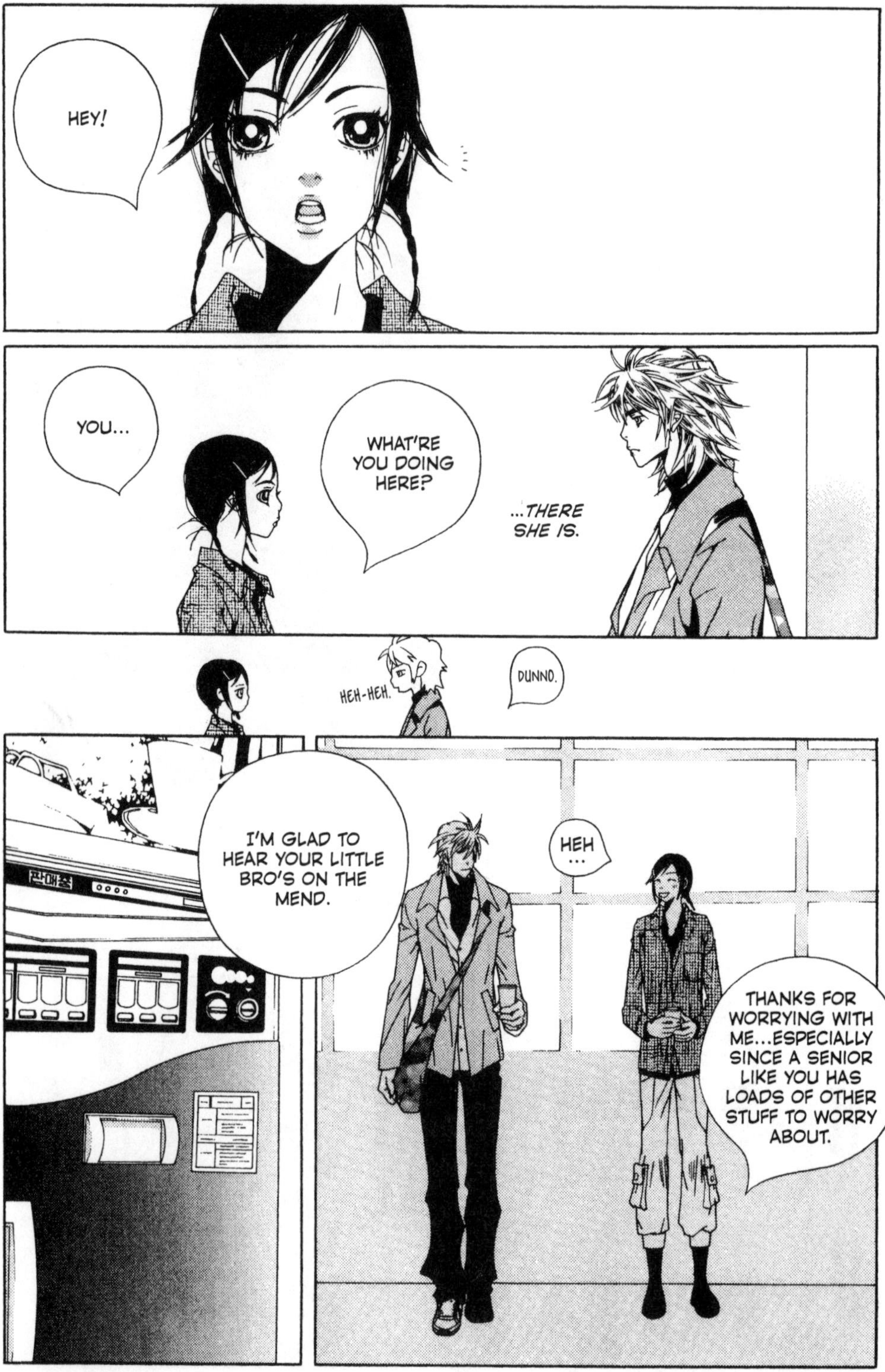
HEY!
YOU...
WHAT'RE YOU DOING HERE?
...THERE SHE IS.
HEH-HEH.
DUNNO.
I'M GLAD TO HEAR YOUR LITTLE BRO'S ON THE MEND.
HEH ...
THANKS FOR WORRYING WITH ME...ESPECIALLY SINCE A SENIOR LIKE YOU HAS LOADS OF OTHER STUFF TO WORRY ABOUT.

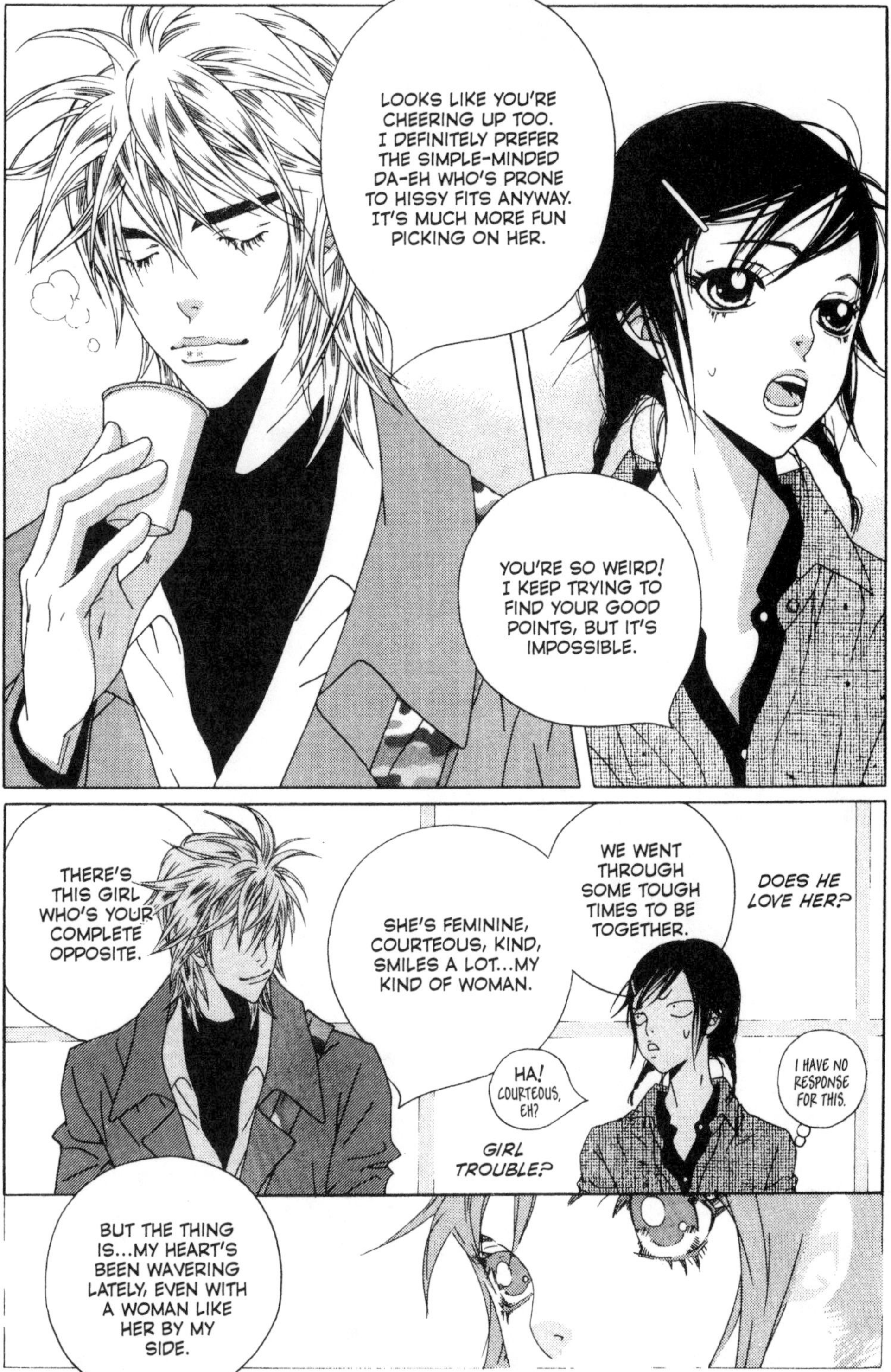
LOOKS LIKE YOU'RE CHEERING UP TOO. I DEFINITELY PREFER THE SIMPLE-MINDED DA-EH WHO'S PRONE TO HISSY FITS ANYWAY. IT'S MUCH MORE FUN PICKING ON HER.
YOU'RE SO WEIRD! I KEEP TRYING TO FIND YOUR GOOD POINTS, BUT IT'S IMPOSSIBLE.
THERE'S THIS GIRL WHO'S YOUR COMPLETE OPPOSITE.
SHE'S FEMININE, COURTEOUS, KIND, SMILES A LOT...MY KIND OF WOMAN.
WE WENT THROUGH SOME TOUGH TIMES TO BE TOGETHER.
DOES HE LOVE HER?
HA! COURTEOUS, EH?
I HAVE NO RESPONSE FOR THIS.
GIRL TROUBLE?
BUT THE THING IS...MY HEART'S BEEN WAVERING LATELY, EVEN WITH A WOMAN LIKE HER BY MY SIDE.

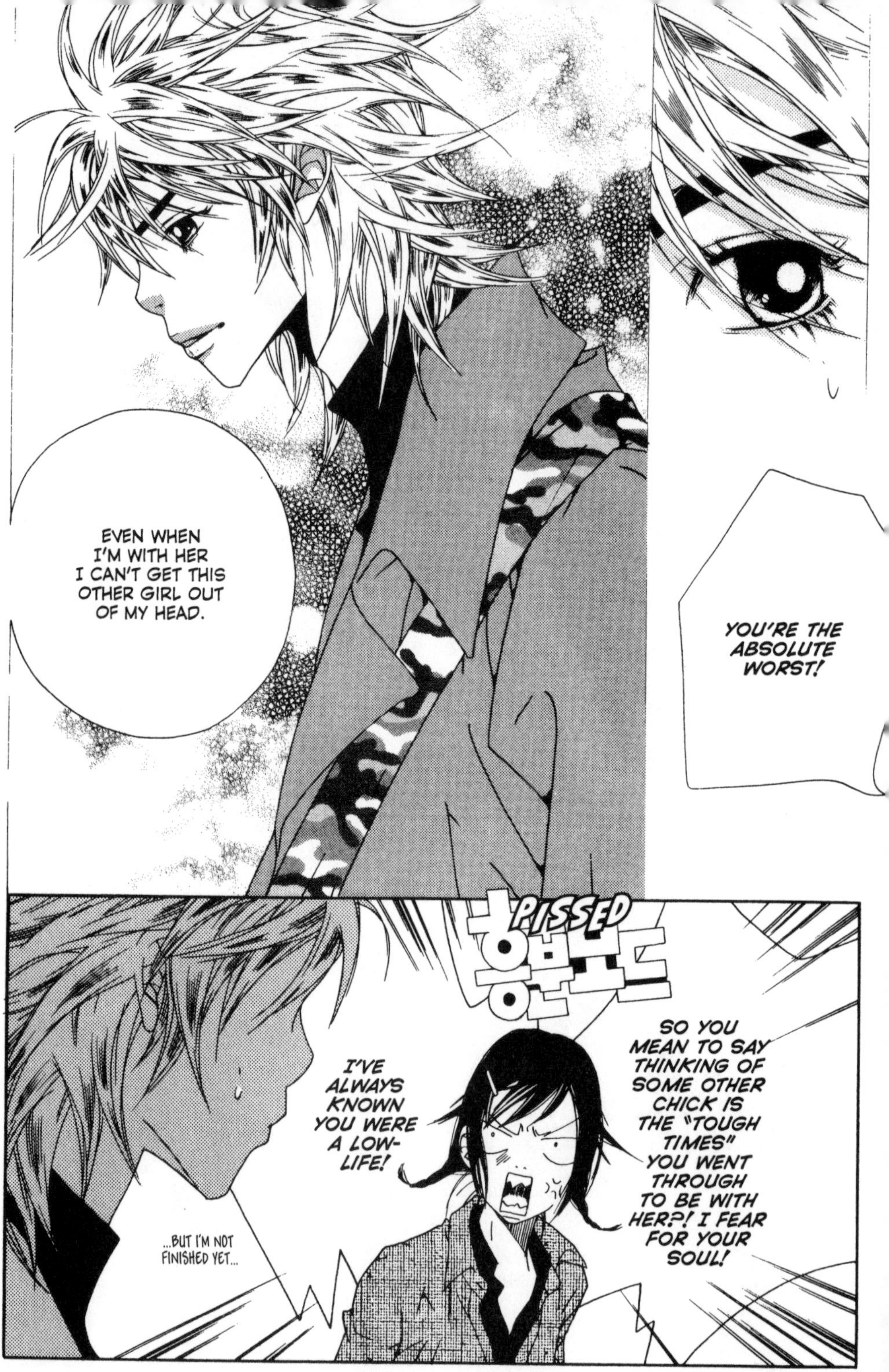
EVEN WHEN I'M WITH HER I CAN'T GET THIS OTHER GIRL OUT OF MY HEAD.
YOU'RE THE ABSOLUTE WORST!
PISSED
I'VE ALWAYS KNOWN YOU WERE A LOW-LIFE!
SO YOU MEAN TO SAY THINKING OF SOME OTHER CHICK IS THE "TOUGH TIMES" YOU WENT THROUGH TO BE WITH HER?! I FEAR FOR YOUR SOUL!
...BUT I'M NOT FINISHED YET...

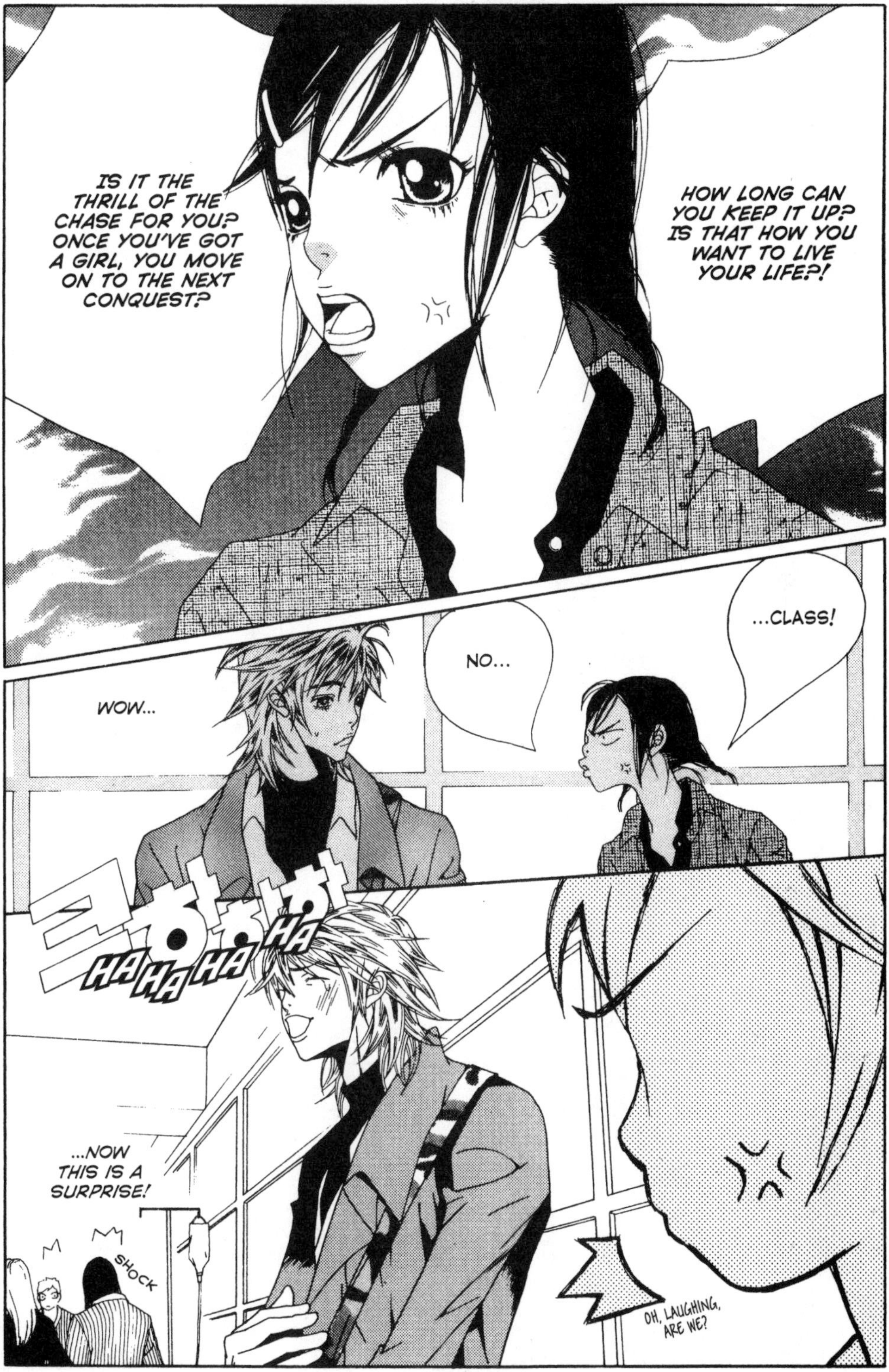
IS IT THE THRILL OF THE CHASE FOR YOU? ONCE YOU'VE GOT A GIRL, YOU MOVE ON TO THE NEXT CONQUEST?
HOW LONG CAN YOU KEEP IT UP? IS THAT HOW YOU WANT TO LIVE YOUR LIFE?!
WOW...
NO...
...CLASS!
HA HA HA HA HA
...NOW THIS IS A SURPRISE!
SHOCK
OH, LAUGHING, ARE WE?

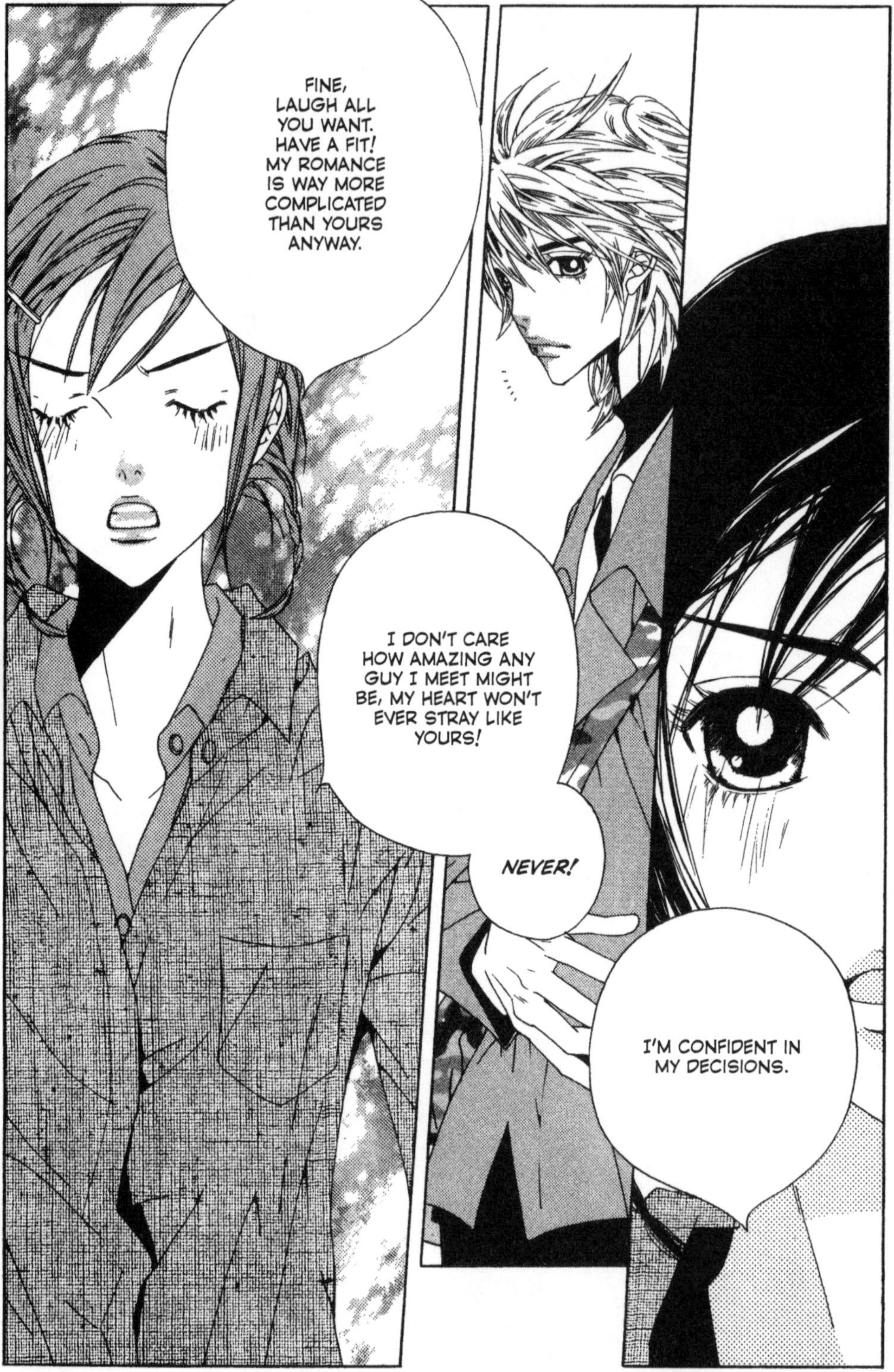
FINE, LAUGH ALL YOU WANT. HAVE A FIT! MY ROMANCE IS WAY MORE COMPLICATED THAN YOURS ANYWAY.
I DON'T CARE HOW AMAZING ANY GUY I MEET MIGHT BE, MY HEART WON'T EVER STRAY LIKE YOURS!
NEVER!
I'M CONFIDENT IN MY DECISIONS.

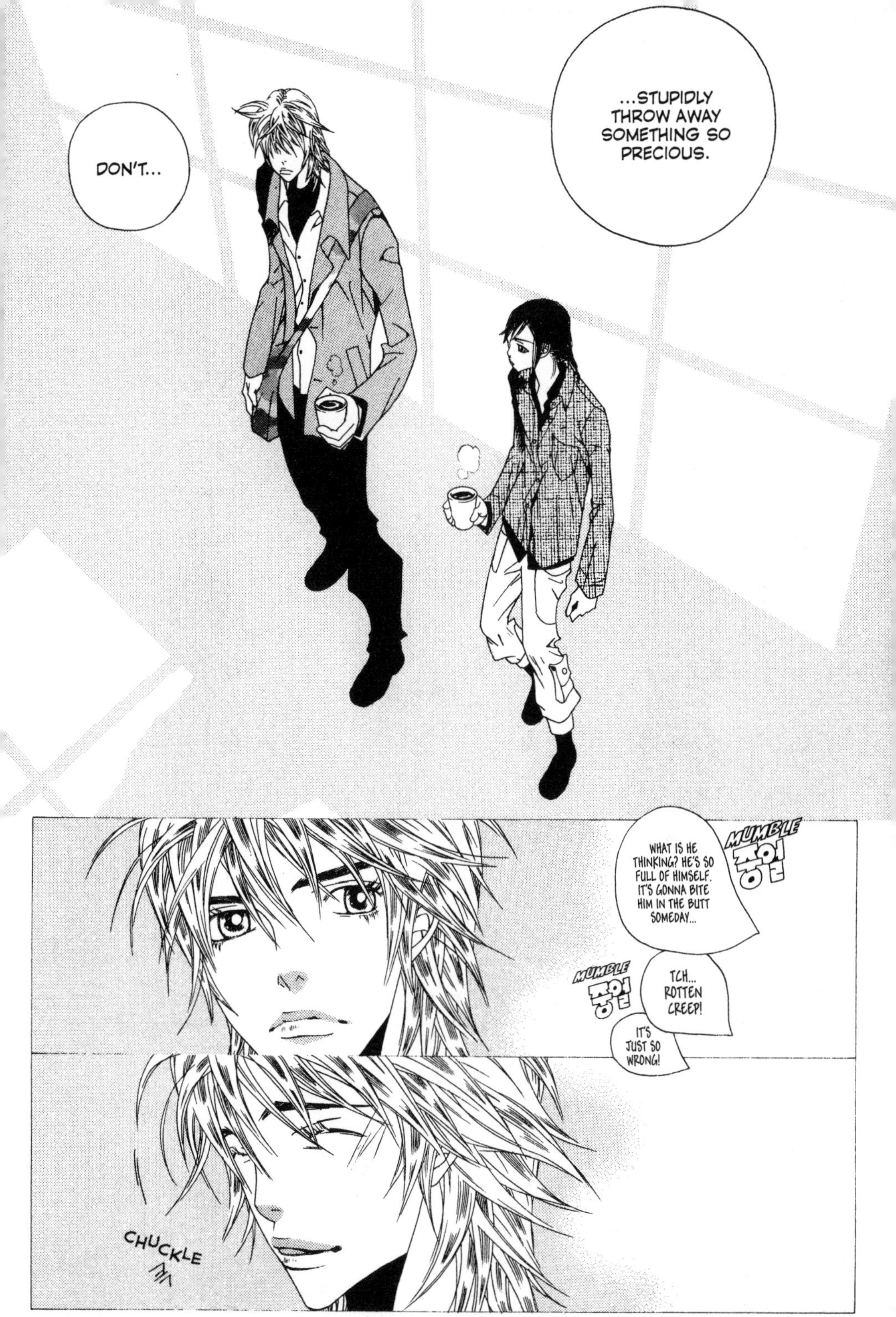
DON'T...
...STUPIDLY THROW AWAY SOMETHING SO PRECIOUS.
MUMBLE
WHAT IS HE THINKING? HE'S SO FULL OF HIMSELF. IT'S GONNA BITE HIM IN THE BUTT SOMEDAY...
MUMBLE
TCH... ROTTEN CREEP!
IT'S JUST SO WRONG!
CHUCKLE

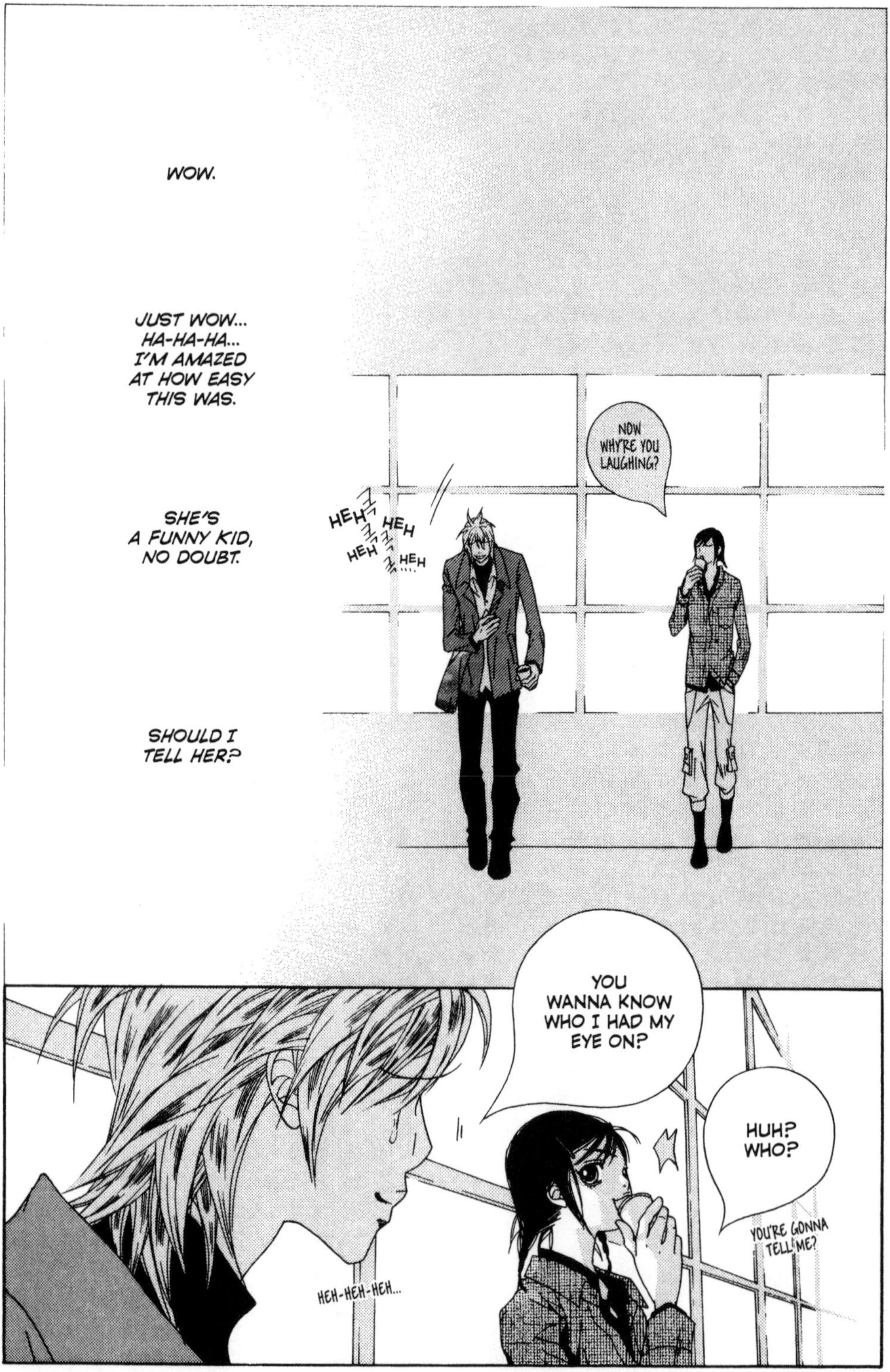
WOW.
JUST WOW... HA-HA-HA... I'M AMAZED AT HOW EASY THIS WAS.
SHE'S A FUNNY KID, NO DOUBT.
SHOULD I TELL HER?
HEH HEH HEH HEH
NOW WHY'RE YOU LAUGHING?
YOU WANNA KNOW WHO I HAD MY EYE ON?
HUH? WHO?
YOU'RE GONNA TELL ME?
HEH-HEH-HEH...

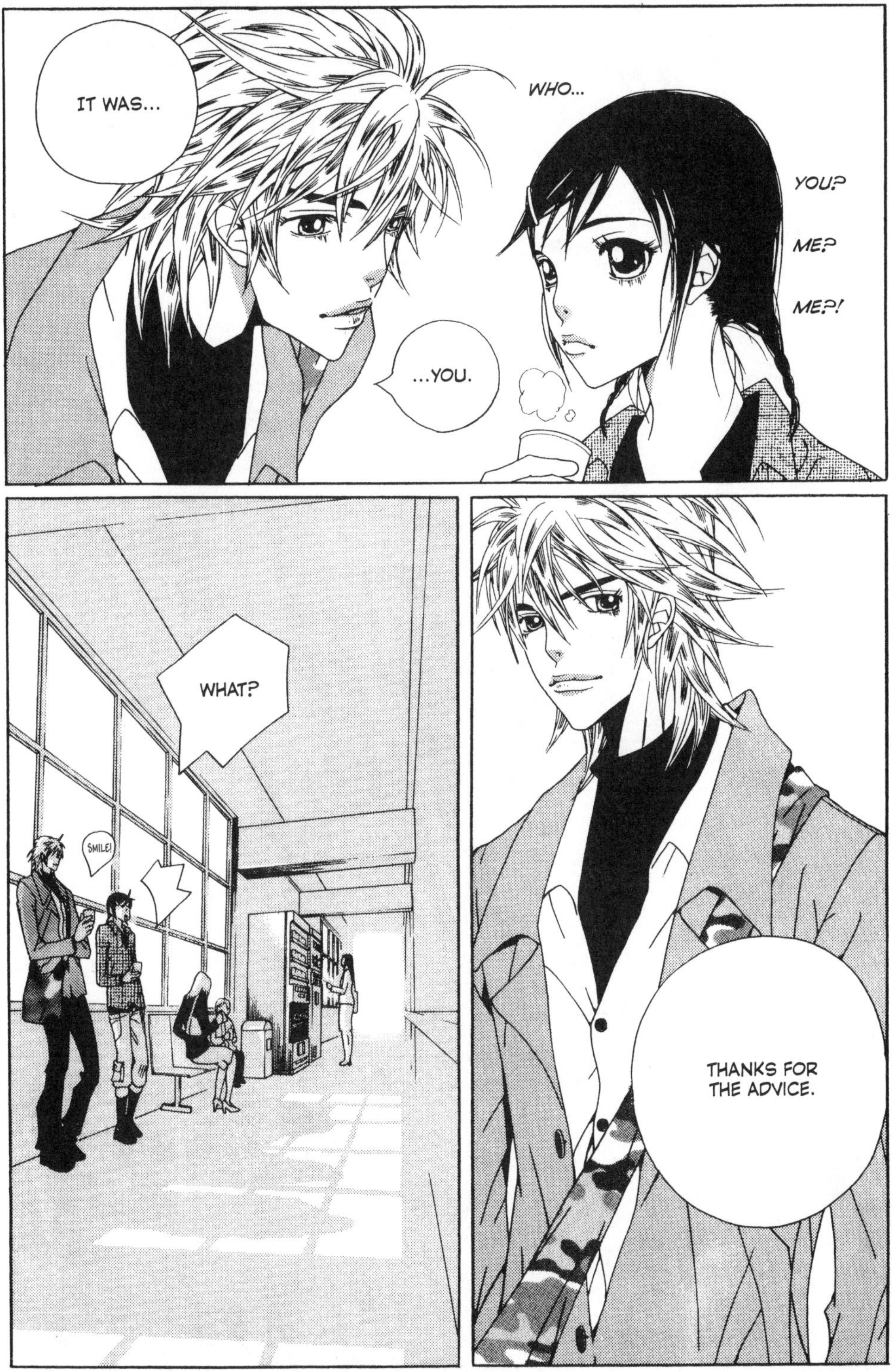
IT WAS...
...YOU.
WHO...
YOU?
ME?
ME?!
WHAT?
SMILE!
THANKS FOR THE ADVICE.

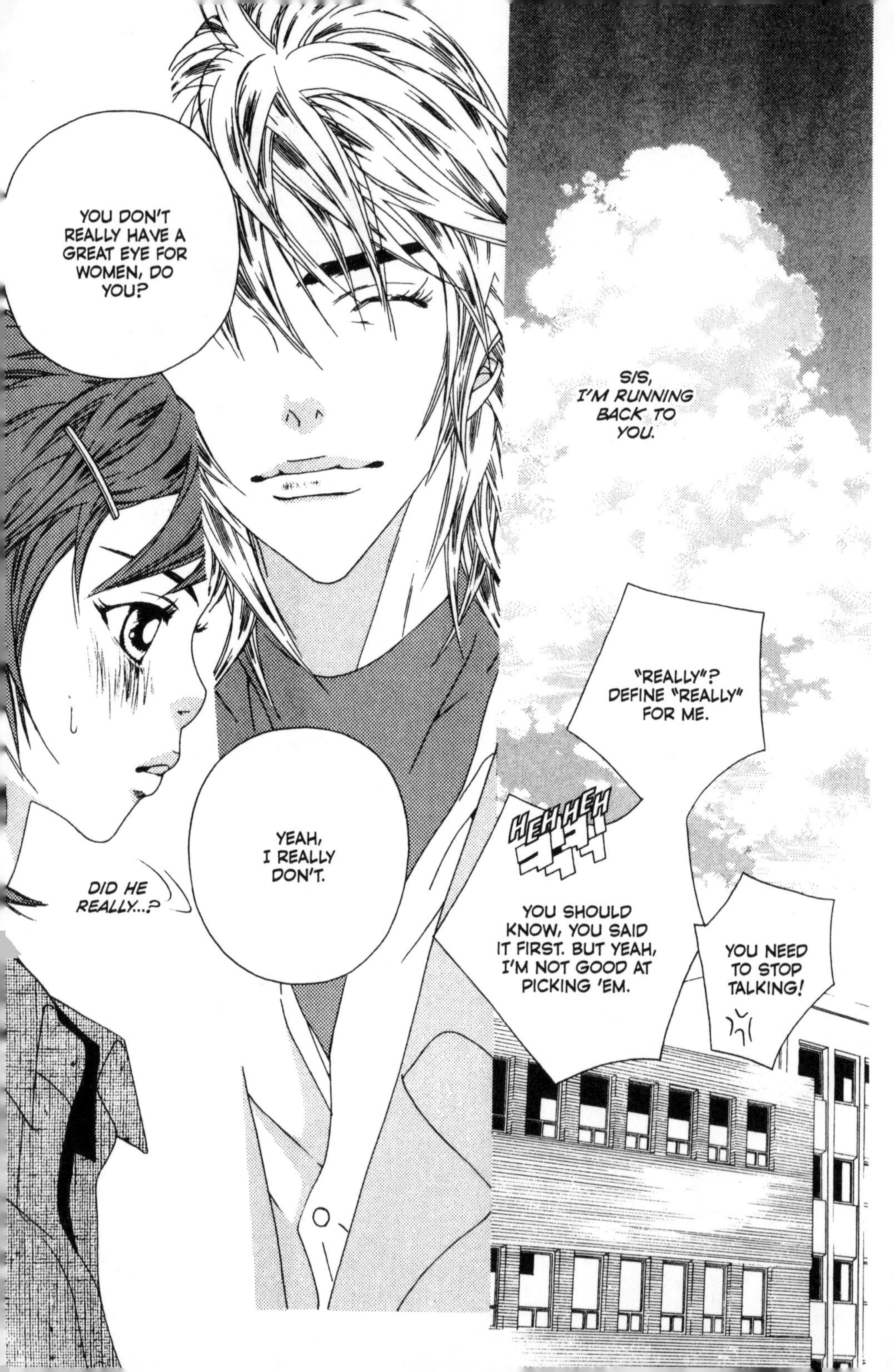
YOU DON'T REALLY HAVE A GREAT EYE FOR WOMEN, DO YOU?
YEAH, I REALLY DON'T.
DID HE REALLY...?
SIS, I'M RUNNING BACK TO YOU.
"REALLY"? DEFINE "REALLY" FOR ME.
HEH HEH
YOU SHOULD KNOW, YOU SAID IT FIRST. BUT YEAH, I'M NOT GOOD AT PICKING 'EM.
YOU NEED TO STOP TALKING!

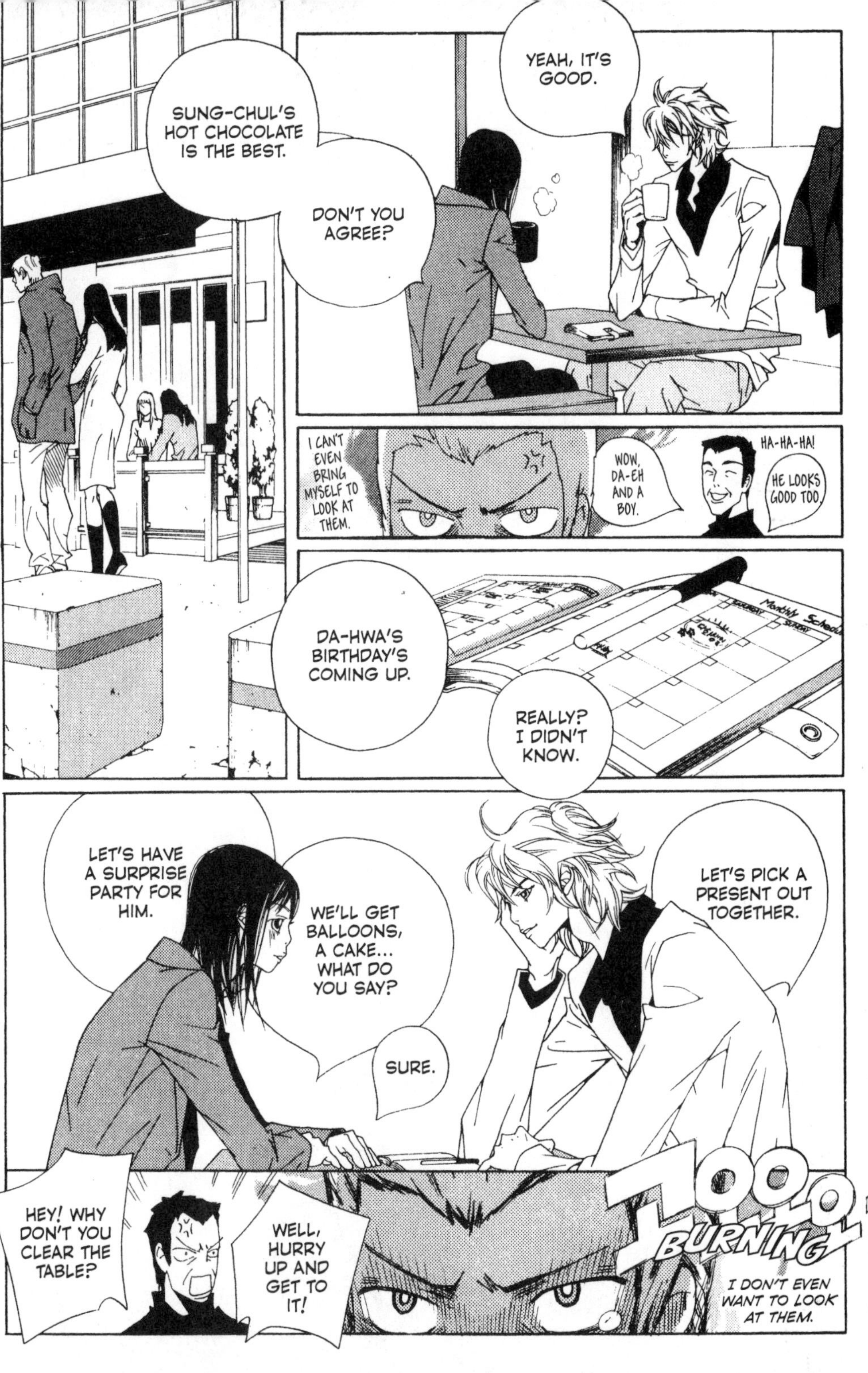
SUNG-CHUL'S HOT CHOCOLATE IS THE BEST.
DON'T YOU AGREE?
YEAH, IT'S GOOD.
I CAN'T EVEN BRING MYSELF TO LOOK AT THEM.
WOW, DA-EH AND A BOY.
HA-HA-HA!
HE LOOKS GOOD TOO.
DA-HWA'S BIRTHDAY'S COMING UP.
REALLY? I DIDN'T KNOW.
LET'S HAVE A SURPRISE PARTY FOR HIM.
WE'LL GET BALLOONS, A CAKE... WHAT DO YOU SAY?
SURE.
LET'S PICK A PRESENT OUT TOGETHER.
HEY! WHY DON'T YOU CLEAR THE TABLE?
WELL, HURRY UP AND GET TO IT!
BURNING
I DON'T EVEN WANT TO LOOK AT THEM.

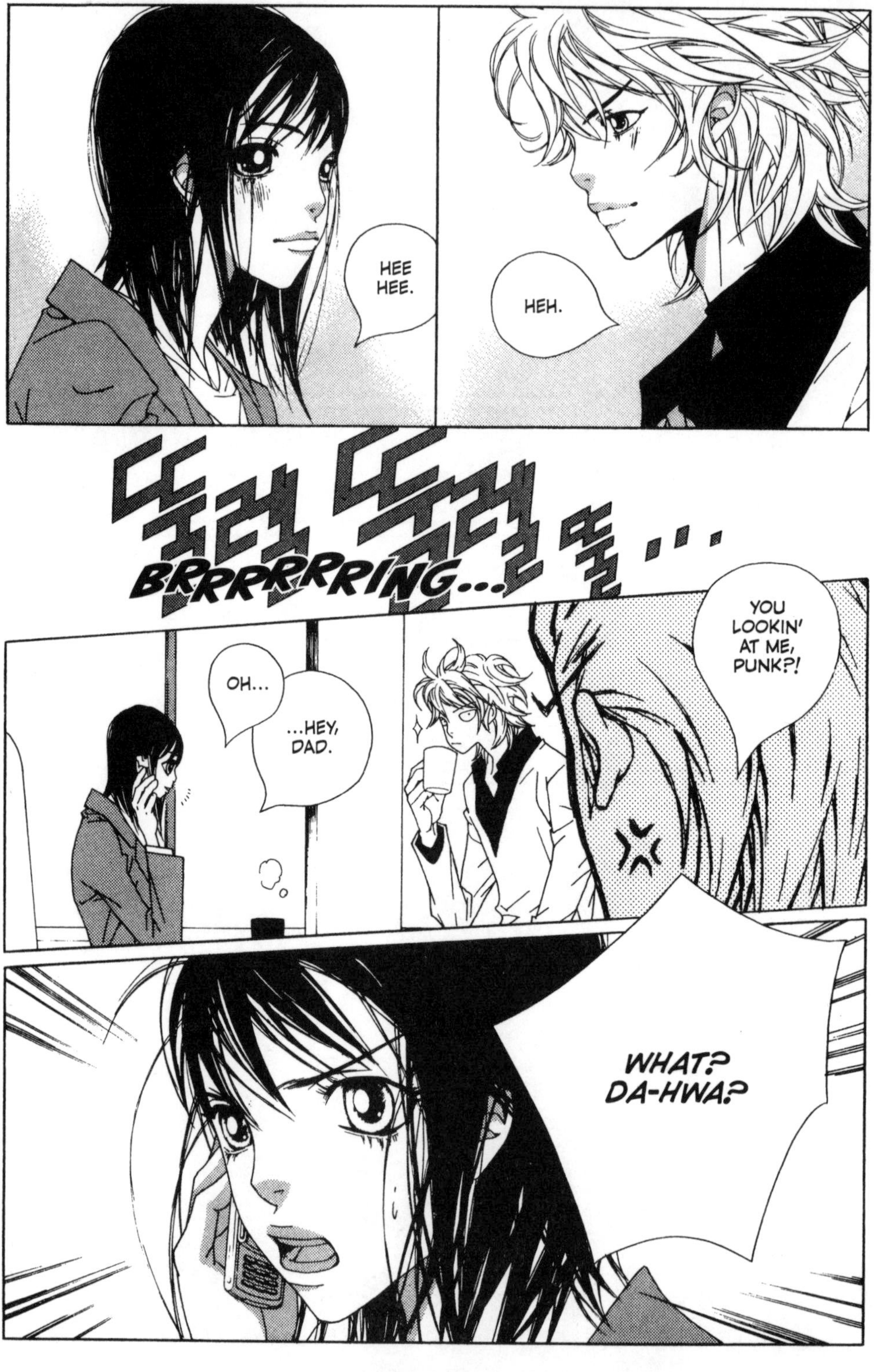
HEE HEE.
HEH.
BRRRRRRING...
OH...
...HEY, DAD.
YOU LOOKIN' AT ME, PUNK?!
WHAT? DA-HWA?

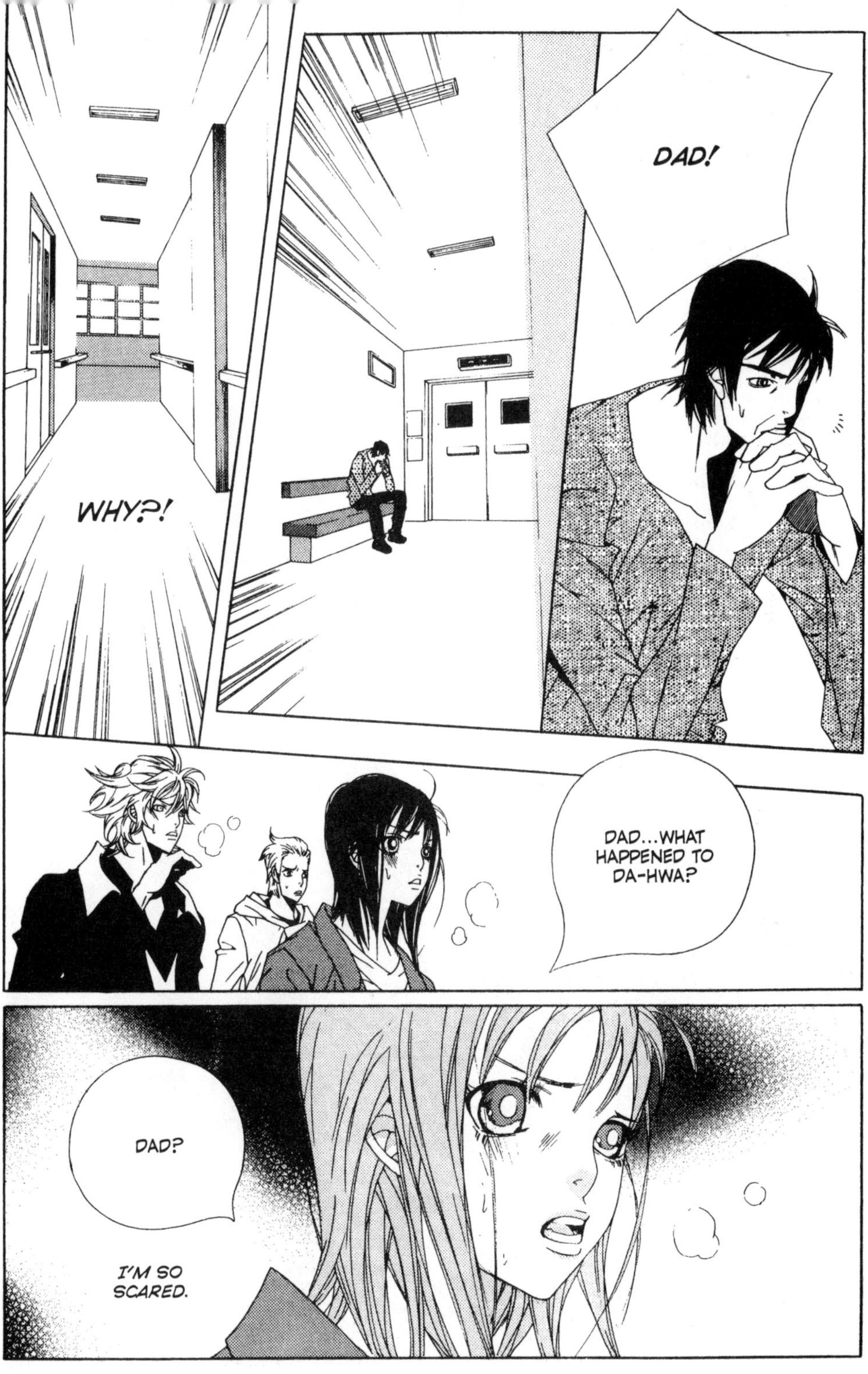
WHY?!
DAD!
DAD...WHAT HAPPENED TO DA-HWA?
DAD?
I'M SO SCARED.

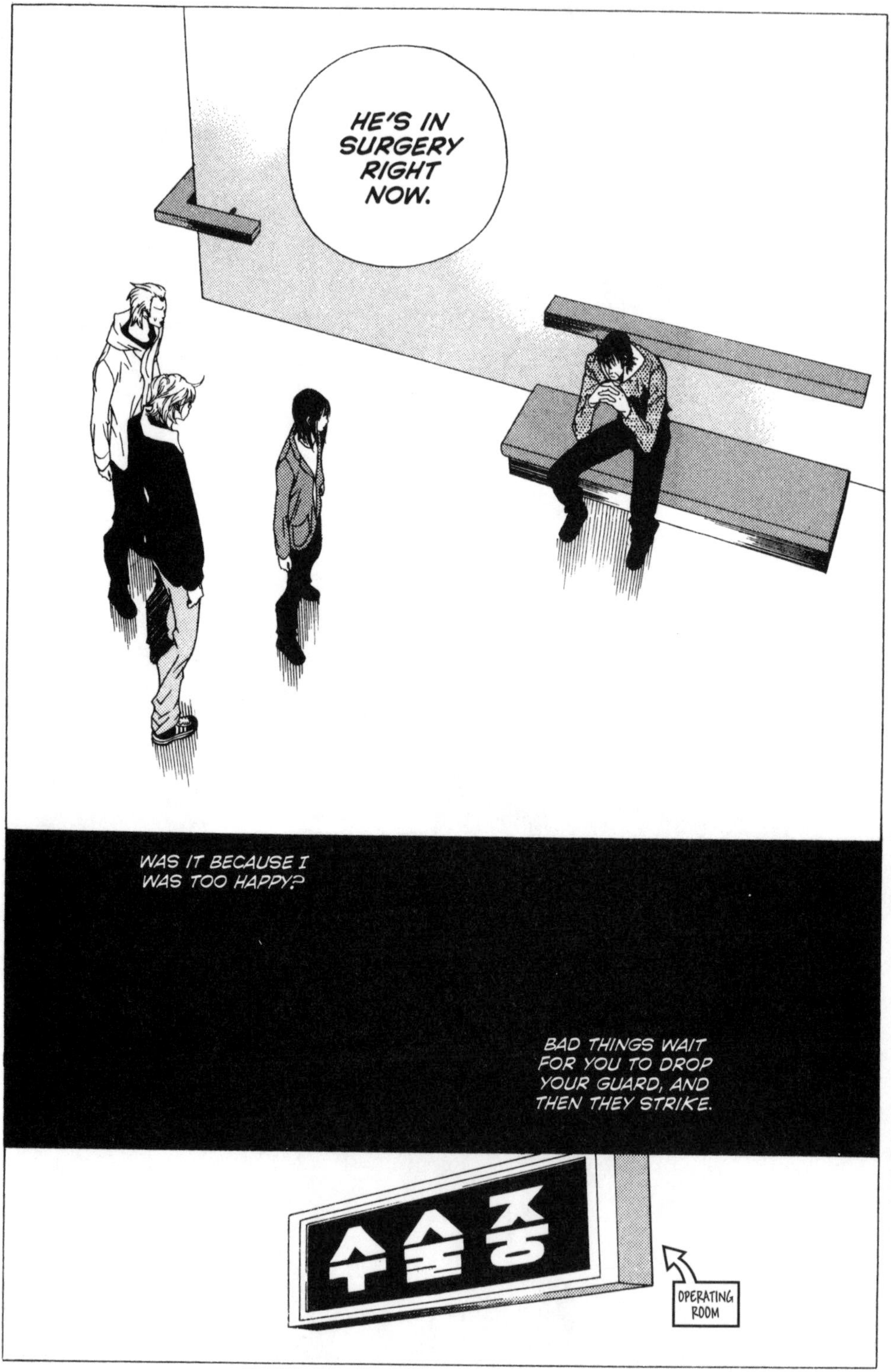
HE'S IN SURGERY RIGHT NOW.
WAS IT BECAUSE I WAS TOO HAPPY?
BAD THINGS WAIT FOR YOU TO DROP YOUR GUARD, AND THEN THEY STRIKE.
수술중
OPERATING ROOM

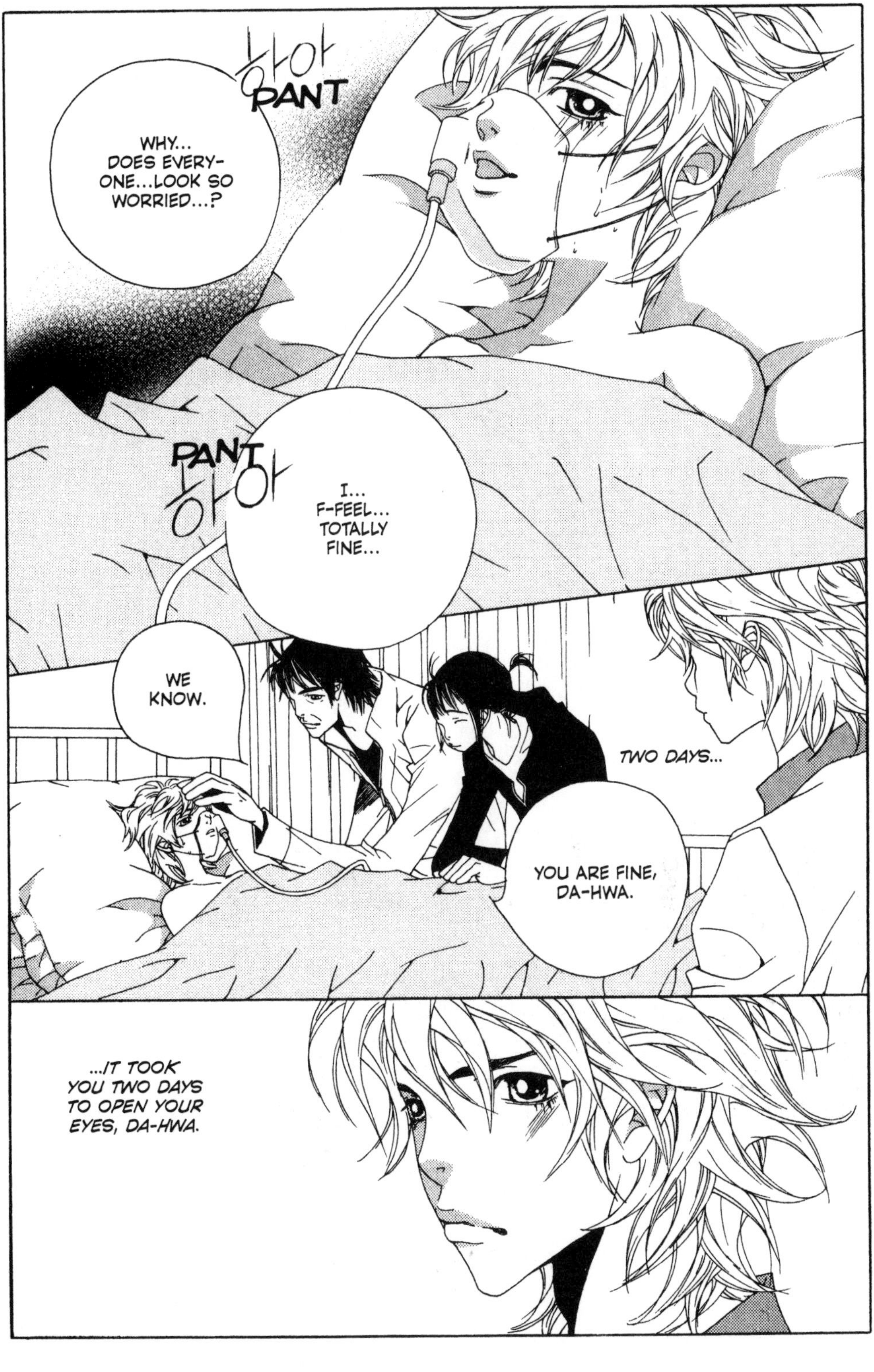
하아
PANT
WHY... DOES EVERY-ONE...LOOK SO WORRIED...?
PANT
하아
I... F-FEEL... TOTALLY FINE...
WE KNOW.
TWO DAYS...
YOU ARE FINE, DA-HWA.
...IT TOOK YOU TWO DAYS TO OPEN YOUR EYES, DA-HWA.

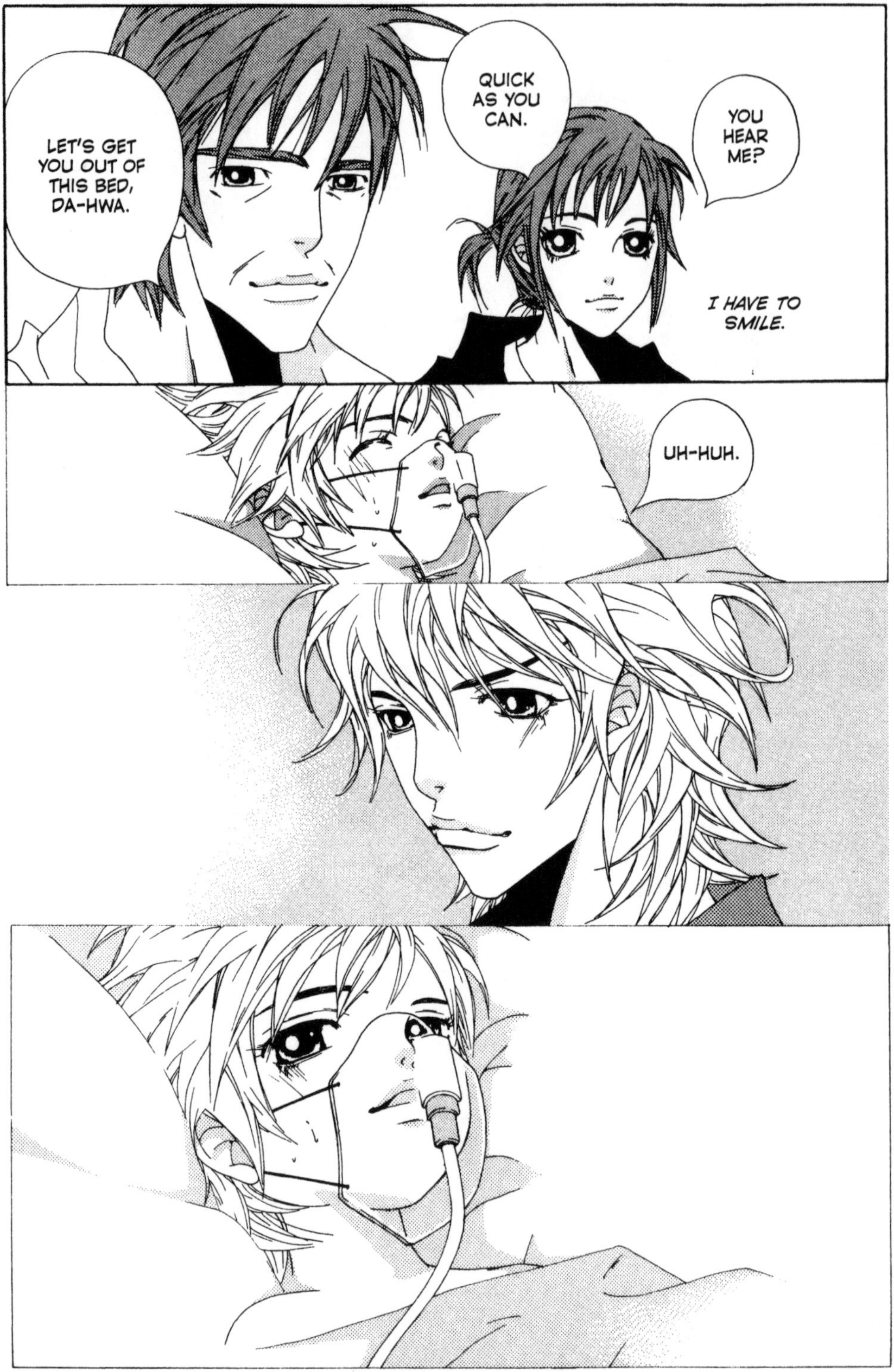
LET'S GET YOU OUT OF THIS BED, DA-HWA.
QUICK AS YOU CAN.
YOU HEAR ME?
I HAVE TO SMILE.
UH-HUH.

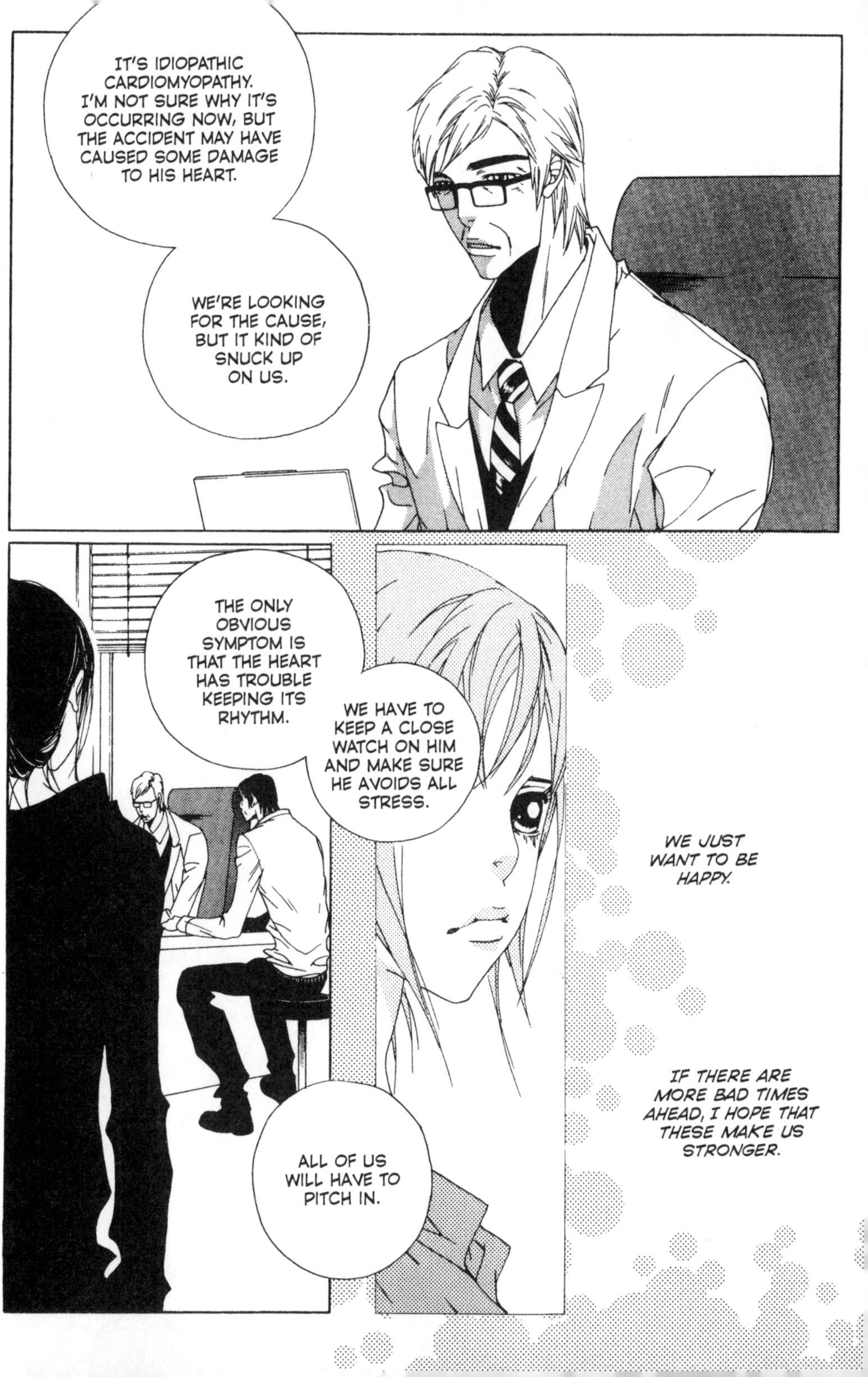
IT'S IDIOPATHIC CARDIOMYOPATHY. I'M NOT SURE WHY IT'S OCCURRING NOW, BUT THE ACCIDENT MAY HAVE CAUSED SOME DAMAGE TO HIS HEART.
WE'RE LOOKING FOR THE CAUSE, BUT IT KIND OF SNUCK UP ON US.
THE ONLY OBVIOUS SYMPTOM IS THAT THE HEART HAS TROUBLE KEEPING ITS RHYTHM.
WE HAVE TO KEEP A CLOSE WATCH ON HIM AND MAKE SURE HE AVOIDS ALL STRESS.
ALL OF US WILL HAVE TO PITCH IN.
WE JUST WANT TO BE HAPPY.
IF THERE ARE MORE BAD TIMES AHEAD, I HOPE THAT THESE MAKE US STRONGER.

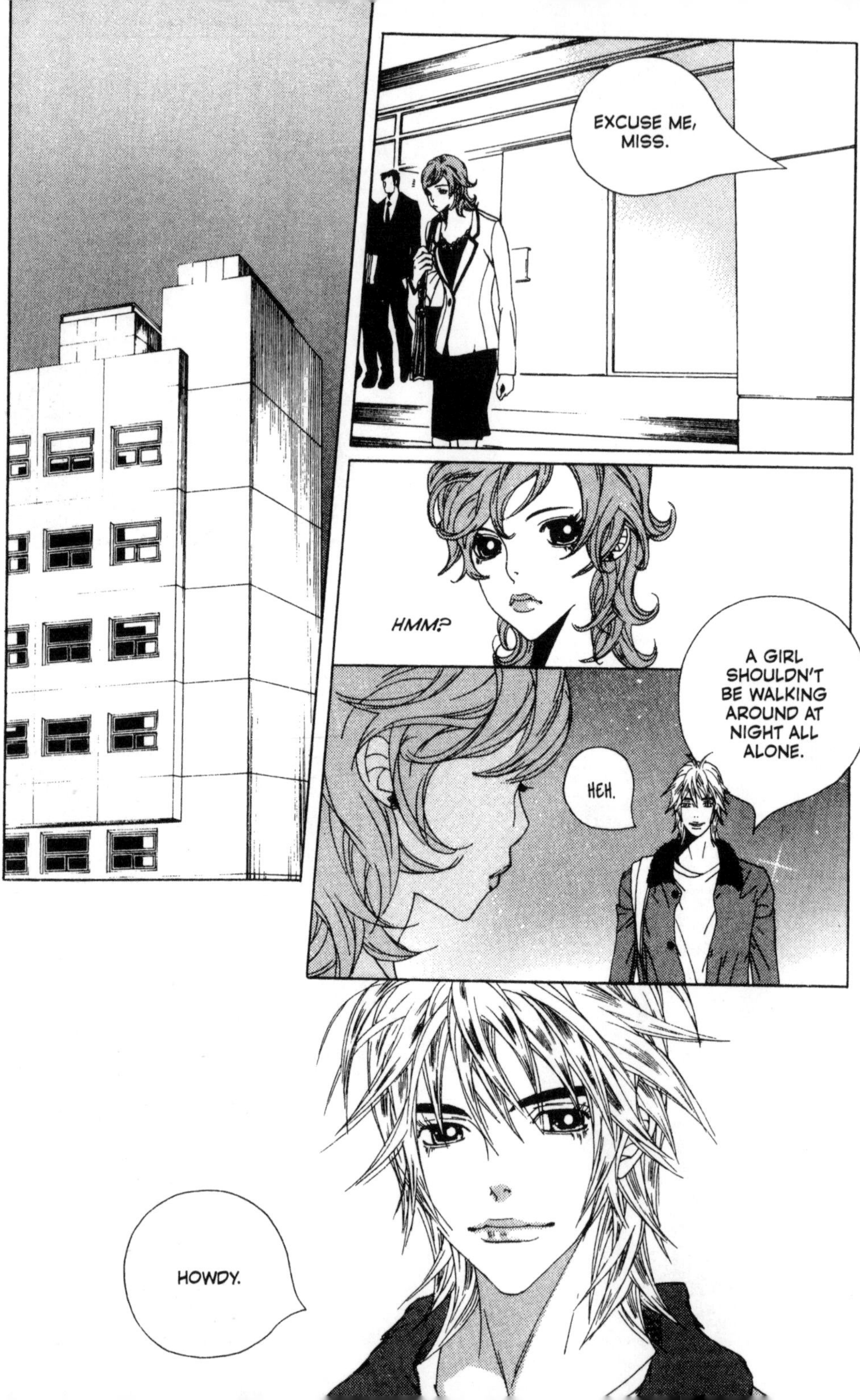
EXCUSE ME, MISS.
HMM?
A GIRL SHOULDN'T BE WALKING AROUND AT NIGHT ALL ALONE.
HEH.
HOWDY.

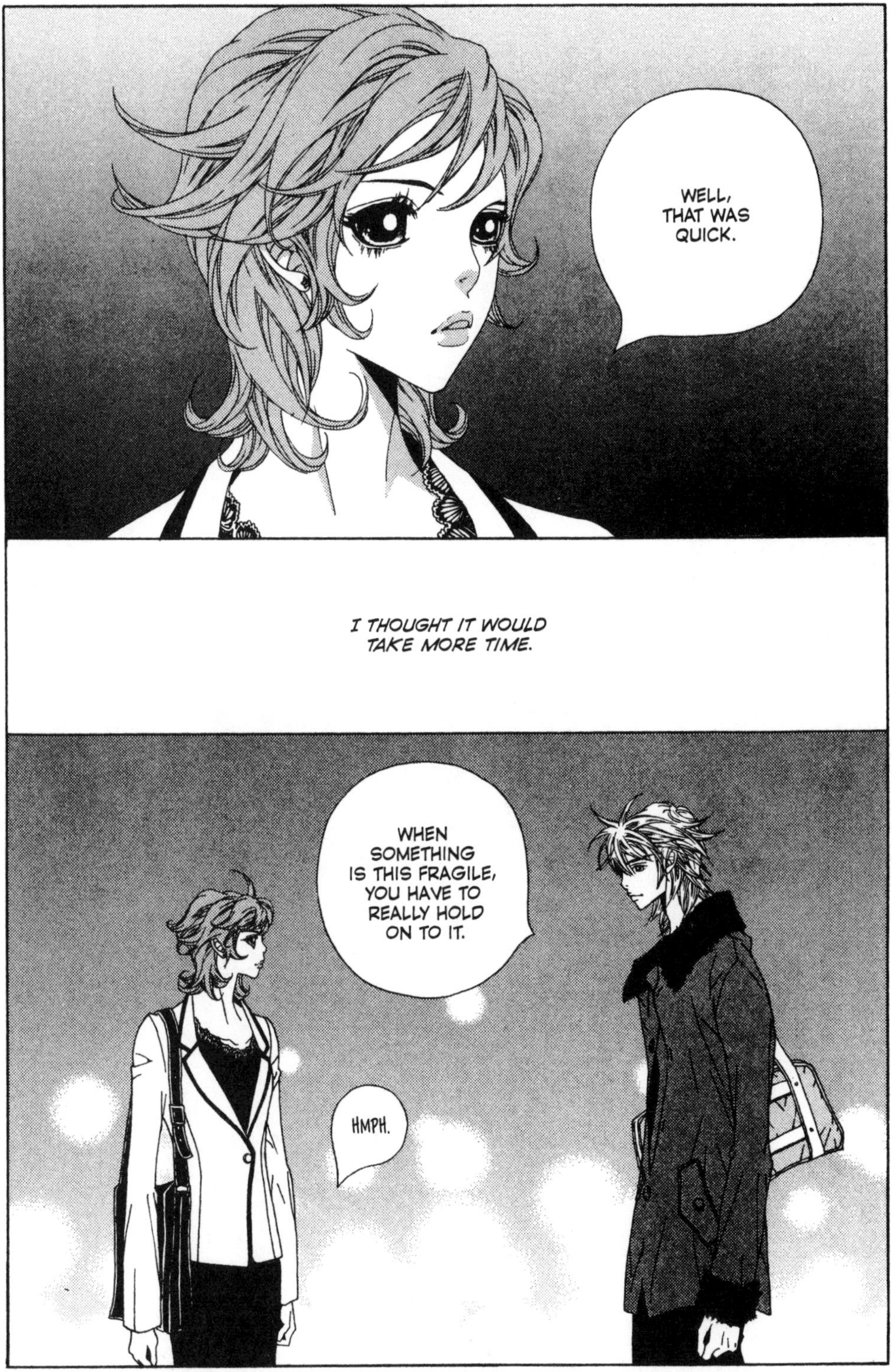
WELL, THAT WAS QUICK.
I THOUGHT IT WOULD TAKE MORE TIME.
WHEN SOMETHING IS THIS FRAGILE, YOU HAVE TO REALLY HOLD ON TO IT.
HMPH.

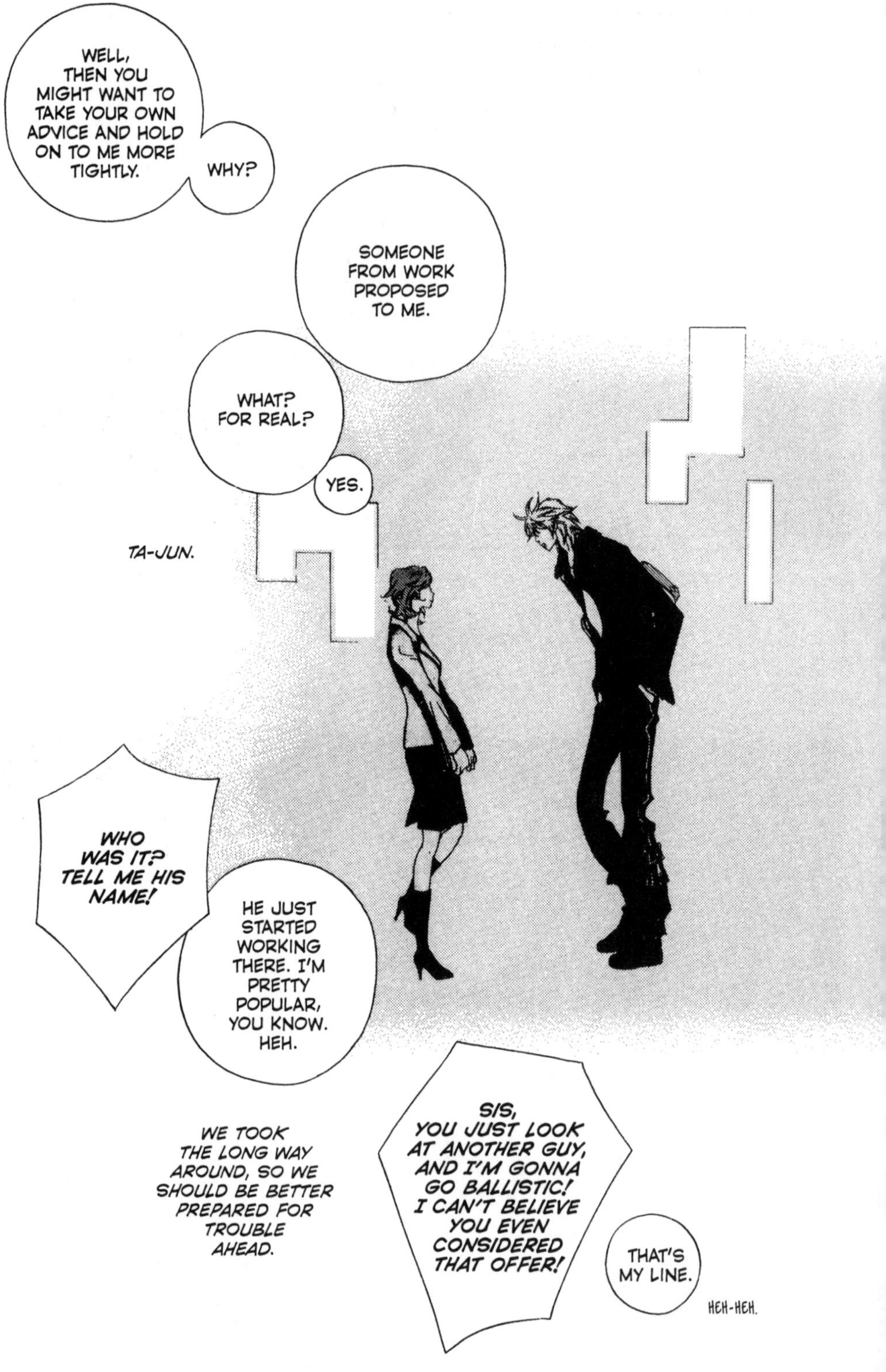
WELL, THEN YOU MIGHT WANT TO TAKE YOUR OWN ADVICE AND HOLD ON TO ME MORE TIGHTLY.
WHY?
SOMEONE FROM WORK PROPOSED TO ME.
WHAT? FOR REAL?
YES.
TA-JUN.
WHO WAS IT? TELL ME HIS NAME!
HE JUST STARTED WORKING THERE. I'M PRETTY POPULAR, YOU KNOW. HEH.
WE TOOK THE LONG WAY AROUND, SO WE SHOULD BE BETTER PREPARED FOR TROUBLE AHEAD.
SIS, YOU JUST LOOK AT ANOTHER GUY, AND I'M GONNA GO BALLISTIC! I CAN'T BELIEVE YOU EVEN CONSIDERED THAT OFFER!
THAT'S MY LINE.
HEH-HEH.

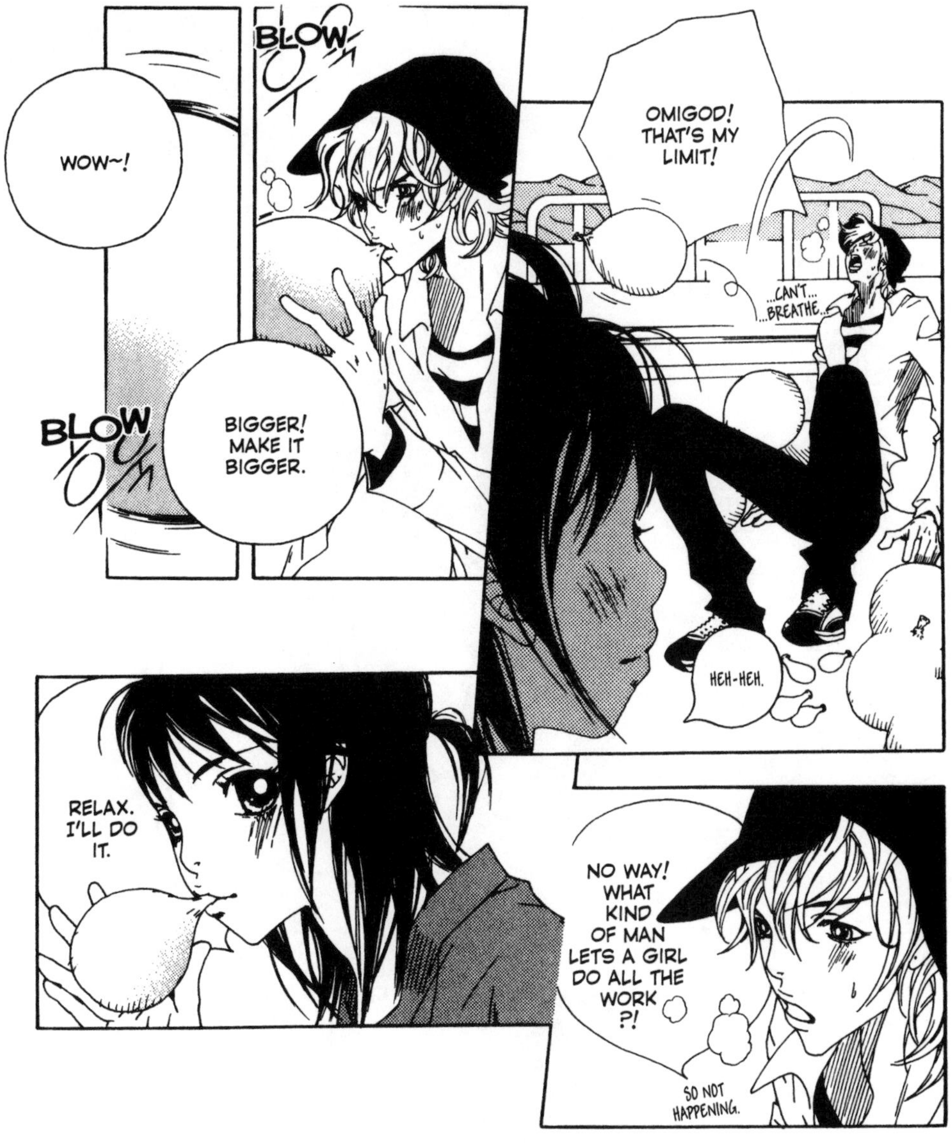
WOW~!
BLOW
BLOW
BIGGER! MAKE IT BIGGER.
OMIGOD! THAT'S MY LIMIT!
...CAN'T... ...BREATHE...
HEH-HEH.
RELAX. I'LL DO IT.
NO WAY! WHAT KIND OF MAN LETS A GIRL DO ALL THE WORK ?!
SO NOT HAPPENING.

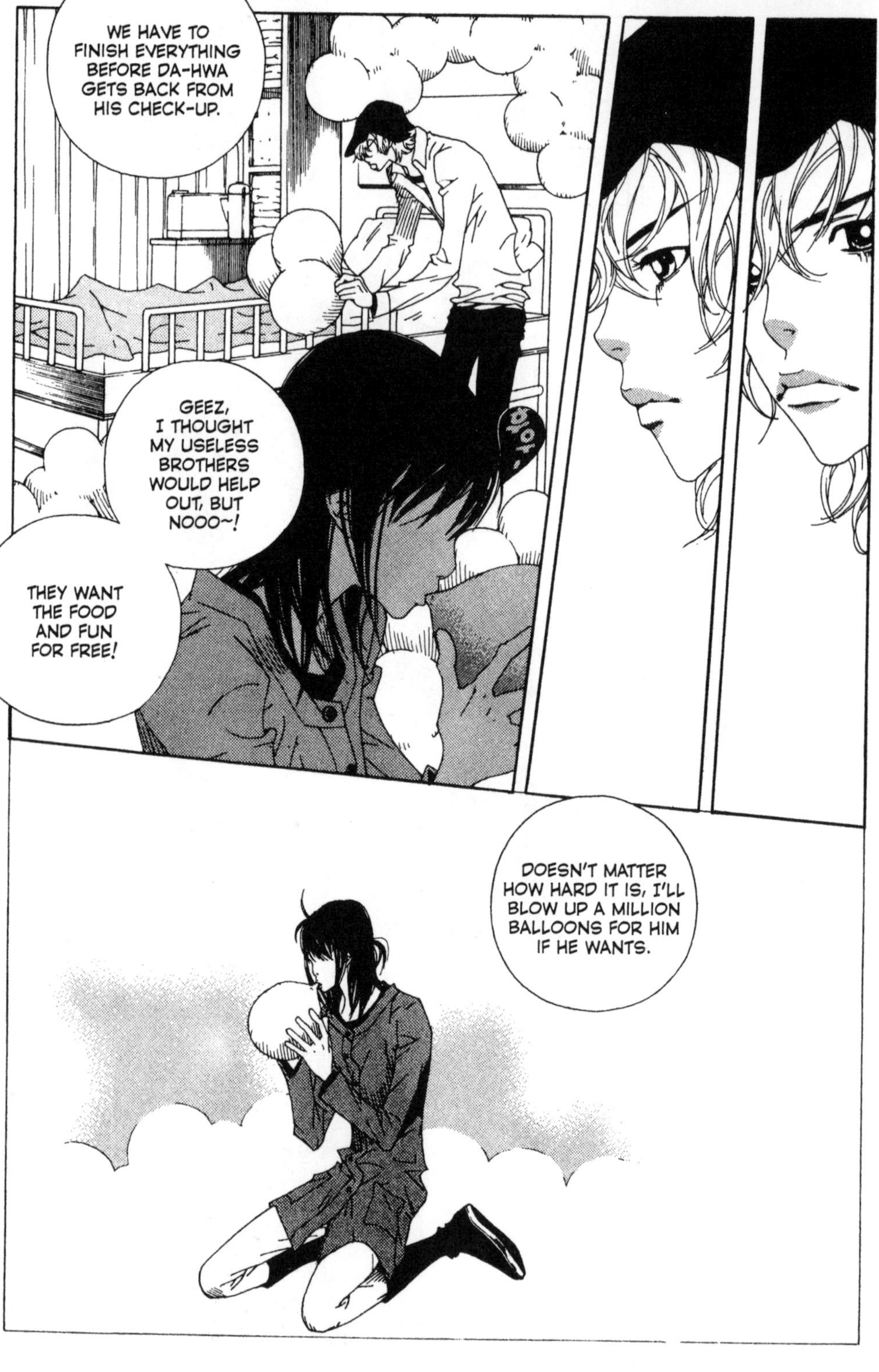
WE HAVE TO FINISH EVERYTHING BEFORE DA-HWA GETS BACK FROM HIS CHECK-UP.
GEEZ, I THOUGHT MY USELESS BROTHERS WOULD HELP OUT, BUT NOOO~!
THEY WANT THE FOOD AND FUN FOR FREE!
DOESN'T MATTER HOW HARD IT IS, I'LL BLOW UP A MILLION BALLOONS FOR HIM IF HE WANTS.

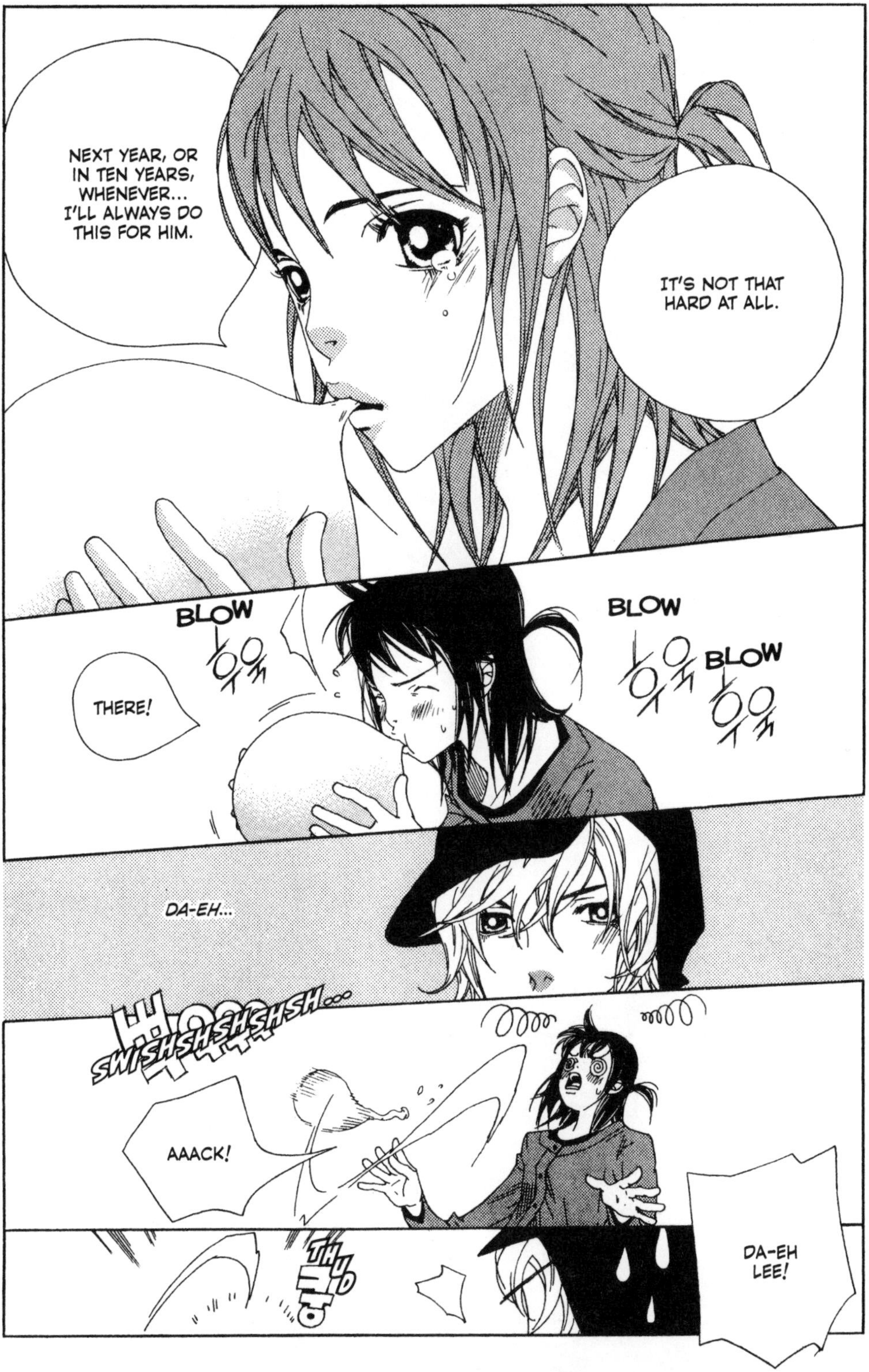
NEXT YEAR, OR IN TEN YEARS, WHENEVER... I'LL ALWAYS DO THIS FOR HIM.
IT'S NOT THAT HARD AT ALL.
BLOW
THERE!
BLOW
BLOW
DA-EH...
SWISHSHSHSHSH...
AAACK!
THUD
DA-EH LEE!

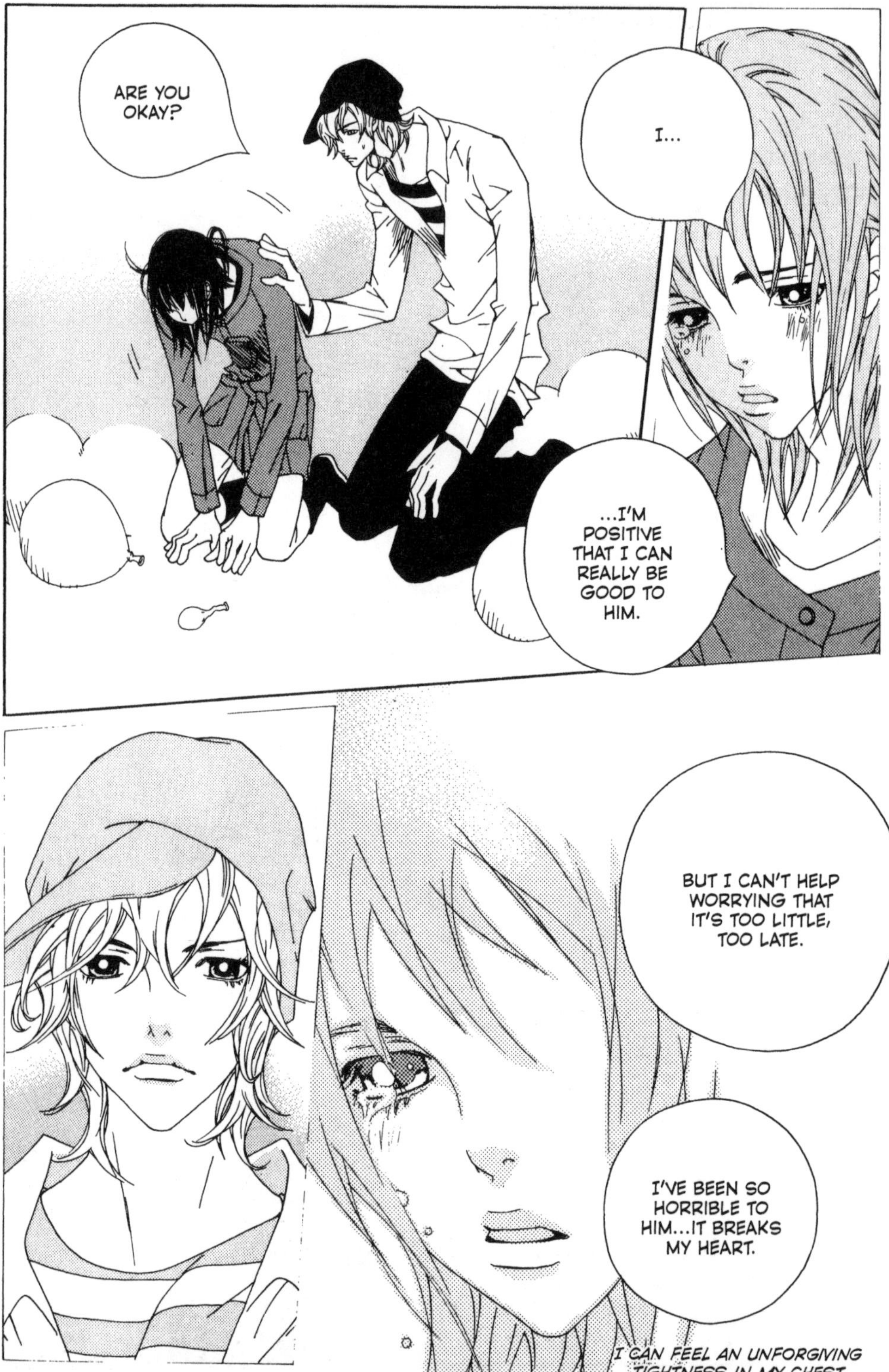
ARE YOU OKAY?
I...
...I'M POSITIVE THAT I CAN REALLY BE GOOD TO HIM.
BUT I CAN'T HELP WORRYING THAT IT'S TOO LITTLE, TOO LATE.
I'VE BEEN SO HORRIBLE TO HIM...IT BREAKS MY HEART.
I CAN FEEL AN UNFORGIVING TIGHTNESS IN MY CHEST.

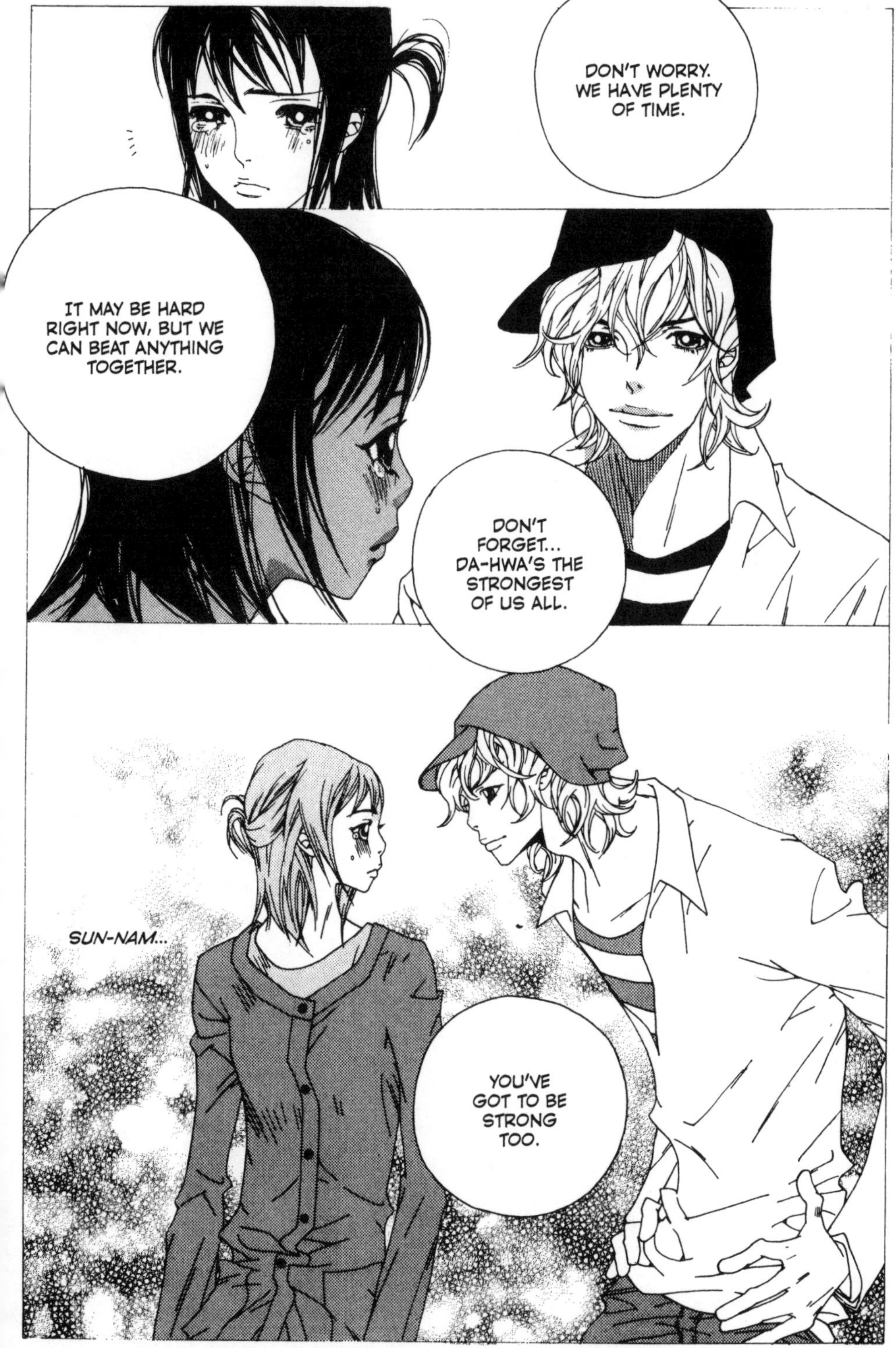
DON'T WORRY. WE HAVE PLENTY OF TIME.
IT MAY BE HARD RIGHT NOW, BUT WE CAN BEAT ANYTHING TOGETHER.
DON'T FORGET... DA-HWA'S THE STRONGEST OF US ALL.
SUN-NAM...
YOU'VE GOT TO BE STRONG TOO.

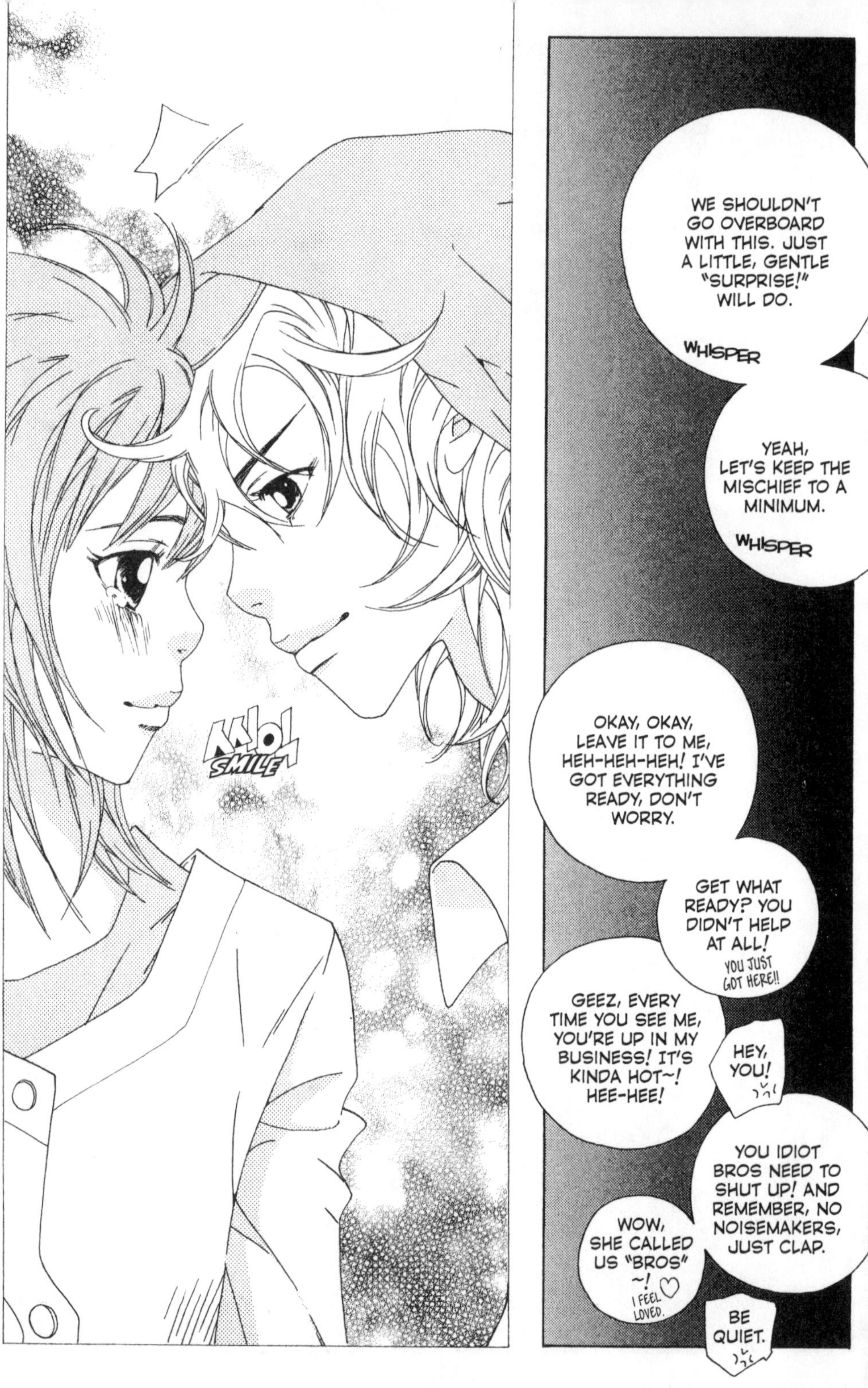
SMILE
WE SHOULDN'T GO OVERBOARD WITH THIS. JUST A LITTLE, GENTLE "SURPRISE!" WILL DO.
WHISPER
YEAH, LET'S KEEP THE MISCHIEF TO A MINIMUM.
WHISPER
OKAY, OKAY, LEAVE IT TO ME, HEH-HEH-HEH! I'VE GOT EVERYTHING READY, DON'T WORRY.
GET WHAT READY? YOU DIDN'T HELP AT ALL!
YOU JUST GOT HERE!!
GEEZ, EVERY TIME YOU SEE ME, YOU'RE UP IN MY BUSINESS! IT'S KINDA HOT~! HEE-HEE!
HEY, YOU!
YOU IDIOT BROS NEED TO SHUT UP! AND REMEMBER, NO NOISEMAKERS, JUST CLAP.
WOW, SHE CALLED US "BROS" ~! ♡
I FEEL LOVED.
BE QUIET.

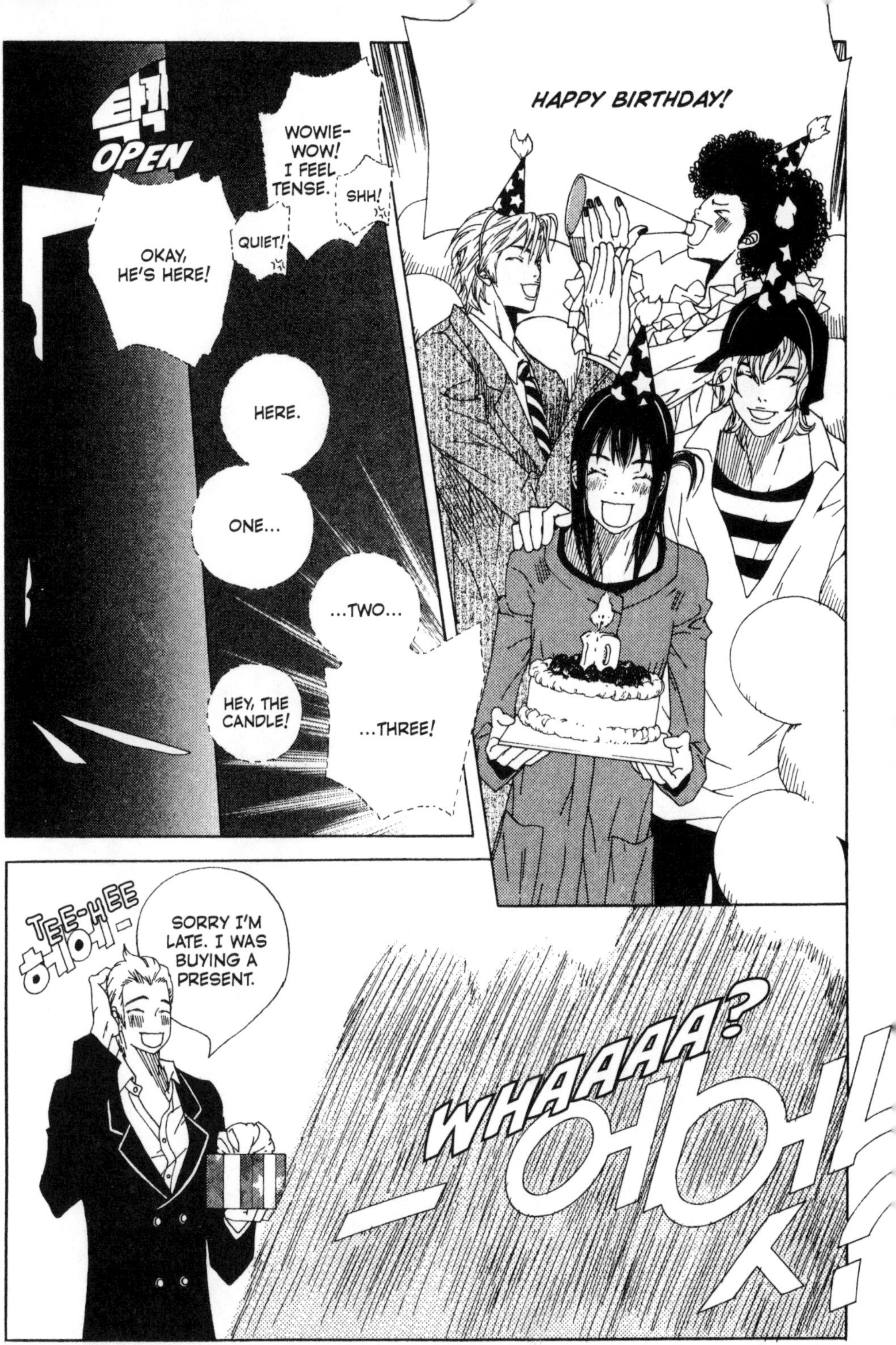
OPEN
OKAY, HE'S HERE!
QUIET!
WOWIE-WOW! I FEEL TENSE.
SHH!
HERE.
ONE...
...TWO...
HEY, THE CANDLE!
...THREE!
HAPPY BIRTHDAY!
TEE-HEE
SORRY I'M LATE. I WAS BUYING A PRESENT.
WHAAAAA?

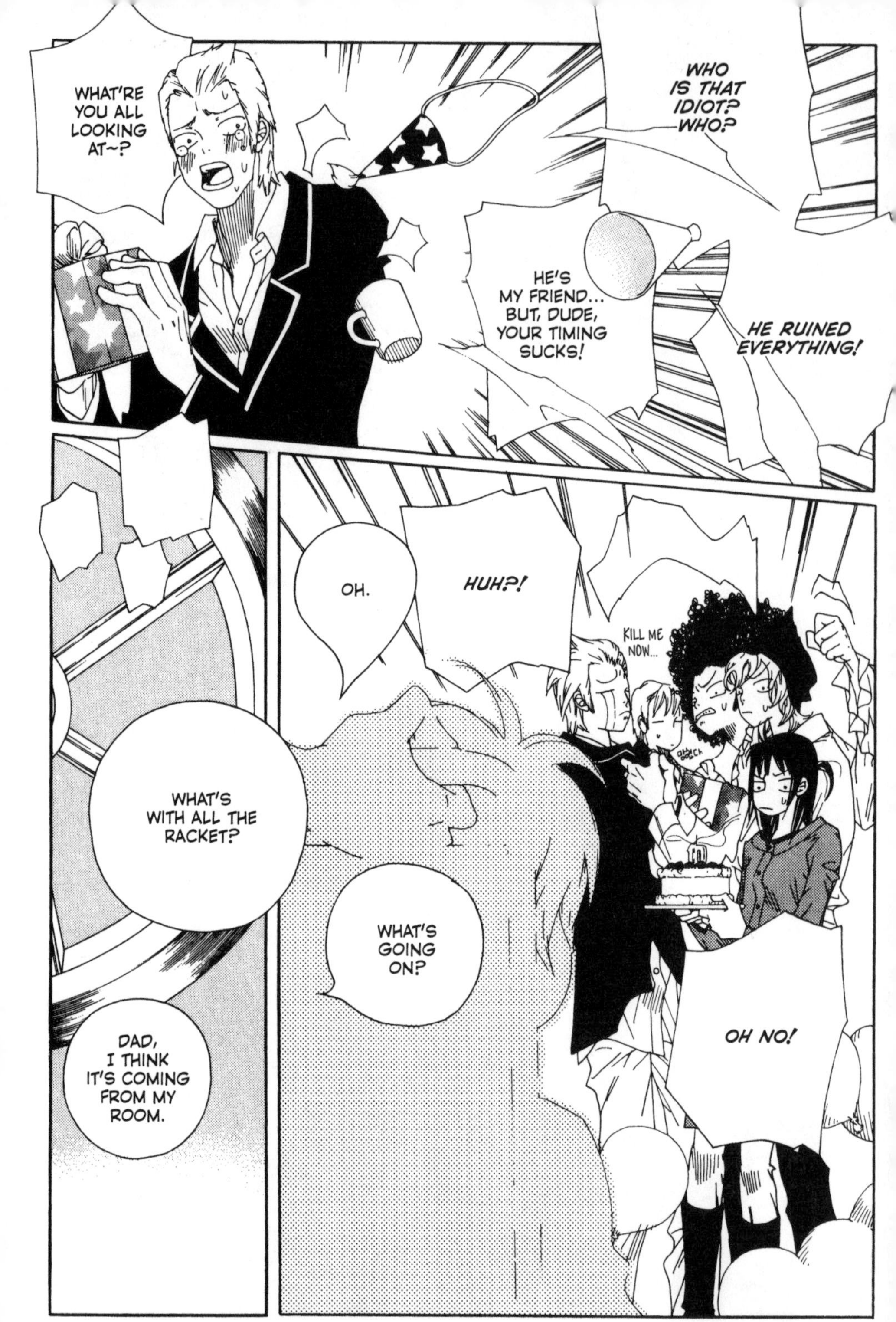
WHAT'RE YOU ALL LOOKING AT~?
WHO IS THAT IDIOT? WHO?
HE'S MY FRIEND... BUT, DUDE, YOUR TIMING SUCKS!
HE RUINED EVERYTHING!
WHAT'S WITH ALL THE RACKET?
DAD, I THINK IT'S COMING FROM MY ROOM.
OH.
HUH?!
KILL ME NOW...
WHAT'S GOING ON?
OH NO!

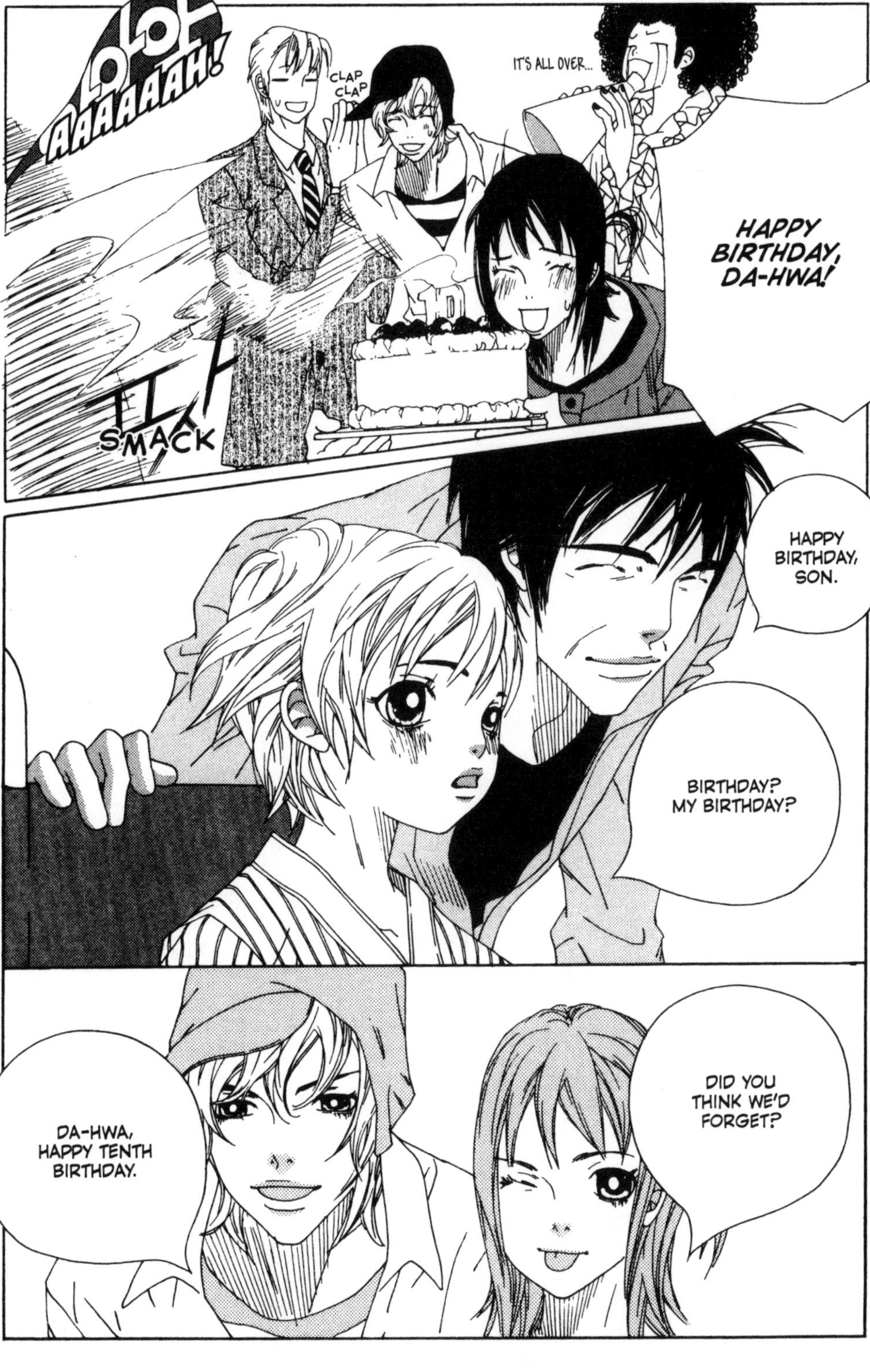
AAAAAAH!
CLAP CLAP
IT'S ALL OVER...
HAPPY BIRTHDAY, DA-HWA!
SMACK
HAPPY BIRTHDAY, SON.
BIRTHDAY? MY BIRTHDAY?
DA-HWA, HAPPY TENTH BIRTHDAY.
DID YOU THINK WE'D FORGET?

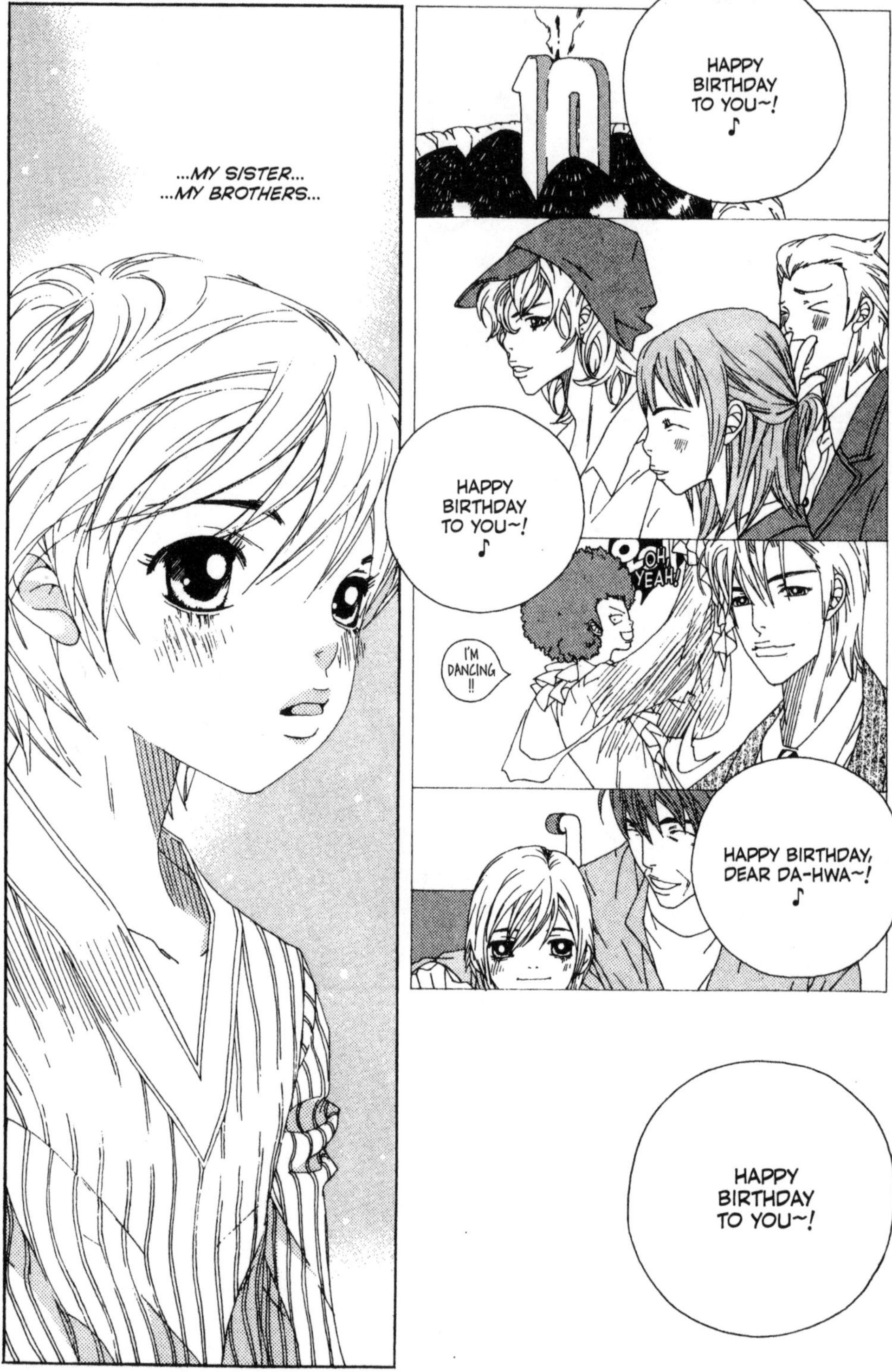
...MY SISTER... ...MY BROTHERS...
HAPPY BIRTHDAY TO YOU~! ♪
HAPPY BIRTHDAY TO YOU~! ♪
OH YEAH!
I'M DANCING !!
HAPPY BIRTHDAY, DEAR DA-HWA~! ♪
HAPPY BIRTHDAY TO YOU~!

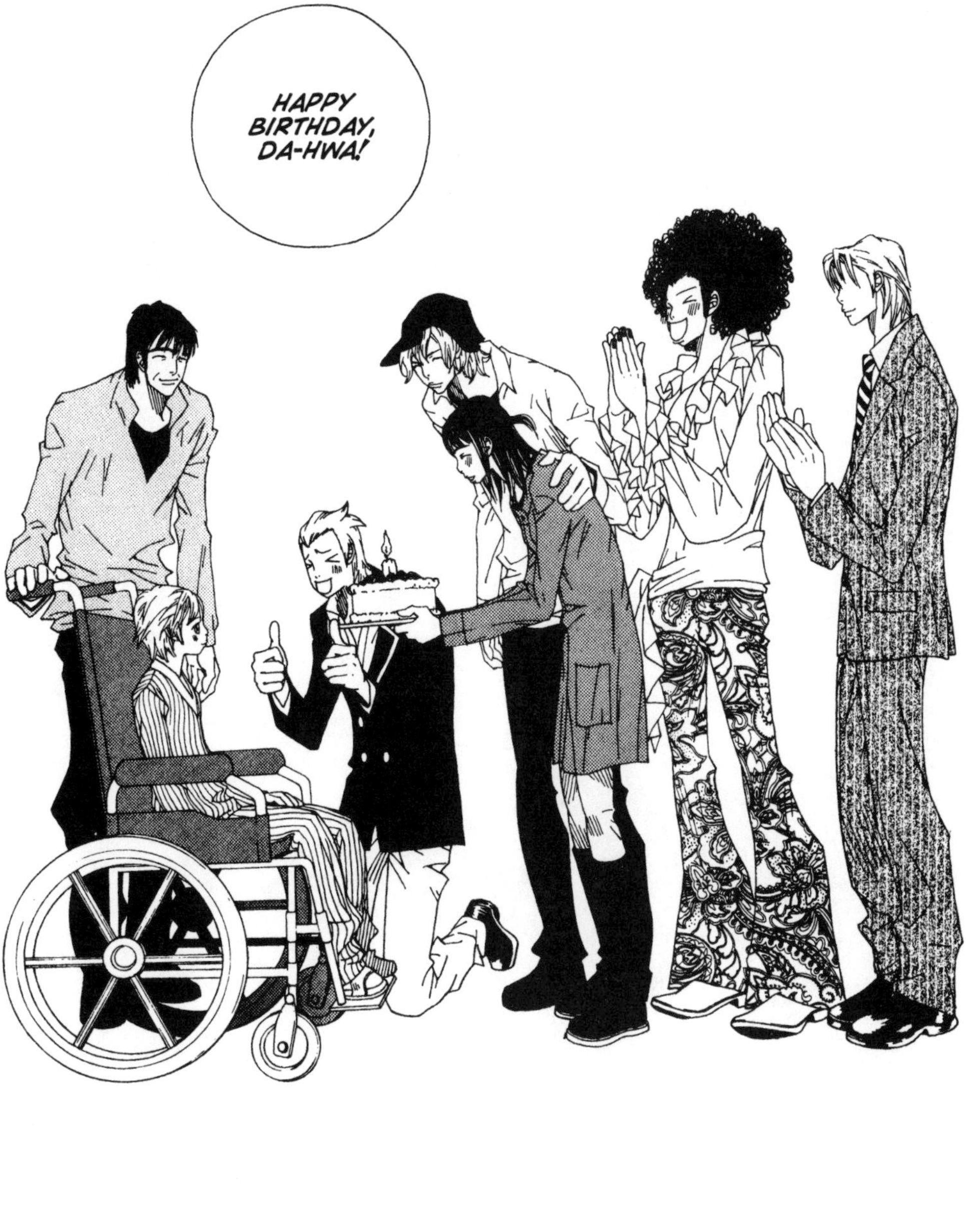
HAPPY BIRTHDAY, DA-HWA!

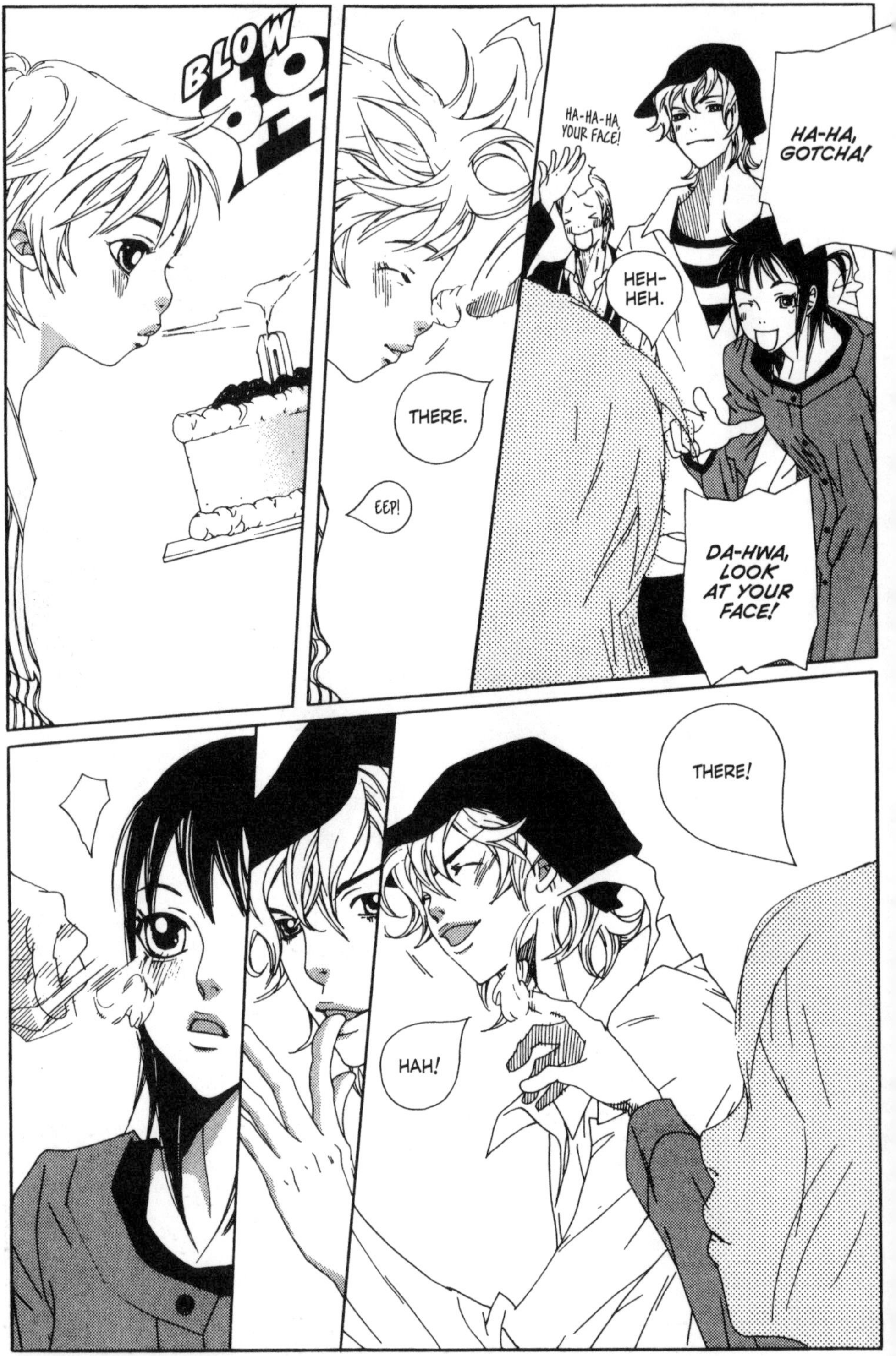
BLOW
THERE.
EEP!
HA-HA-HA YOUR FACE!
HA-HA, GOTCHA!
HEH-HEH.
DA-HWA, LOOK AT YOUR FACE!
THERE!
HAH!

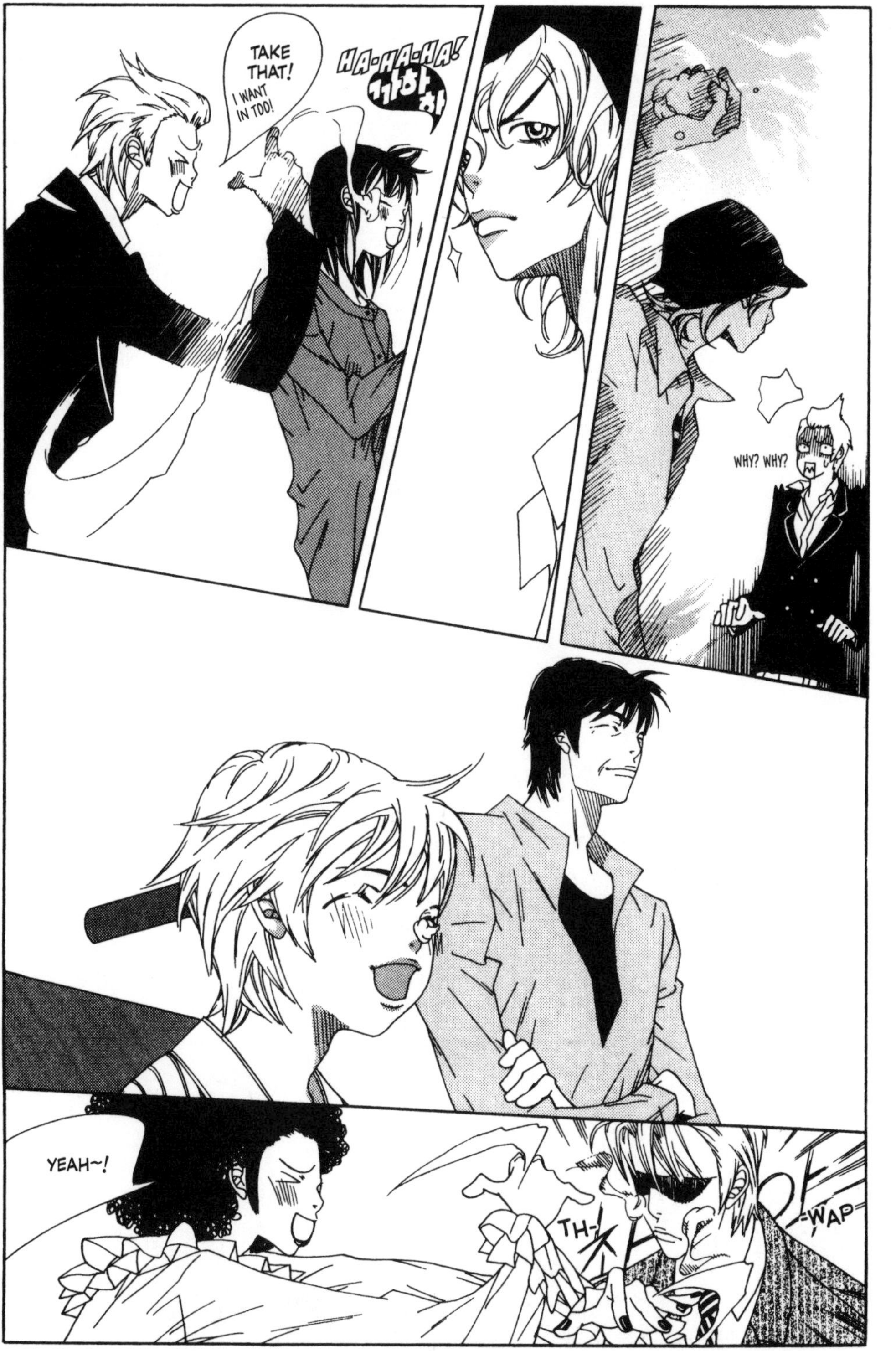
TAKE THAT!
I WANT IN TOO!
HA-HA-HA!
까하하
WHY? WHY?
YEAH~!
TH-
-WAP

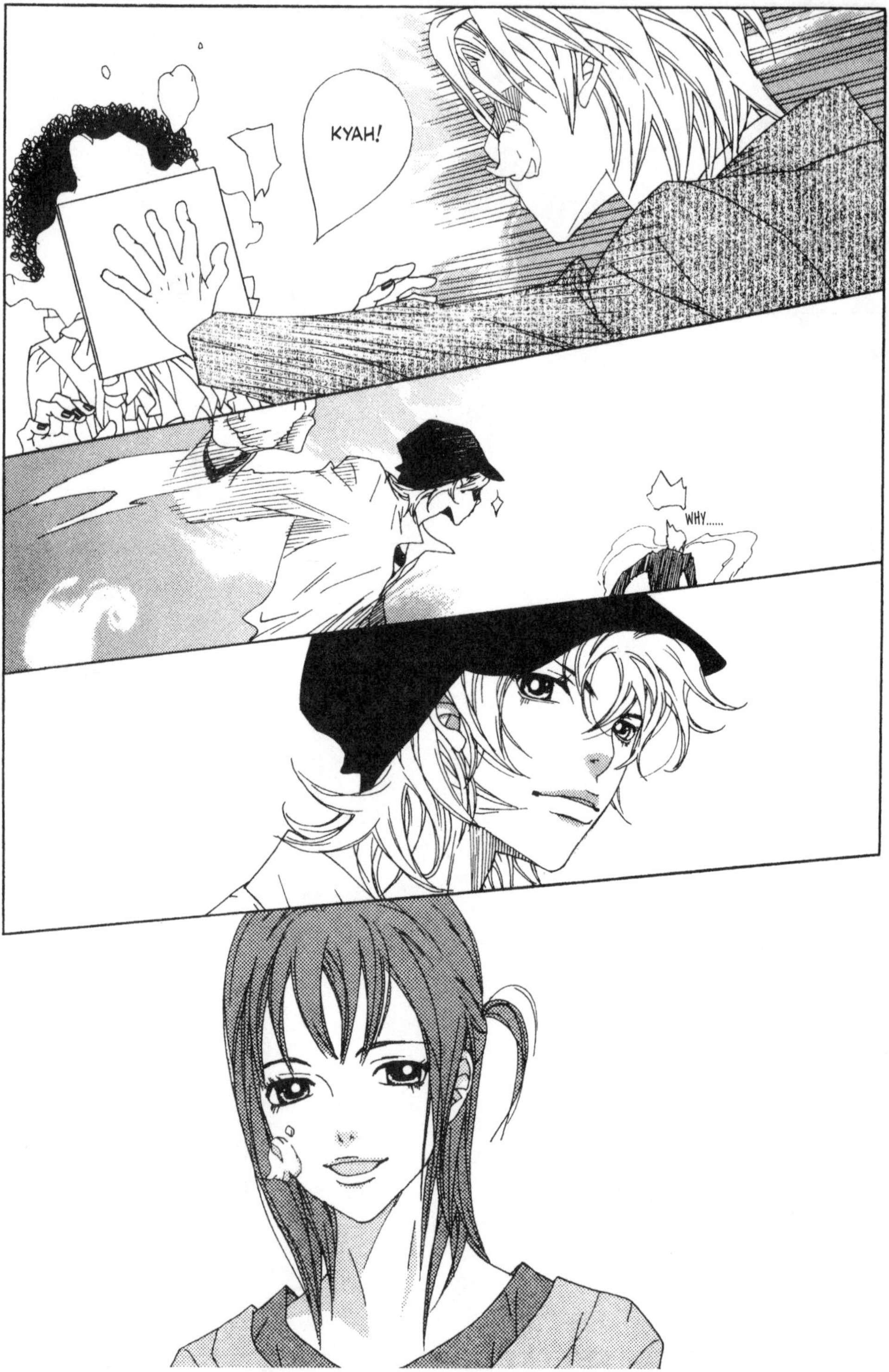
KYAH!
WHY......

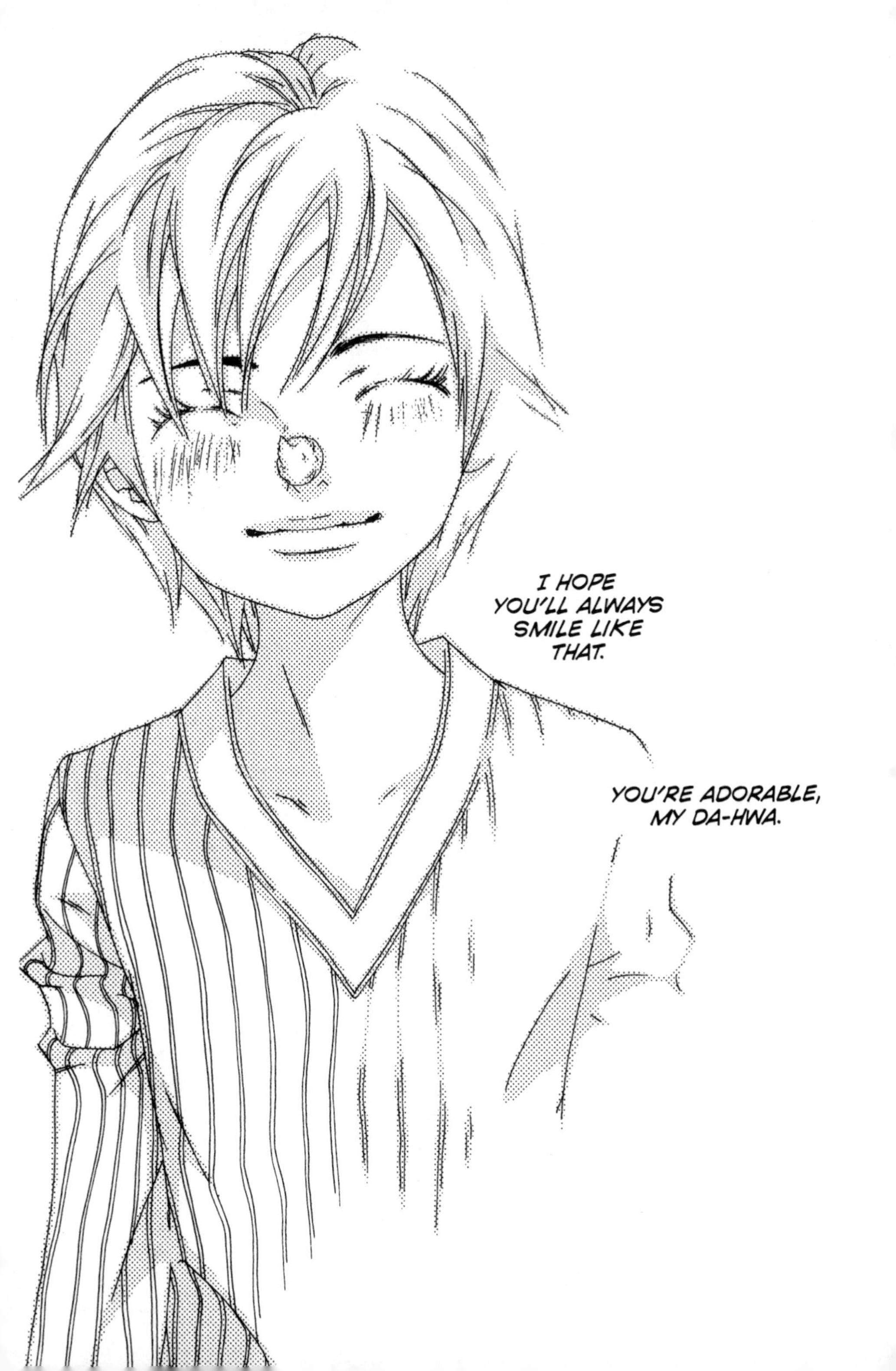
I HOPE YOU'LL ALWAYS SMILE LIKE THAT.
YOU'RE ADORABLE, MY DA-HWA.

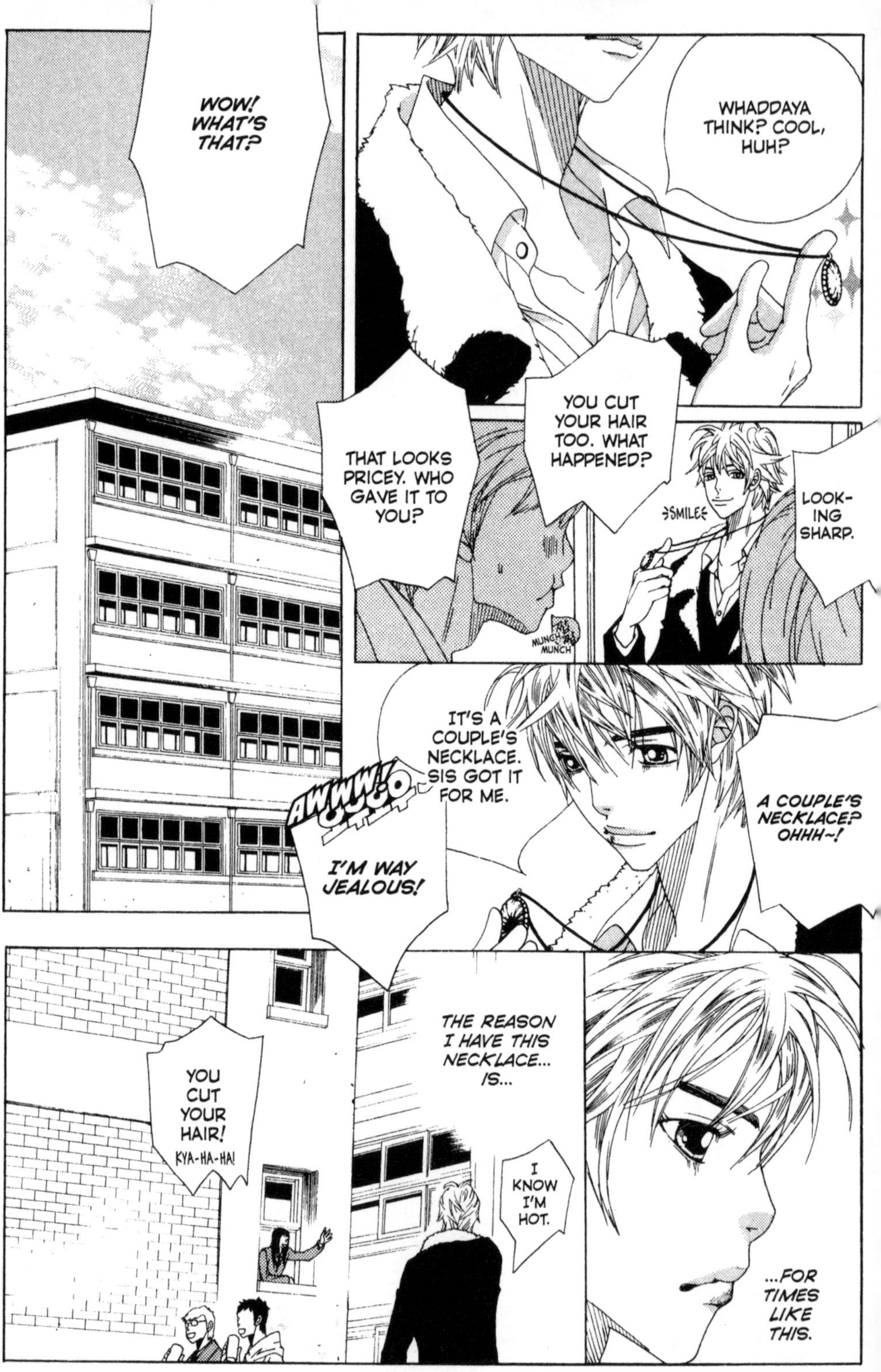
WOW! WHAT'S THAT?
WHADDAYA THINK? COOL, HUH?
THAT LOOKS PRICEY. WHO GAVE IT TO YOU?
MUNCH MUNCH
YOU CUT YOUR HAIR TOO. WHAT HAPPENED?
SMILE
LOOKING SHARP.
AWWW!
IT'S A COUPLE'S NECKLACE. SIS GOT IT FOR ME.
I'M WAY JEALOUS!
A COUPLE'S NECKLACE? OHHH~!
YOU CUT YOUR HAIR!
KYA-HA-HA!
THE REASON I HAVE THIS NECKLACE... IS...
I KNOW I'M HOT.
...FOR TIMES LIKE THIS.

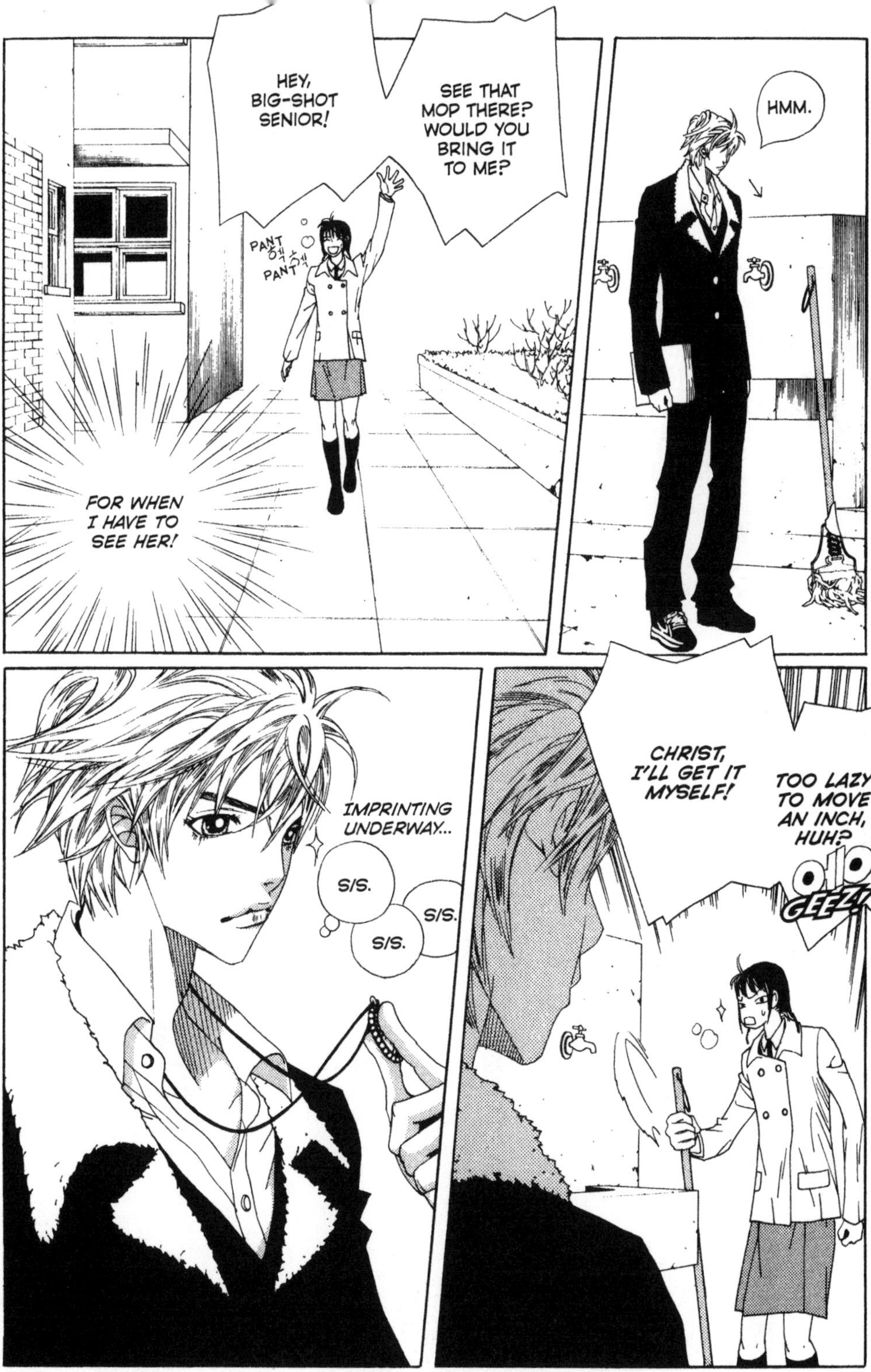
HEY, BIG-SHOT SENIOR!
SEE THAT MOP THERE? WOULD YOU BRING IT TO ME?
PANT 헉 PANT 헉
FOR WHEN I HAVE TO SEE HER!
HMM.
IMPRINTING UNDERWAY...
SIS.
SIS.
SIS.
CHRIST, I'LL GET IT MYSELF!
TOO LAZY TO MOVE AN INCH, HUH?
아이 GEEZ!

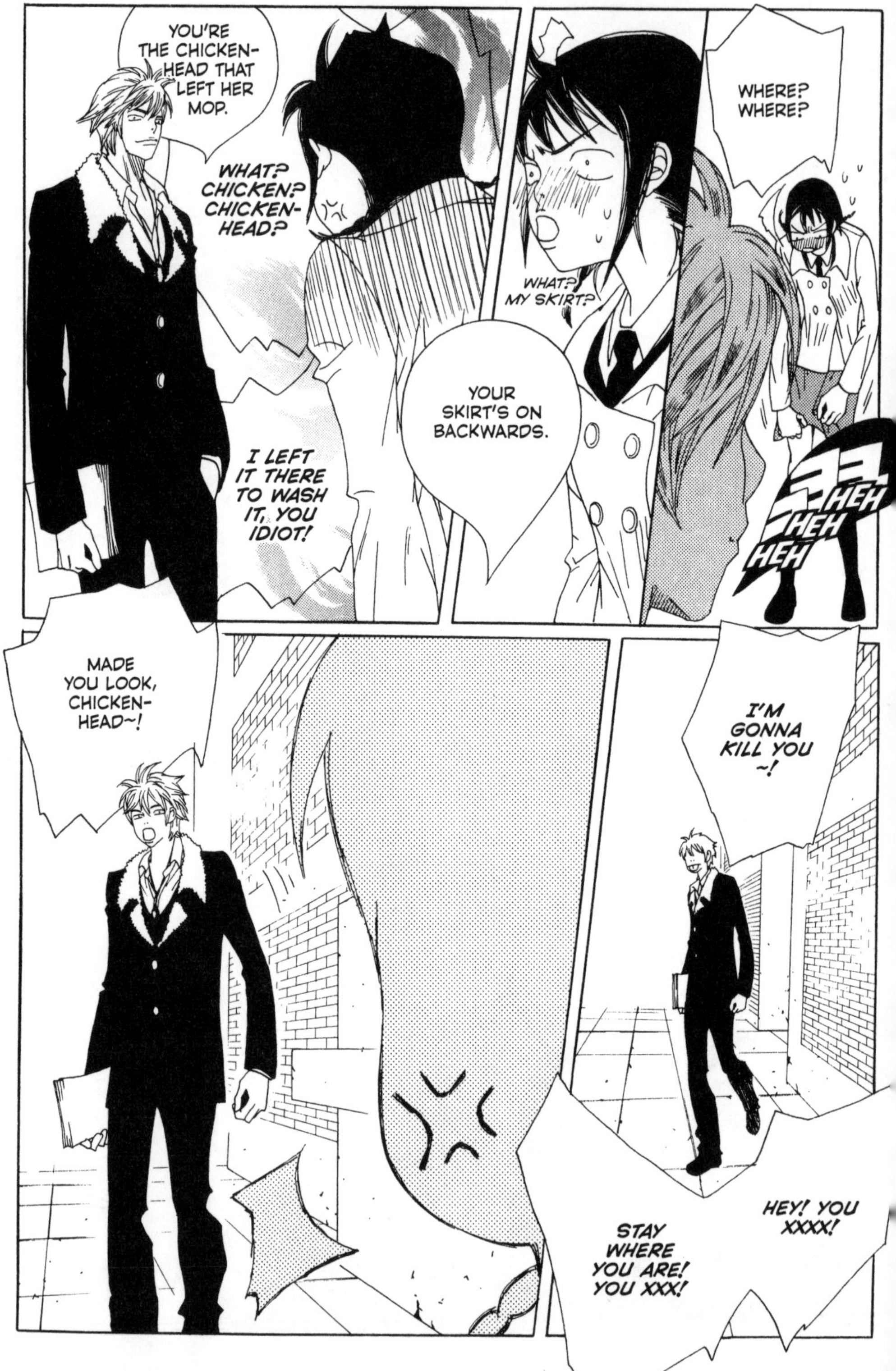
YOU'RE THE CHICKEN-HEAD THAT LEFT HER MOP.
WHAT? CHICKEN? CHICKEN-HEAD?
I LEFT IT THERE TO WASH IT, YOU IDIOT!
YOUR SKIRT'S ON BACKWARDS.
WHAT? MY SKIRT?
WHERE? WHERE?
HEH HEH HEH
MADE YOU LOOK, CHICKEN-HEAD~!
I'M GONNA KILL YOU ~!
STAY WHERE YOU ARE! YOU XXX!
HEY! YOU XXXX!

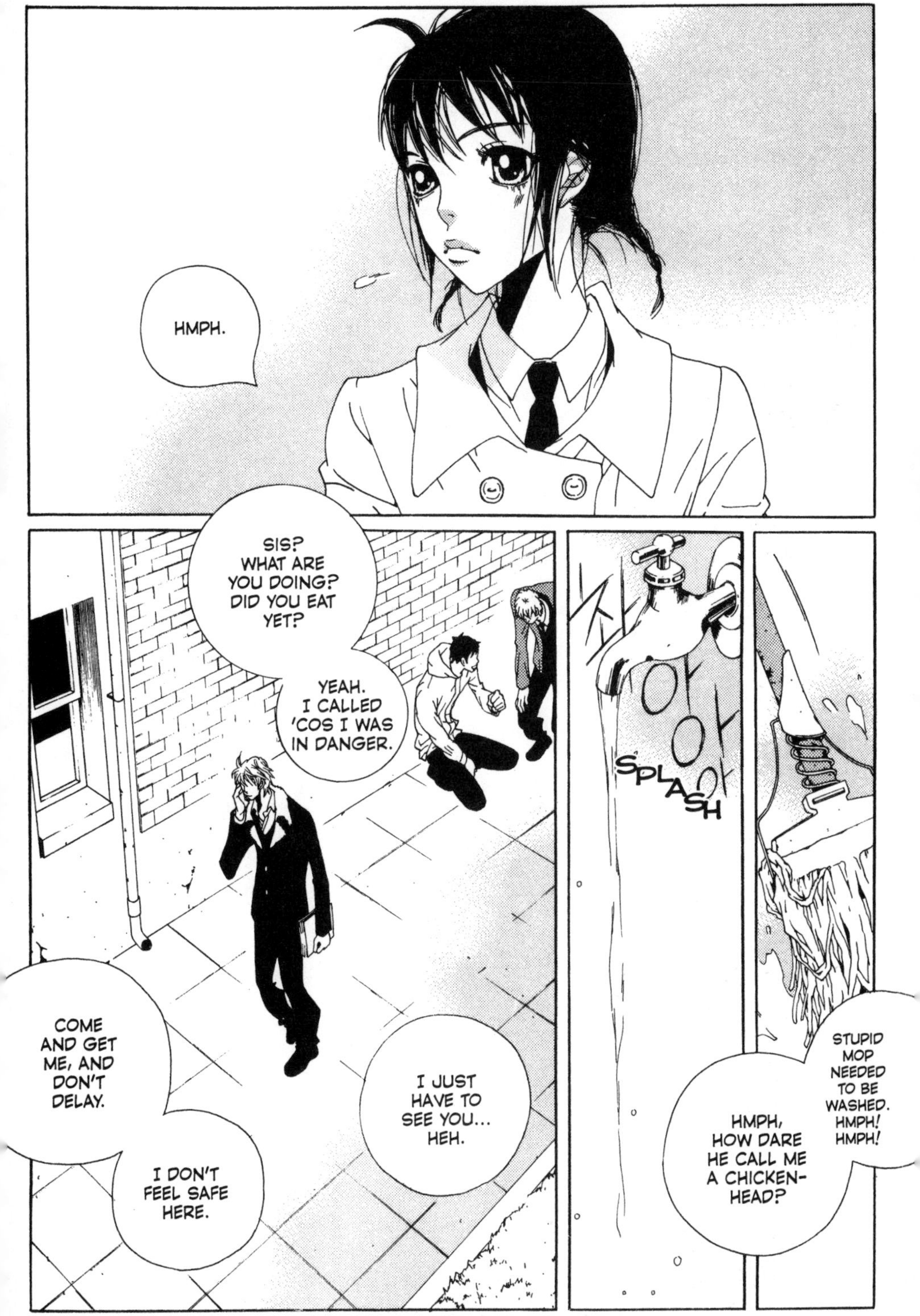
HMPH.
SIS? WHAT ARE YOU DOING? DID YOU EAT YET?
YEAH. I CALLED 'COS I WAS IN DANGER.
COME AND GET ME, AND DON'T DELAY.
I DON'T FEEL SAFE HERE.
I JUST HAVE TO SEE YOU... HEH.
SPLASH
STUPID MOP NEEDED TO BE WASHED. HMPH! HMPH!
HMPH, HOW DARE HE CALL ME A CHICKEN-HEAD?

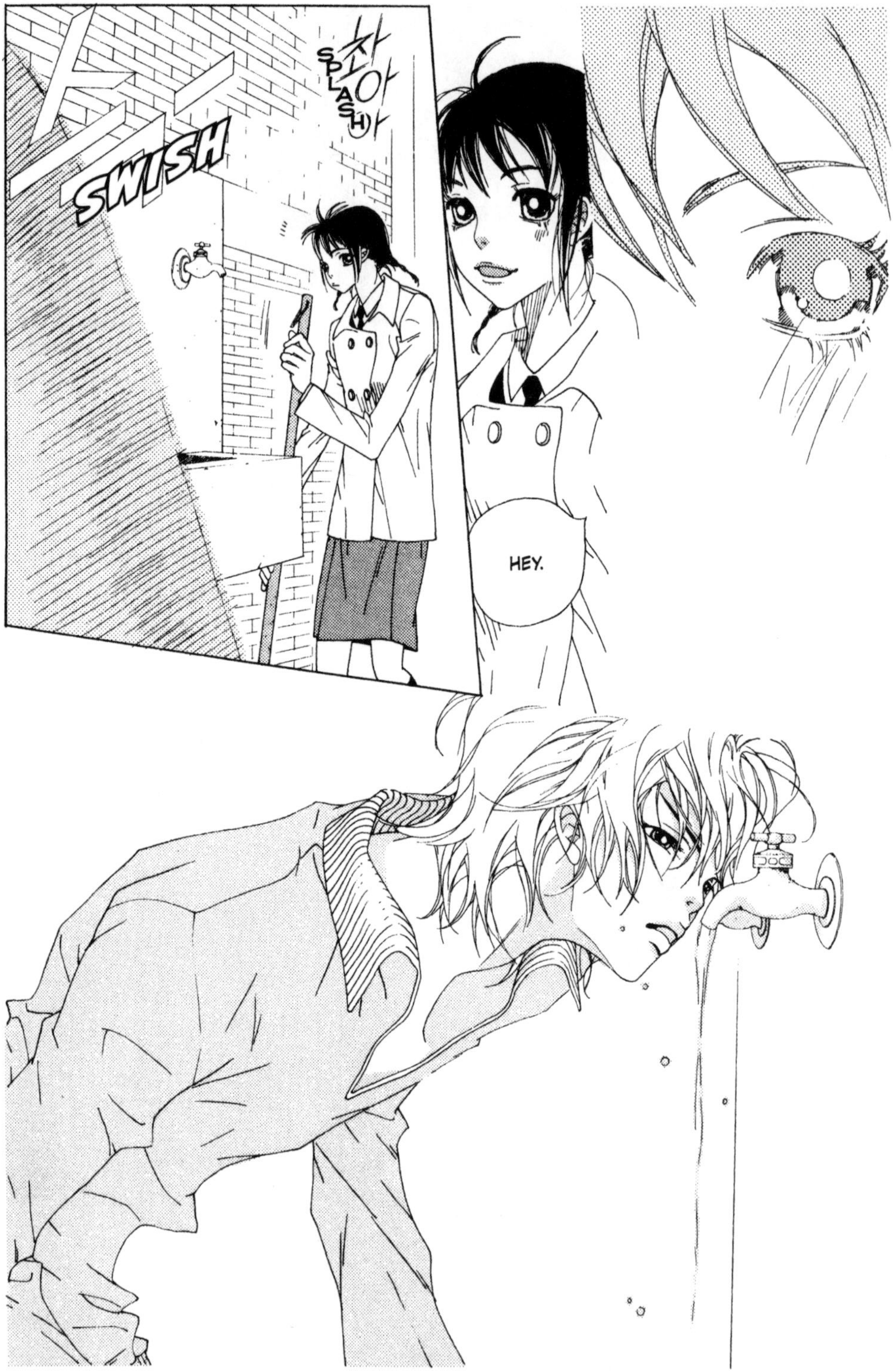
SPLASH
SWISH
HEY.

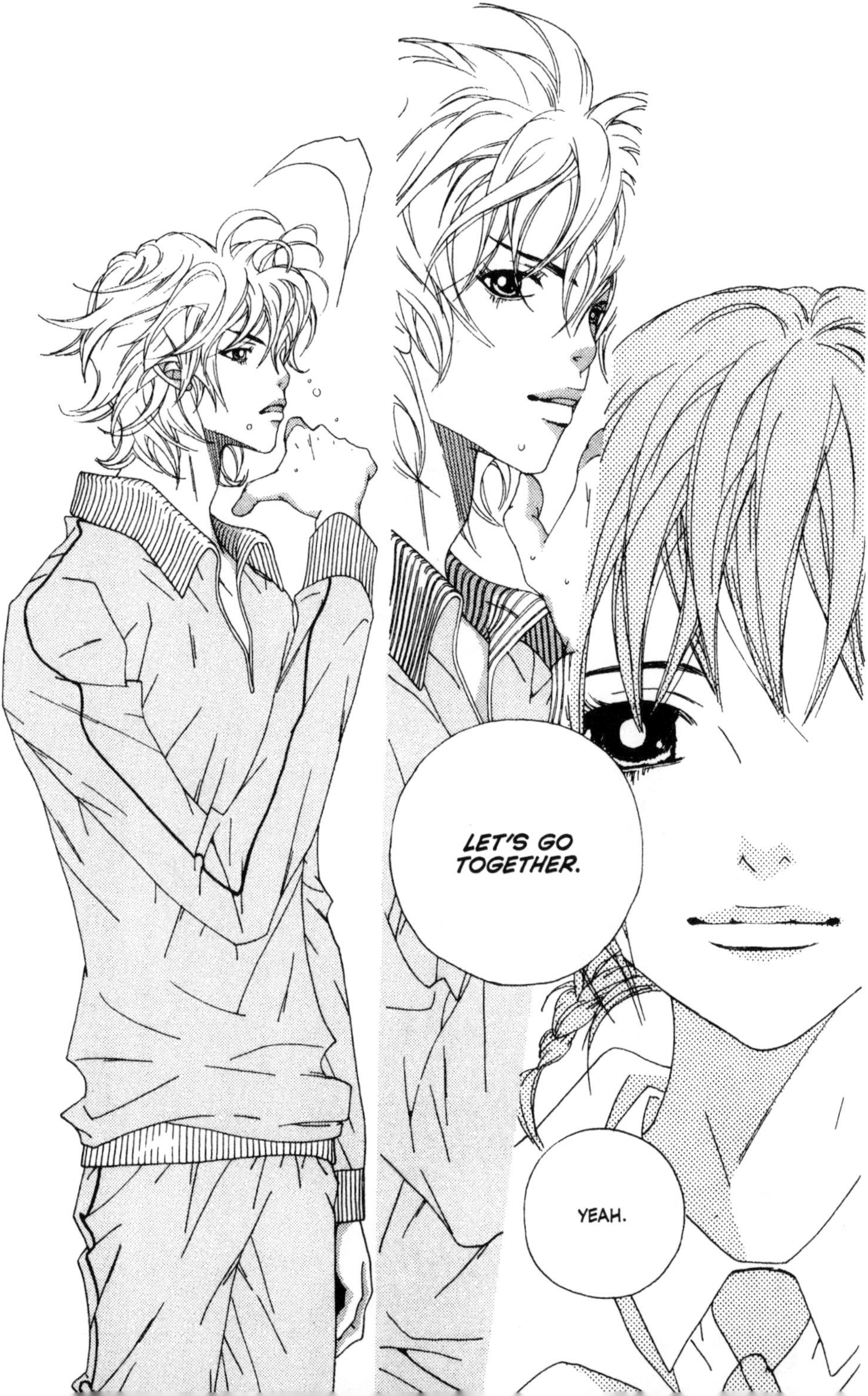
LET'S GO TOGETHER.
YEAH.

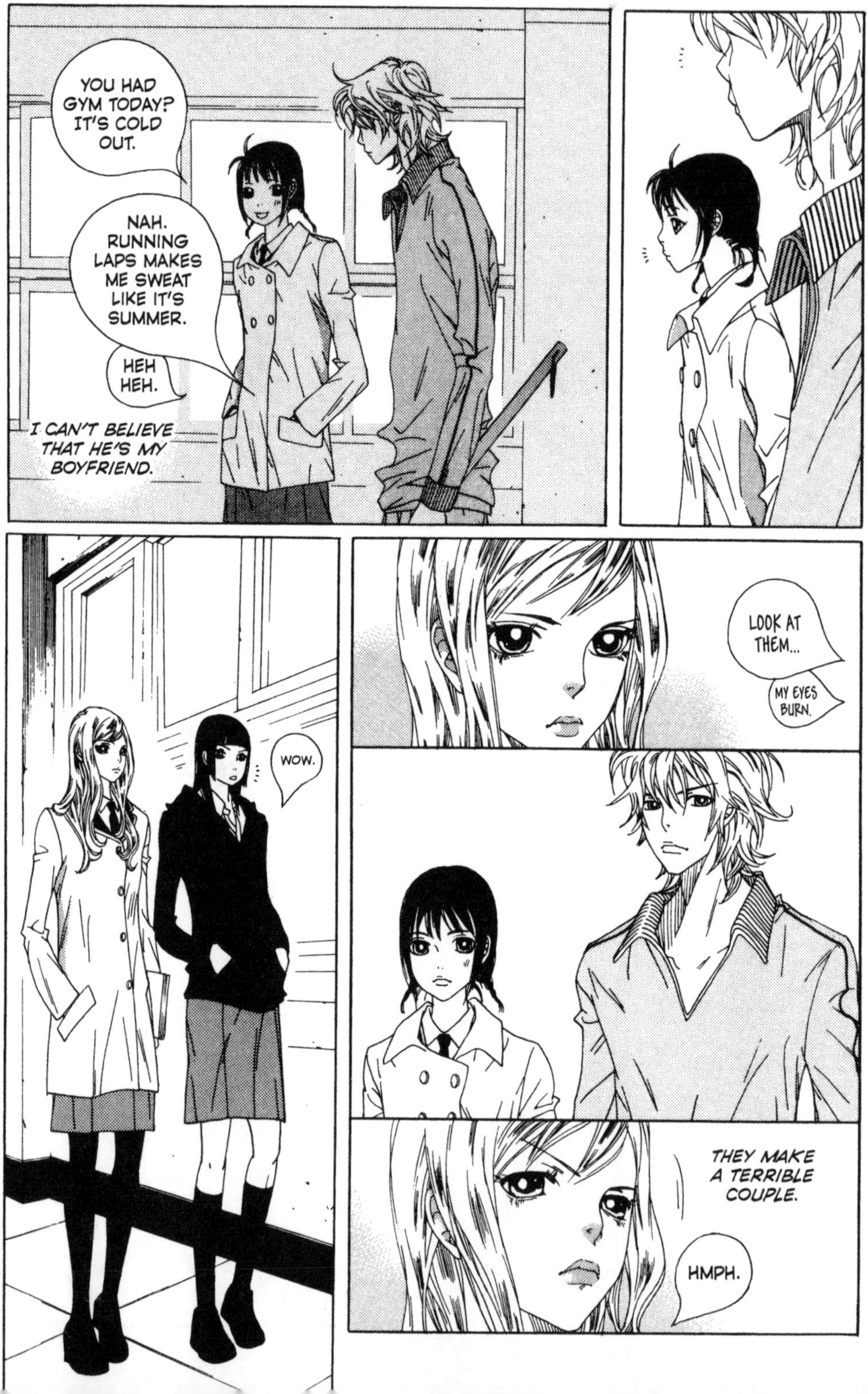
YOU HAD GYM TODAY? IT'S COLD OUT.
NAH. RUNNING LAPS MAKES ME SWEAT LIKE IT'S SUMMER.
HEH HEH.
I CAN'T BELIEVE THAT HE'S MY BOYFRIEND.
WOW.
LOOK AT THEM...
MY EYES BURN.
THEY MAKE A TERRIBLE COUPLE.
HMPH.

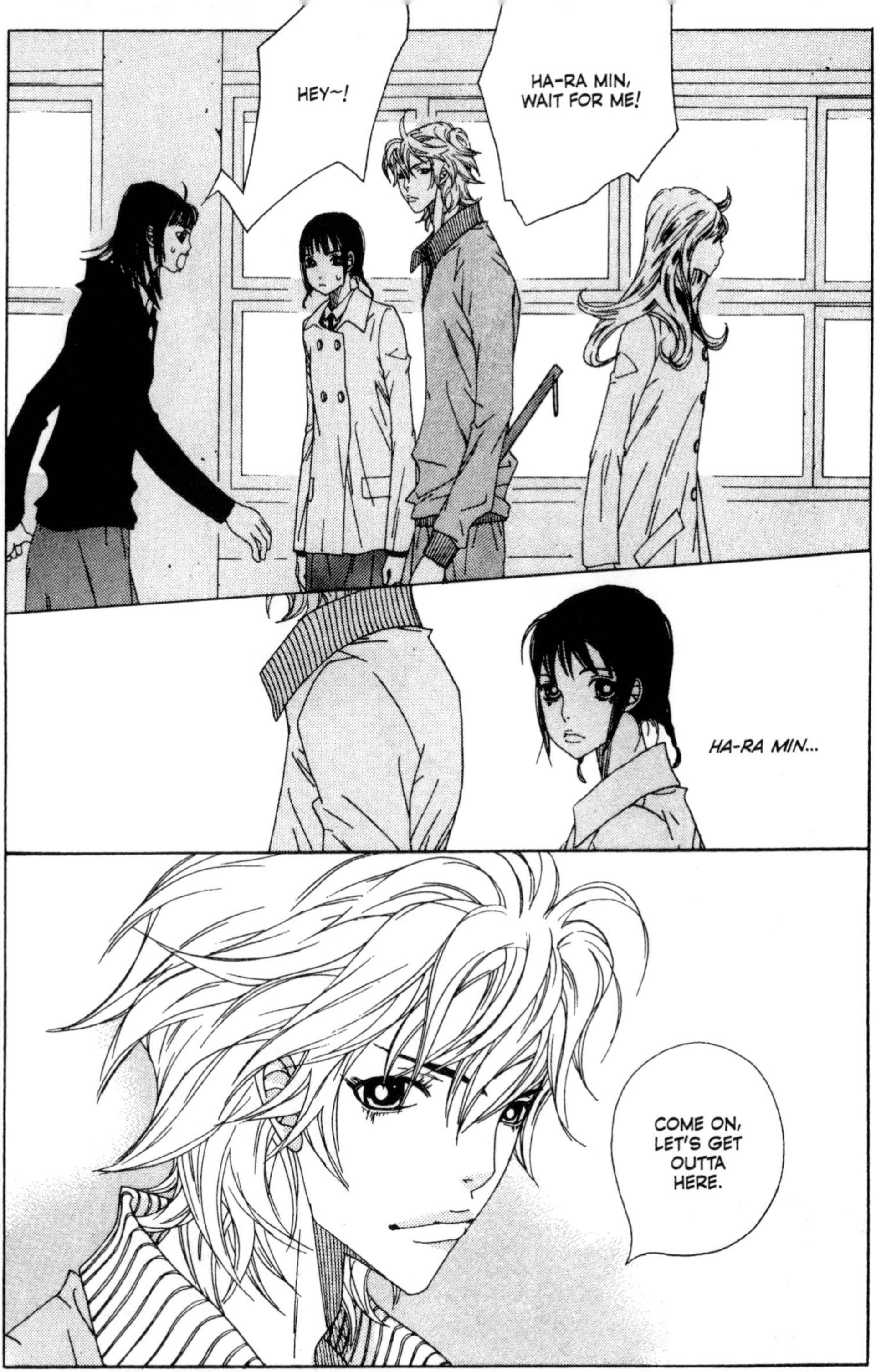
HEY~!
HA-RA MIN, WAIT FOR ME!
HA-RA MIN...
COME ON, LET'S GET OUTTA HERE.

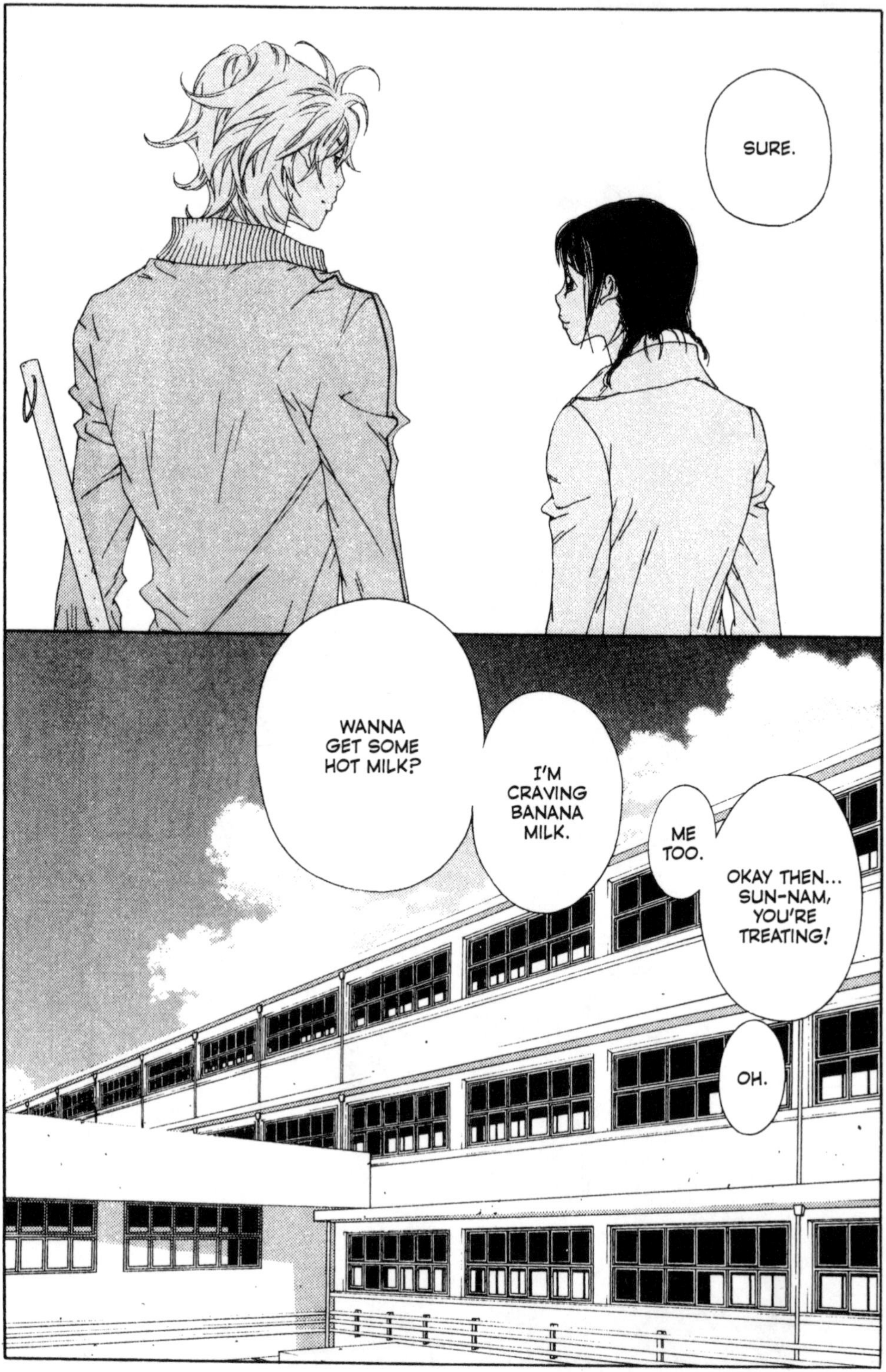
SURE.
WANNA GET SOME HOT MILK?
I'M CRAVING BANANA MILK.
ME TOO.
OKAY THEN... SUN-NAM, YOU'RE TREATING!
OH.

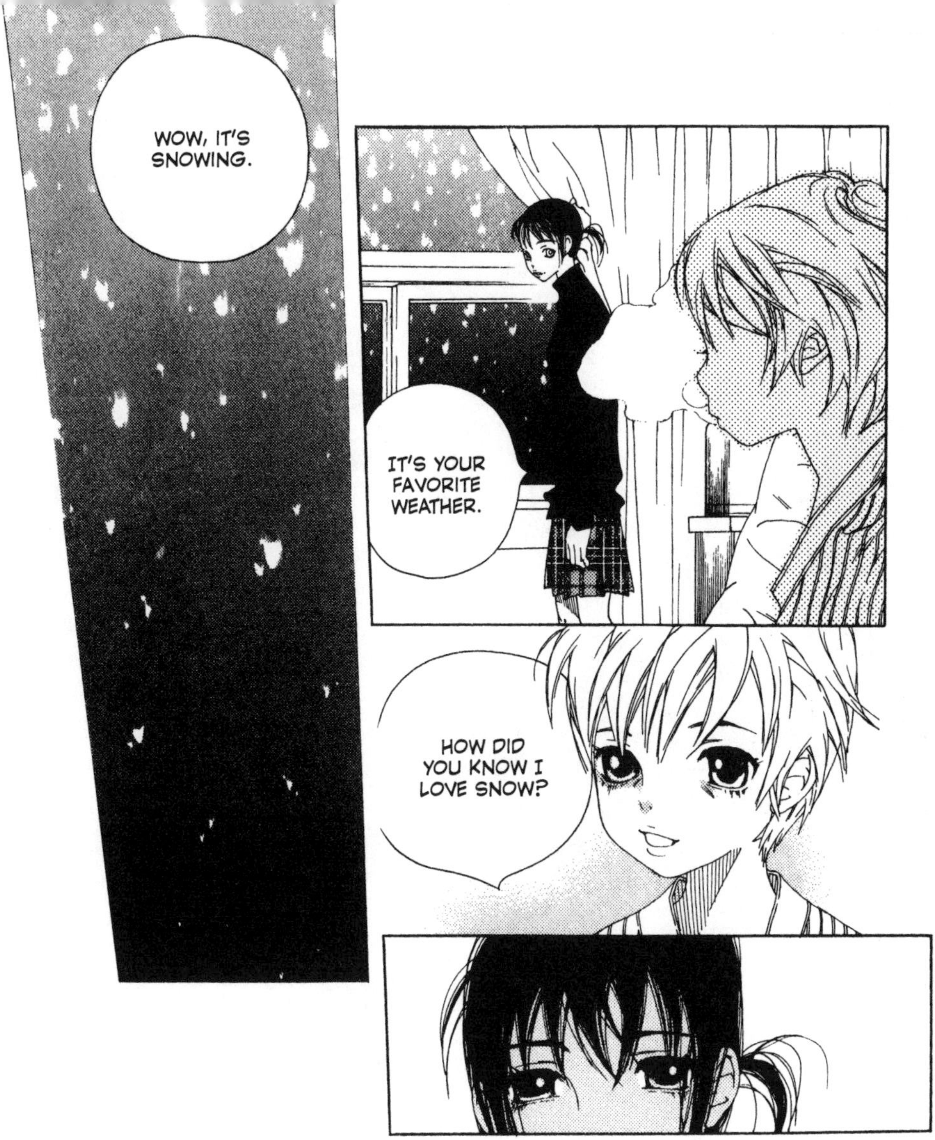
WOW, IT'S SNOWING.
IT'S YOUR FAVORITE WEATHER.
HOW DID YOU KNOW I LOVE SNOW?

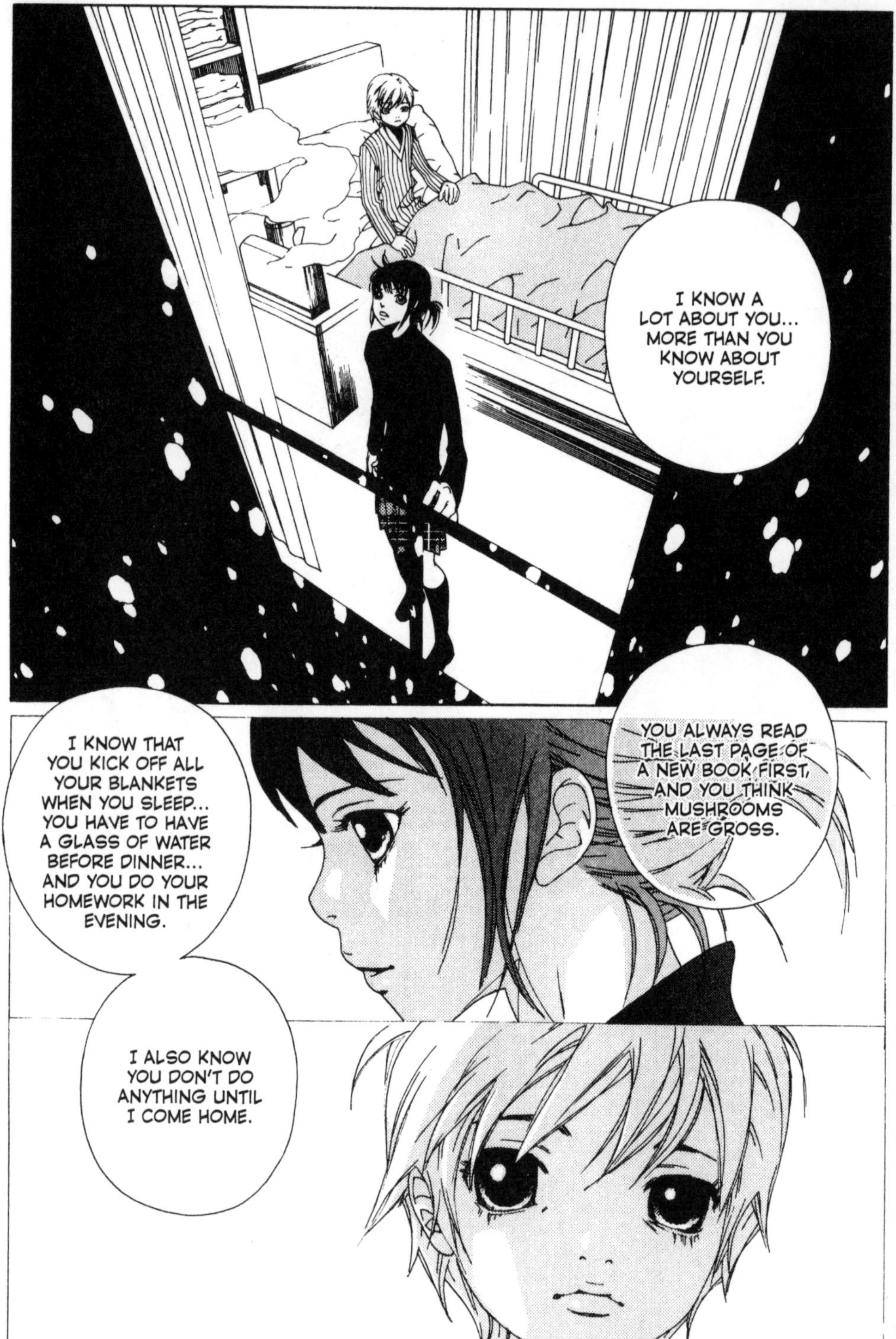
I KNOW A LOT ABOUT YOU... MORE THAN YOU KNOW ABOUT YOURSELF.
I KNOW THAT YOU KICK OFF ALL YOUR BLANKETS WHEN YOU SLEEP... YOU HAVE TO HAVE A GLASS OF WATER BEFORE DINNER... AND YOU DO YOUR HOMEWORK IN THE EVENING.
YOU ALWAYS READ THE LAST PAGE OF A NEW BOOK FIRST, AND YOU THINK MUSHROOMS ARE GROSS.
I ALSO KNOW YOU DON'T DO ANYTHING UNTIL I COME HOME.

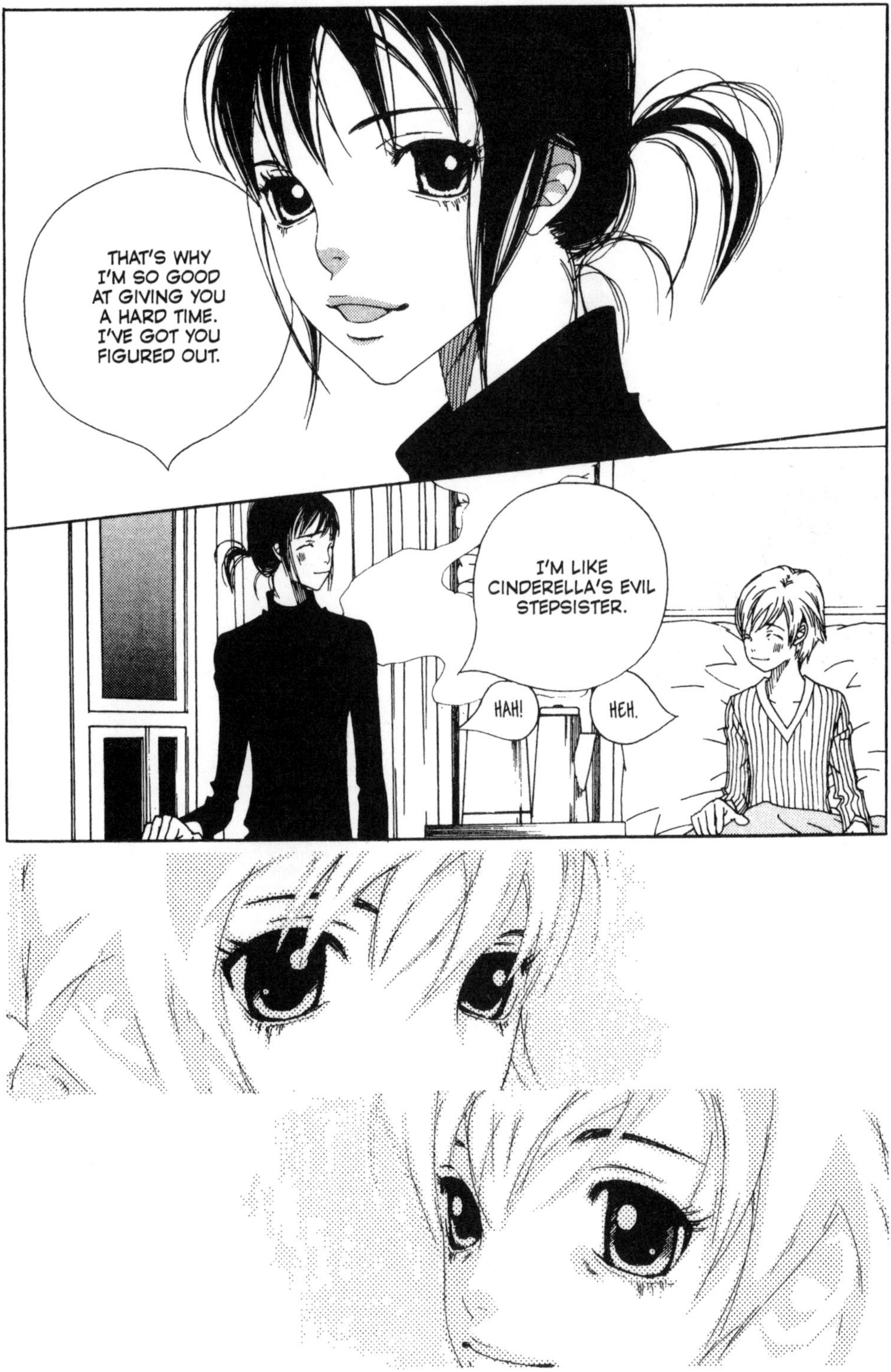
THAT'S WHY I'M SO GOOD AT GIVING YOU A HARD TIME. I'VE GOT YOU FIGURED OUT.
I'M LIKE CINDERELLA'S EVIL STEPSISTER.
HAH!
HEH.

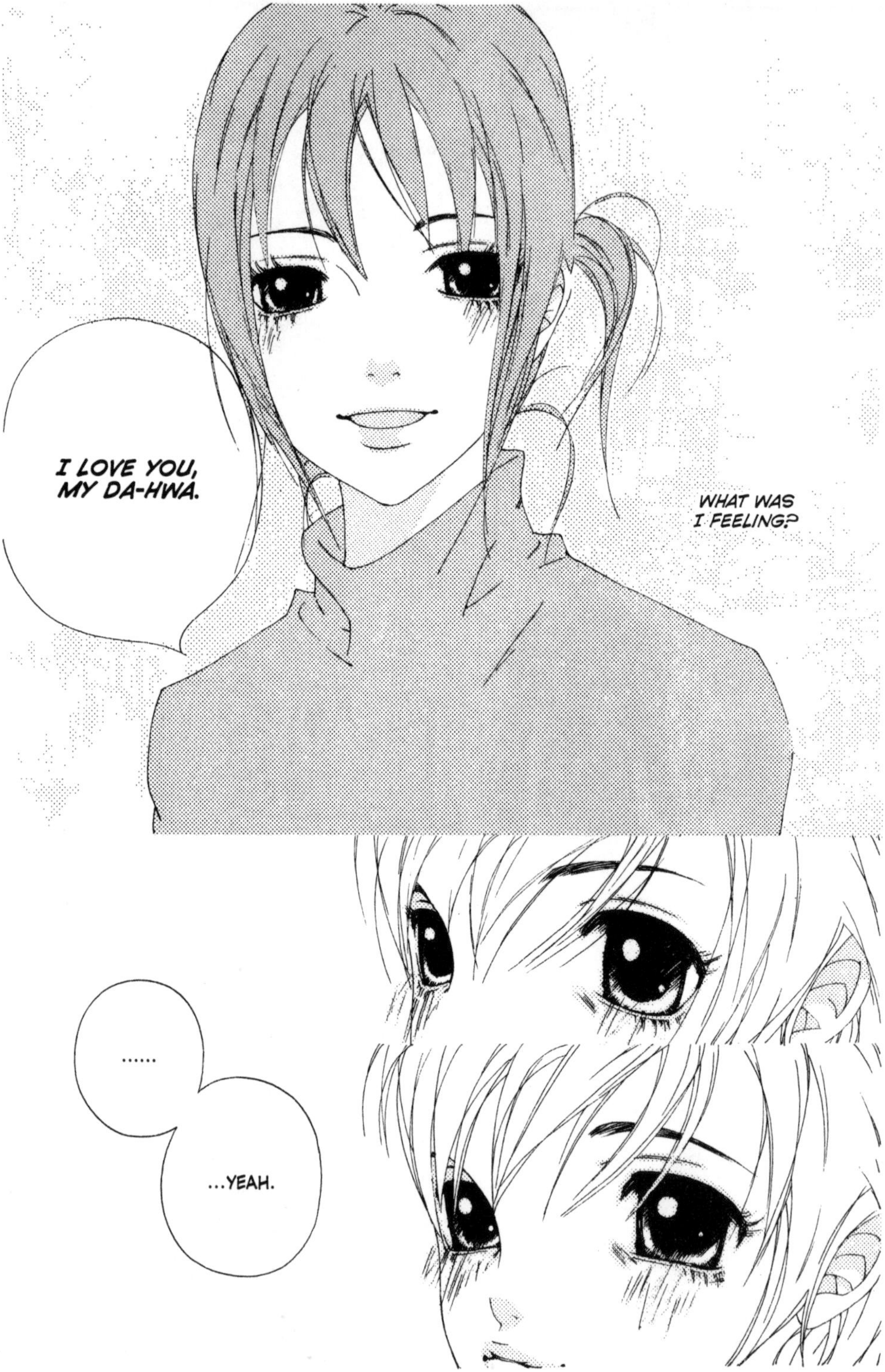
I LOVE YOU, MY DA-HWA.
WHAT WAS I FEELING?
......
...YEAH.

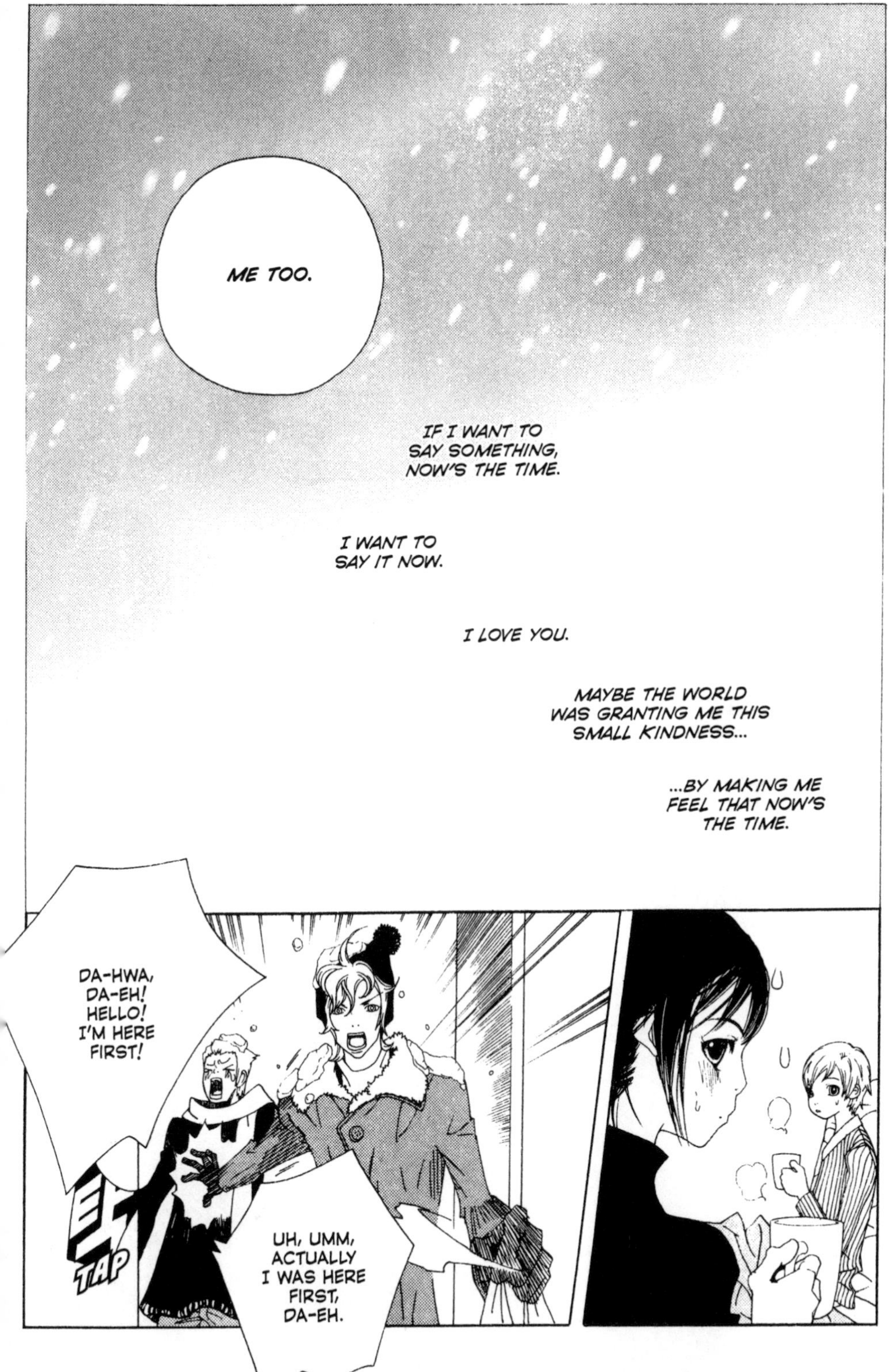
ME TOO.
IF I WANT TO SAY SOMETHING, NOW'S THE TIME.
I WANT TO SAY IT NOW.
I LOVE YOU.
MAYBE THE WORLD WAS GRANTING ME THIS SMALL KINDNESS...
...BY MAKING ME FEEL THAT NOW'S THE TIME.
DA-HWA, DA-EH! HELLO! I'M HERE FIRST!
TAP
UH, UMM, ACTUALLY I WAS HERE FIRST, DA-EH.

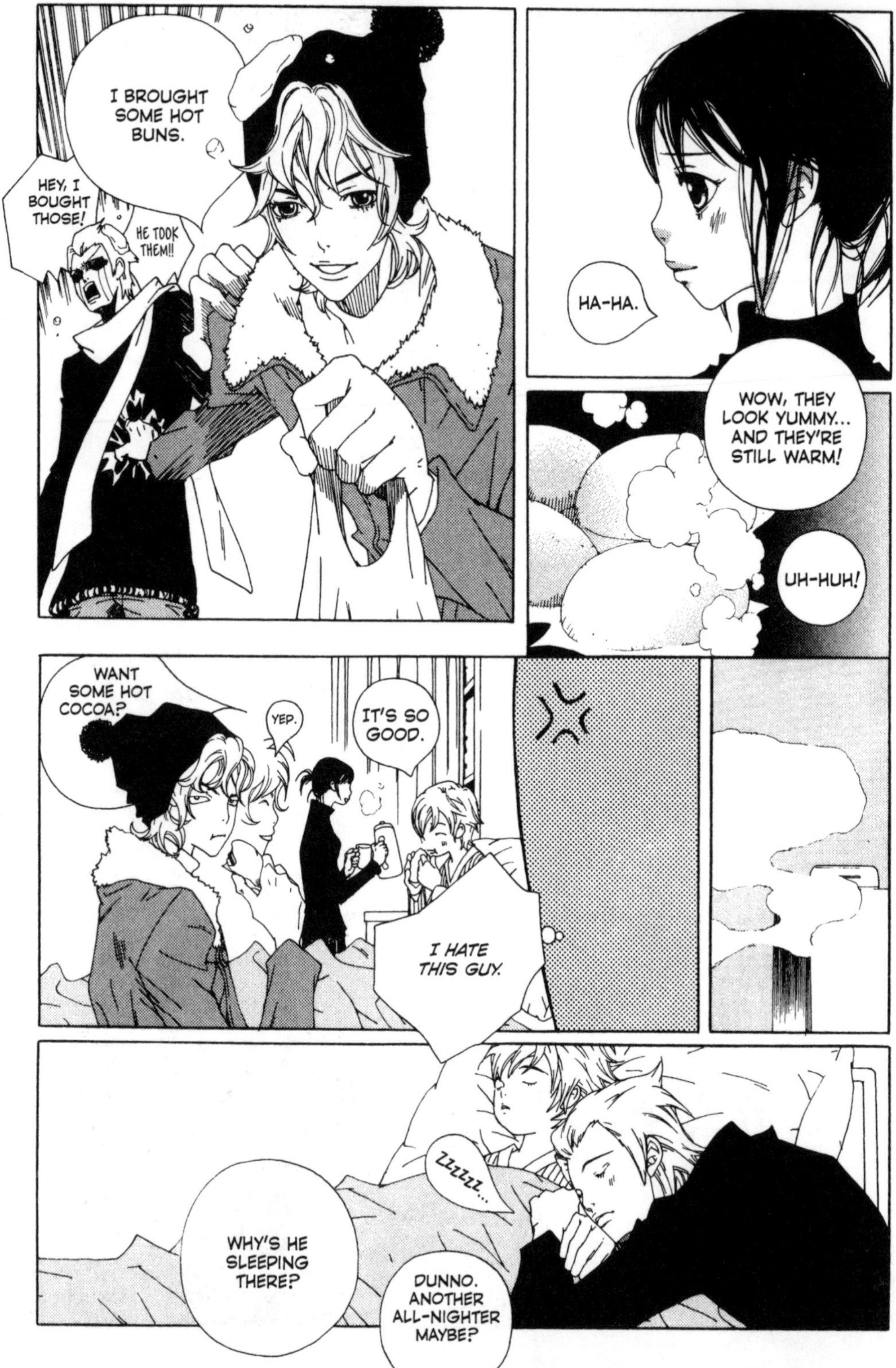

I BROUGHT SOME HOT BUNS.
HEY, I BOUGHT THOSE!
HE TOOK THEM!!
HA-HA.
WOW, THEY LOOK YUMMY... AND THEY'RE STILL WARM!
UH-HUH!
WANT SOME HOT COCOA?
YEP.
IT'S SO GOOD.
I HATE THIS GUY.
ZZZZZZ...
WHY'S HE SLEEPING THERE?
DUNNO. ANOTHER ALL-NIGHTER MAYBE?

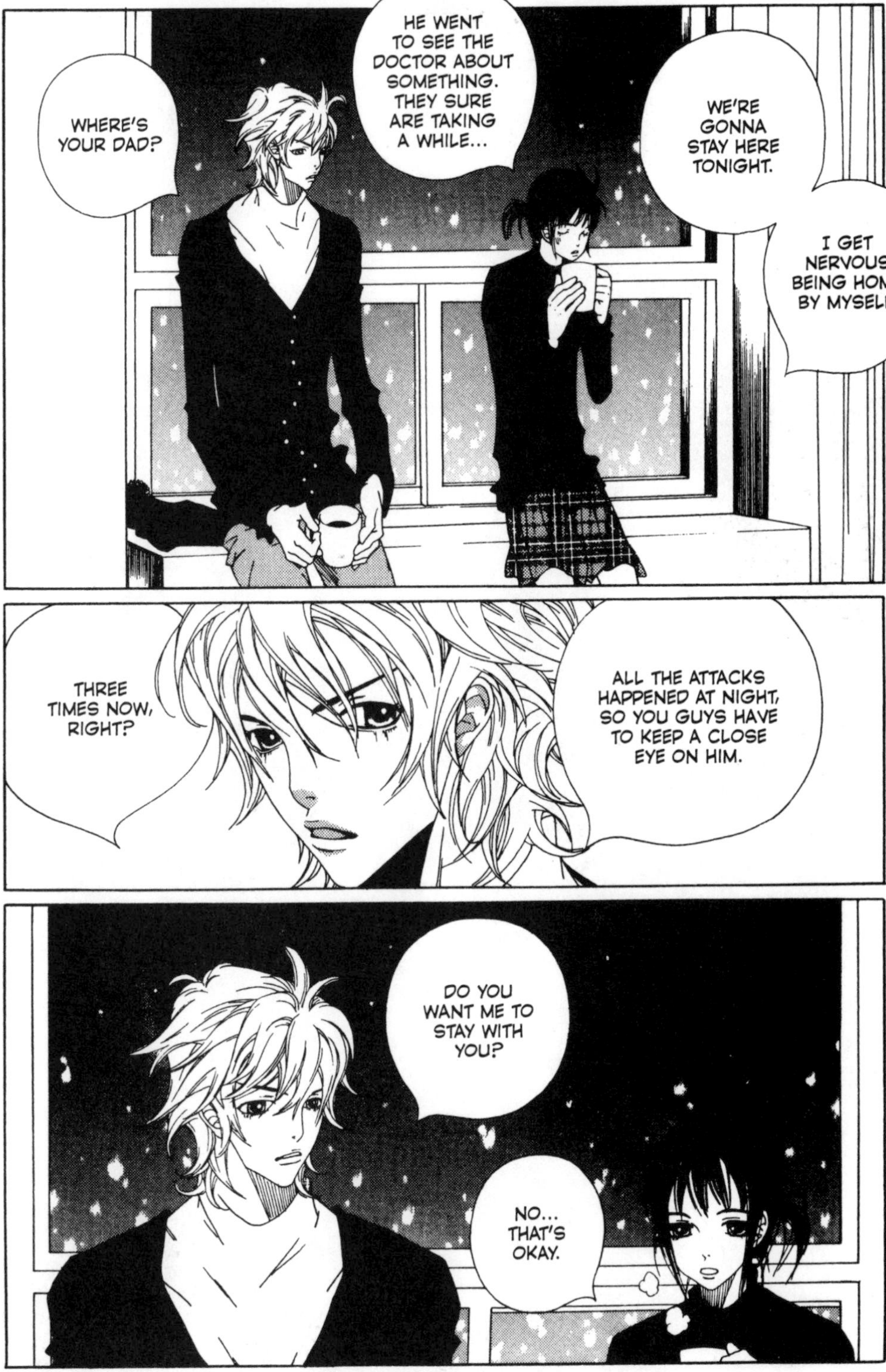
WHERE'S YOUR DAD?
HE WENT TO SEE THE DOCTOR ABOUT SOMETHING. THEY SURE ARE TAKING A WHILE...
WE'RE GONNA STAY HERE TONIGHT.
I GET NERVOUS BEING HOME BY MYSELF.
THREE TIMES NOW, RIGHT?
ALL THE ATTACKS HAPPENED AT NIGHT, SO YOU GUYS HAVE TO KEEP A CLOSE EYE ON HIM.
DO YOU WANT ME TO STAY WITH YOU?
NO... THAT'S OKAY.

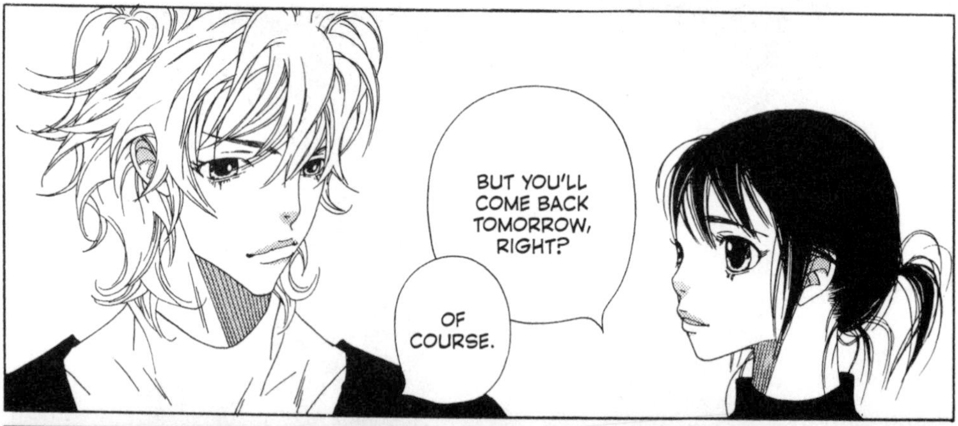
BUT YOU'LL COME BACK TOMORROW, RIGHT?
OF COURSE.

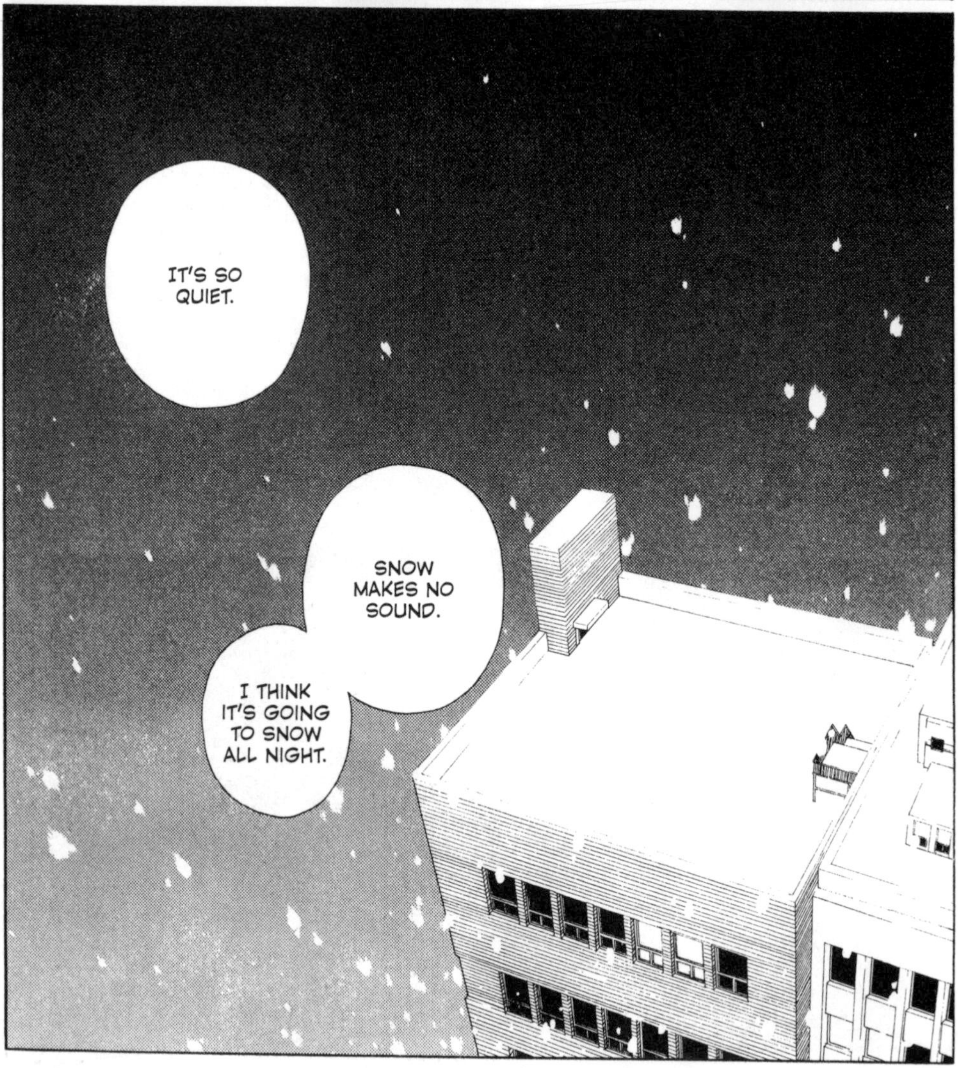
IT'S SO QUIET.
SNOW MAKES NO SOUND.
I THINK IT'S GOING TO SNOW ALL NIGHT.

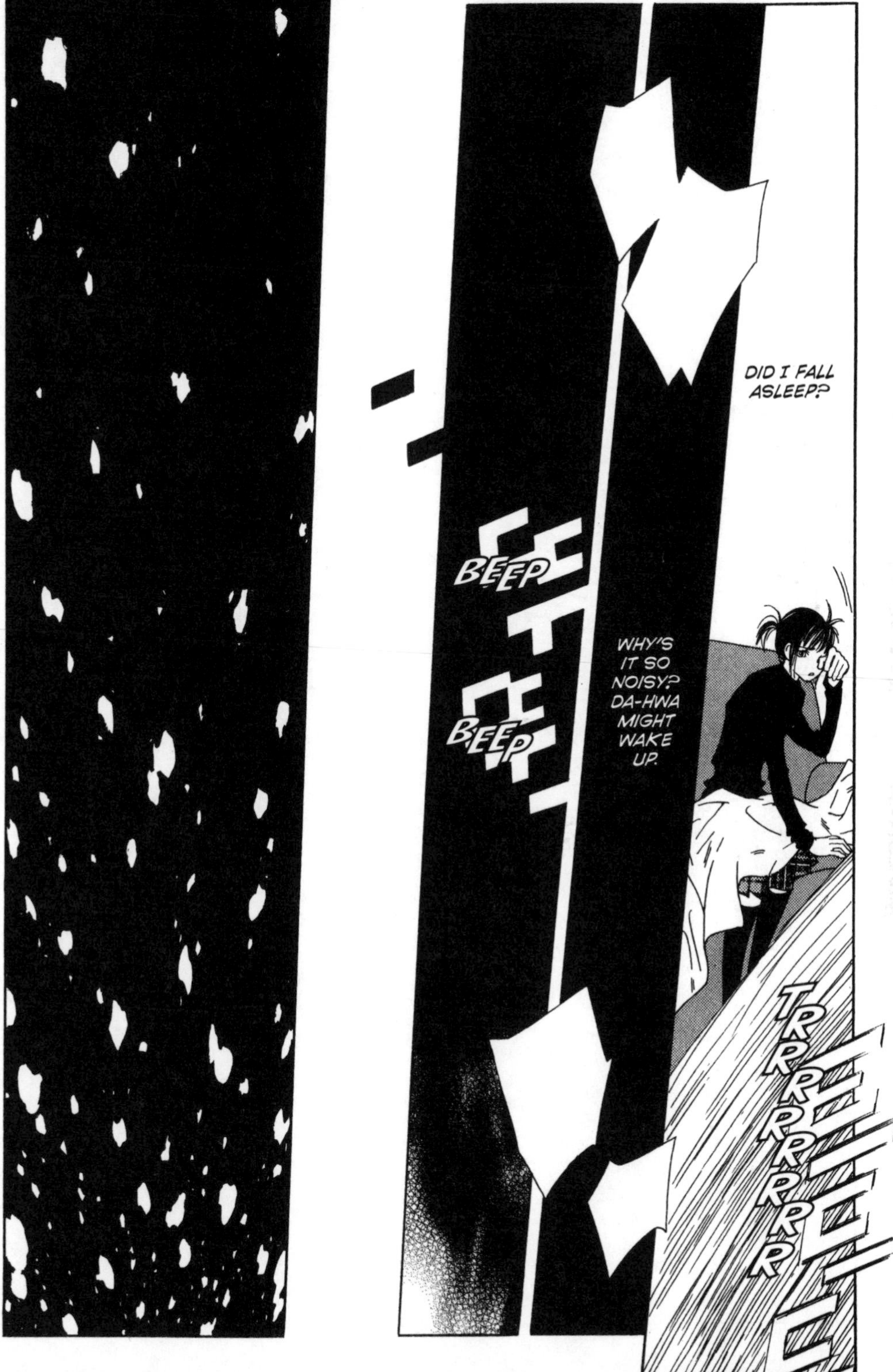
DID I FALL ASLEEP?
BEEP
WHY'S IT SO NOISY? DA-HWA MIGHT WAKE UP.
BEEP
TRRRRRRR

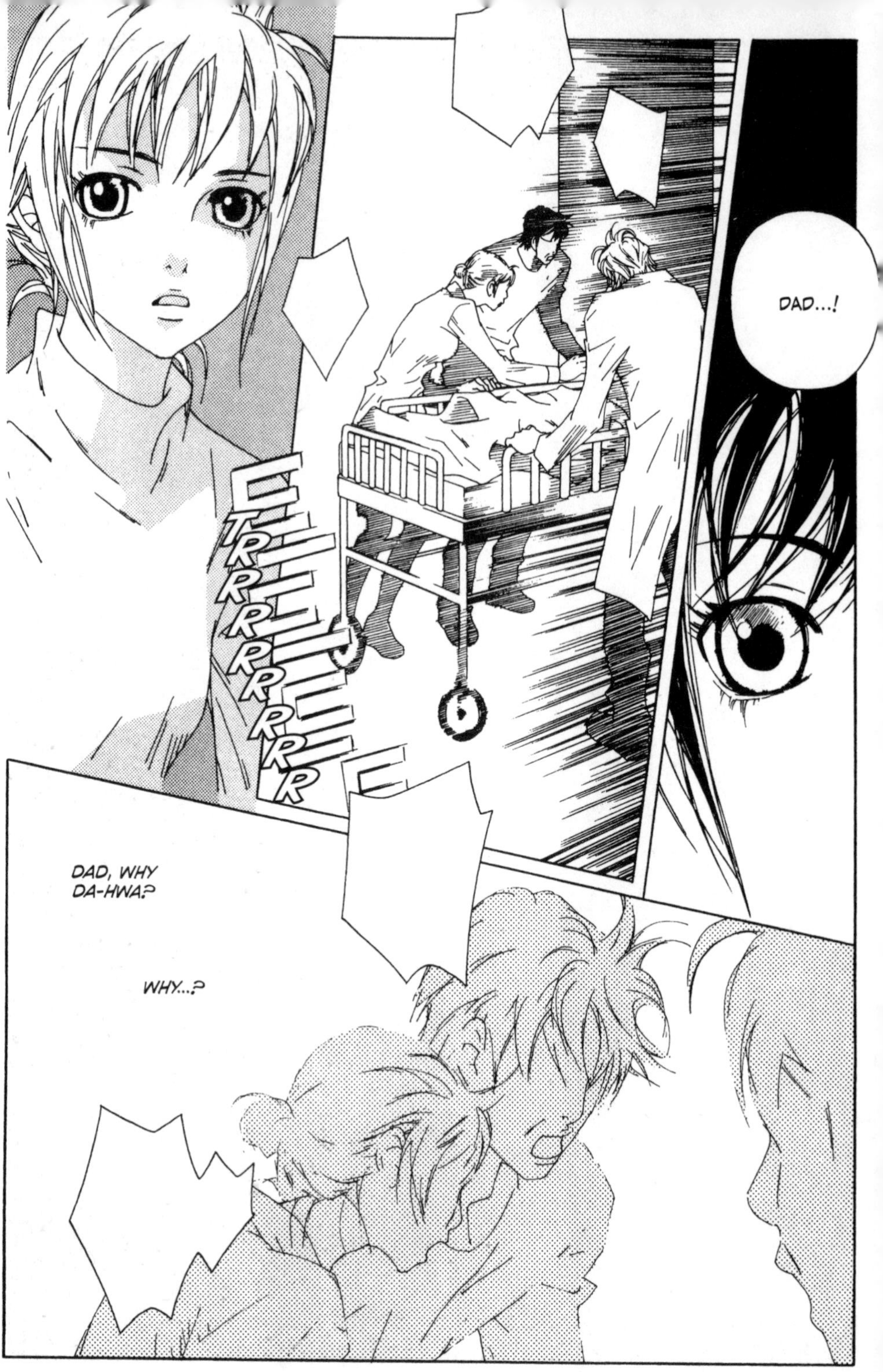
TRRRRRRRR
DAD...!
DAD, WHY DA-HWA?
WHY...?

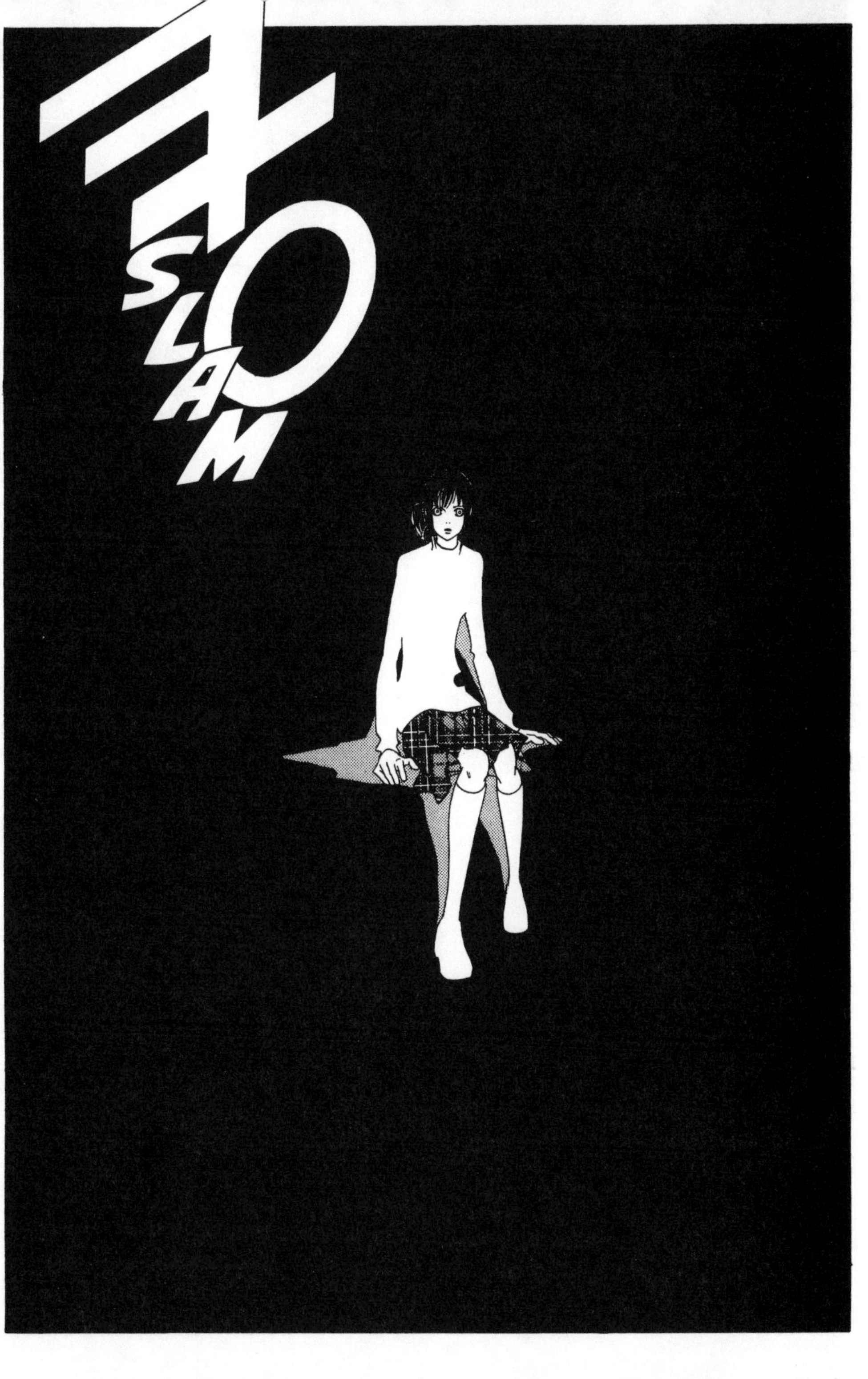
SLAM

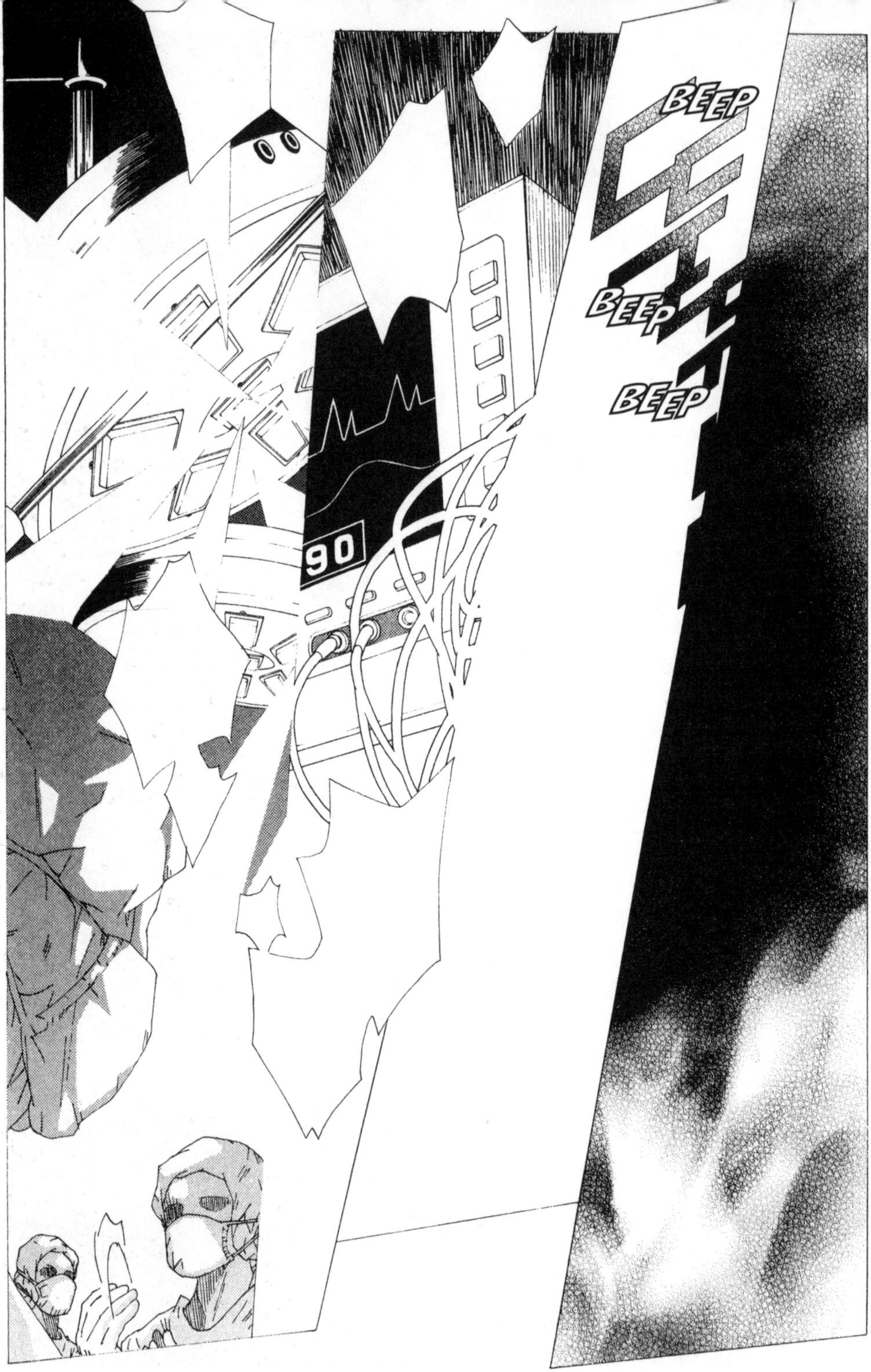
BEEP
BEEP
BEEP
90

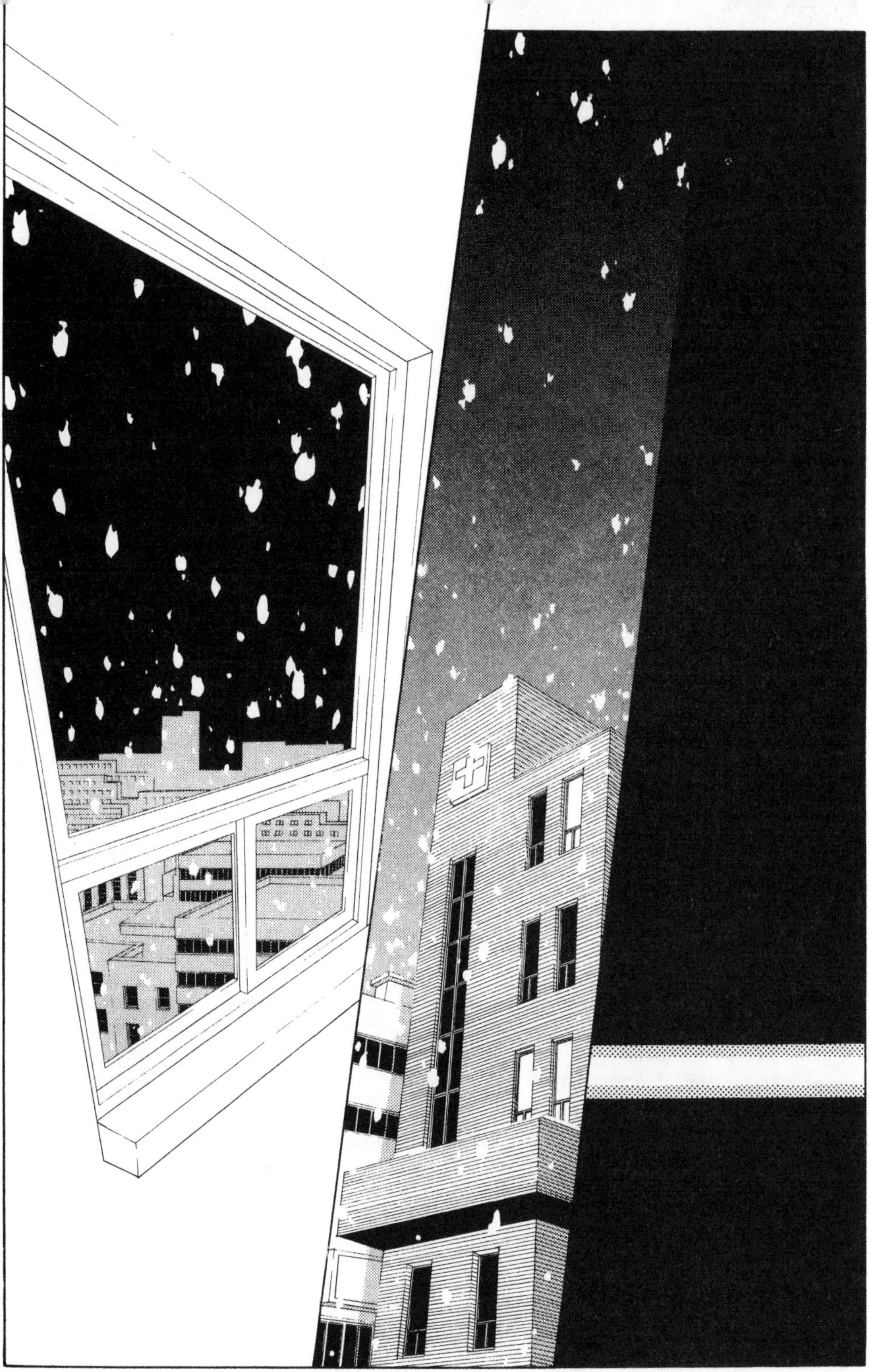

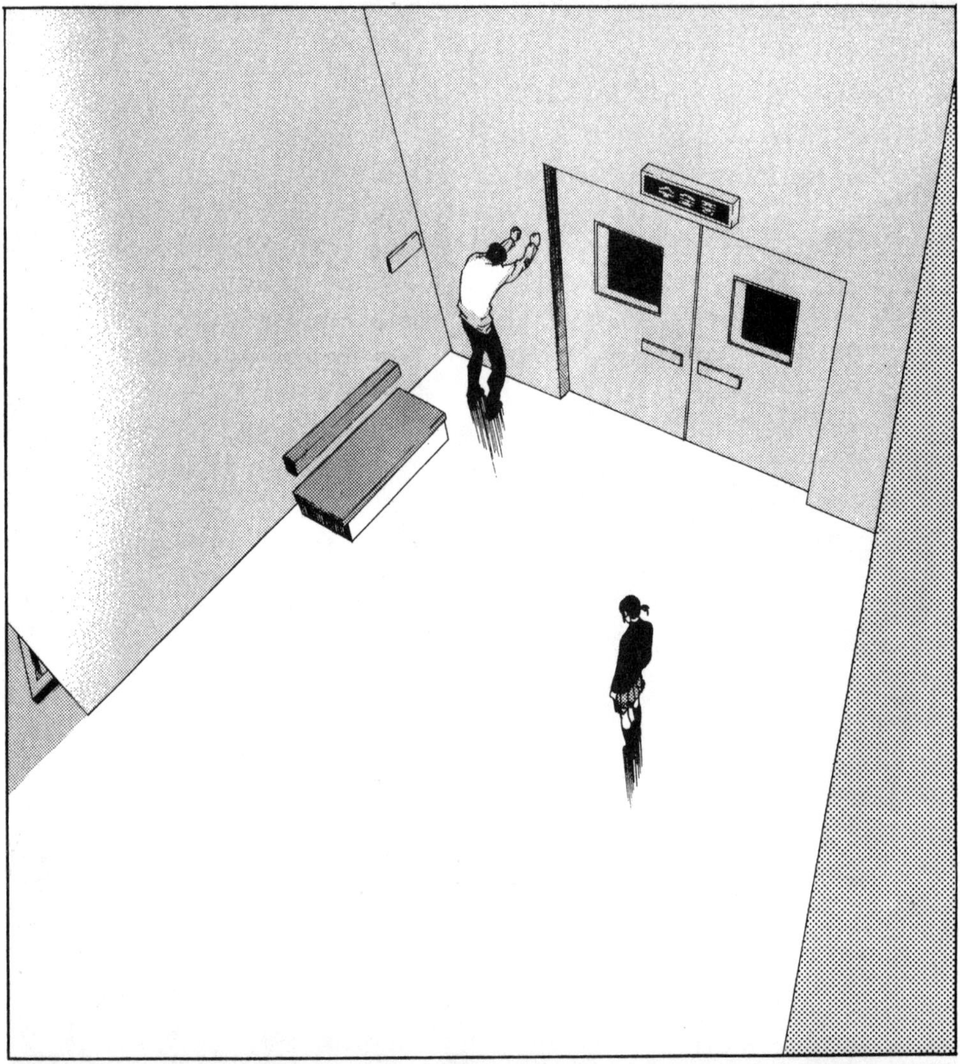
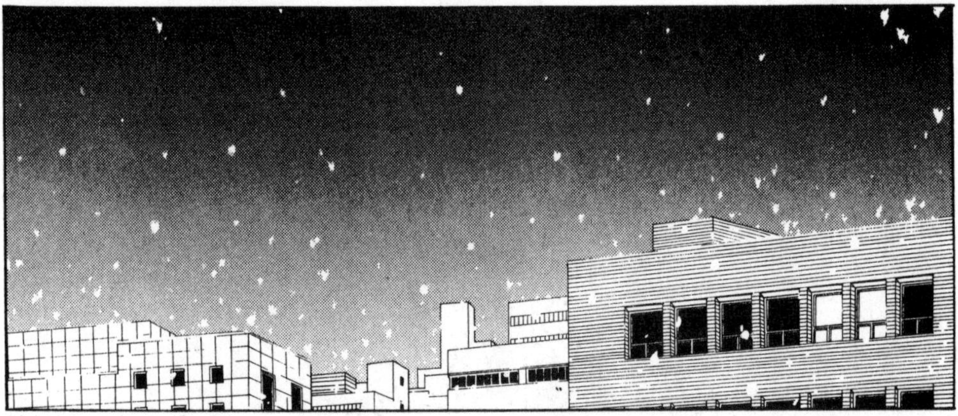

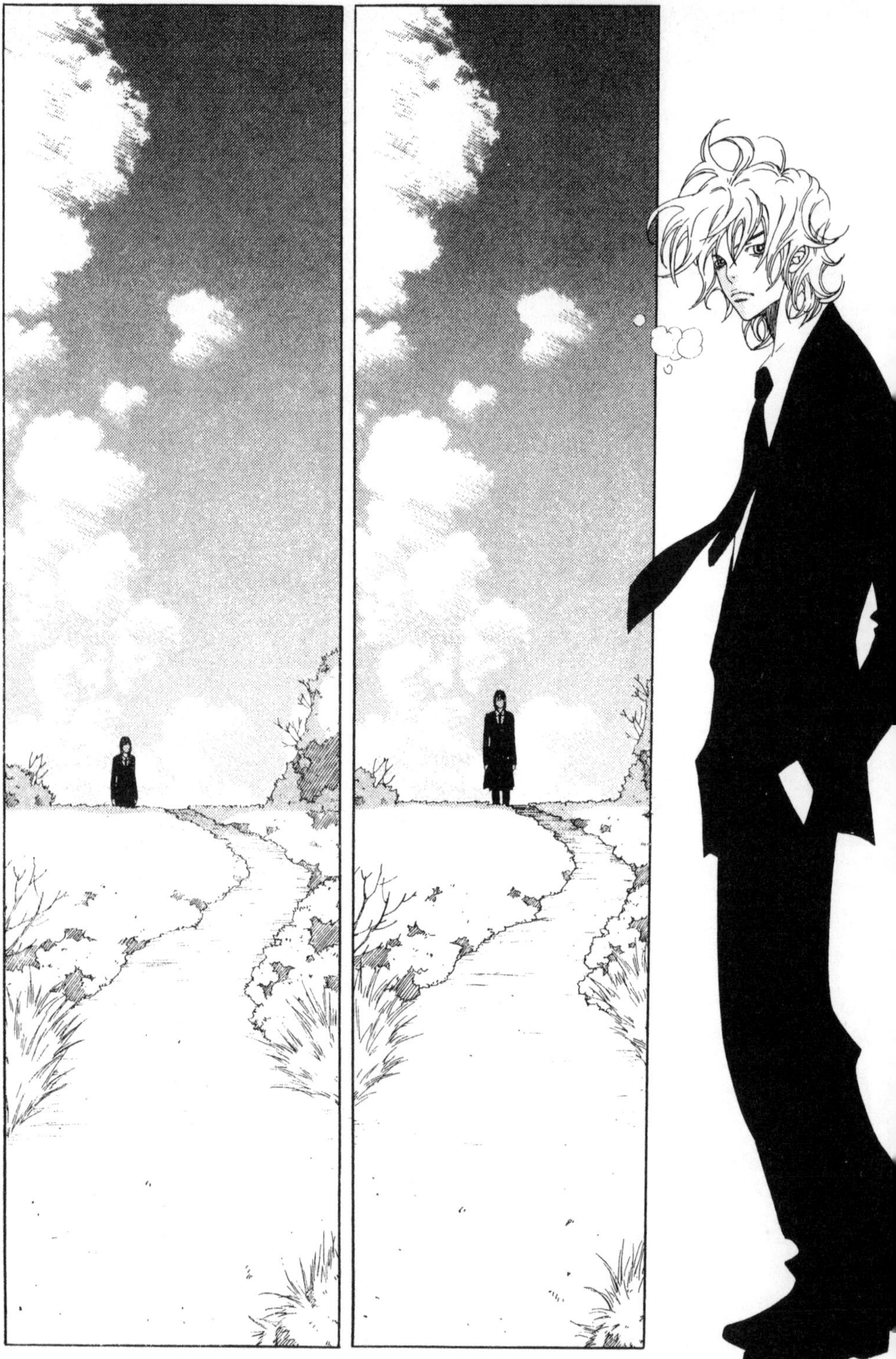

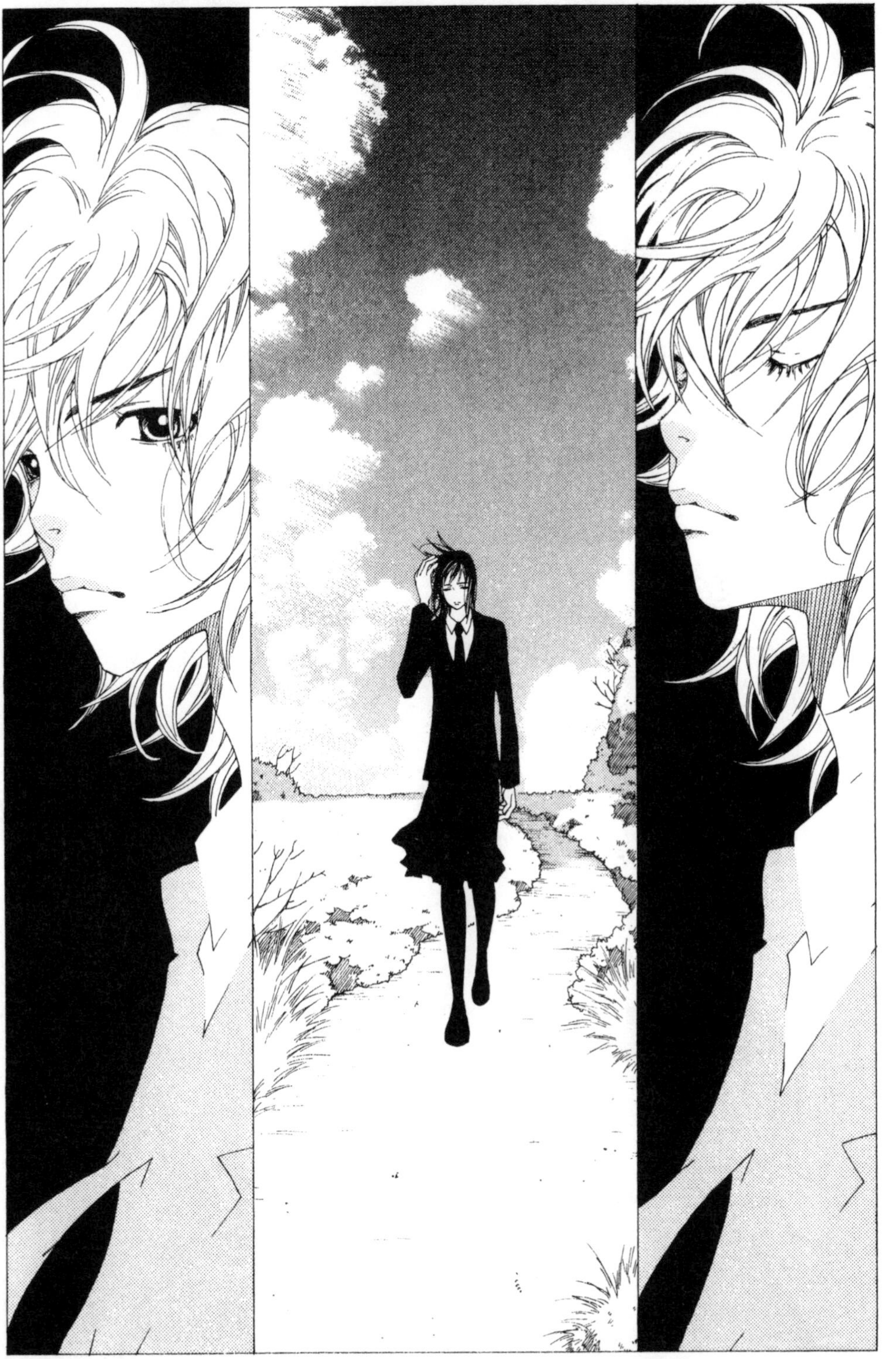

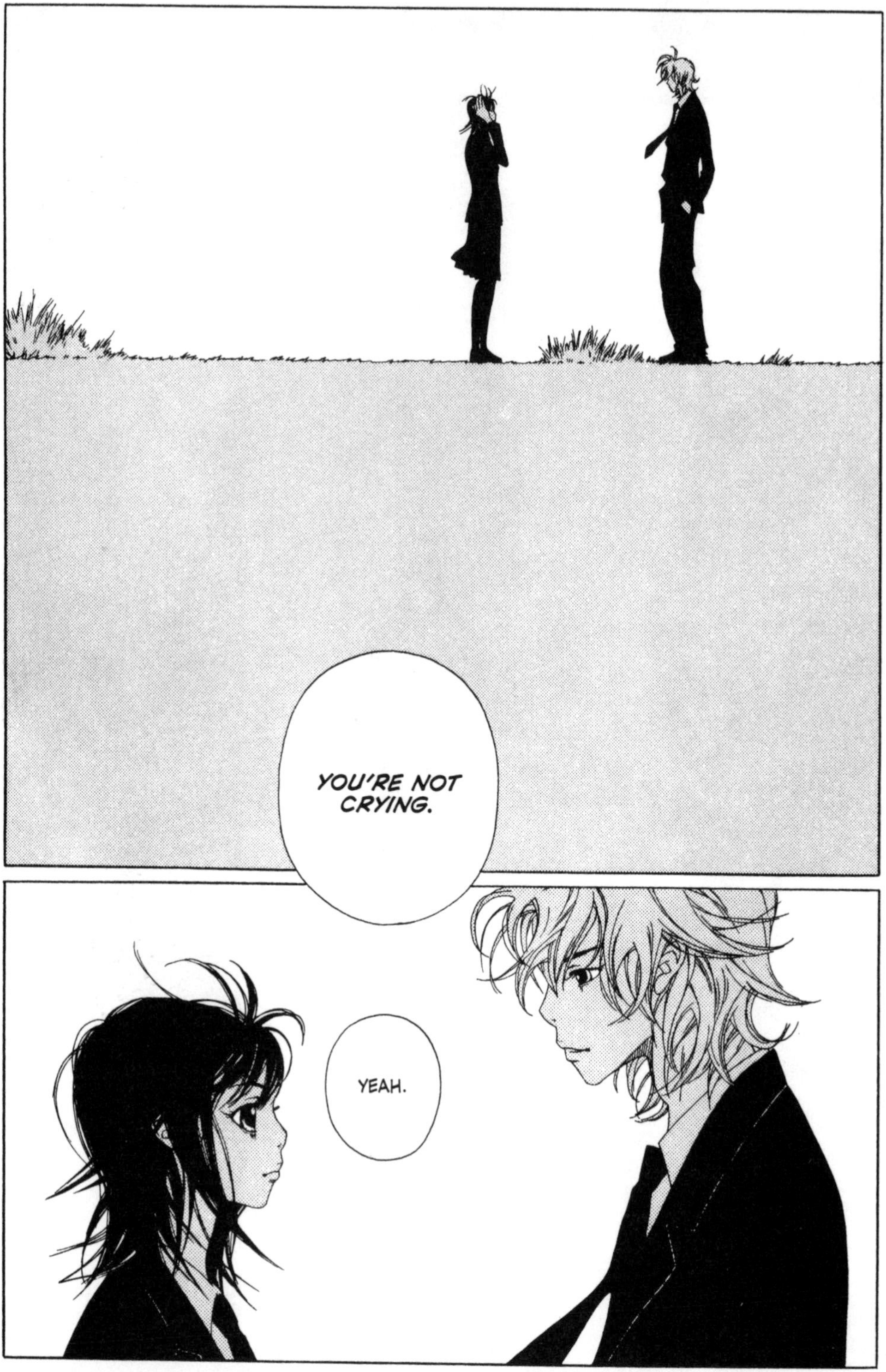
YOU'RE NOT CRYING.
YEAH.

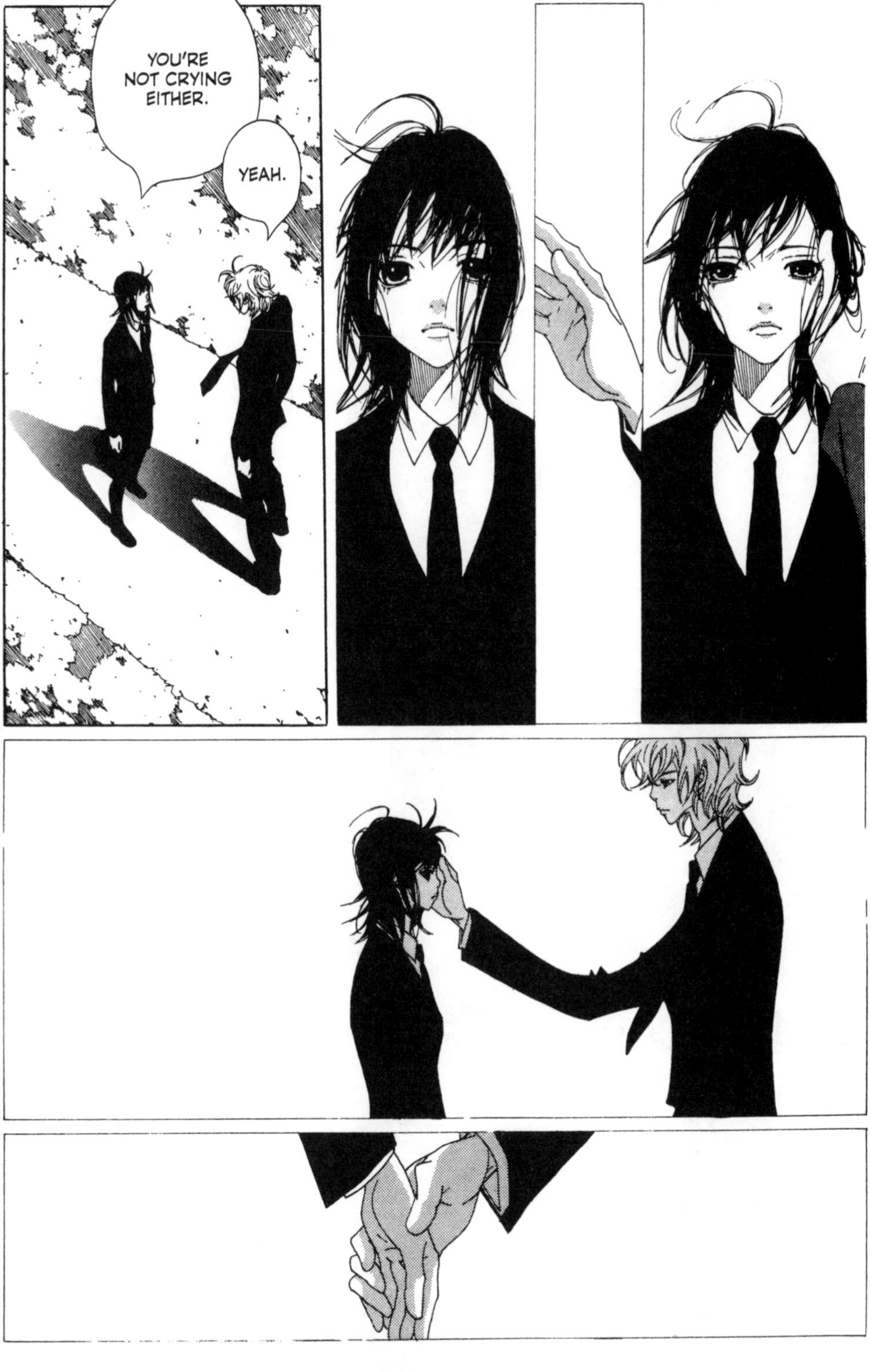
YOU'RE NOT CRYING EITHER.
YEAH.

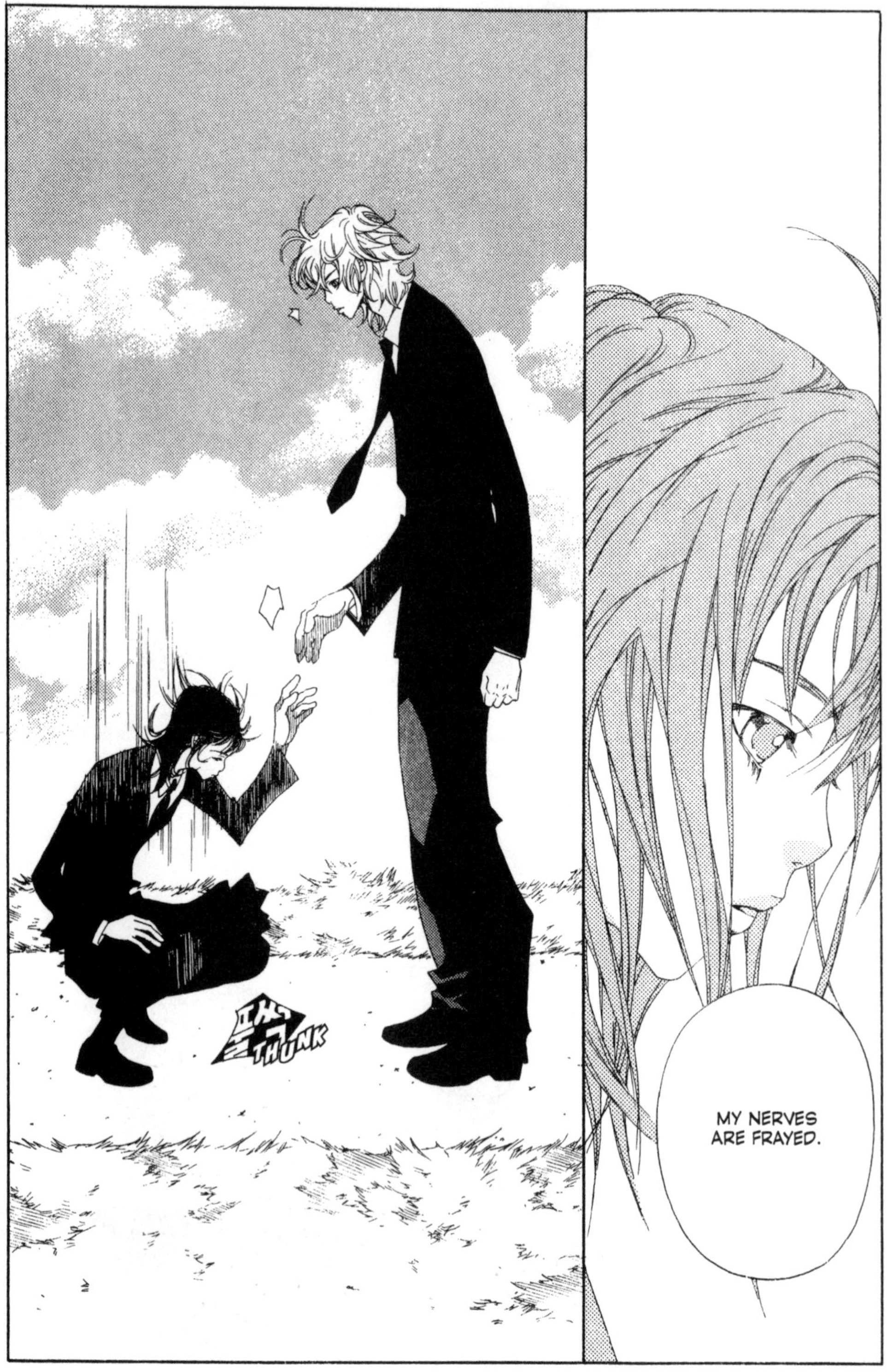
THUNK
MY NERVES ARE FRAYED.

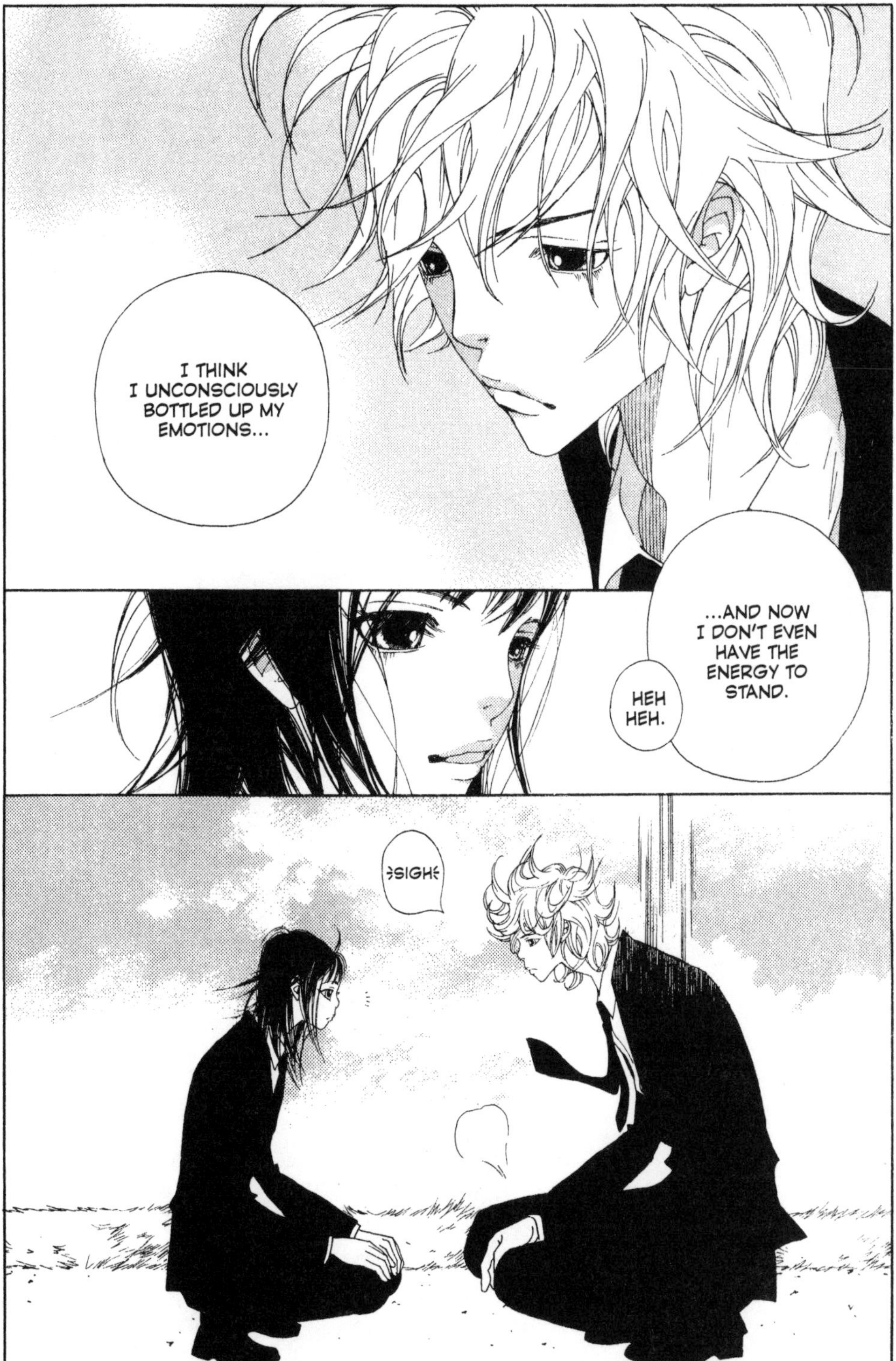
I THINK I UNCONSCIOUSLY BOTTLED UP MY EMOTIONS...
...AND NOW I DON'T EVEN HAVE THE ENERGY TO STAND.
HEH HEH.
SIGH

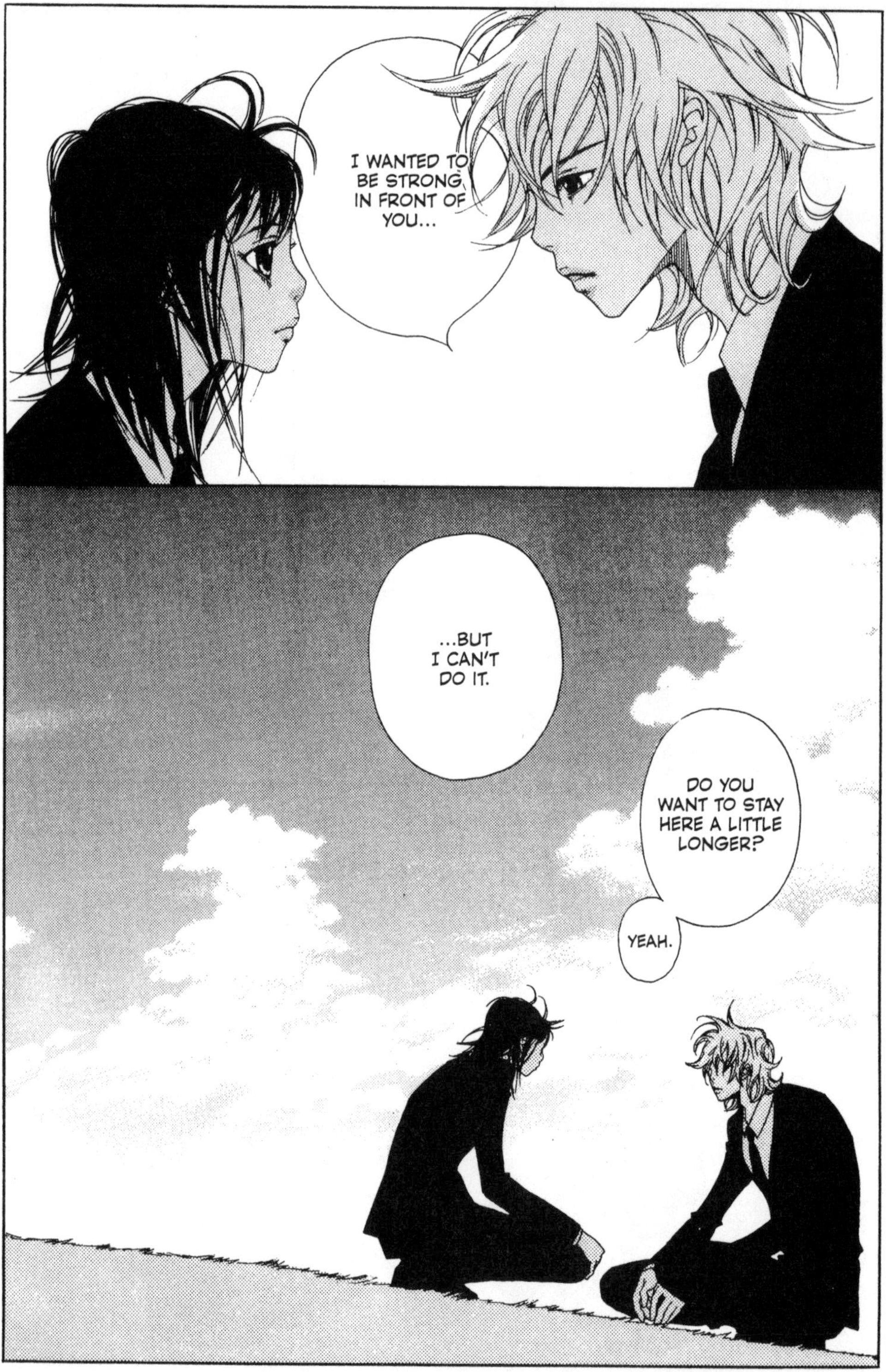
I WANTED TO BE STRONG IN FRONT OF YOU...
...BUT I CAN'T DO IT.
DO YOU WANT TO STAY HERE A LITTLE LONGER?
YEAH.

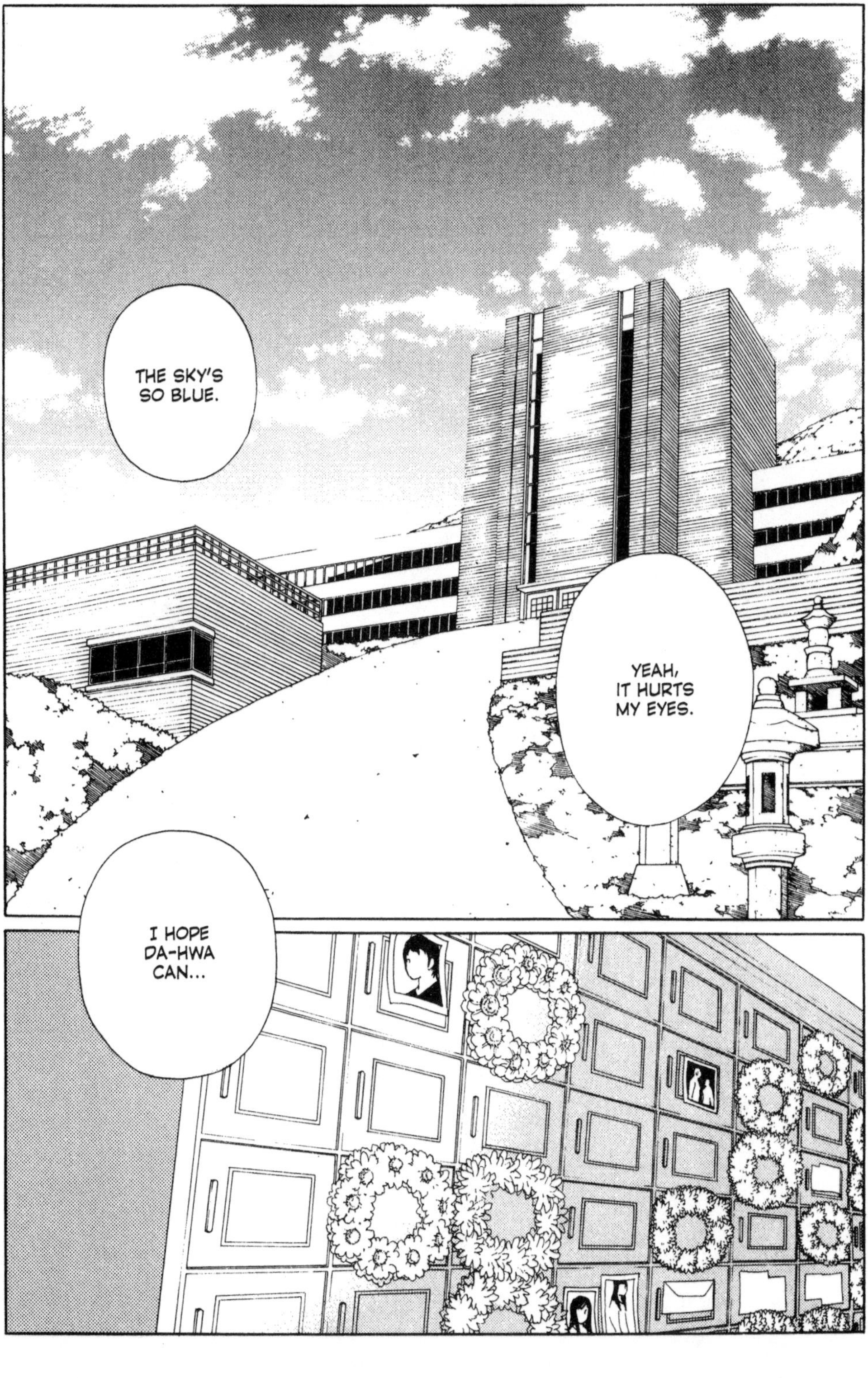
THE SKY'S SO BLUE.
YEAH, IT HURTS MY EYES.
I HOPE DA-HWA CAN...

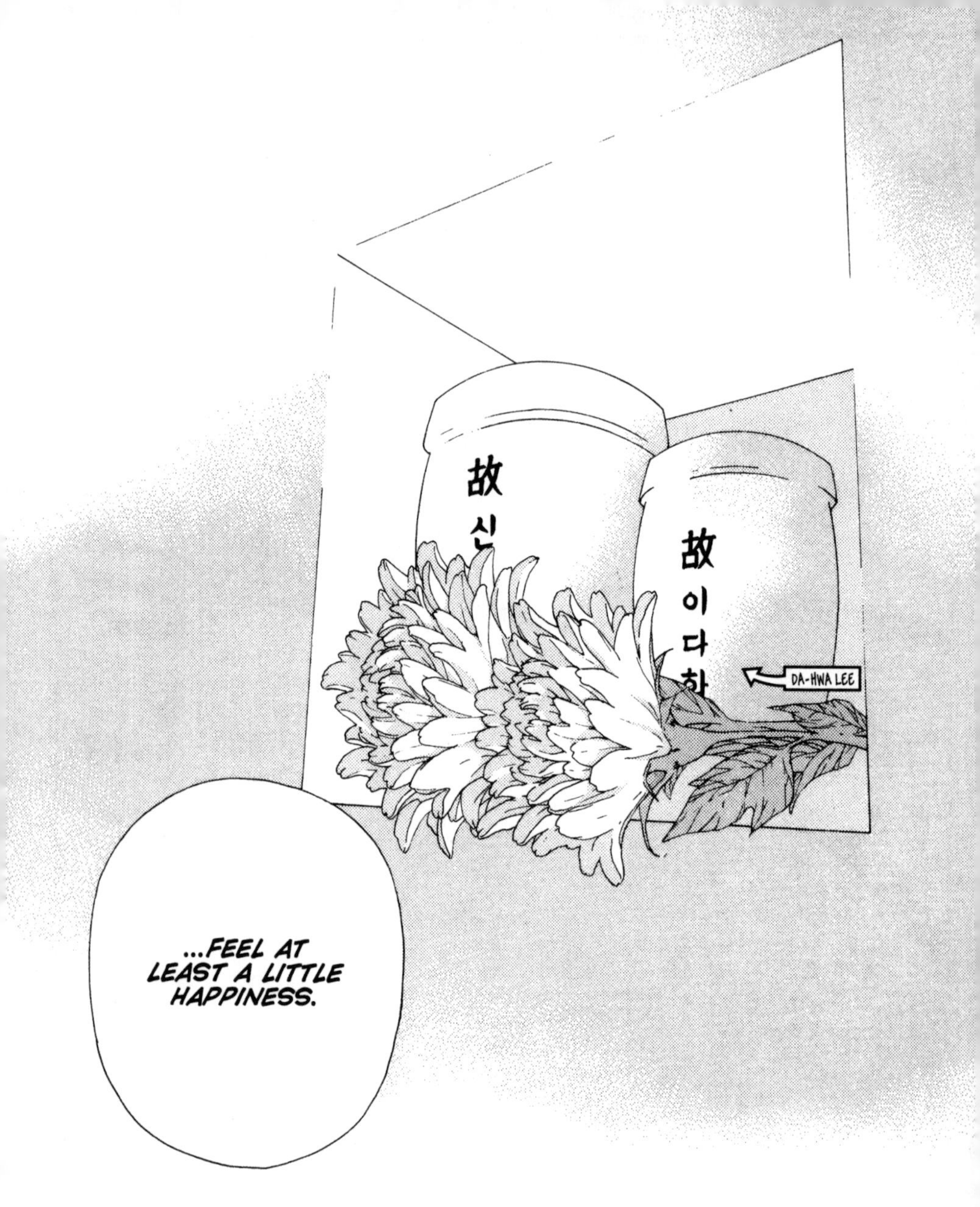
故 신
故 이다하
DA-HWA LEE
...FEEL AT LEAST A LITTLE HAPPINESS.

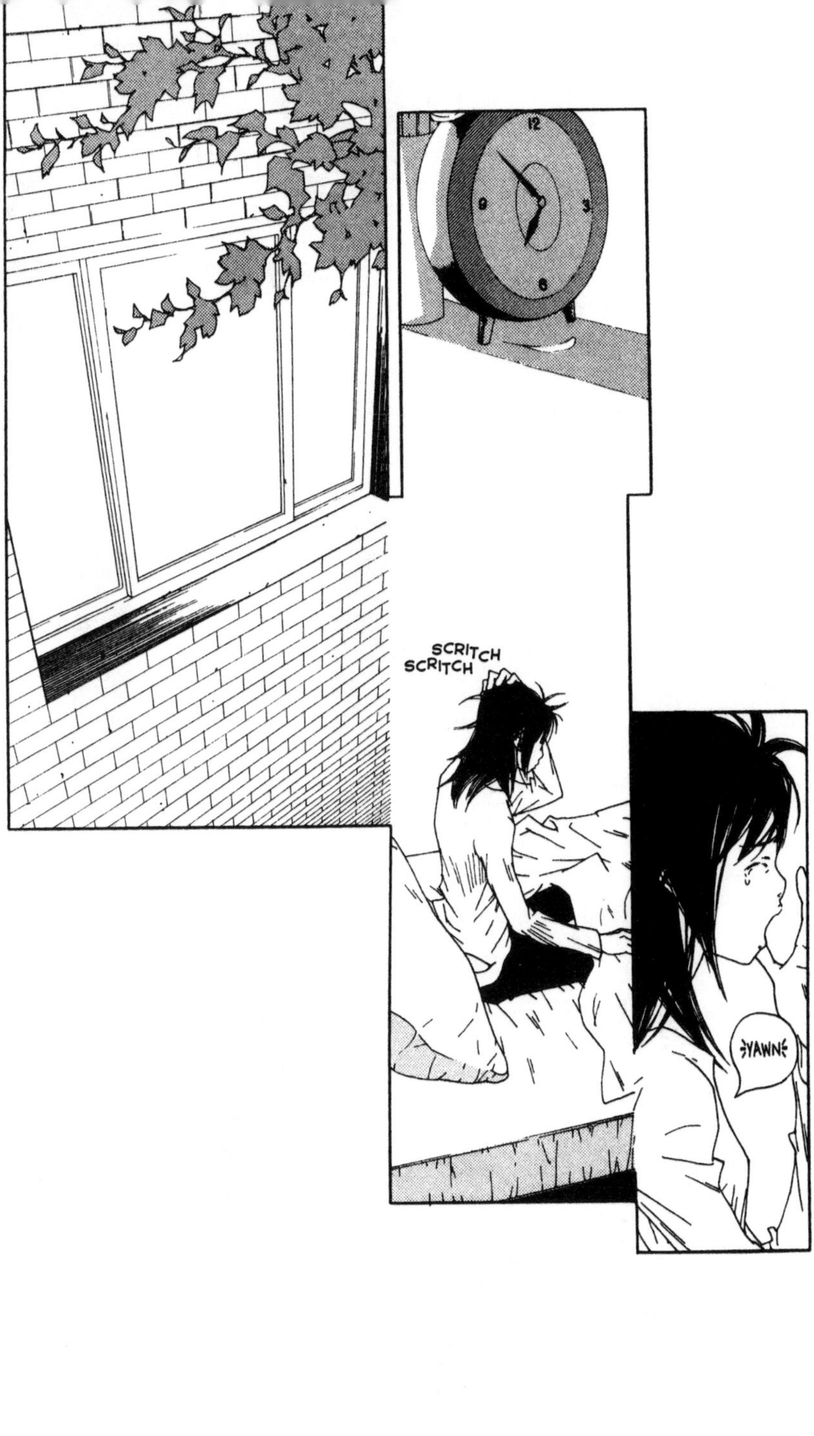
SCRITCH
SCRITCH
YAWN

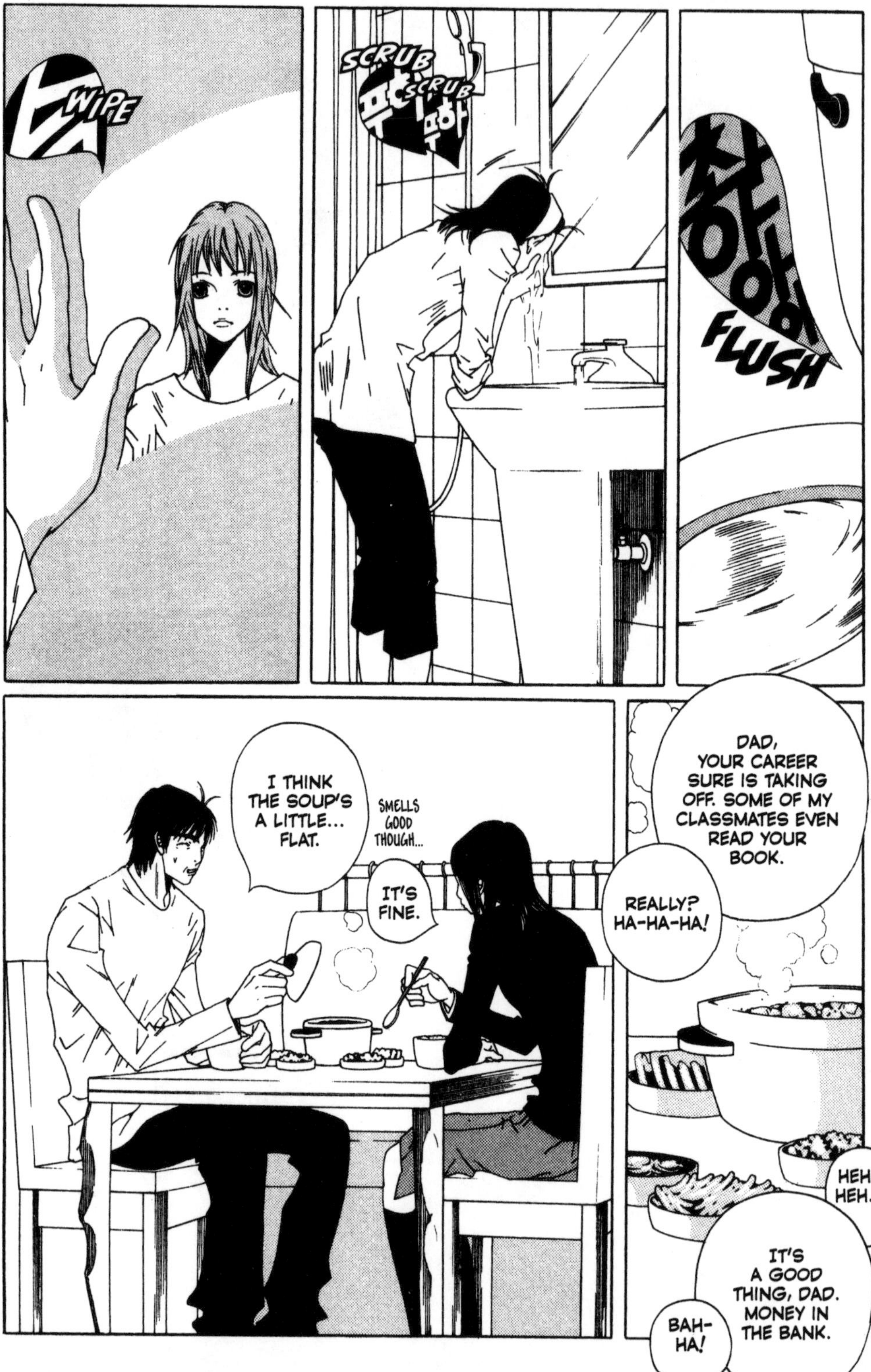
WIPE
SCRUB
SCRUB
FLUSH
I THINK THE SOUP'S A LITTLE... FLAT.
SMELLS GOOD THOUGH...
IT'S FINE.
DAD, YOUR CAREER SURE IS TAKING OFF. SOME OF MY CLASSMATES EVEN READ YOUR BOOK.
REALLY? HA-HA-HA!
HEH HEH.
IT'S A GOOD THING, DAD. MONEY IN THE BANK.
BAH-HA!

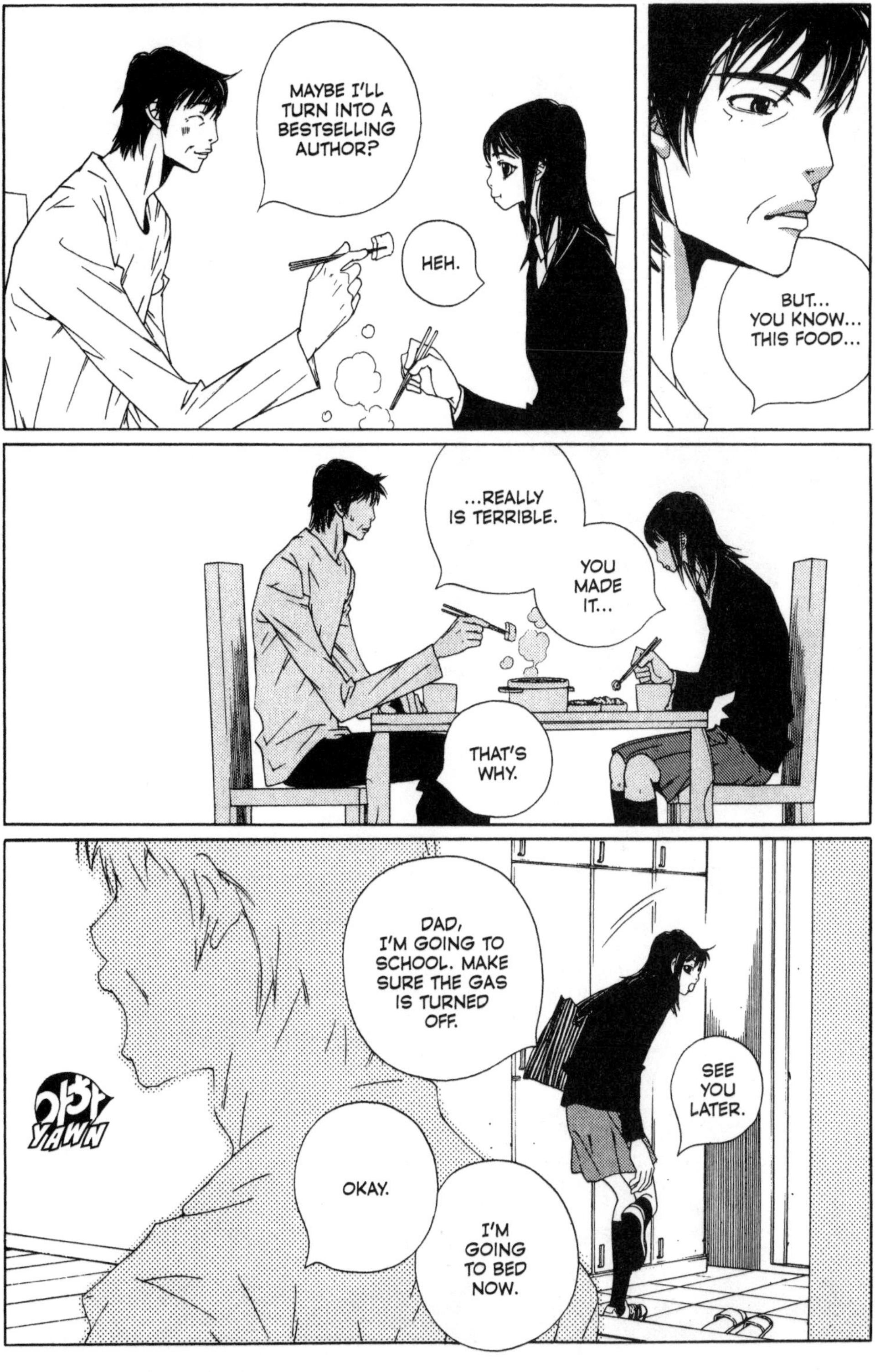
MAYBE I'LL TURN INTO A BESTSELLING AUTHOR?
HEH.
BUT... YOU KNOW... THIS FOOD...
...REALLY IS TERRIBLE.
YOU MADE IT...
THAT'S WHY.
DAD, I'M GOING TO SCHOOL. MAKE SURE THE GAS IS TURNED OFF.
SEE YOU LATER.
YAWN
OKAY.
I'M GOING TO BED NOW.

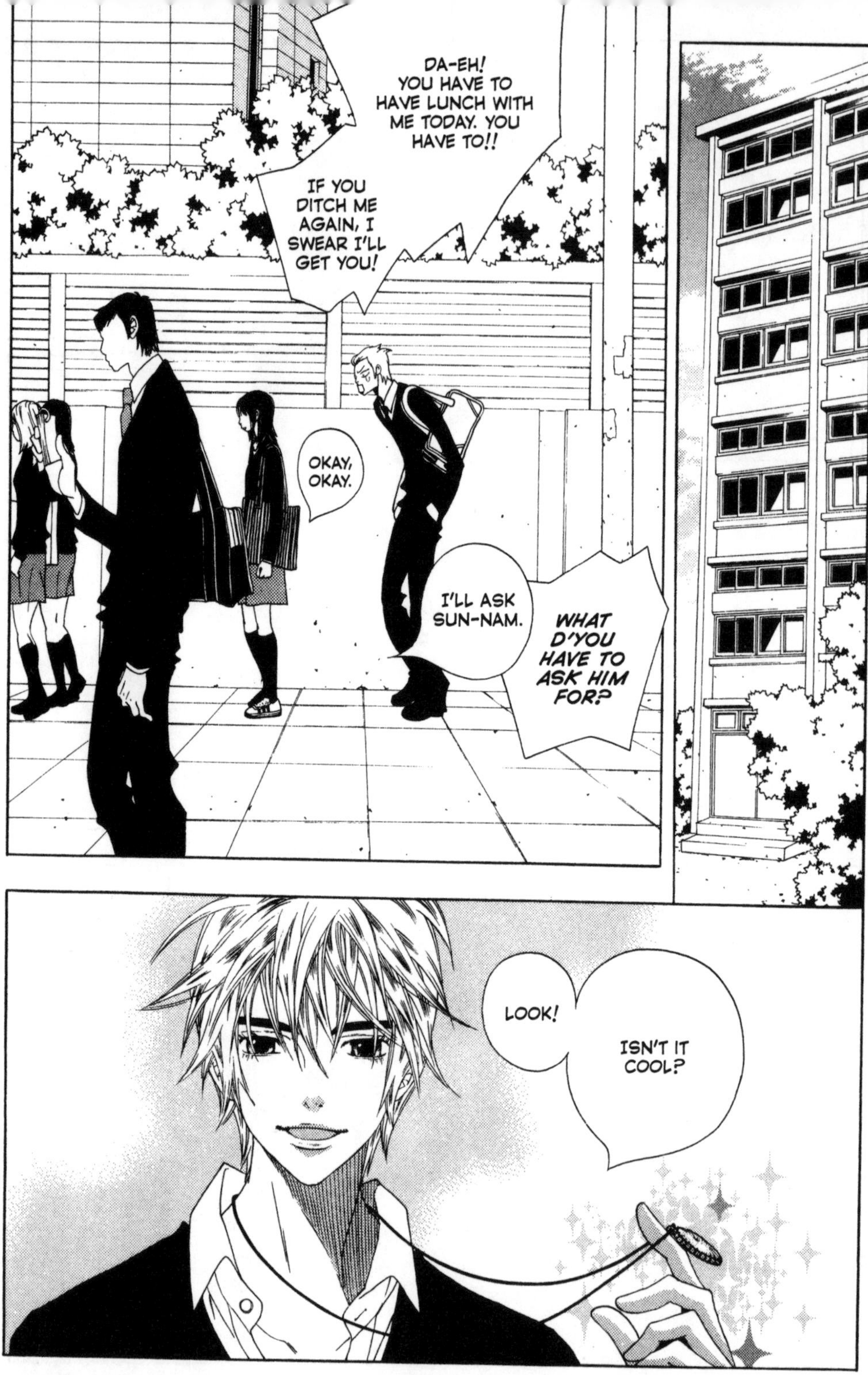
DA-EH! YOU HAVE TO HAVE LUNCH WITH ME TODAY. YOU HAVE TO!!
IF YOU DITCH ME AGAIN, I SWEAR I'LL GET YOU!
OKAY, OKAY.
I'LL ASK SUN-NAM.
WHAT D'YOU HAVE TO ASK HIM FOR?
LOOK!
ISN'T IT COOL?

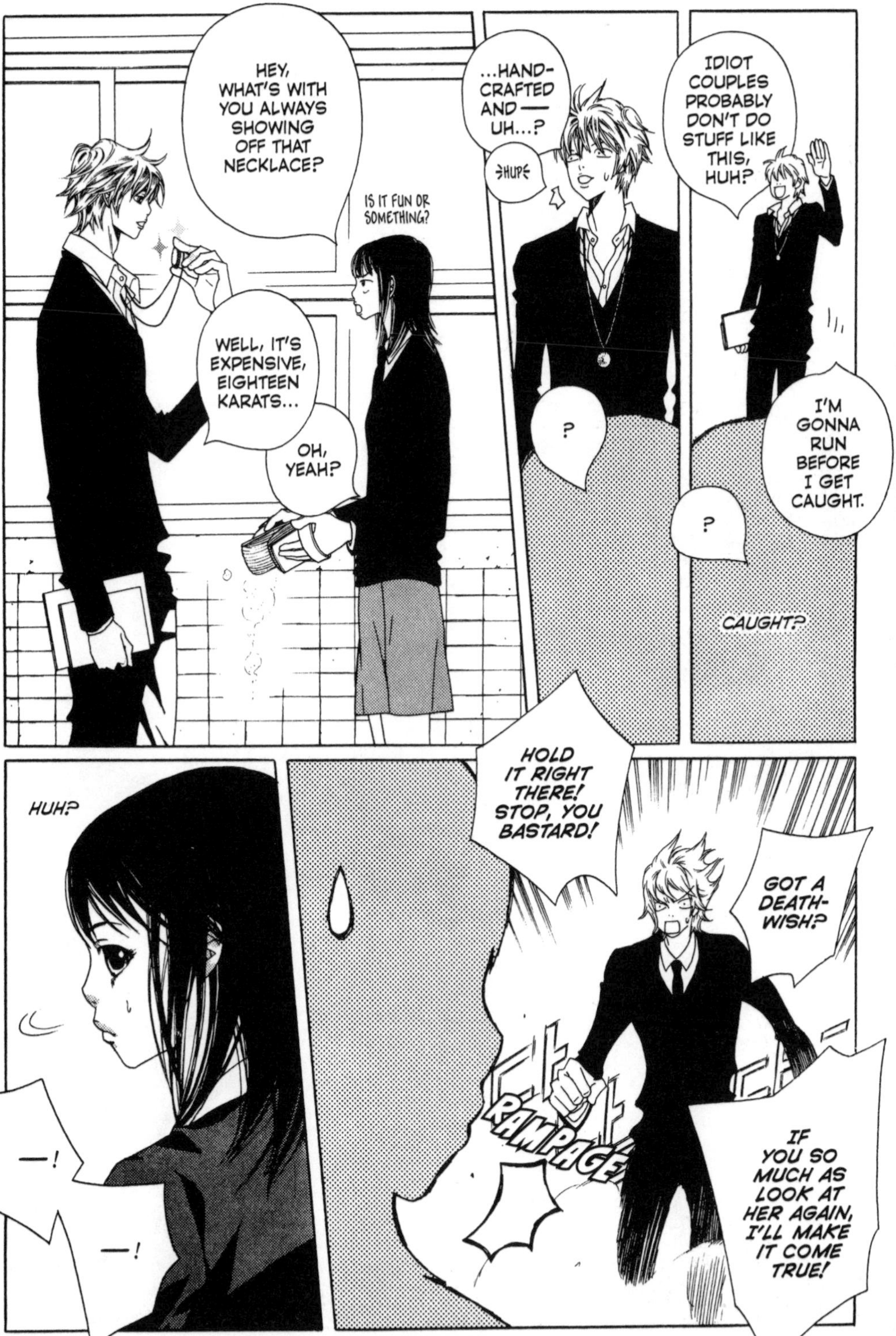
HEY, WHAT'S WITH YOU ALWAYS SHOWING OFF THAT NECKLACE?
IS IT FUN OR SOMETHING?
WELL, IT'S EXPENSIVE, EIGHTEEN KARATS...
OH, YEAH?
...HAND-CRAFTED AND — UH...?
HUP
?
IDIOT COUPLES PROBABLY DON'T DO STUFF LIKE THIS, HUH?
I'M GONNA RUN BEFORE I GET CAUGHT.
?
CAUGHT?
HUH?
—!
—!
HOLD IT RIGHT THERE! STOP, YOU BASTARD!
GOT A DEATH-WISH?
RAMPAGE
IF YOU SO MUCH AS LOOK AT HER AGAIN, I'LL MAKE IT COME TRUE!

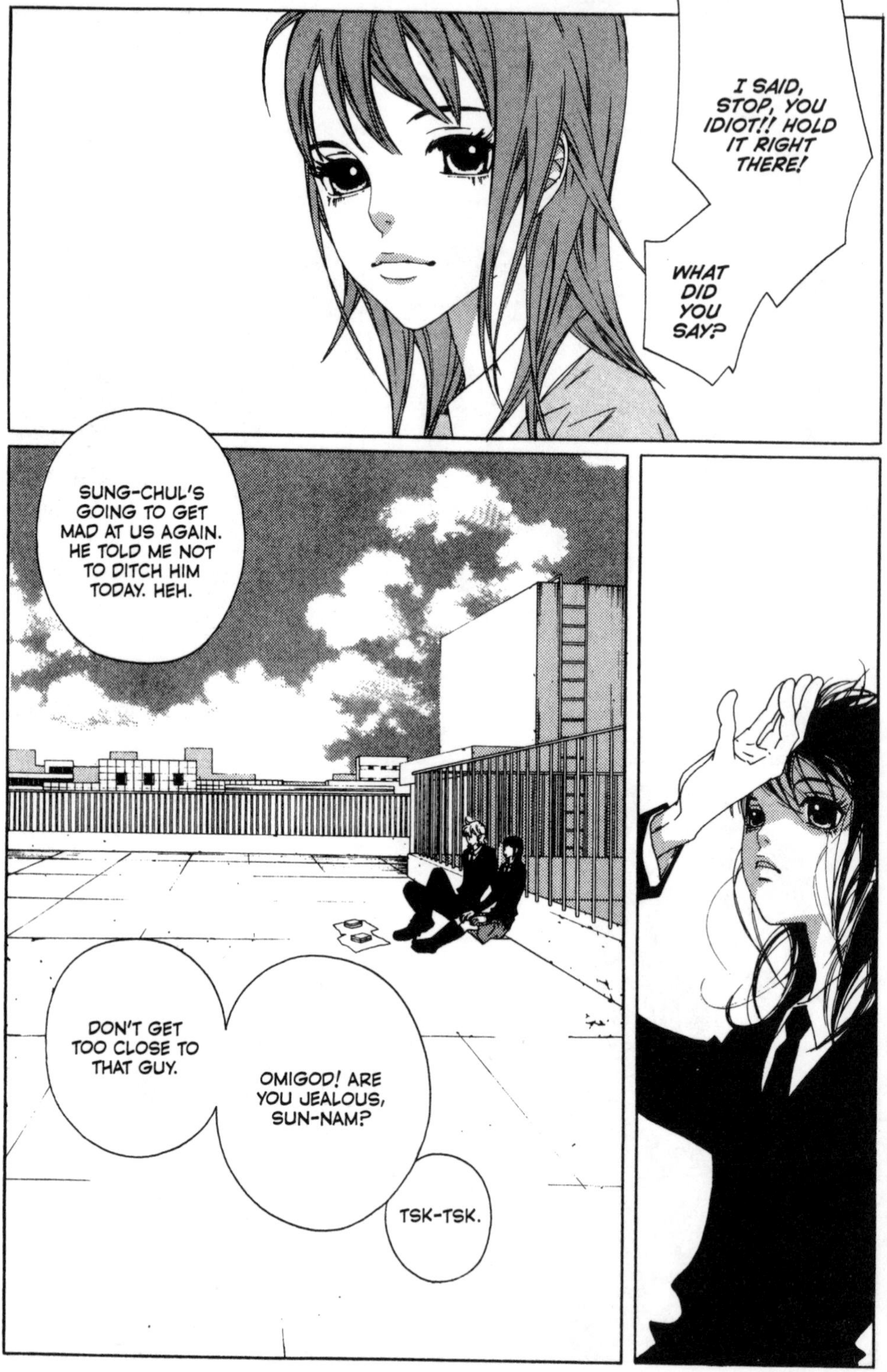
I SAID, STOP, YOU IDIOT!! HOLD IT RIGHT THERE!
WHAT DID YOU SAY?
SUNG-CHUL'S GOING TO GET MAD AT US AGAIN. HE TOLD ME NOT TO DITCH HIM TODAY. HEH.
DON'T GET TOO CLOSE TO THAT GUY.
OMIGOD! ARE YOU JEALOUS, SUN-NAM?
TSK-TSK.

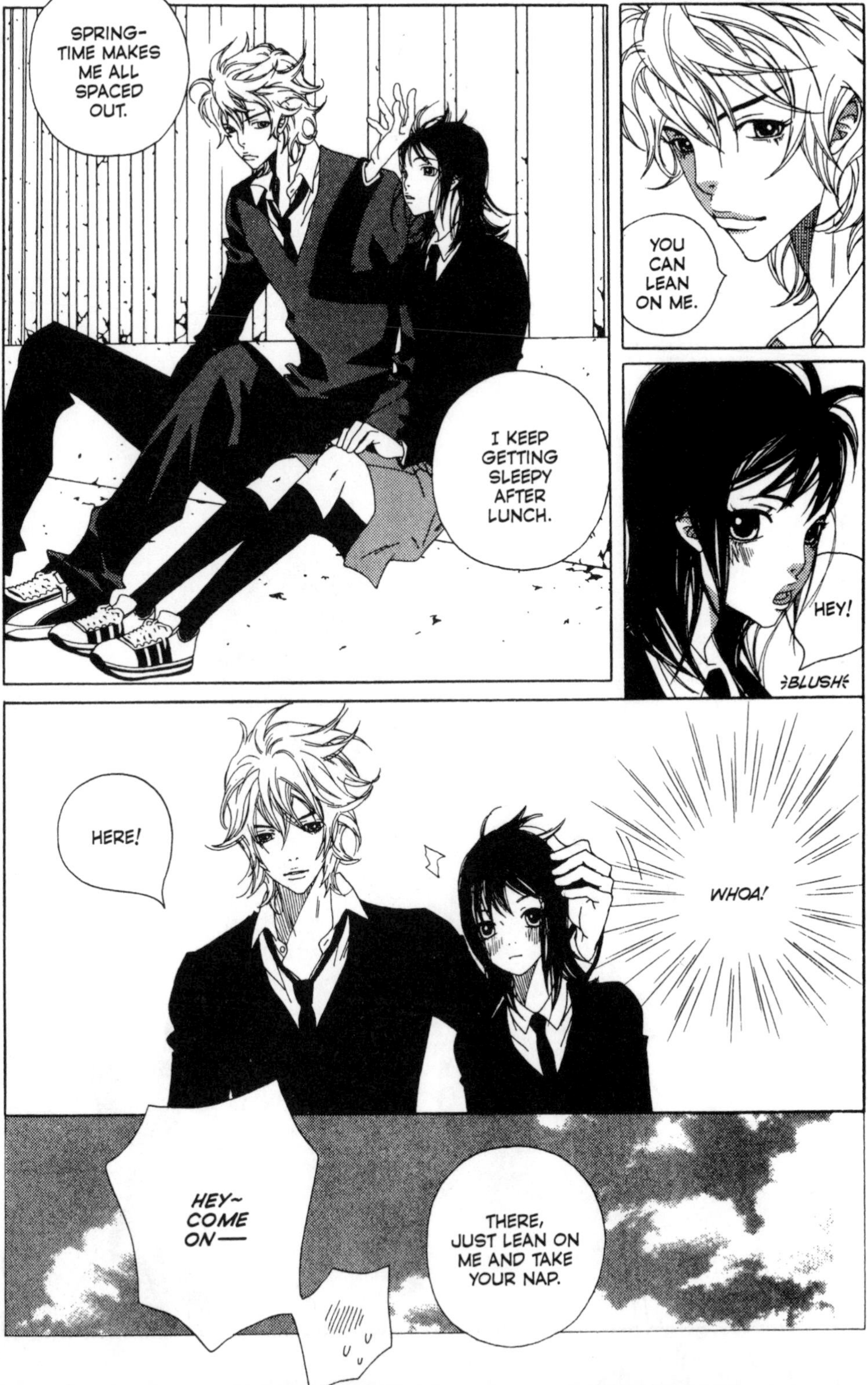
SPRING-TIME MAKES ME ALL SPACED OUT.
I KEEP GETTING SLEEPY AFTER LUNCH.
YOU CAN LEAN ON ME.
HEY!
BLUSH
HERE!
WHOA!
HEY~ COME ON—
THERE, JUST LEAN ON ME AND TAKE YOUR NAP.

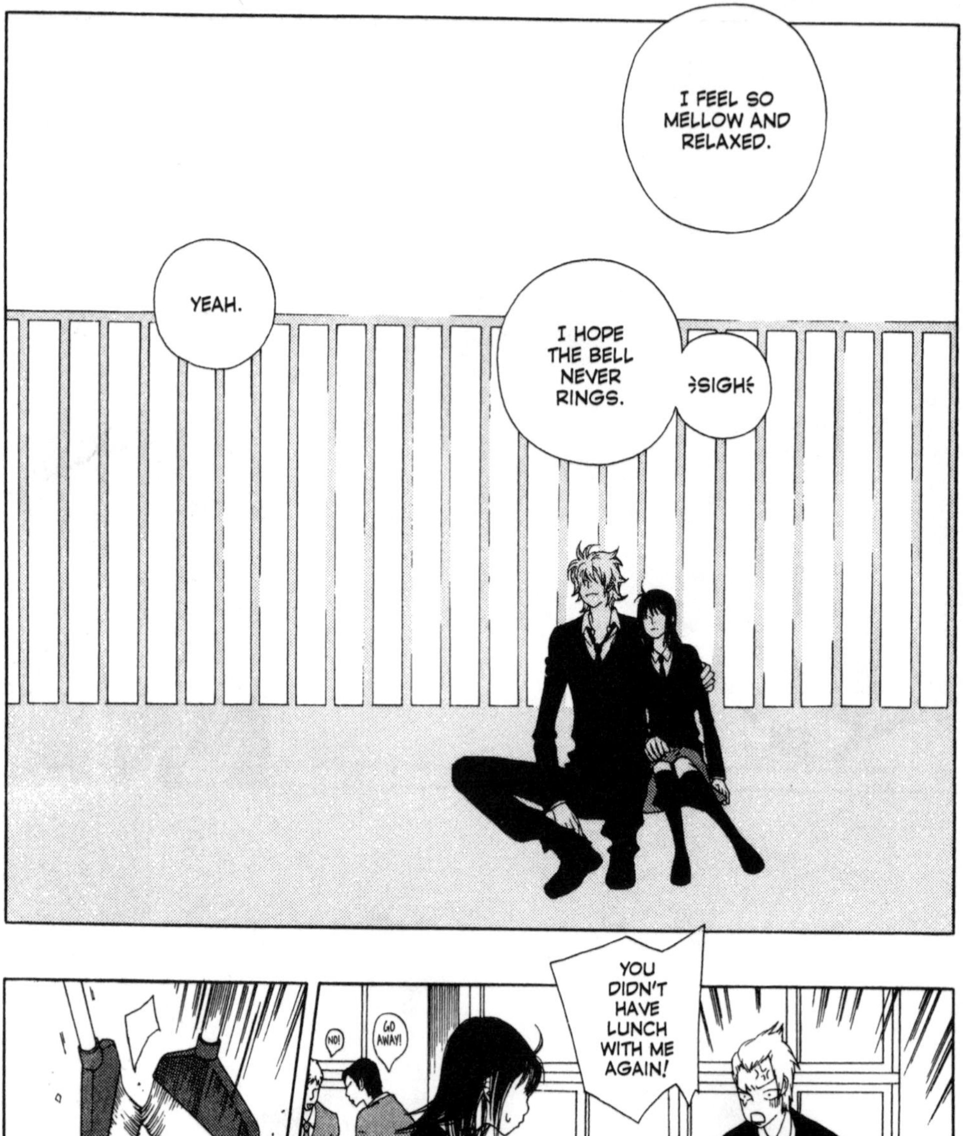
I FEEL SO MELLOW AND RELAXED.
YEAH.
I HOPE THE BELL NEVER RINGS.
SIGH

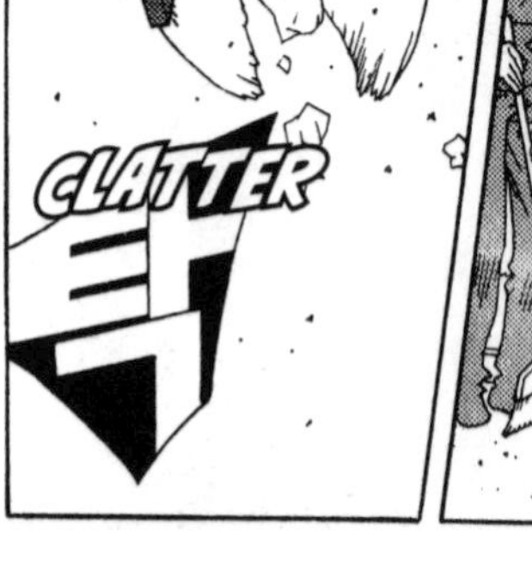
CLATTER

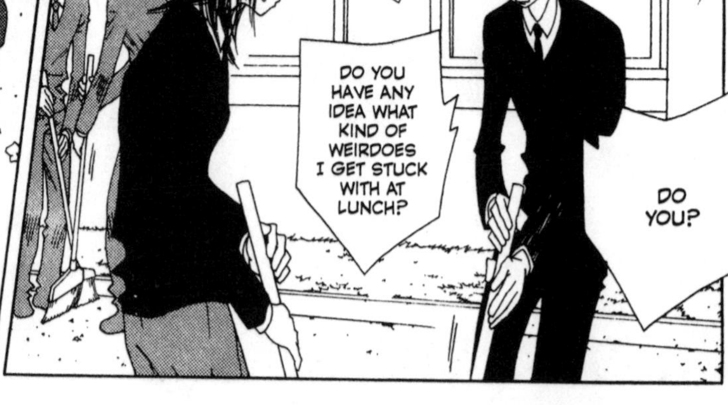
NO!
GO AWAY!
YOU DIDN'T HAVE LUNCH WITH ME AGAIN!
DO YOU HAVE ANY IDEA WHAT KIND OF WEIRDOES I GET STUCK WITH AT LUNCH?
DO YOU?

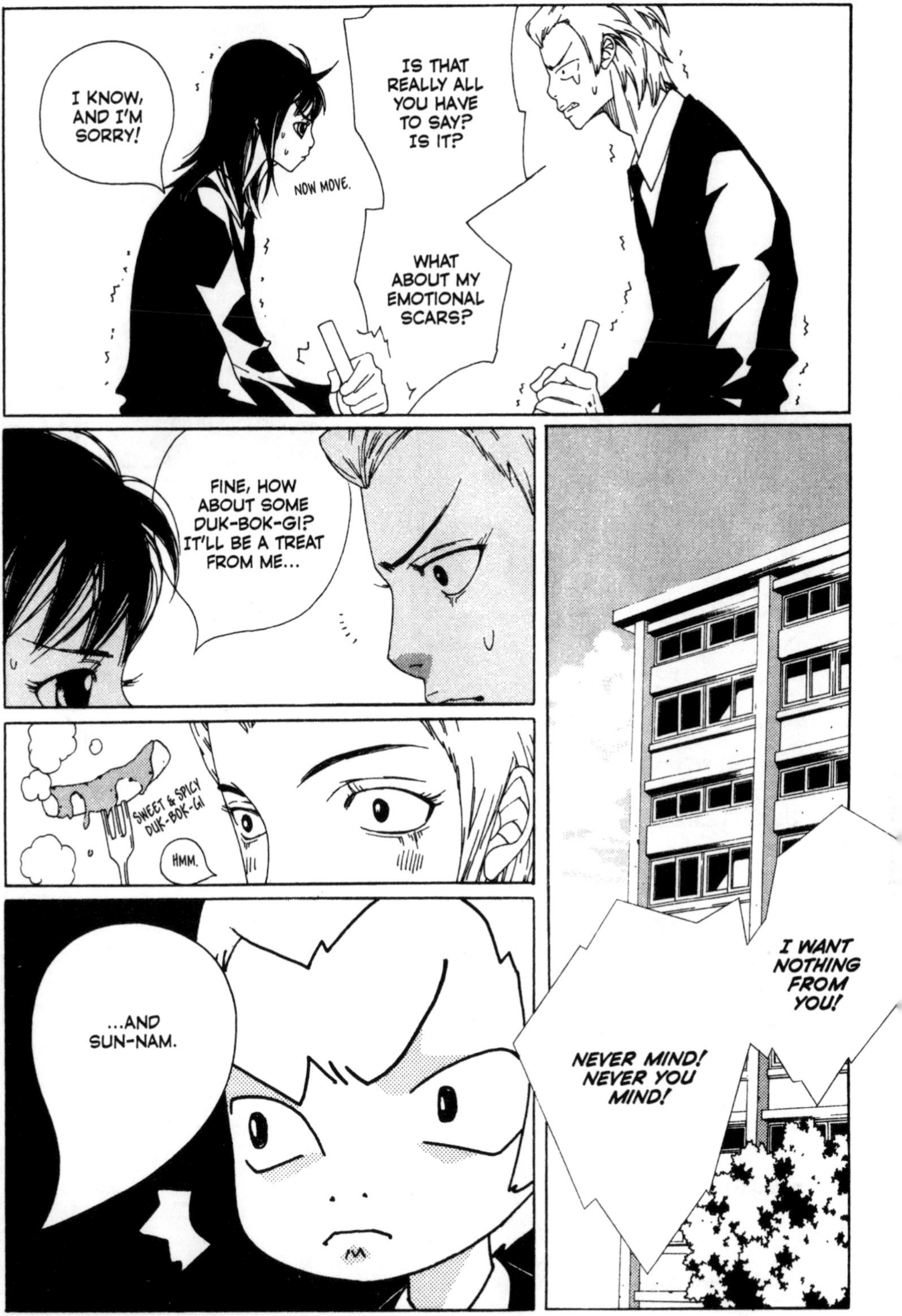
I KNOW, AND I'M SORRY!
NOW MOVE.
IS THAT REALLY ALL YOU HAVE TO SAY? IS IT?
WHAT ABOUT MY EMOTIONAL SCARS?
FINE, HOW ABOUT SOME DUK-BOK-GI? IT'LL BE A TREAT FROM ME...
SWEET & SPICY DUK-BOK-GI
HMM.
...AND SUN-NAM.
I WANT NOTHING FROM YOU!
NEVER MIND! NEVER YOU MIND!

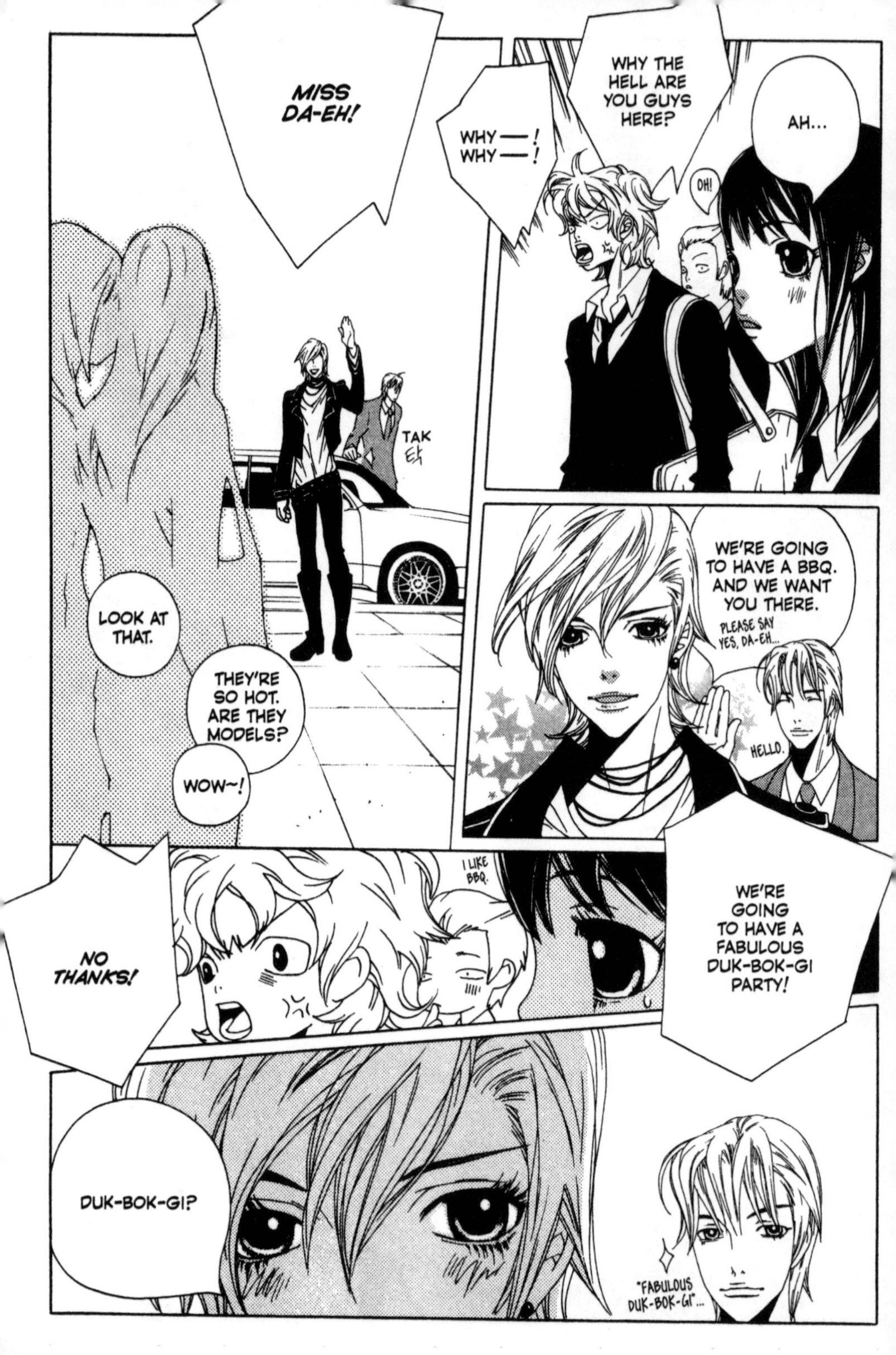
MISS DA-EH!
TAK
탁
LOOK AT THAT.
THEY'RE SO HOT. ARE THEY MODELS?
WOW~!
WHY—! WHY—!
WHY THE HELL ARE YOU GUYS HERE?
OH!
AH...
WE'RE GOING TO HAVE A BBQ. AND WE WANT YOU THERE.
PLEASE SAY YES, DA-EH...
HELLO.
NO THANKS!
I LIKE BBQ.
WE'RE GOING TO HAVE A FABULOUS DUK-BOK-GI PARTY!
DUK-BOK-GI?
"FABULOUS DUK-BOK-GI"...

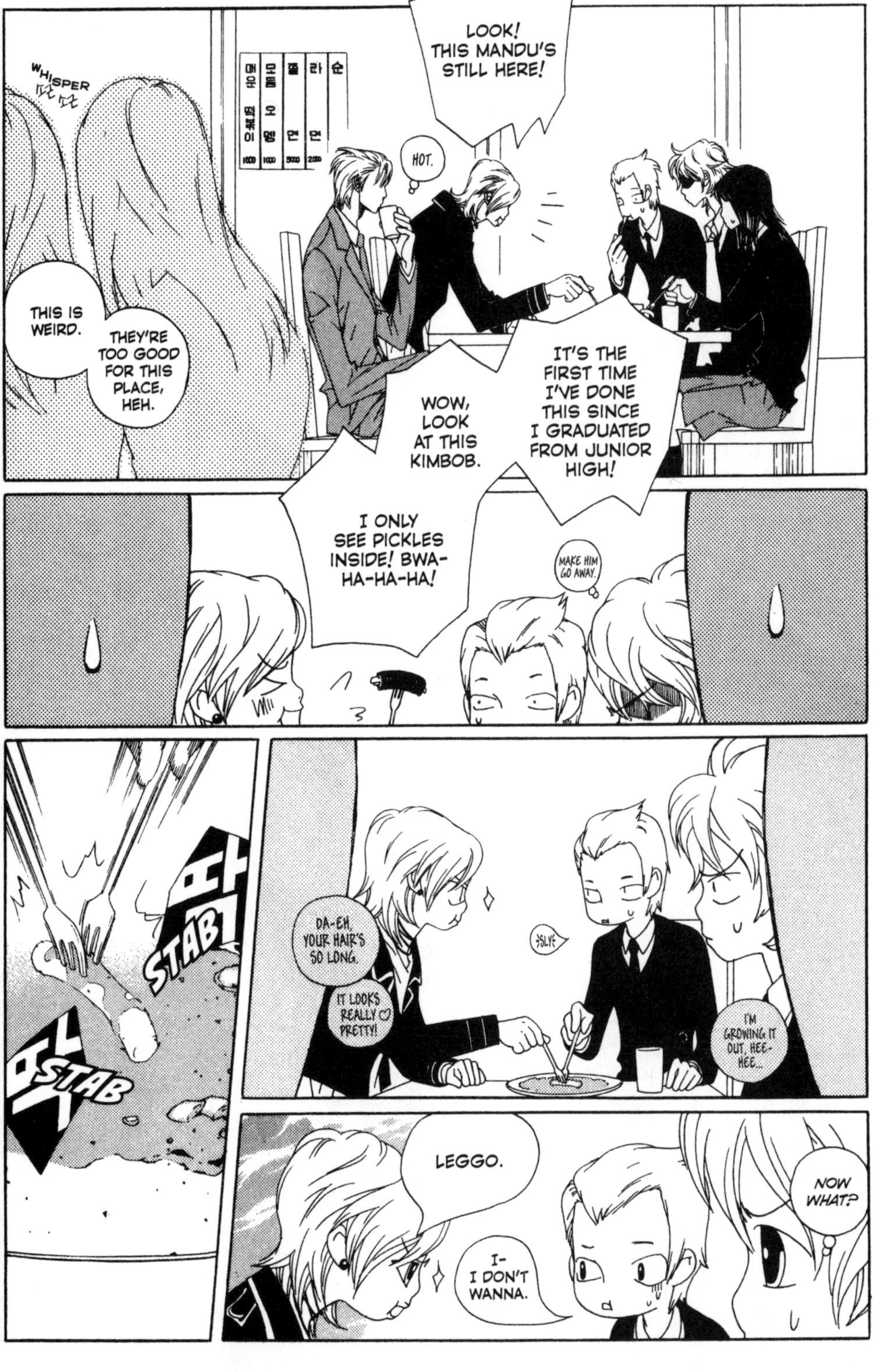
WHISPER
THIS IS WEIRD.
THEY'RE TOO GOOD FOR THIS PLACE, HEH.
LOOK! THIS MANDU'S STILL HERE!
HOT.
WOW, LOOK AT THIS KIMBOB.
IT'S THE FIRST TIME I'VE DONE THIS SINCE I GRADUATED FROM JUNIOR HIGH!
I ONLY SEE PICKLES INSIDE! BWA-HA-HA-HA!
MAKE HIM GO AWAY.
STAB
STAB
DA-EH, YOUR HAIR'S SO LONG.
IT LOOKS REALLY ♡ PRETTY!
SLY
I'M GROWING IT OUT, HEE-HEE...
LEGGO.
I- I DON'T WANNA.
NOW WHAT?

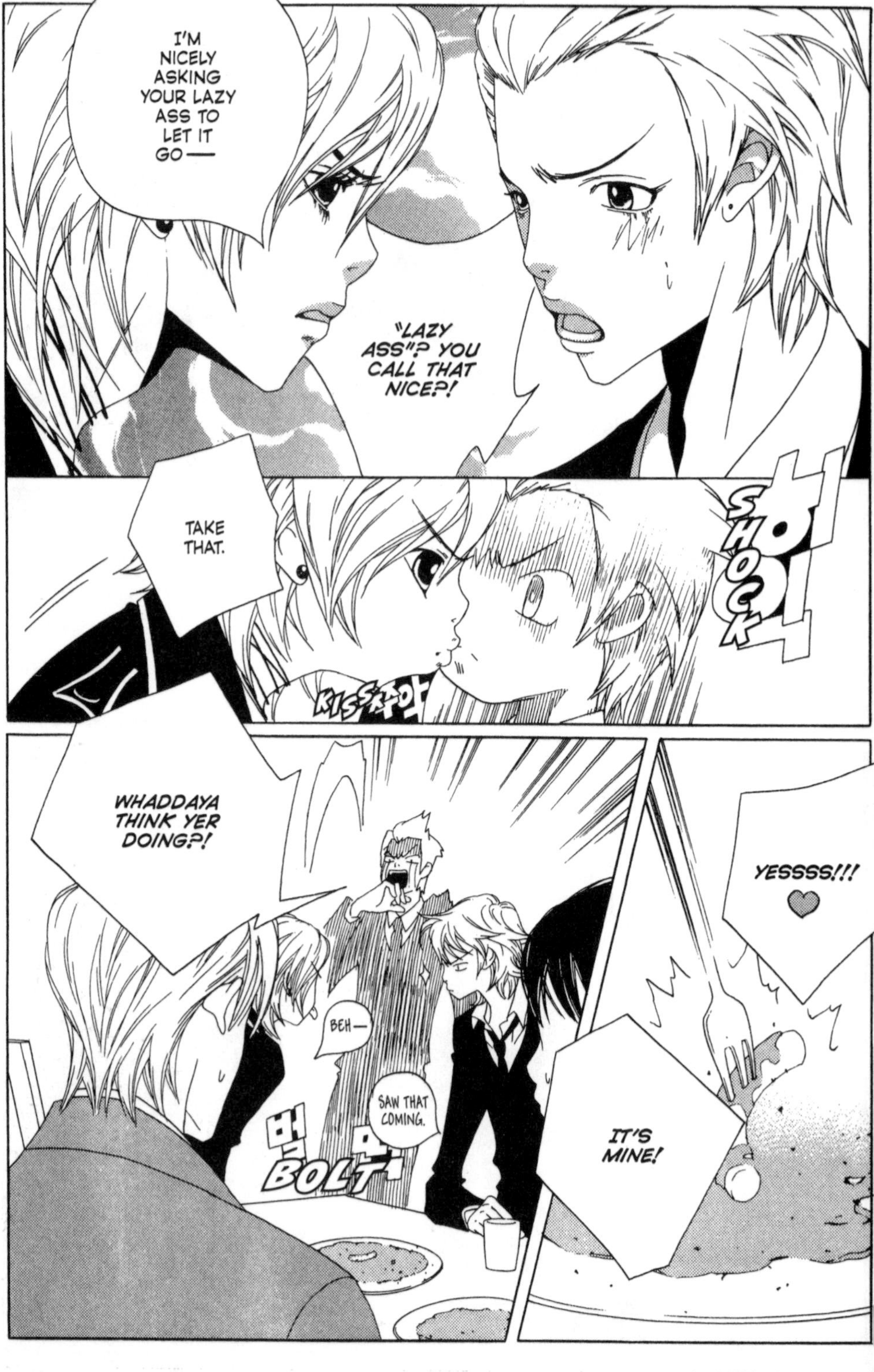
I'M NICELY ASKING YOUR LAZY ASS TO LET IT GO—
"LAZY ASS"? YOU CALL THAT NICE?!
TAKE THAT.
SHOCK
KISS
WHADDAYA THINK YER DOING?!
BEH—
SAW THAT COMING.
BOLT
YESSSS!!!
IT'S MINE!

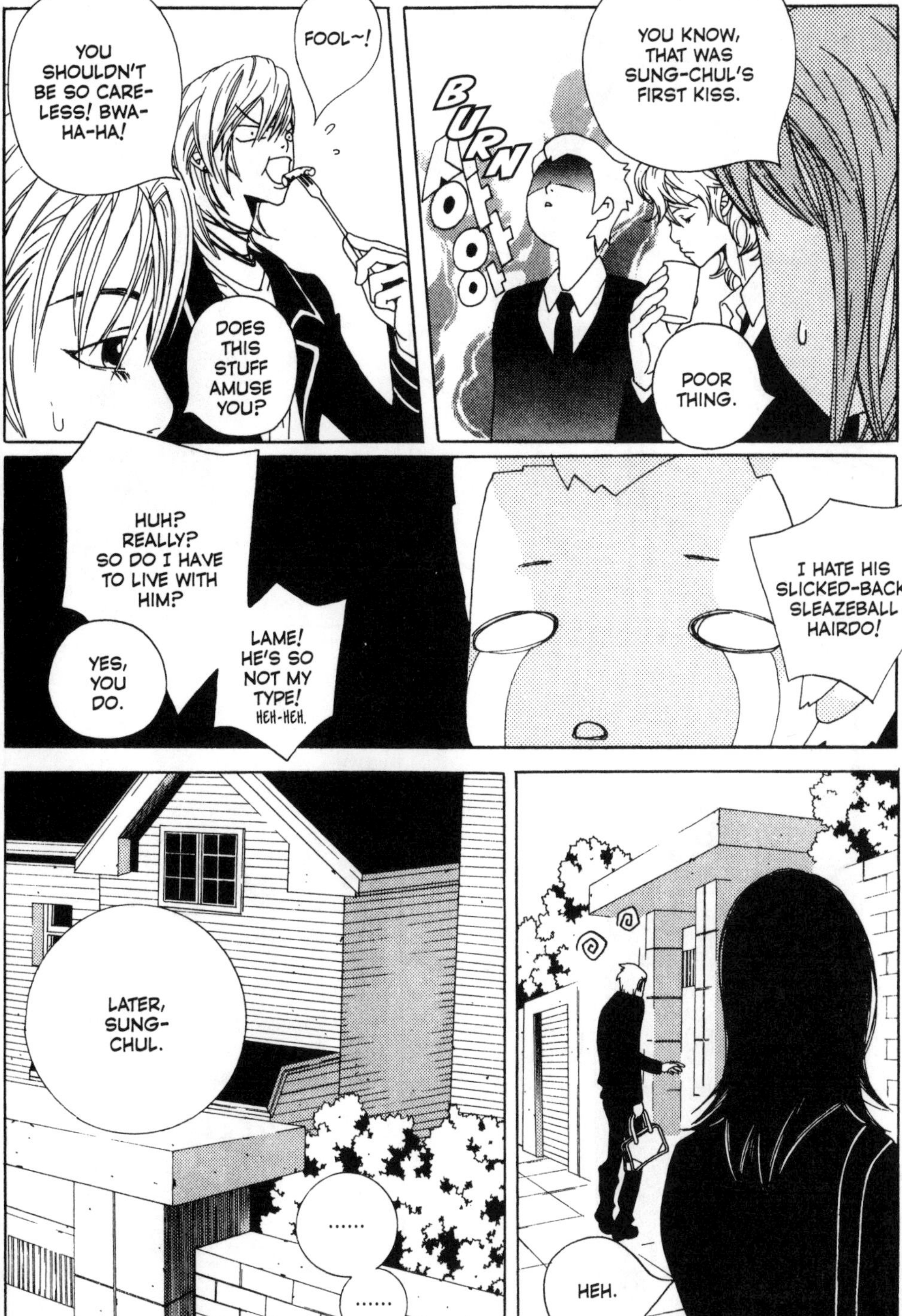
YOU SHOULDN'T BE SO CARE-LESS! BWA-HA-HA!
FOOL~!
DOES THIS STUFF AMUSE YOU?
YOU KNOW, THAT WAS SUNG-CHUL'S FIRST KISS.
BURN
POOR THING.
HUH? REALLY? SO DO I HAVE TO LIVE WITH HIM?
YES, YOU DO.
LAME! HE'S SO NOT MY TYPE! HEH-HEH.
I HATE HIS SLICKED-BACK, SLEAZEBALL HAIRDO!
LATER, SUNG-CHUL.
......
......
HEH.

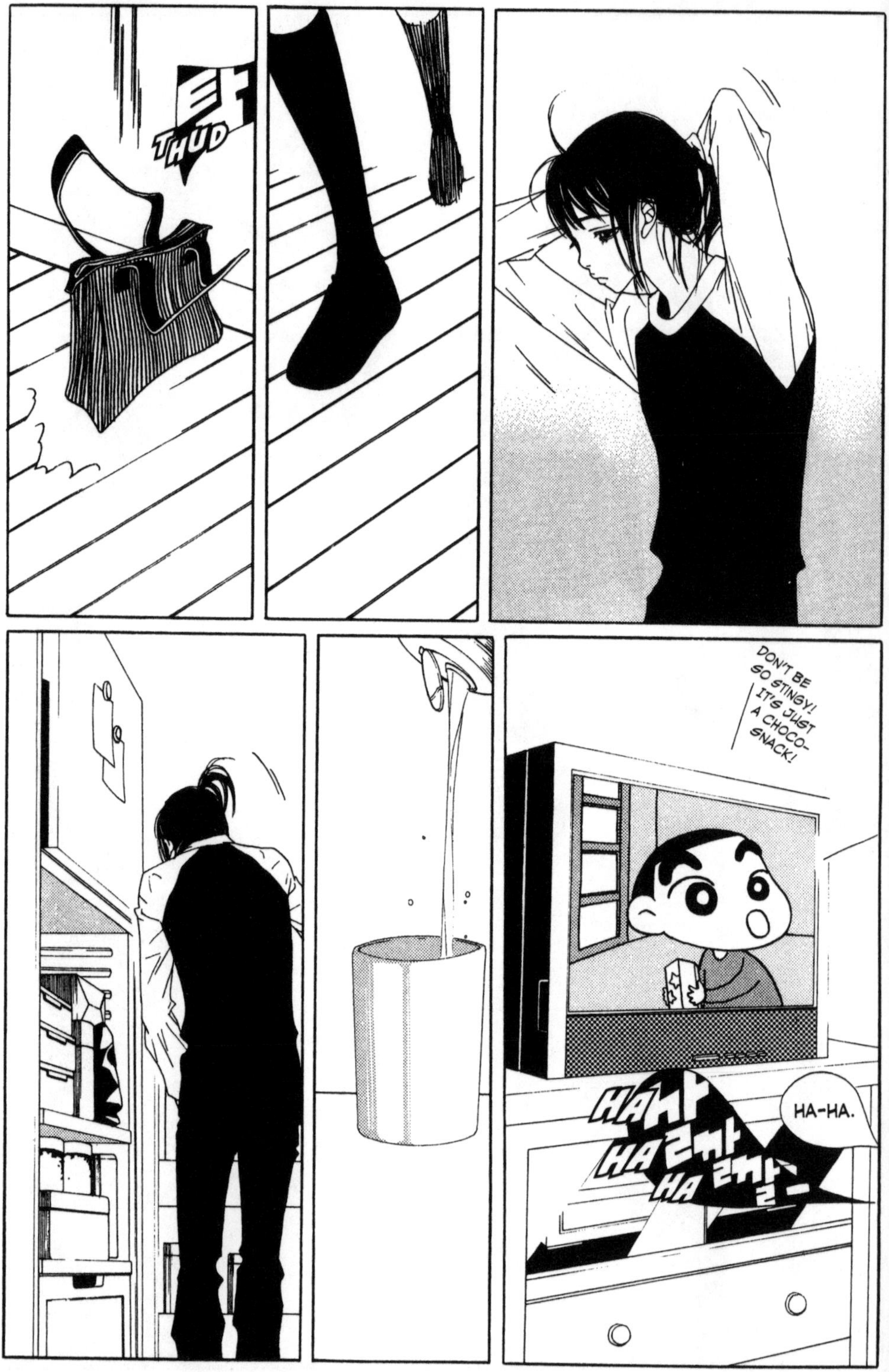
THUD
DON'T BE SO STINGY! IT'S JUST A CHOCO-SNACK!
HA
HA
HA
HA-HA.

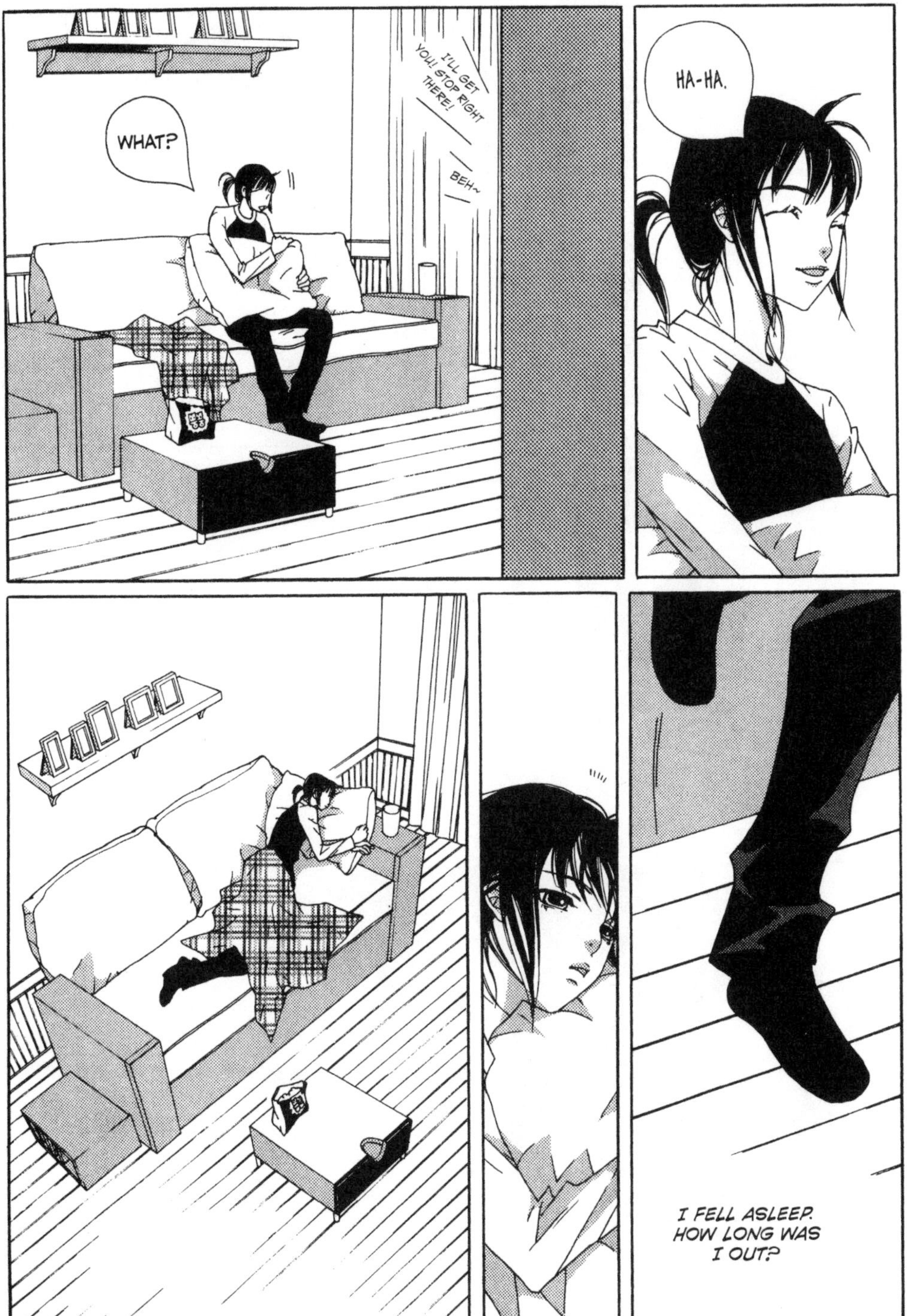
I'LL GET YOU! STOP RIGHT THERE!
BEH~
WHAT?
HA-HA.
I FELL ASLEEP. HOW LONG WAS I OUT?

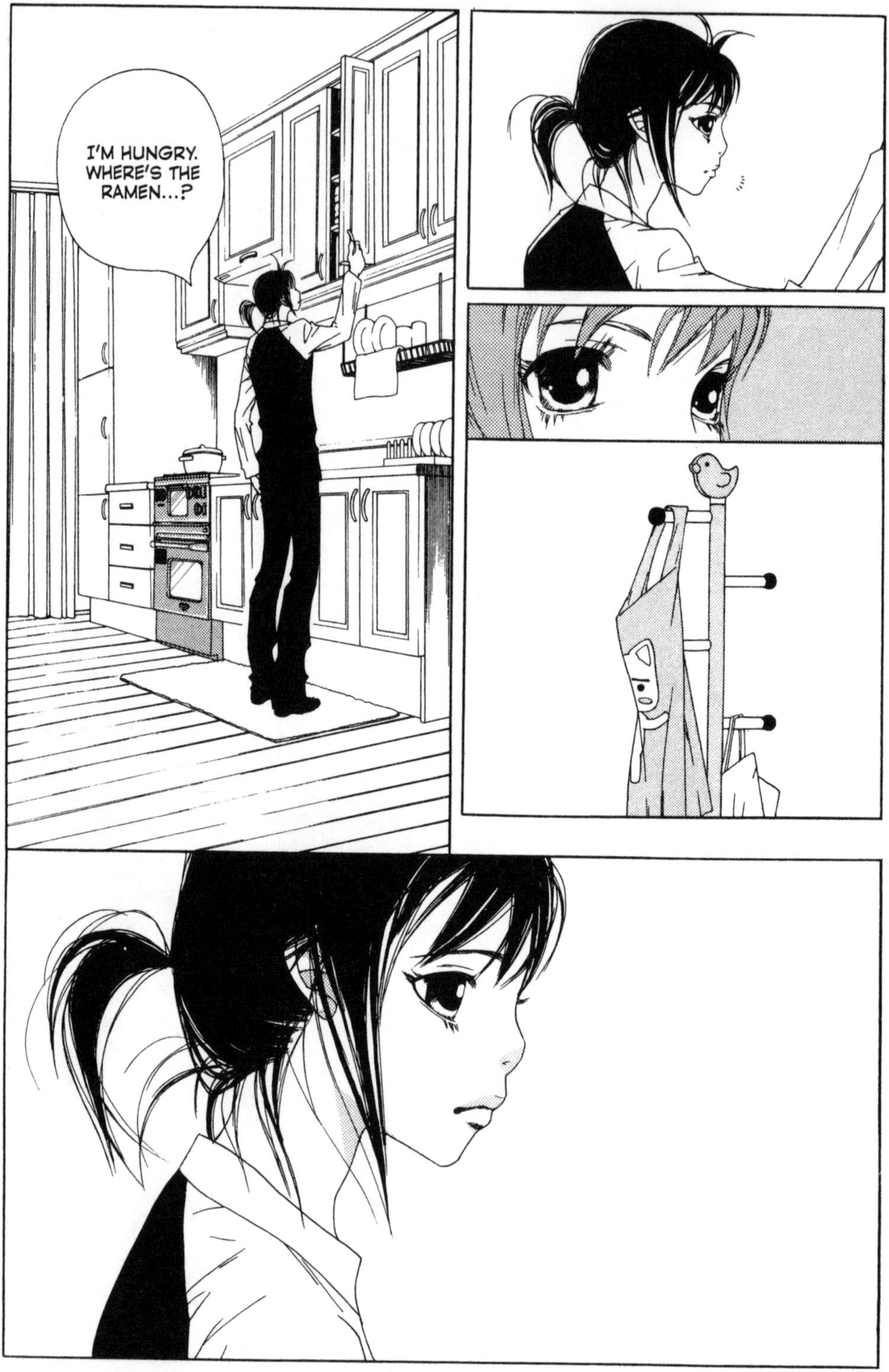
I'M HUNGRY. WHERE'S THE RAMEN...?

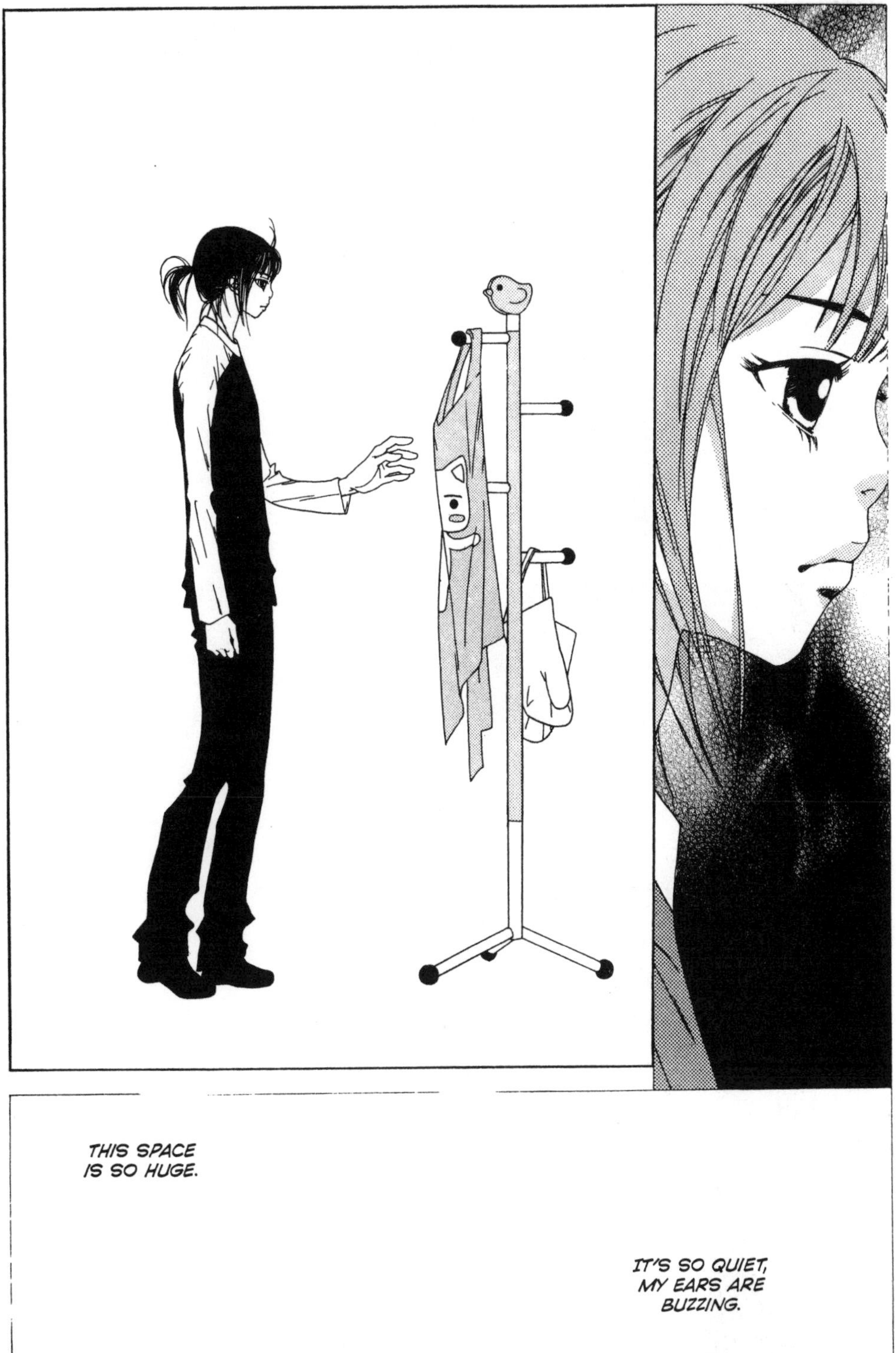
THIS SPACE IS SO HUGE.
IT'S SO QUIET, MY EARS ARE BUZZING.

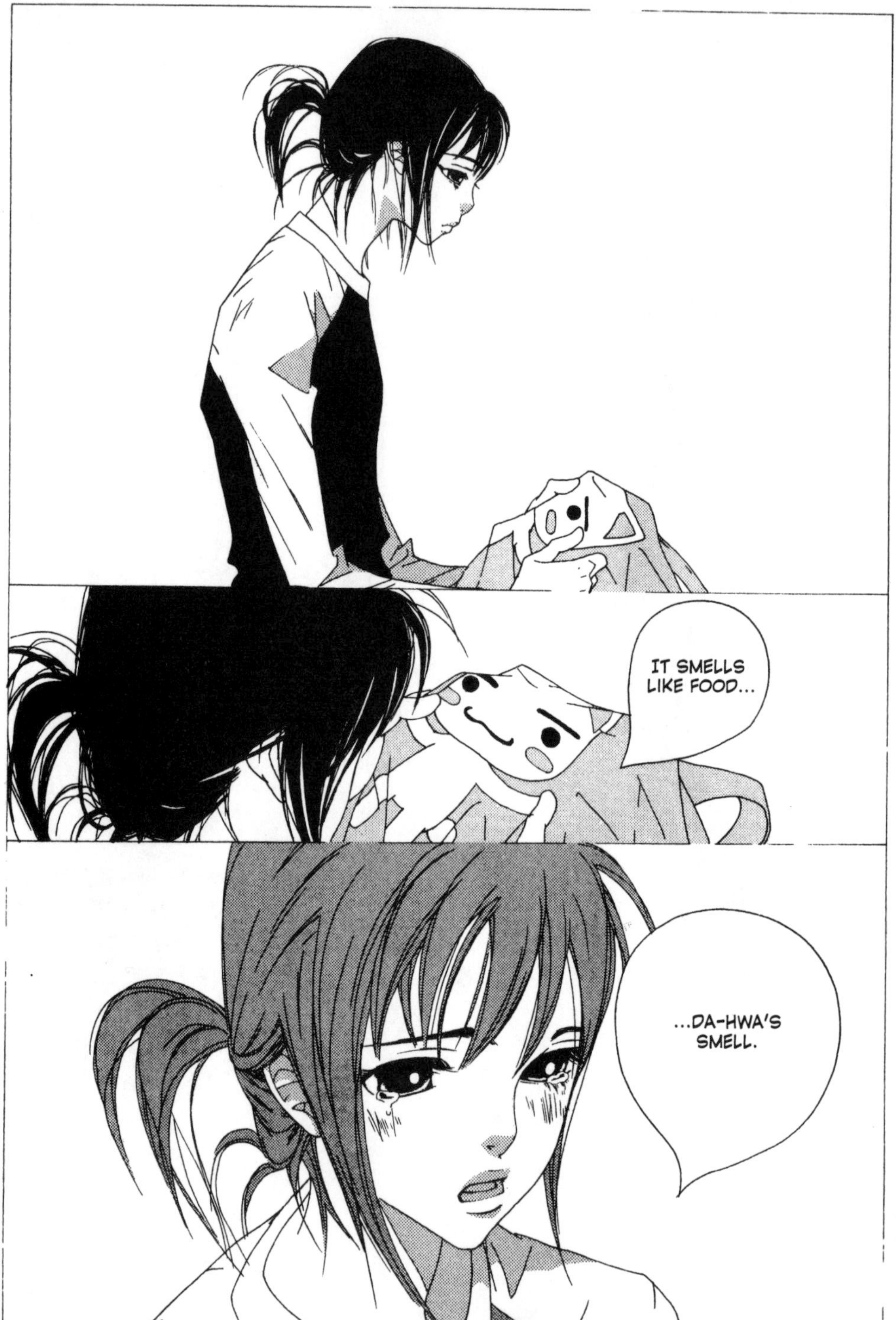
IT SMELLS LIKE FOOD...
...DA-HWA'S SMELL.

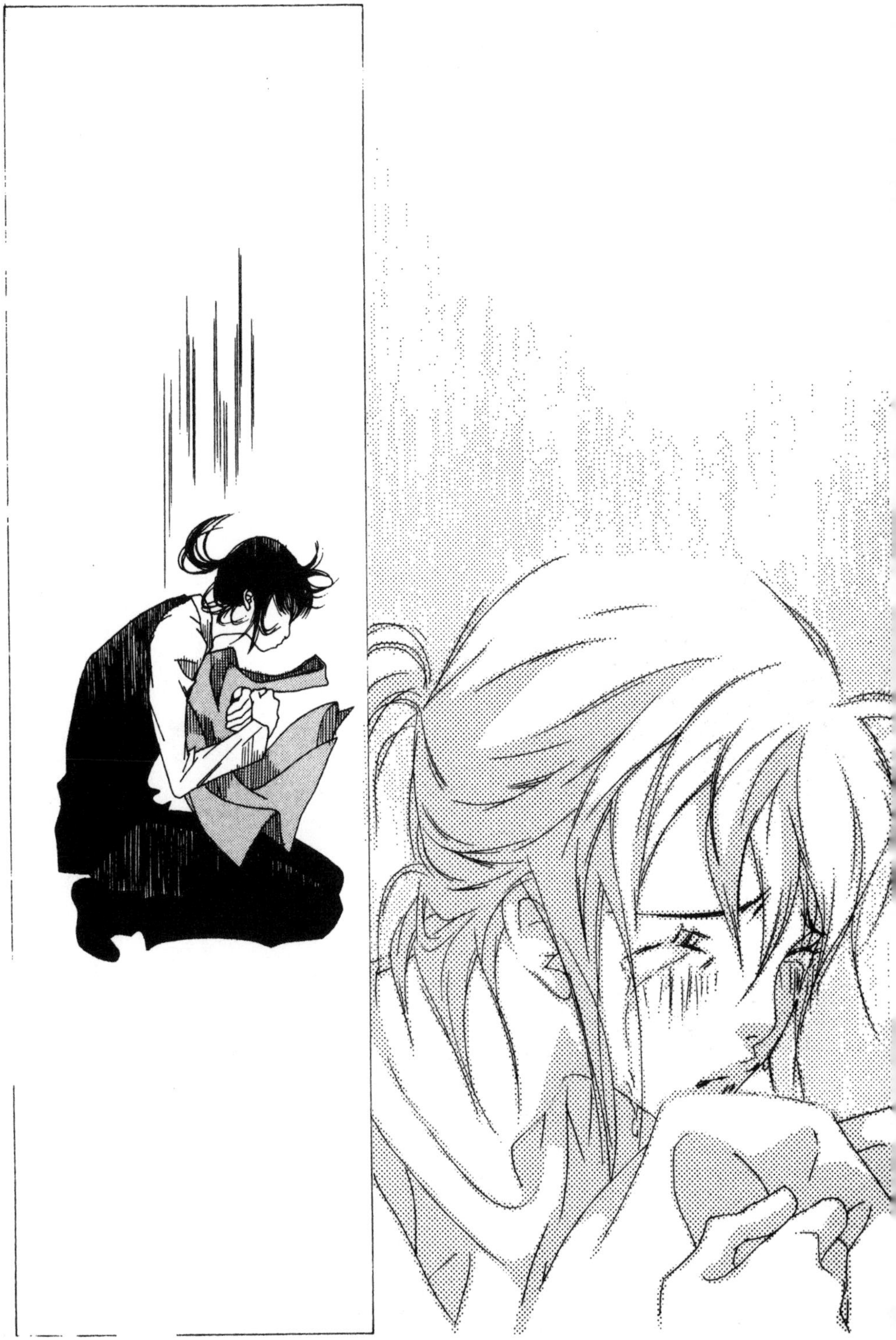

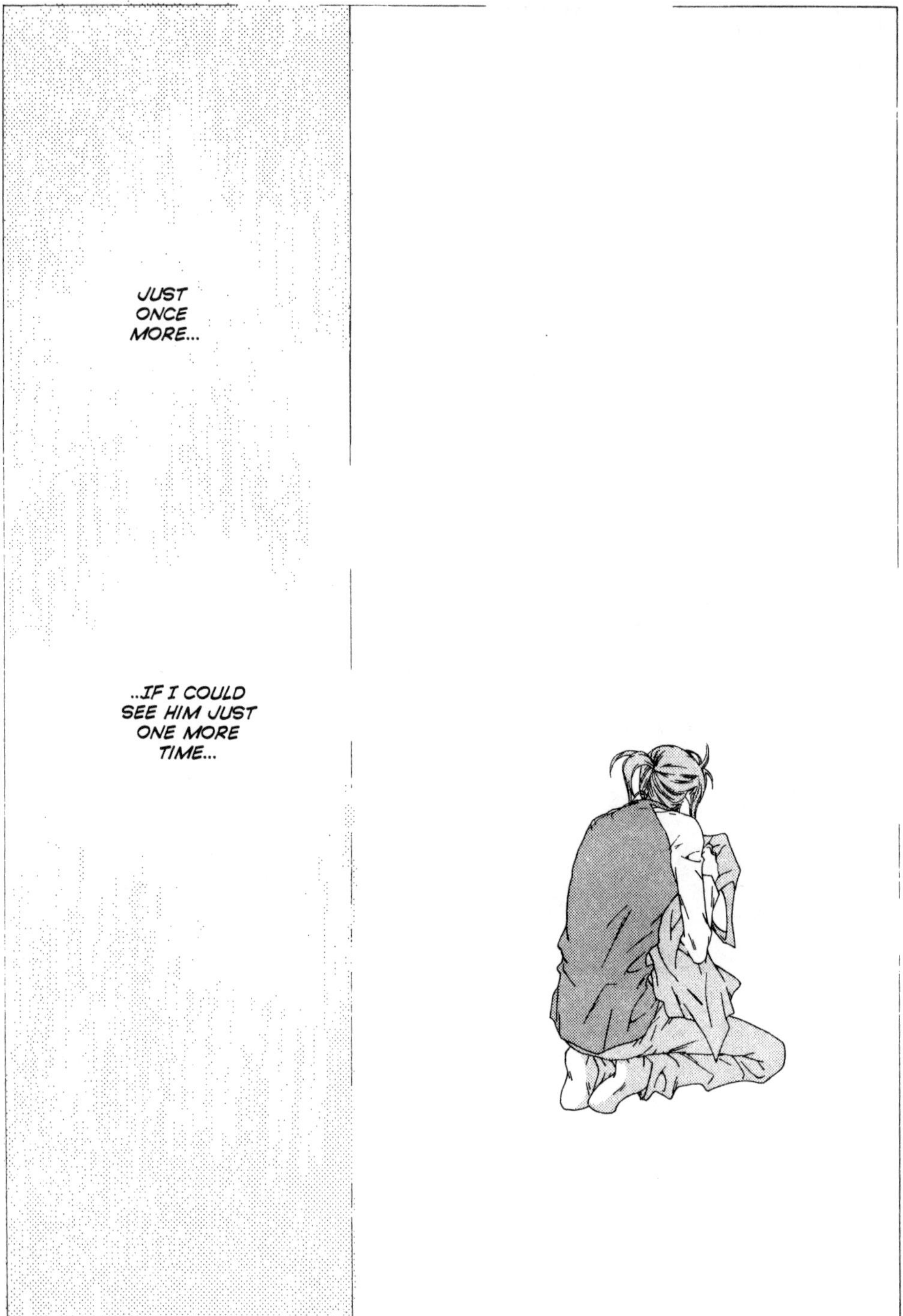
JUST ONCE MORE...
...IF I COULD SEE HIM JUST ONE MORE TIME...

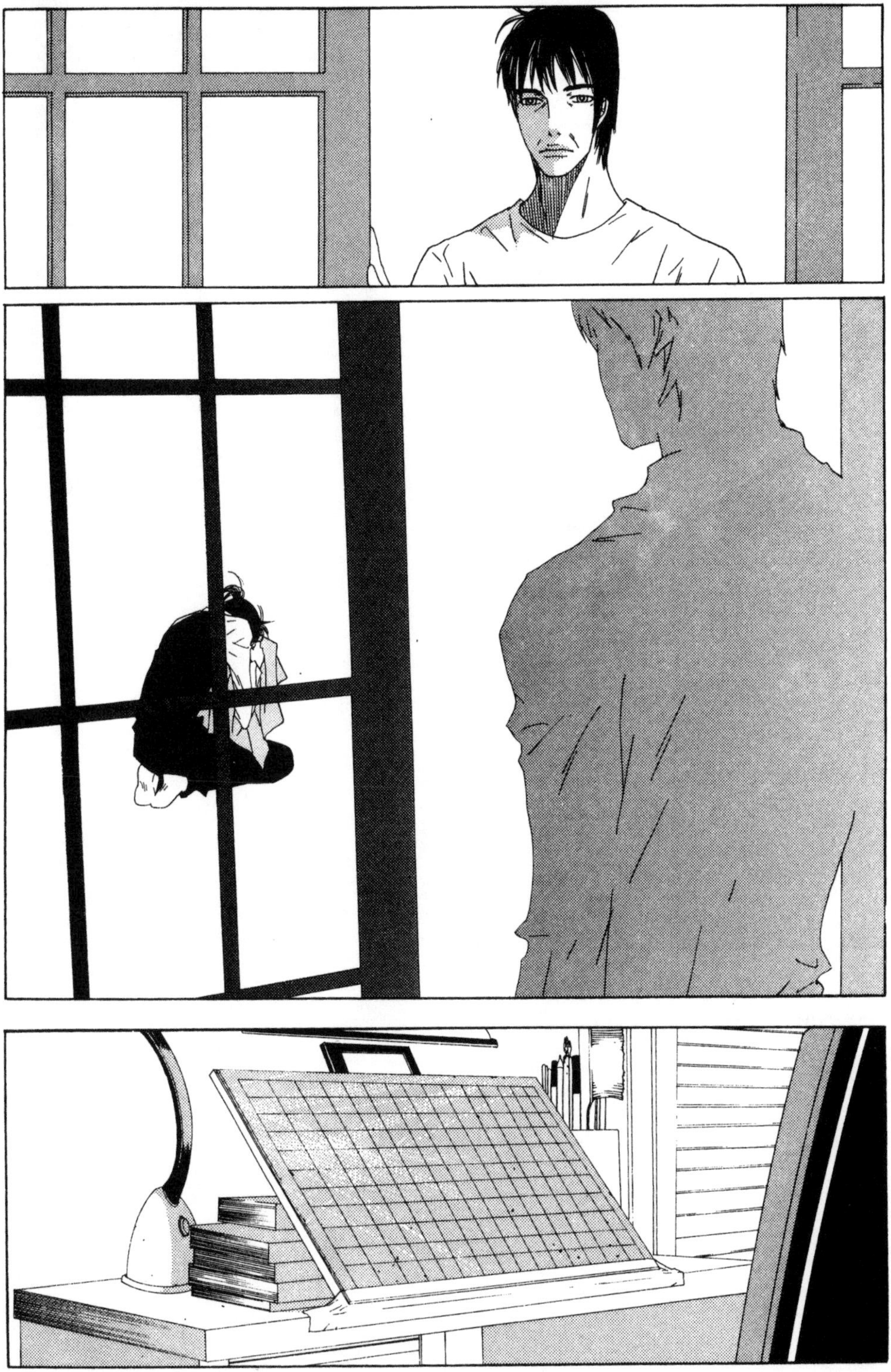

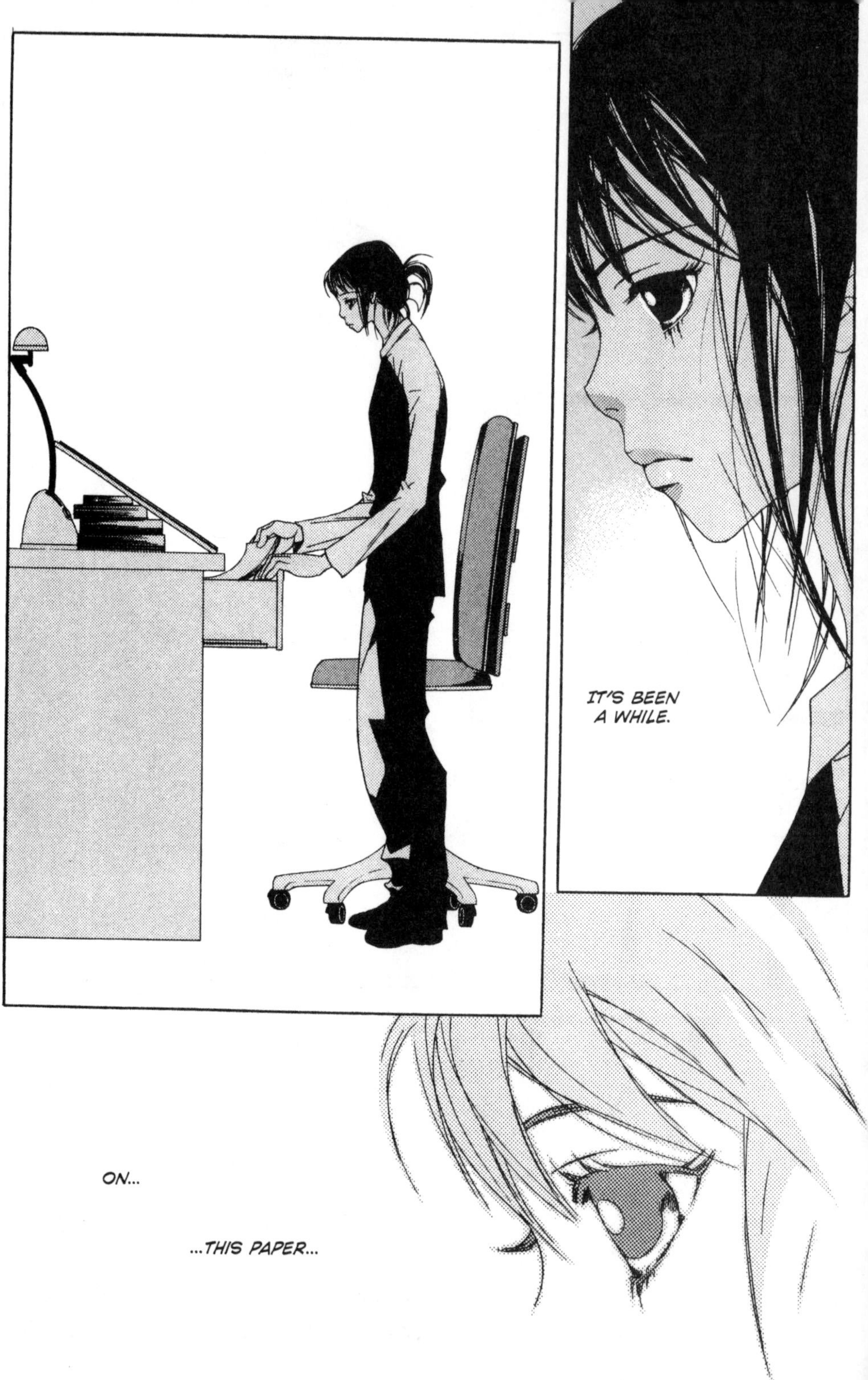
IT'S BEEN A WHILE.
ON...
...THIS PAPER...

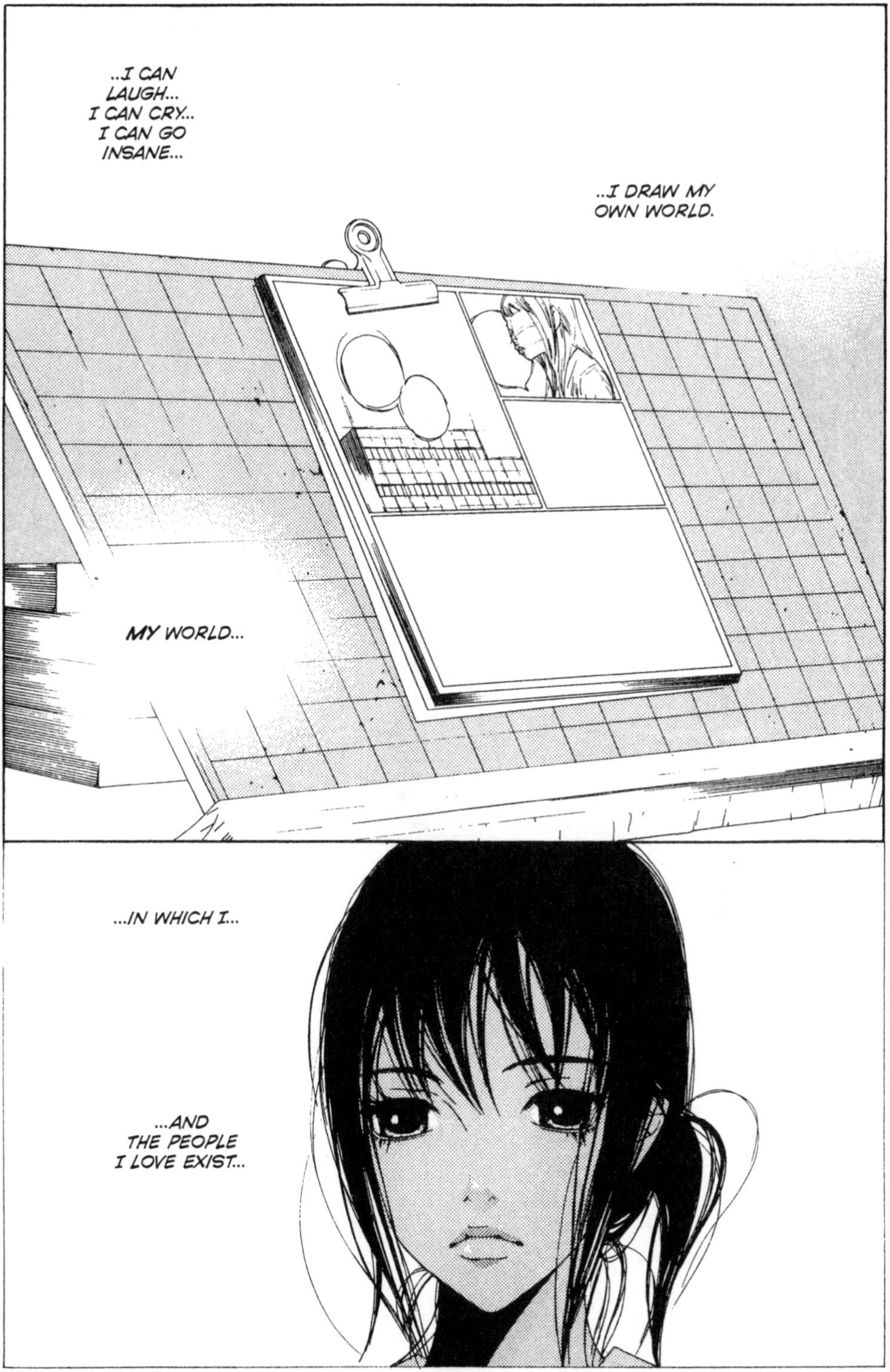
...I CAN LAUGH... I CAN CRY... I CAN GO INSANE...
...I DRAW MY OWN WORLD.
MY WORLD...
...IN WHICH I...
...AND THE PEOPLE I LOVE EXIST...

*...THE
WORLD
IN WHICH
I DREAM.*

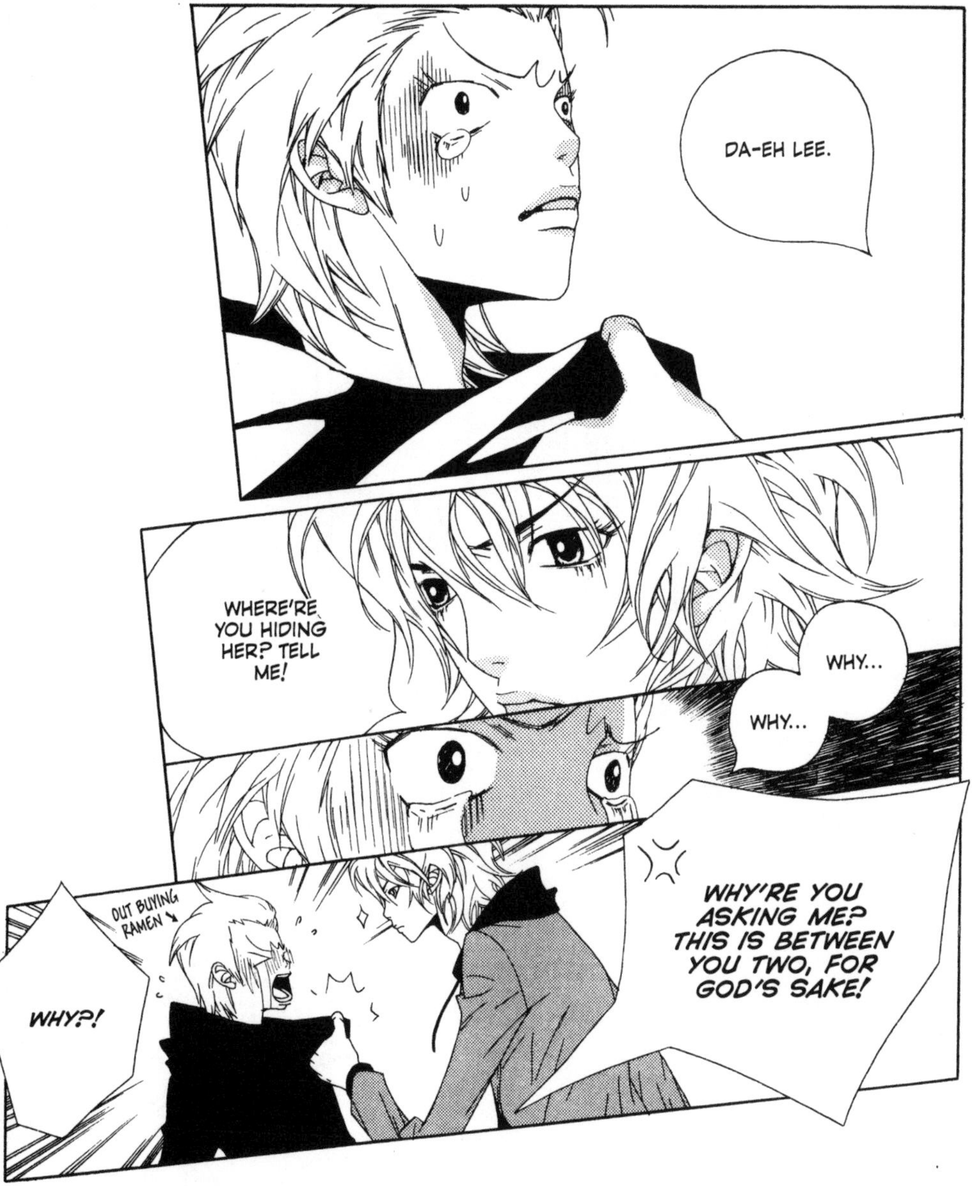
DA-EH LEE.
WHERE'RE YOU HIDING HER? TELL ME!
WHY...
WHY...
OUT BUYING RAMEN
WHY?!
WHY'RE YOU ASKING ME? THIS IS BETWEEN YOU TWO, FOR GOD'S SAKE!

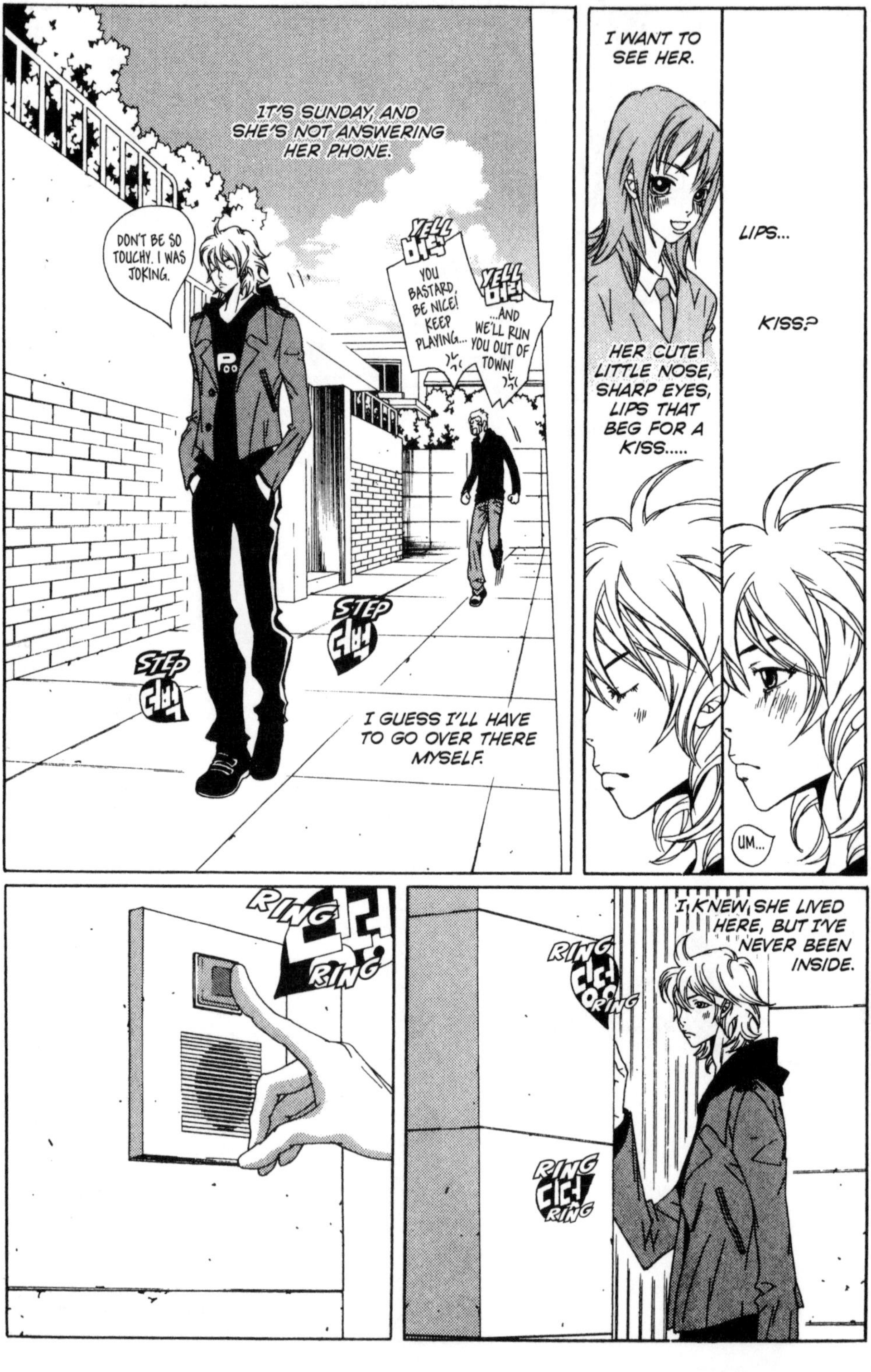
IT'S SUNDAY, AND SHE'S NOT ANSWERING HER PHONE.
DON'T BE SO TOUCHY. I WAS JOKING.
YELL
YOU BASTARD, BE NICE! KEEP PLAYING...
YELL
...AND WE'LL RUN YOU OUT OF TOWN!
STEP
STEP
I GUESS I'LL HAVE TO GO OVER THERE MYSELF.
I WANT TO SEE HER.
HER CUTE LITTLE NOSE, SHARP EYES, LIPS THAT BEG FOR A KISS.....
LIPS...
KISS?
UM...
RING
RING
RING
RING
RING
RING
I KNEW SHE LIVED HERE, BUT I'VE NEVER BEEN INSIDE.

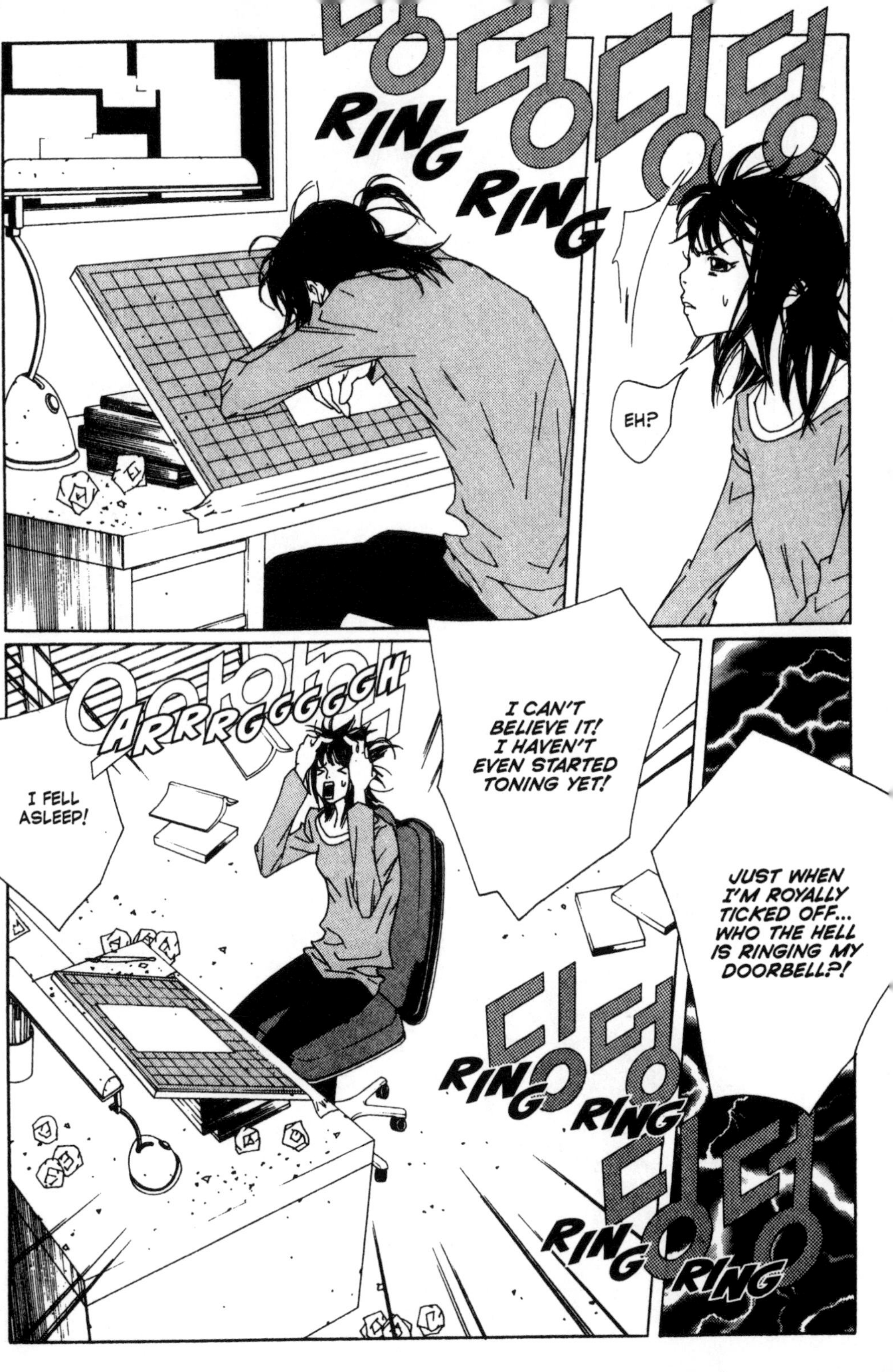
RING RING
EH?
ARRRGGGGGH
I FELL ASLEEP!
I CAN'T BELIEVE IT! I HAVEN'T EVEN STARTED TONING YET!
JUST WHEN I'M ROYALLY TICKED OFF... WHO THE HELL IS RINGING MY DOORBELL?!
RING RING
RING RING

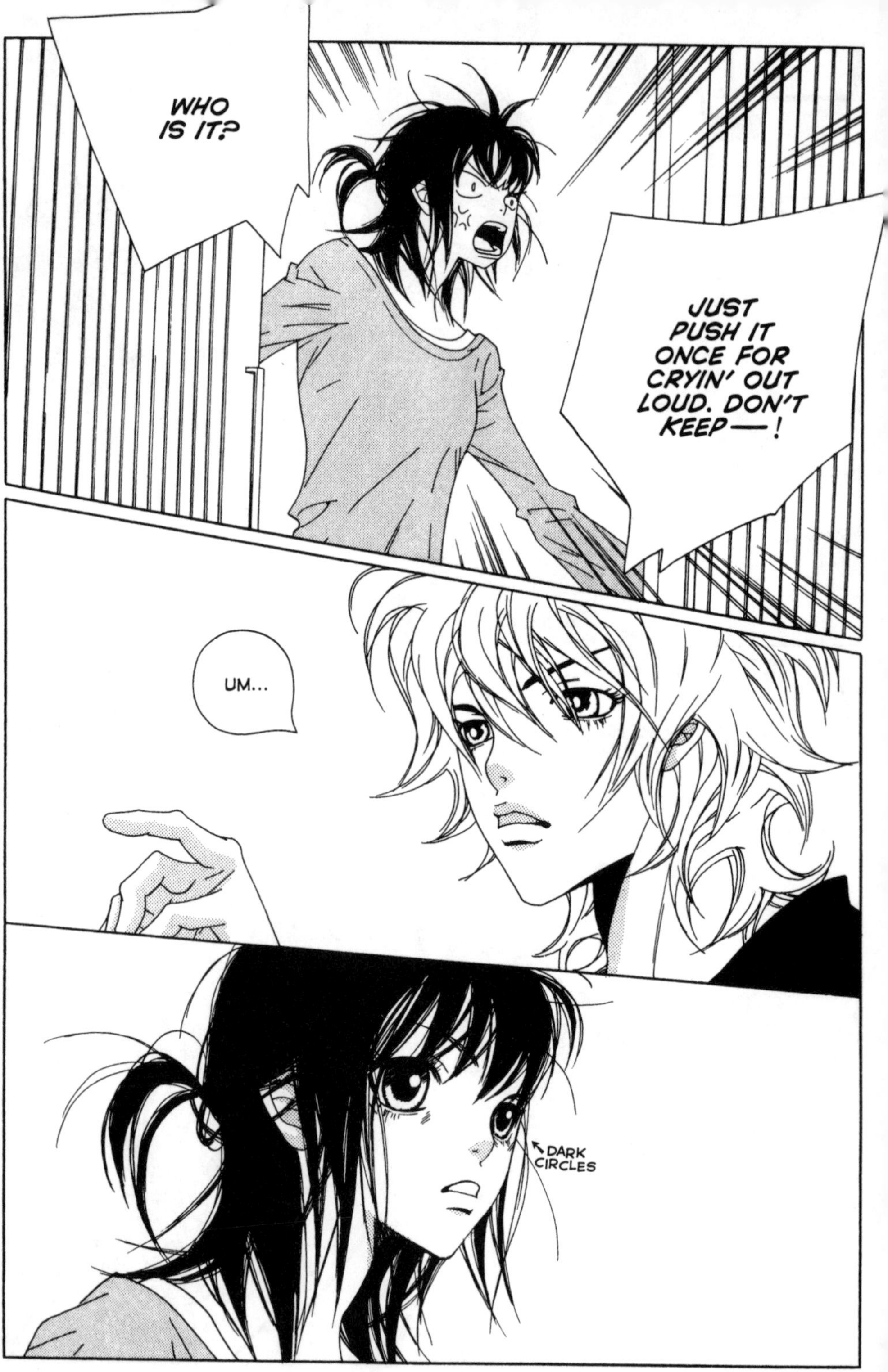
WHO IS IT?
JUST PUSH IT ONCE FOR CRYIN' OUT LOUD. DON'T KEEP—!
UM...
DARK CIRCLES

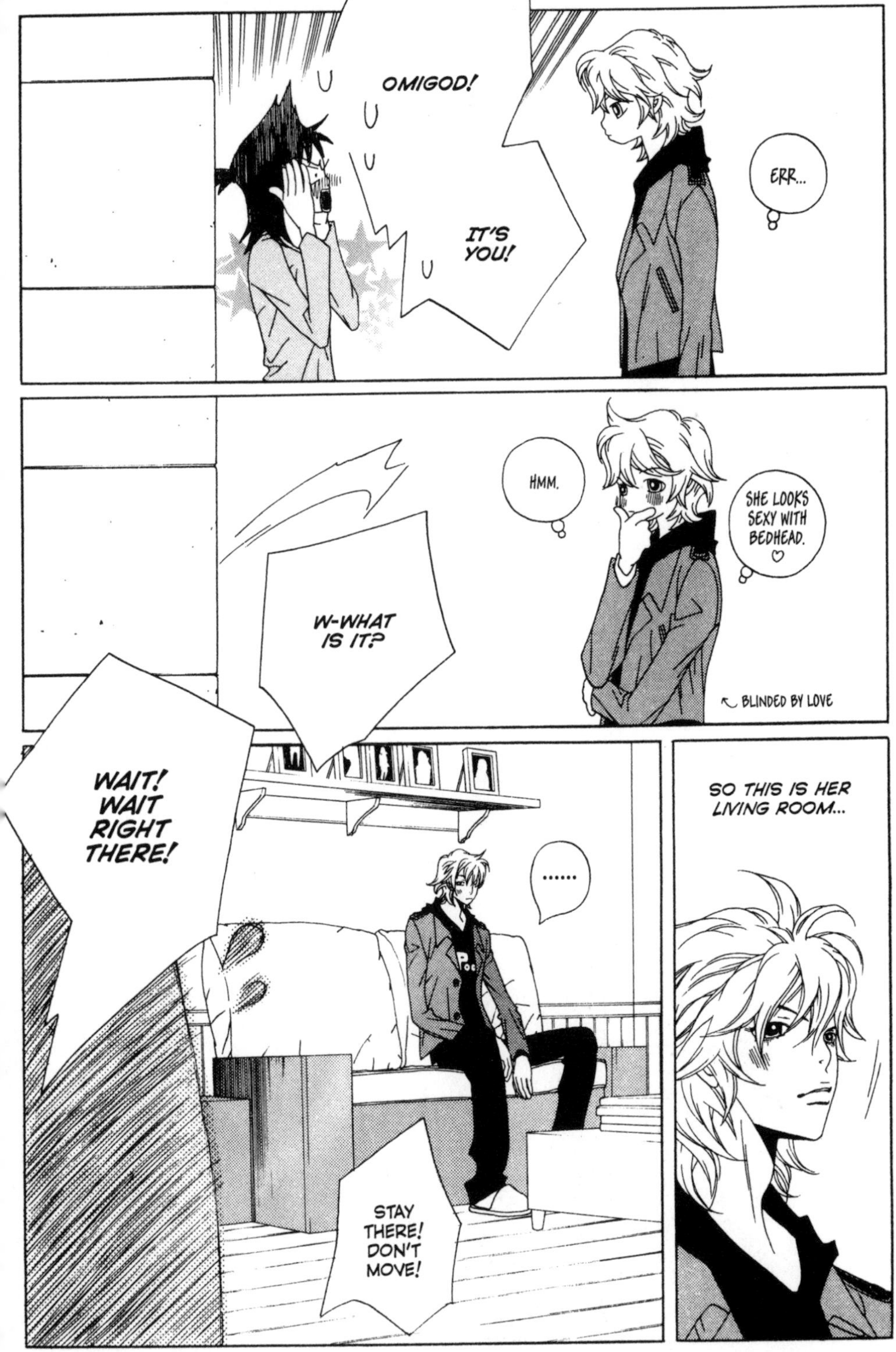
OMIGOD!
IT'S YOU!
ERR...
W-WHAT IS IT?
HMM.
SHE LOOKS SEXY WITH BEDHEAD. ♡
BLINDED BY LOVE
WAIT! WAIT RIGHT THERE!
......
STAY THERE! DON'T MOVE!
SO THIS IS HER LIVING ROOM...

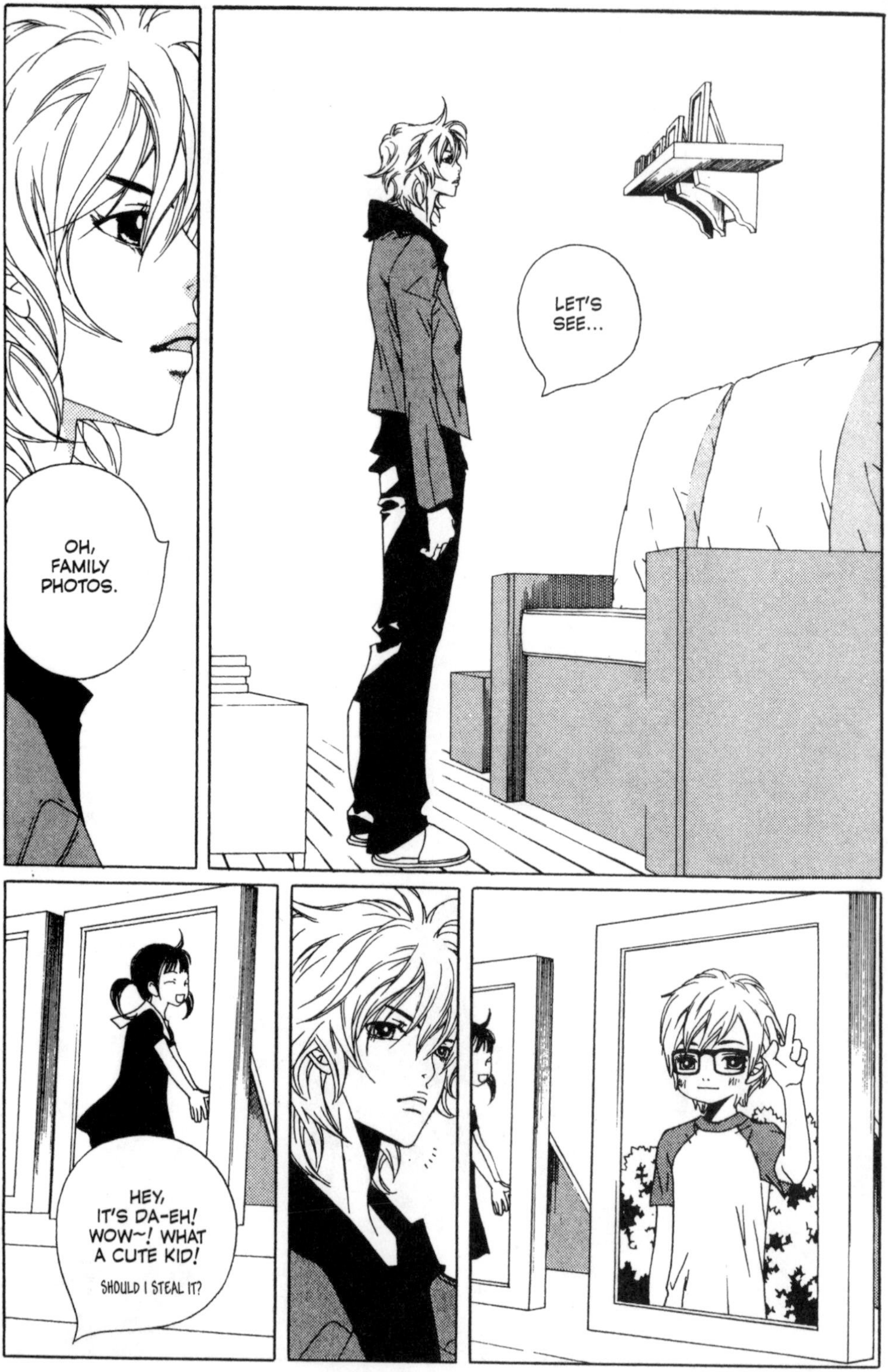
OH, FAMILY PHOTOS.
LET'S SEE...
HEY, IT'S DA-EH! WOW~! WHAT A CUTE KID!
SHOULD I STEAL IT?

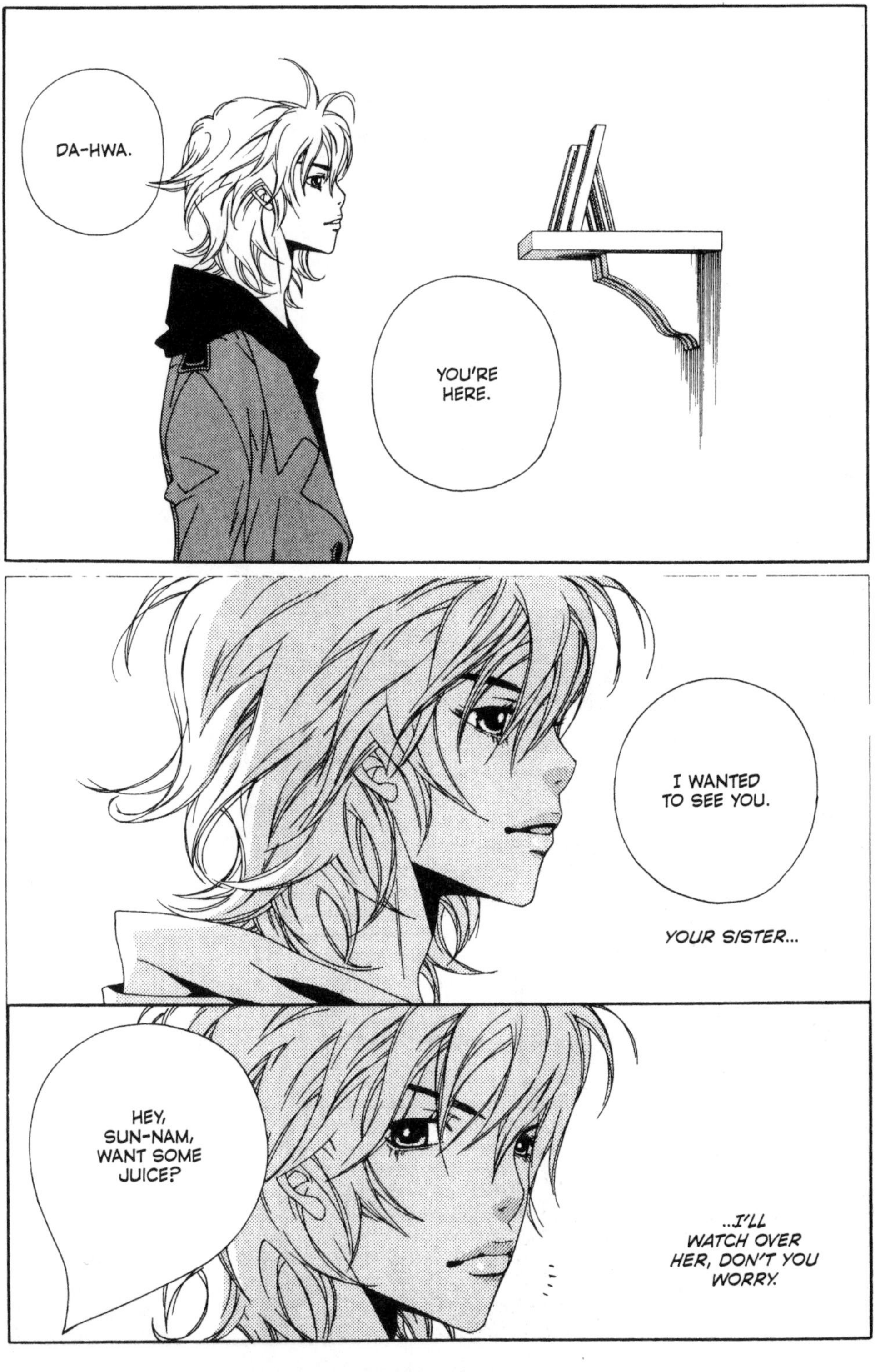
DA-HWA.
YOU'RE HERE.
I WANTED TO SEE YOU.
YOUR SISTER...
HEY, SUN-NAM, WANT SOME JUICE?
...I'LL WATCH OVER HER, DON'T YOU WORRY.

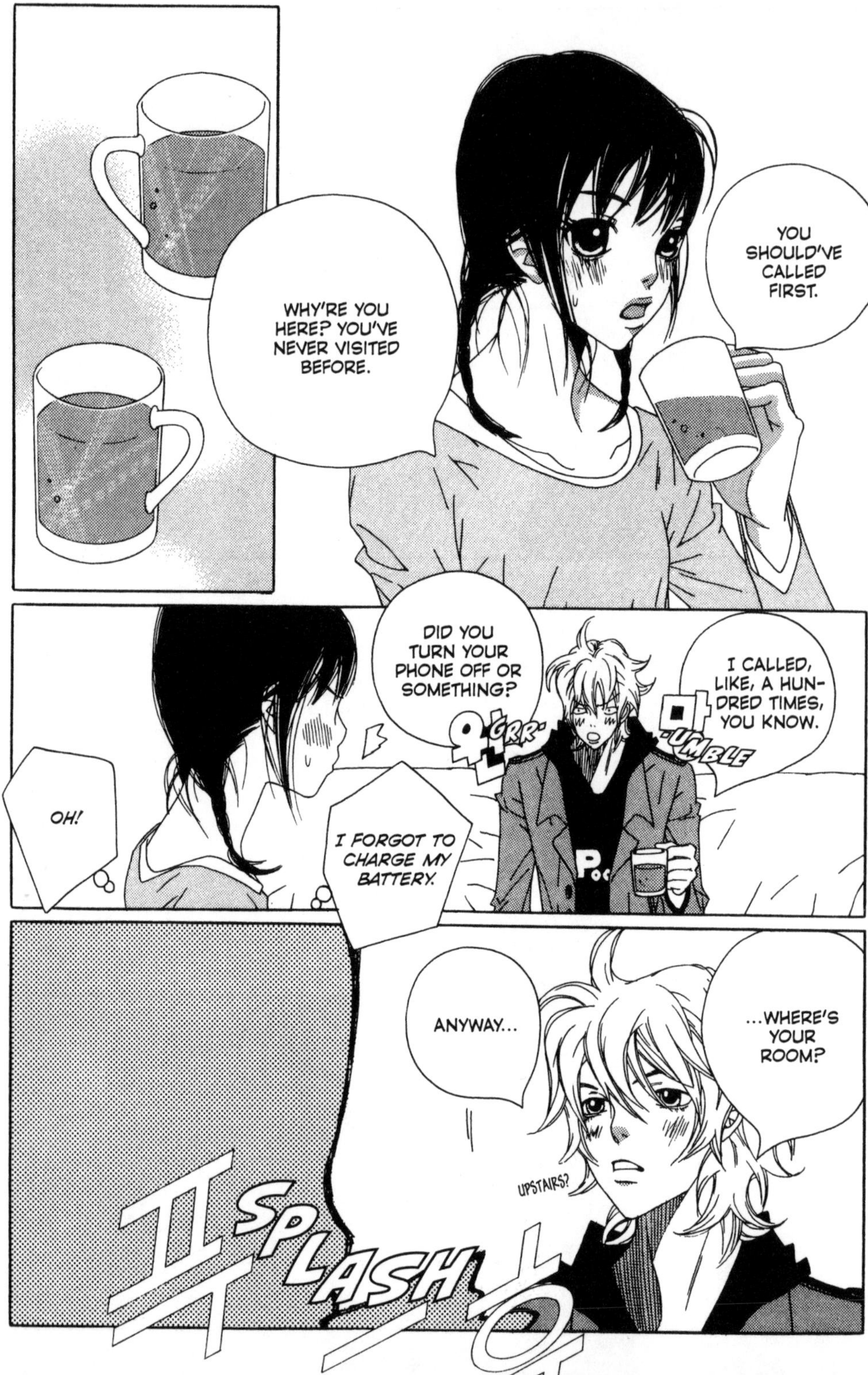
WHY'RE YOU HERE? YOU'VE NEVER VISITED BEFORE.
YOU SHOULD'VE CALLED FIRST.
DID YOU TURN YOUR PHONE OFF OR SOMETHING?
GRR-
-UMBLE
I CALLED, LIKE, A HUN-DRED TIMES, YOU KNOW.
OH!
I FORGOT TO CHARGE MY BATTERY.
ANYWAY...
...WHERE'S YOUR ROOM?
UPSTAIRS?
SPLASH

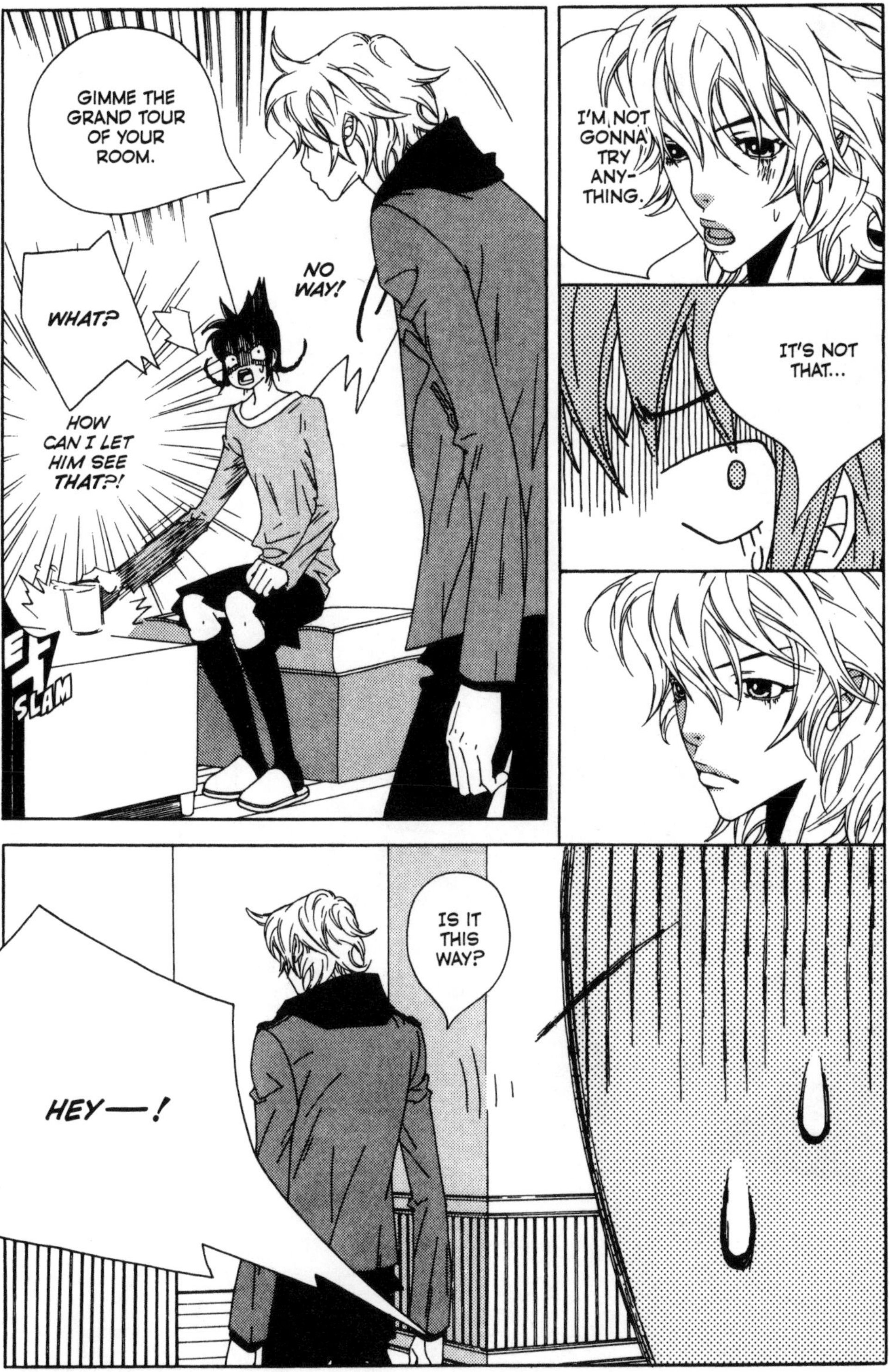
GIMME THE GRAND TOUR OF YOUR ROOM.
WHAT?
NO WAY!
HOW CAN I LET HIM SEE THAT?!
SLAM
I'M NOT GONNA TRY ANY-THING.
IT'S NOT THAT...
HEY—!
IS IT THIS WAY?

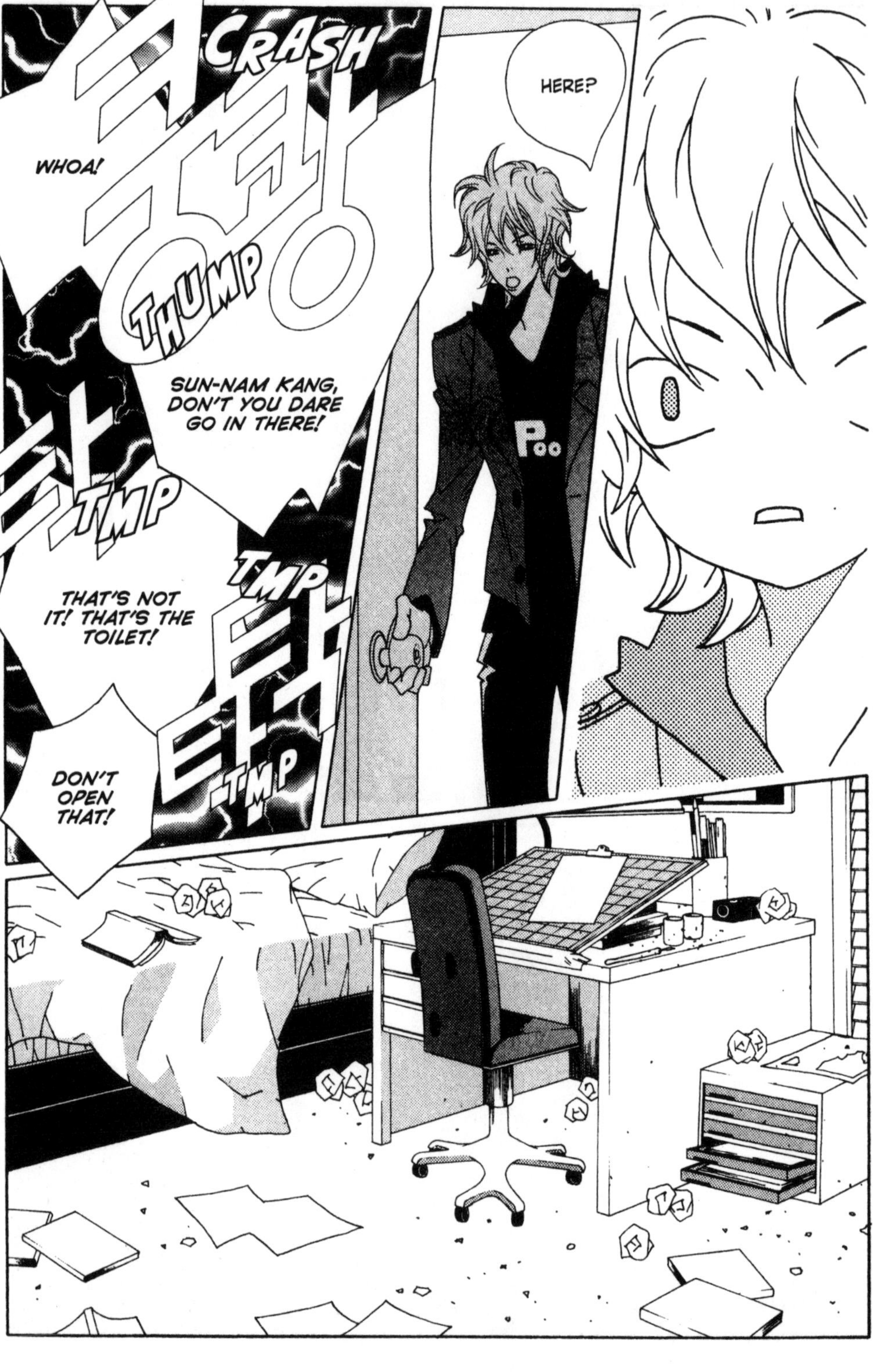
CRASH
WHOA!
THUMP
SUN-NAM KANG, DON'T YOU DARE GO IN THERE!
TMP
TMP
THAT'S NOT IT! THAT'S THE TOILET!
TMP
DON'T OPEN THAT!
HERE?
Poo

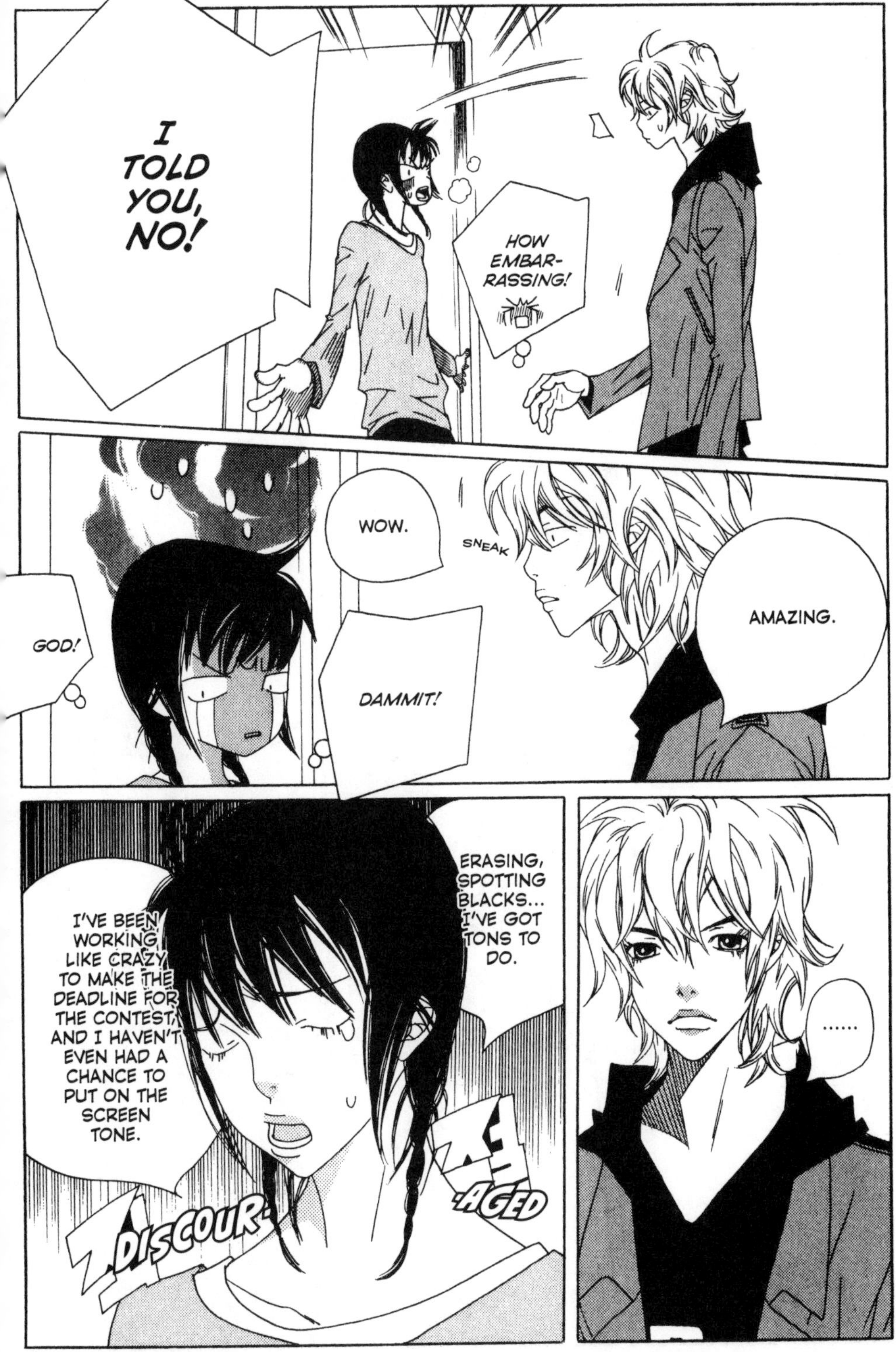
I TOLD YOU, NO!
HOW EMBAR-RASSING!
GOD!
WOW.
DAMMIT!
SNEAK
AMAZING.
I'VE BEEN WORKING LIKE CRAZY TO MAKE THE DEADLINE FOR THE CONTEST, AND I HAVEN'T EVEN HAD A CHANCE TO PUT ON THE SCREEN TONE.
ERASING, SPOTTING BLACKS... I'VE GOT TONS TO DO.
DISCOUR- -AGED
......

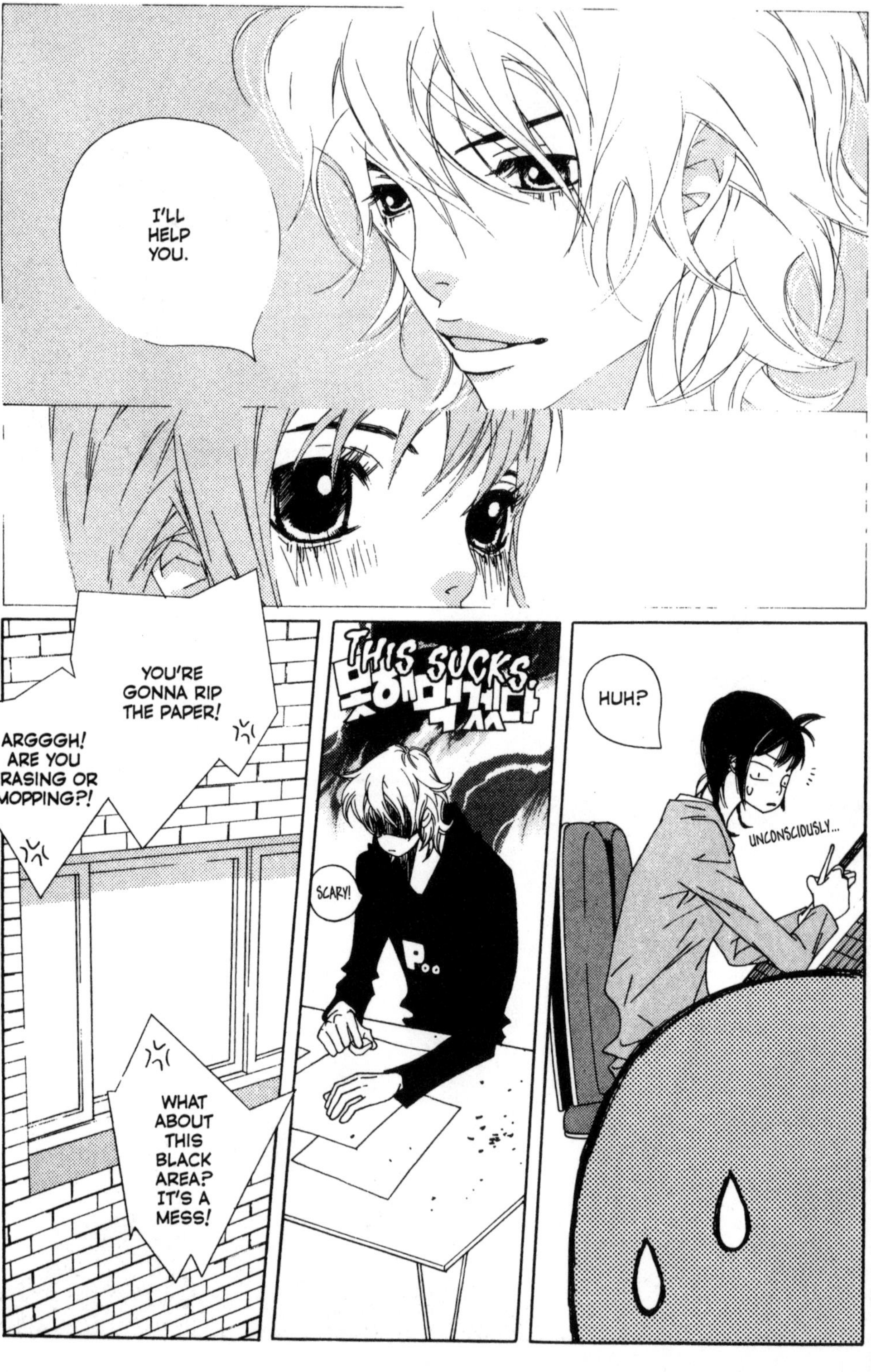
I'LL HELP YOU.
ARGGGH! ARE YOU ERASING OR MOPPING?!
YOU'RE GONNA RIP THE PAPER!
WHAT ABOUT THIS BLACK AREA? IT'S A MESS!
THIS SUCKS.
SCARY!
HUH?
UNCONSCIOUSLY...

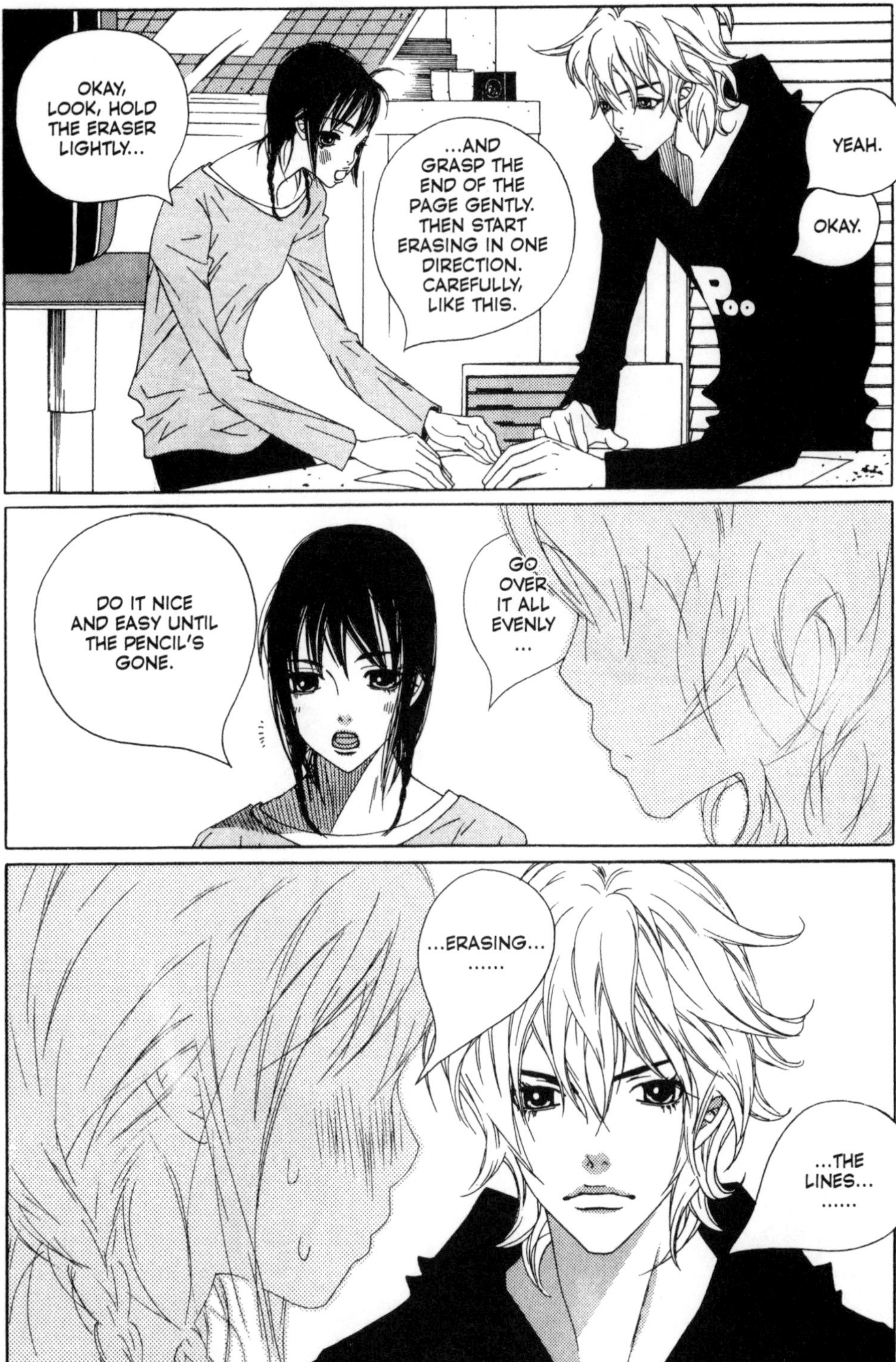
OKAY, LOOK, HOLD THE ERASER LIGHTLY...
...AND GRASP THE END OF THE PAGE GENTLY. THEN START ERASING IN ONE DIRECTION. CAREFULLY, LIKE THIS.
YEAH.
OKAY.
DO IT NICE AND EASY UNTIL THE PENCIL'S GONE.
GO OVER IT ALL EVENLY ...
...ERASING... ......
...THE LINES... ......

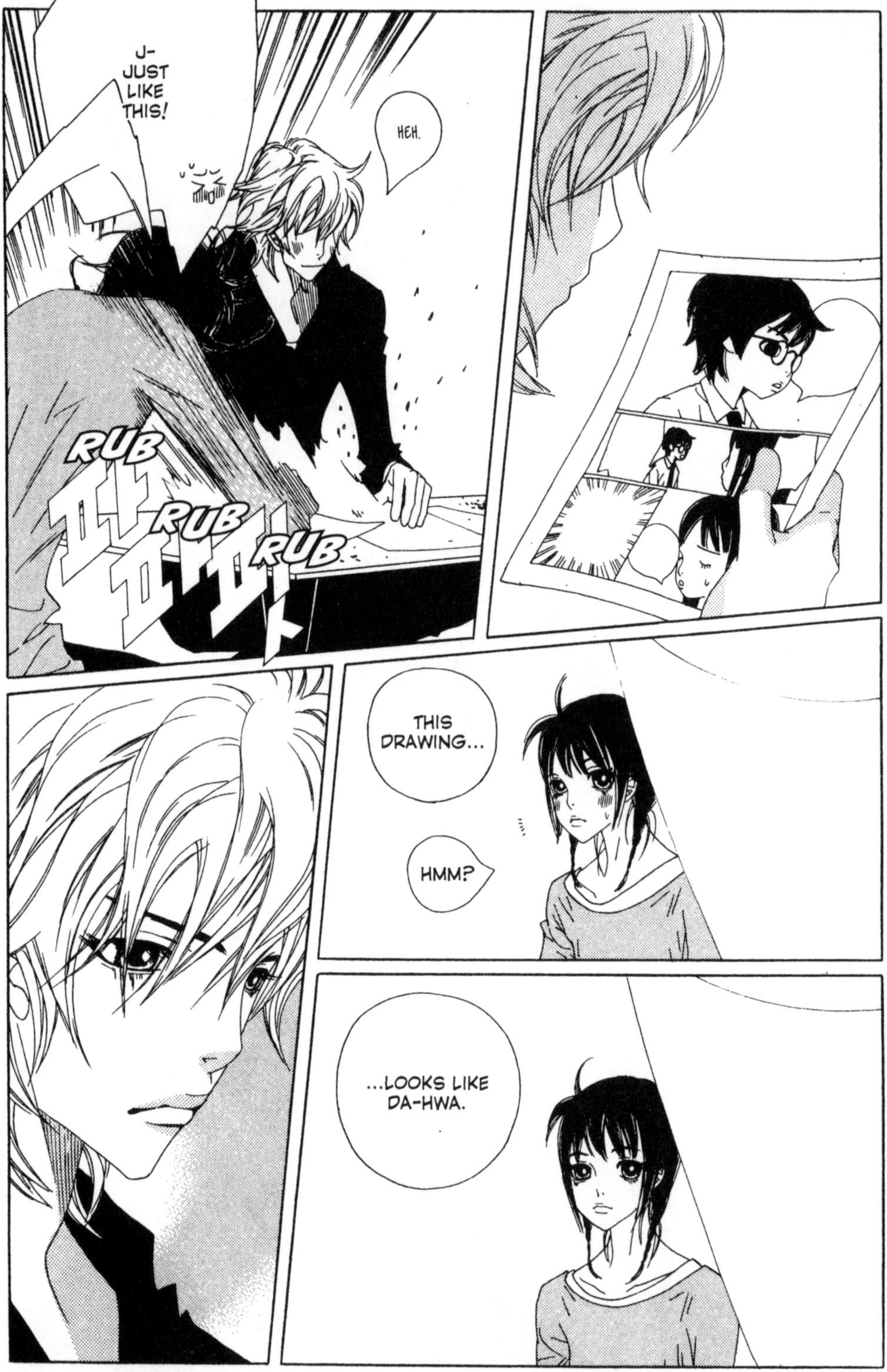
J-
JUST
LIKE
THIS!
HEH.
RUB
RUB
RUB
THIS
DRAWING...
HMM?
...LOOKS LIKE
DA-HWA.

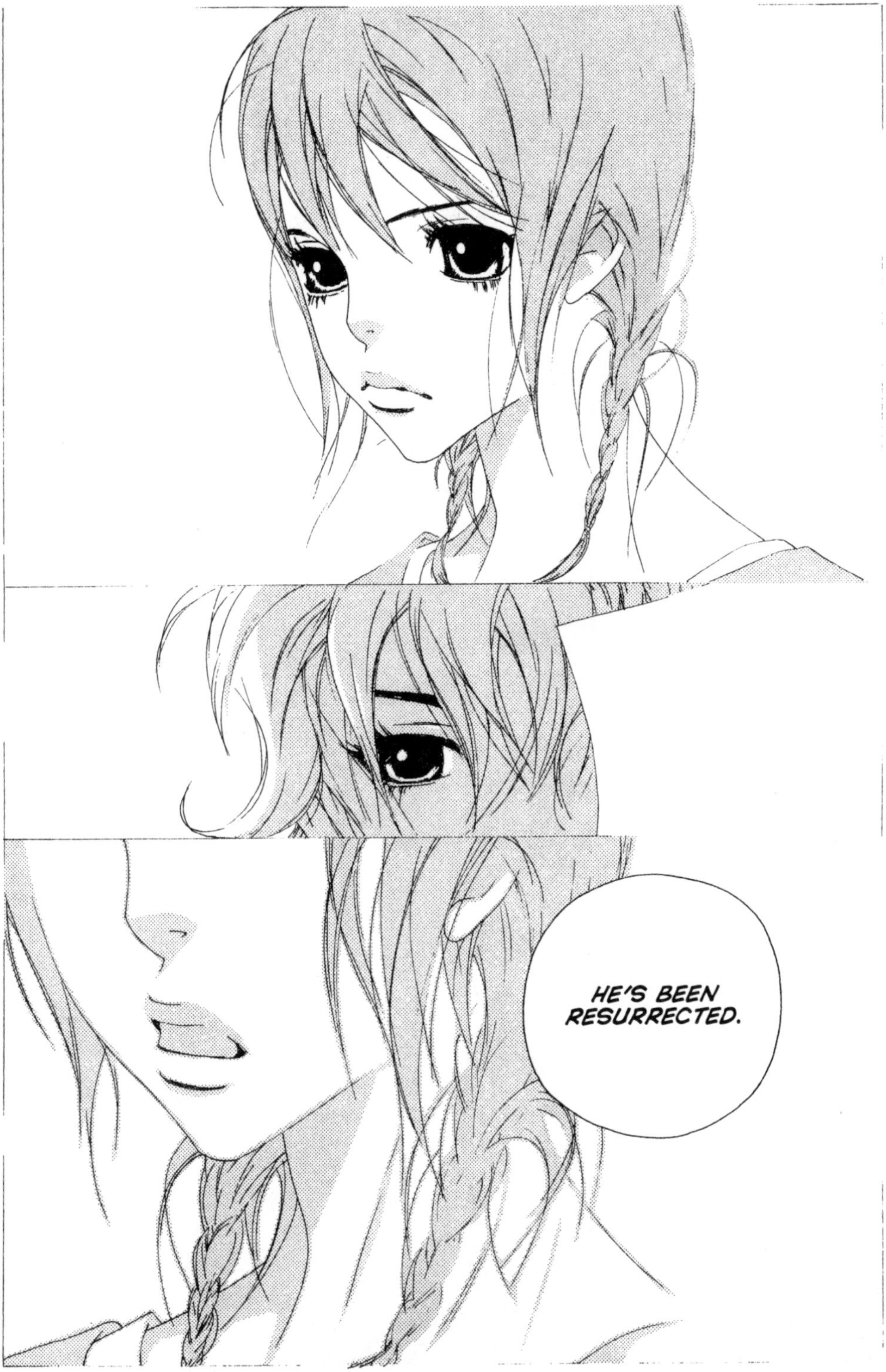
HE'S BEEN RESURRECTED.

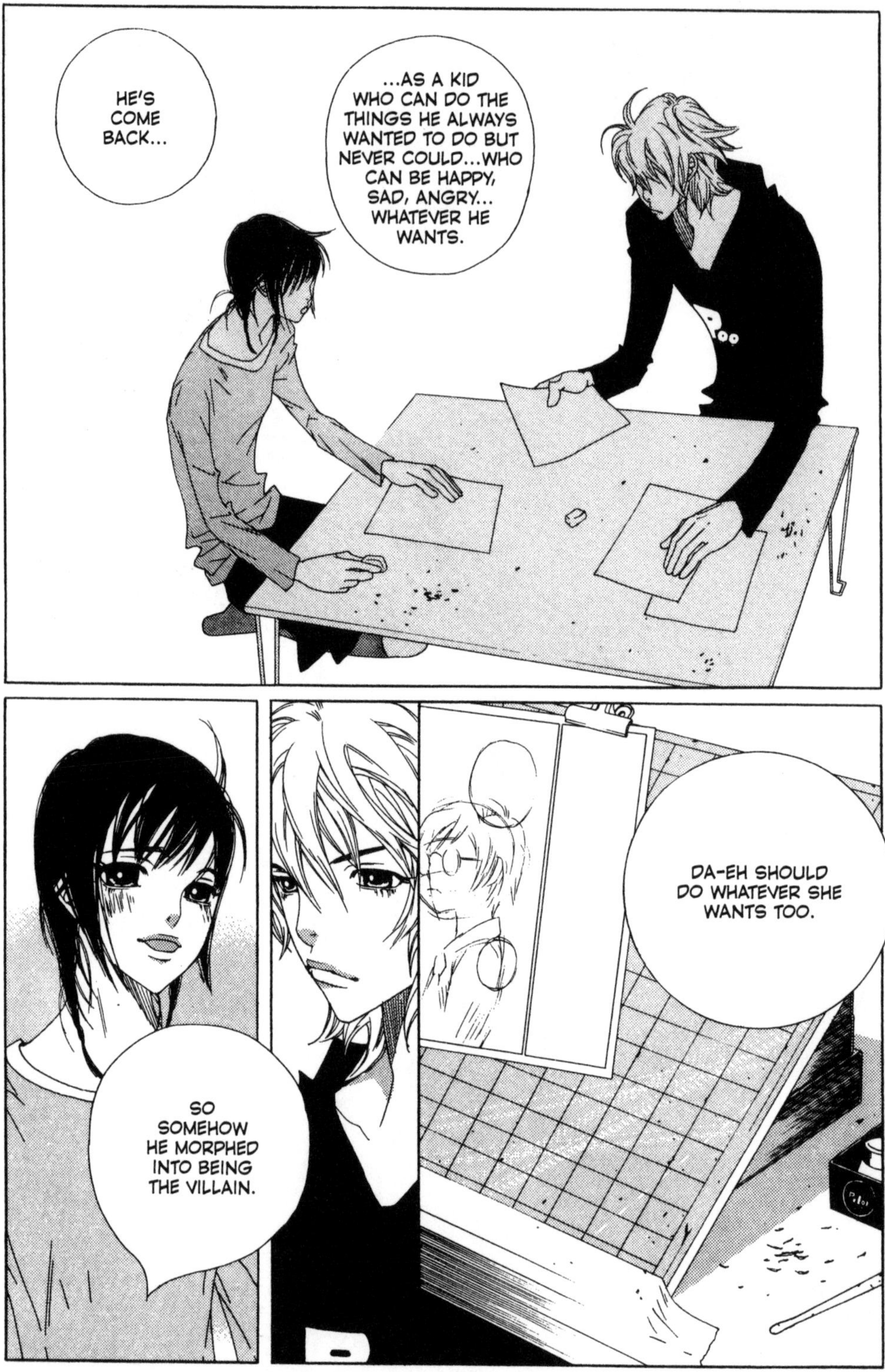
HE'S COME BACK...
...AS A KID WHO CAN DO THE THINGS HE ALWAYS WANTED TO DO BUT NEVER COULD...WHO CAN BE HAPPY, SAD, ANGRY... WHATEVER HE WANTS.
SO SOMEHOW HE MORPHED INTO BEING THE VILLAIN.
DA-EH SHOULD DO WHATEVER SHE WANTS TOO.

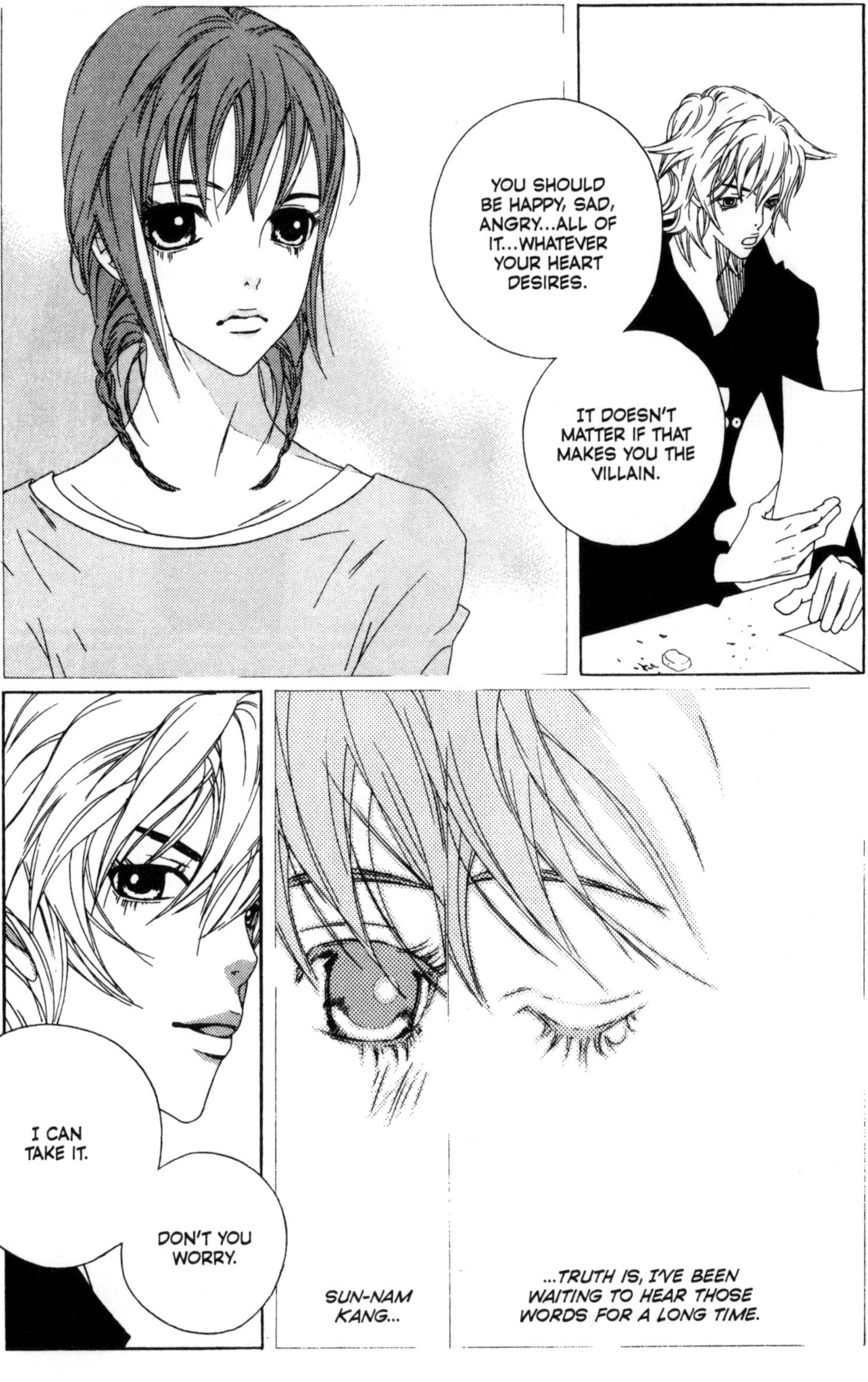
YOU SHOULD BE HAPPY, SAD, ANGRY...ALL OF IT...WHATEVER YOUR HEART DESIRES.
IT DOESN'T MATTER IF THAT MAKES YOU THE VILLAIN.
I CAN TAKE IT.
DON'T YOU WORRY.
SUN-NAM KANG...
...TRUTH IS, I'VE BEEN WAITING TO HEAR THOSE WORDS FOR A LONG TIME.

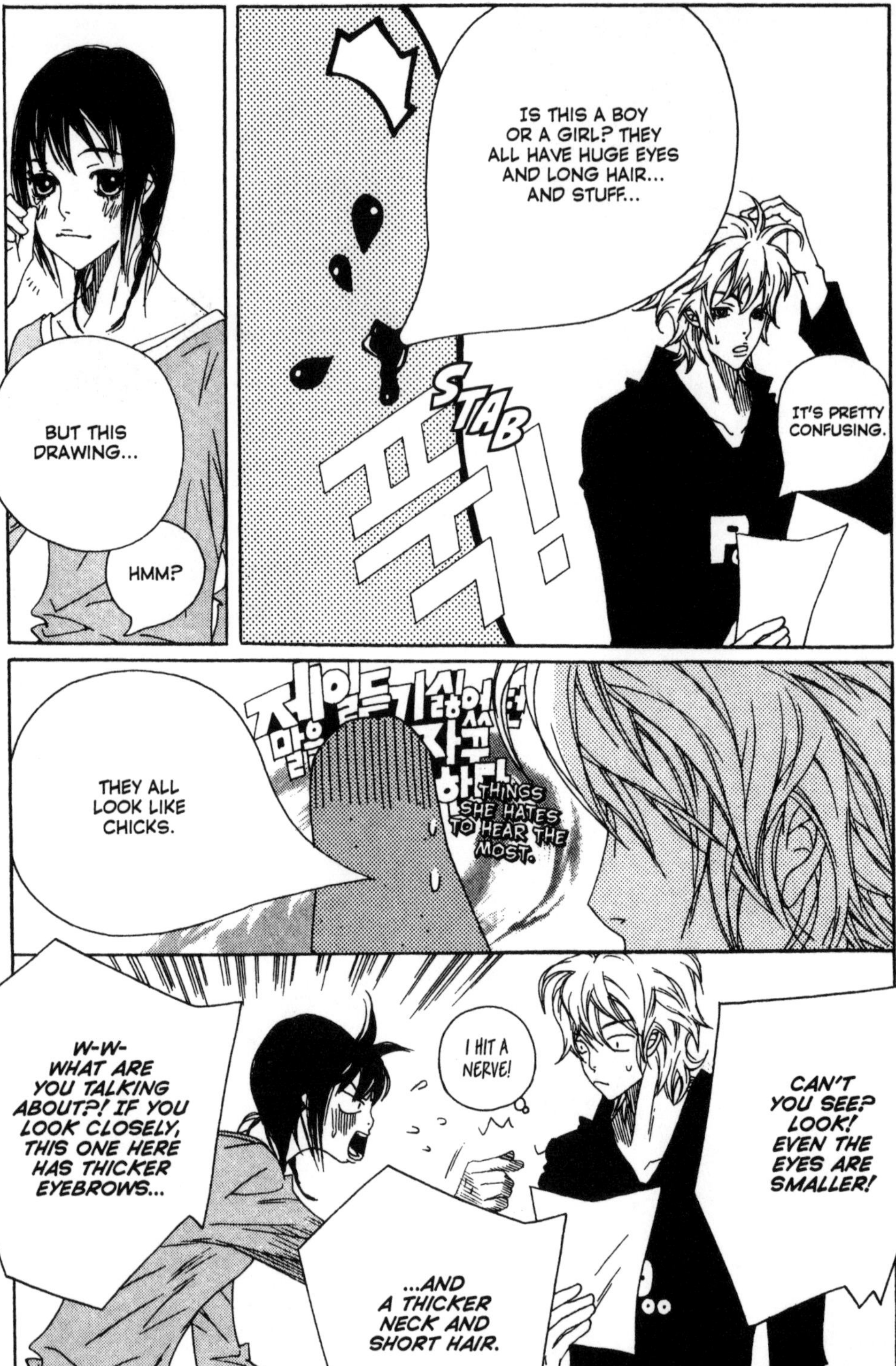
BUT THIS DRAWING...
HMM?
IS THIS A BOY OR A GIRL? THEY ALL HAVE HUGE EYES AND LONG HAIR... AND STUFF...
IT'S PRETTY CONFUSING.
STAB
THEY ALL LOOK LIKE CHICKS.
THINGS SHE HATES TO HEAR THE MOST.
W-W-WHAT ARE YOU TALKING ABOUT?! IF YOU LOOK CLOSELY, THIS ONE HERE HAS THICKER EYEBROWS...
I HIT A NERVE!
CAN'T YOU SEE? LOOK! EVEN THE EYES ARE SMALLER!
...AND A THICKER NECK AND SHORT HAIR.

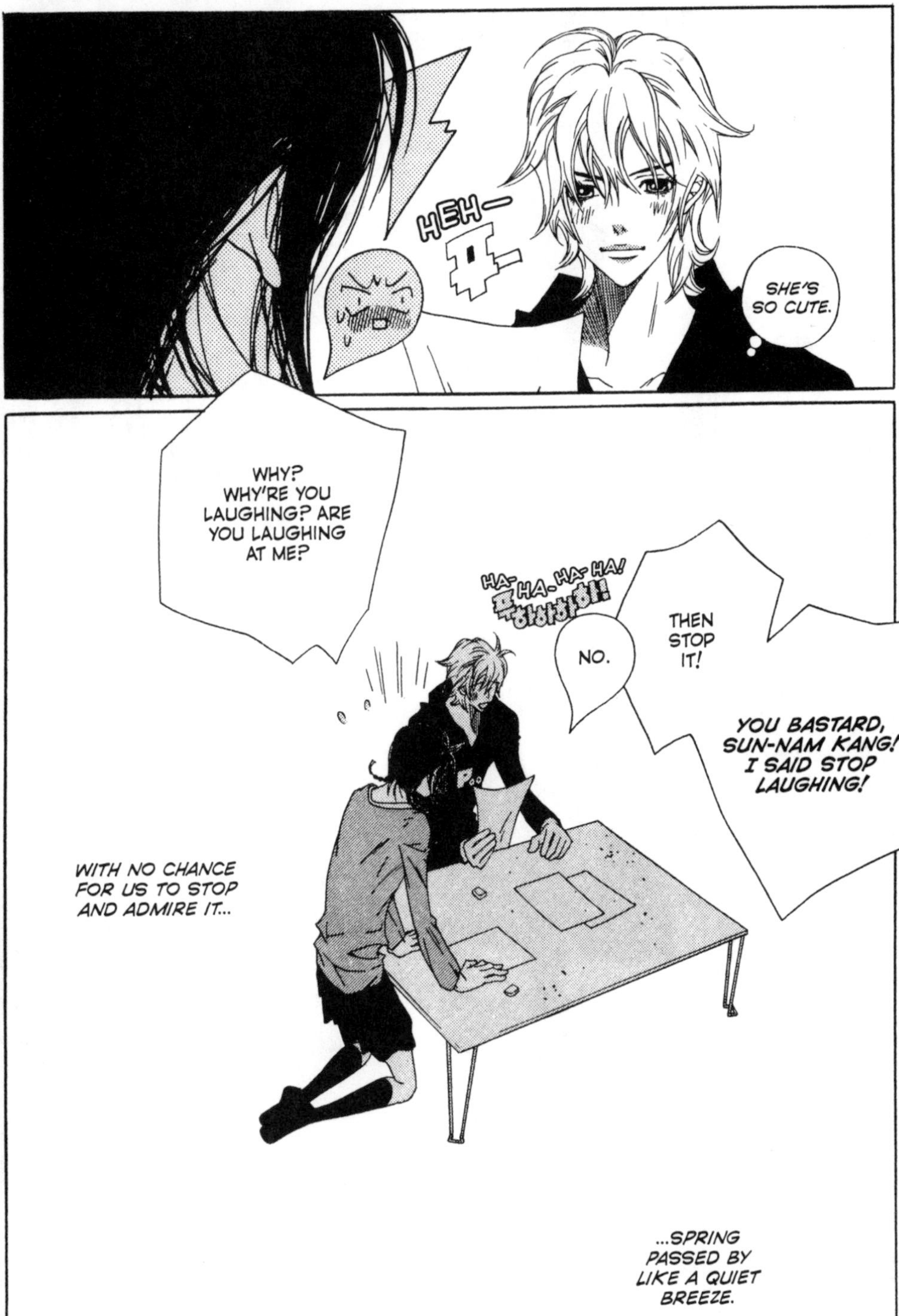
HEH—
SHE'S SO CUTE.
WHY? WHY'RE YOU LAUGHING? ARE YOU LAUGHING AT ME?
HA-HA-HA-HA!
NO.
THEN STOP IT!
YOU BASTARD, SUN-NAM KANG! I SAID STOP LAUGHING!
WITH NO CHANCE FOR US TO STOP AND ADMIRE IT...
...SPRING PASSED BY LIKE A QUIET BREEZE.

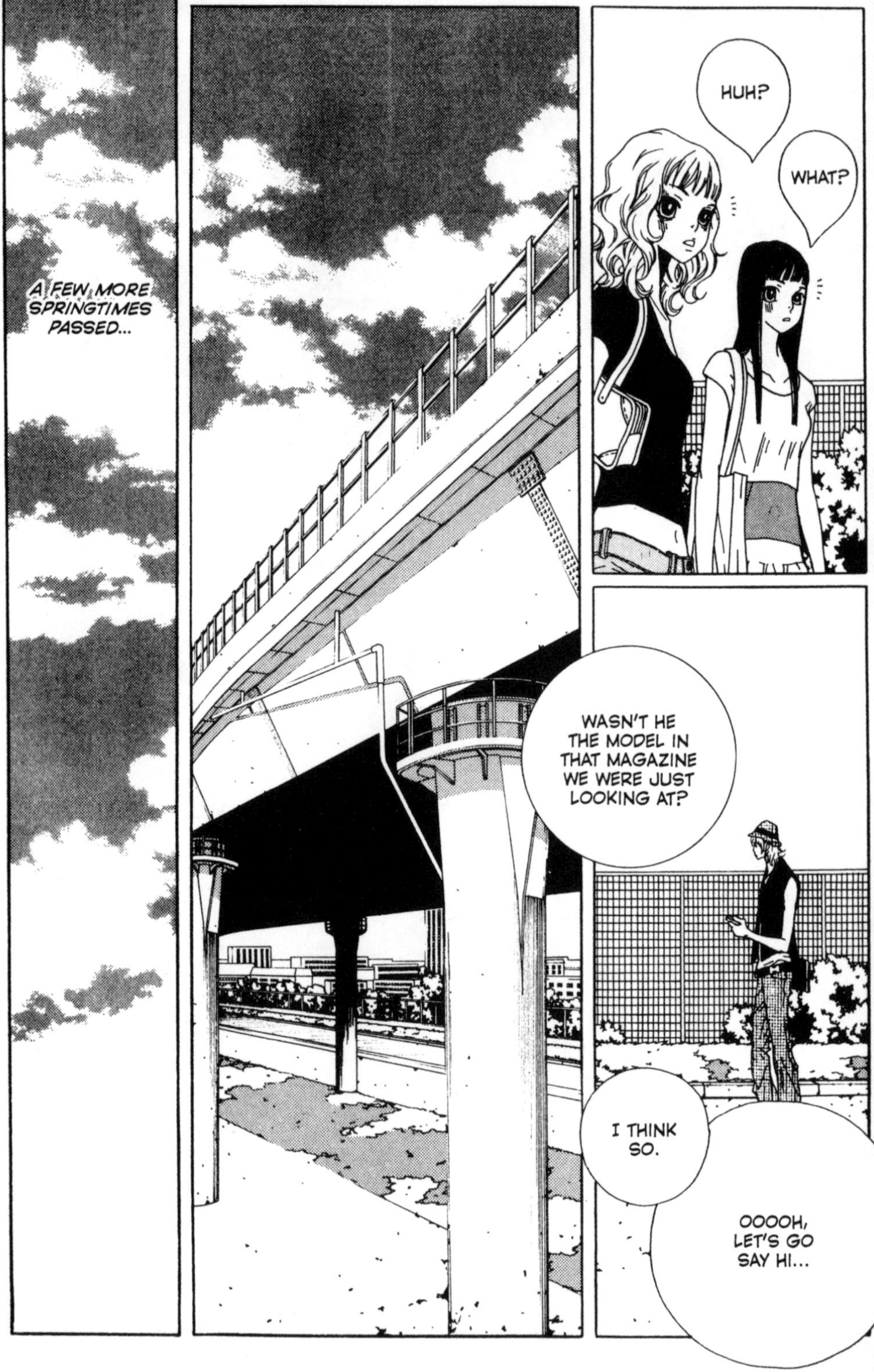
A FEW MORE SPRINGTIMES PASSED...
HUH?
WHAT?
WASN'T HE THE MODEL IN THAT MAGAZINE WE WERE JUST LOOKING AT?
I THINK SO.
OOOOH, LET'S GO SAY HI...

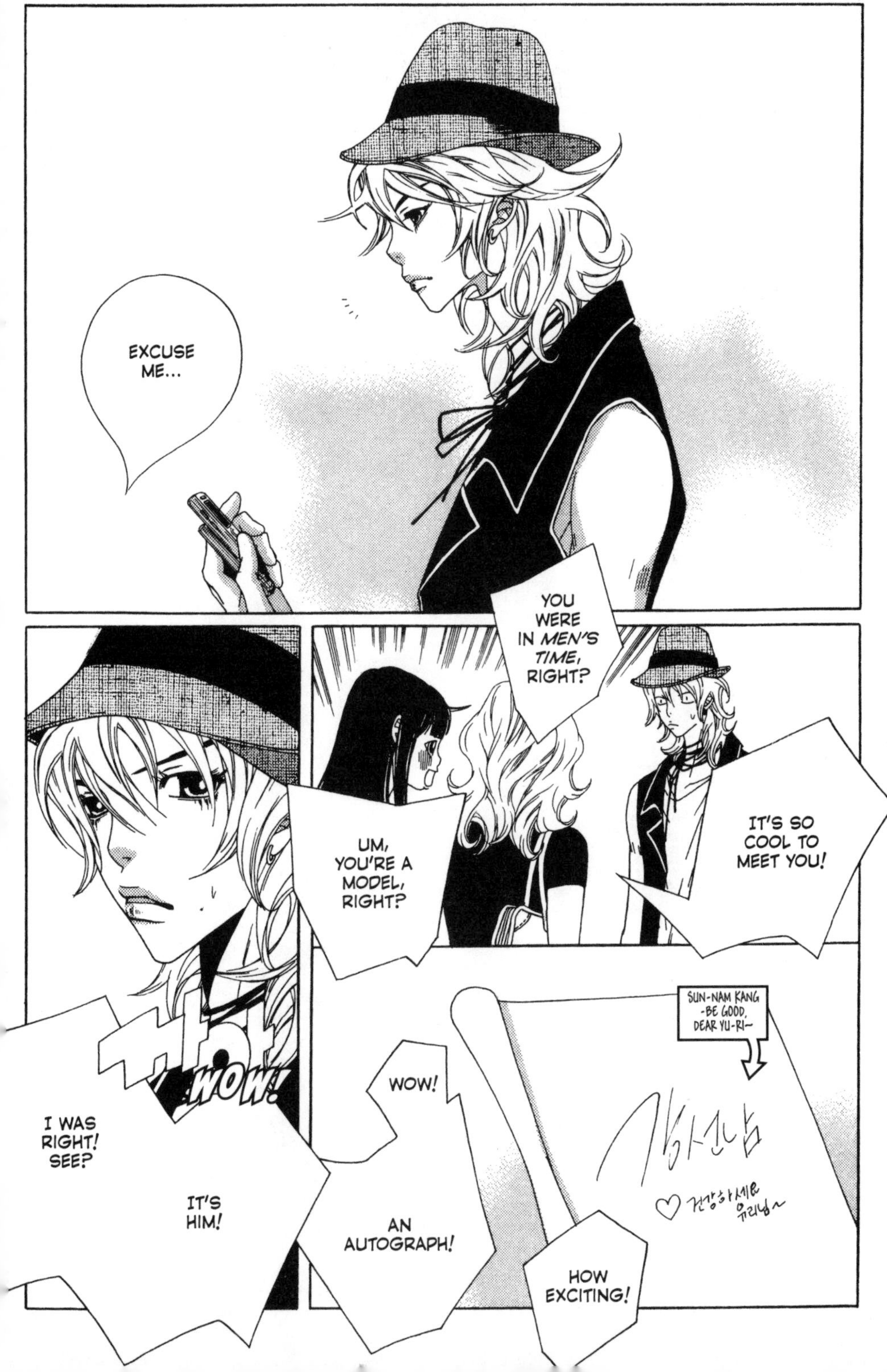
EXCUSE ME...
WOW!
I WAS RIGHT! SEE?
IT'S HIM!
YOU WERE IN *MEN'S TIME*, RIGHT?
UM, YOU'RE A MODEL, RIGHT?
IT'S SO COOL TO MEET YOU!
WOW!
AN AUTOGRAPH!
HOW EXCITING!
SUN-NAM KANG -BE GOOD, DEAR YU-RI~
강선남
건강하세요 유리님~

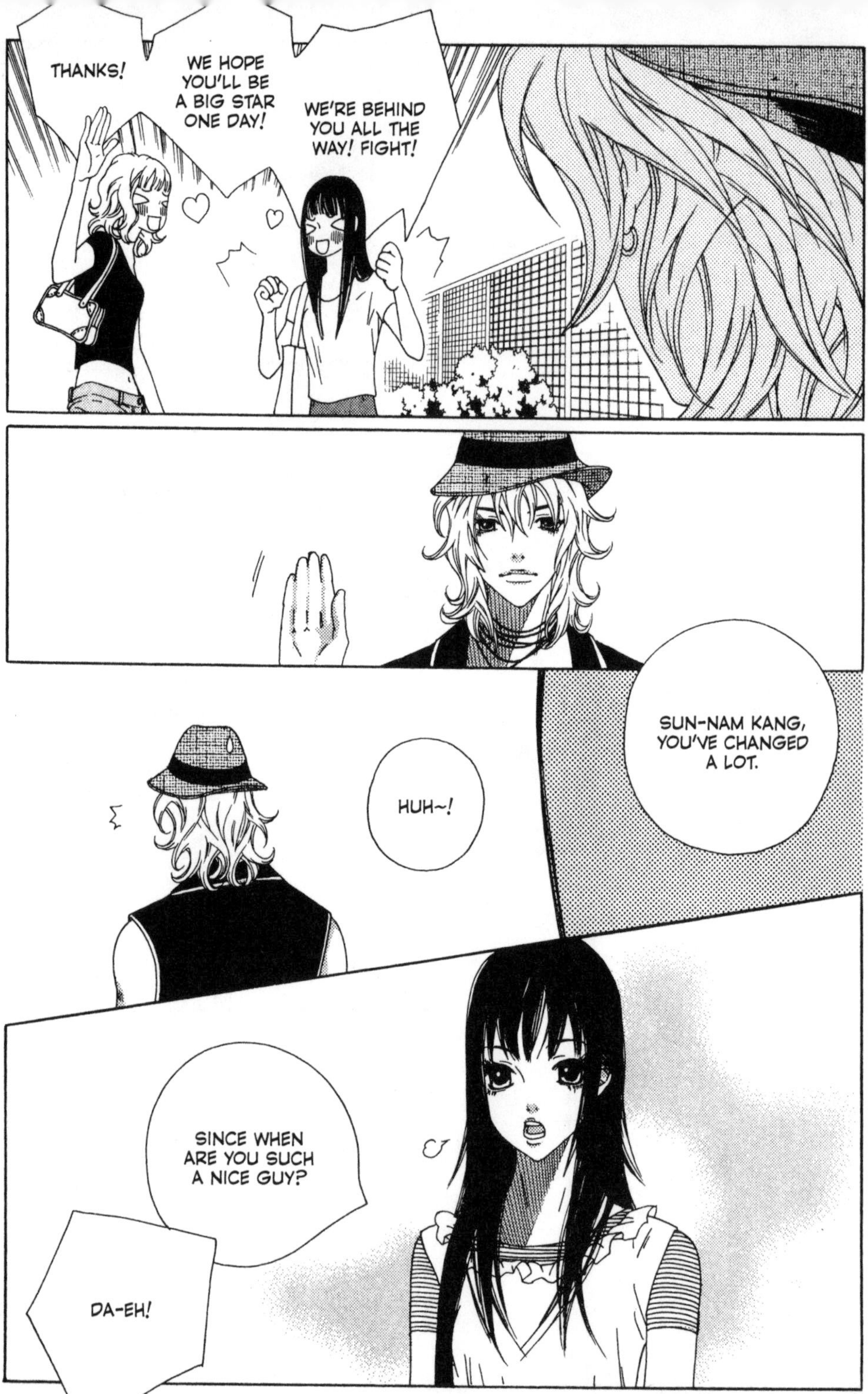
THANKS!
WE HOPE YOU'LL BE A BIG STAR ONE DAY!
WE'RE BEHIND YOU ALL THE WAY! FIGHT!
HUH~!
SUN-NAM KANG, YOU'VE CHANGED A LOT.
SINCE WHEN ARE YOU SUCH A NICE GUY?
DA-EH!

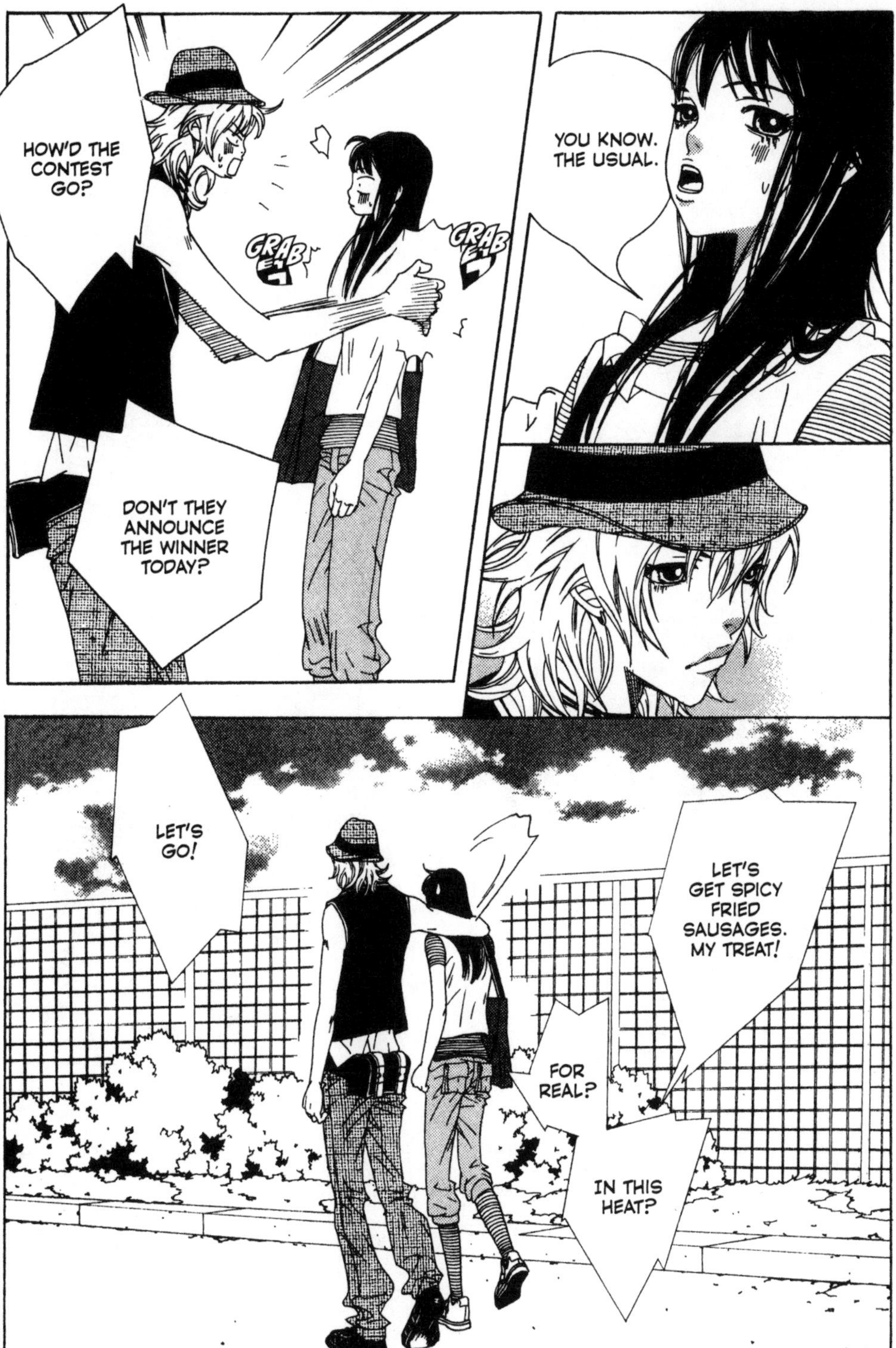
HOW'D THE CONTEST GO?
GRAB
GRAB
DON'T THEY ANNOUNCE THE WINNER TODAY?
YOU KNOW. THE USUAL.
LET'S GO!
LET'S GET SPICY FRIED SAUSAGES. MY TREAT!
FOR REAL?
IN THIS HEAT?

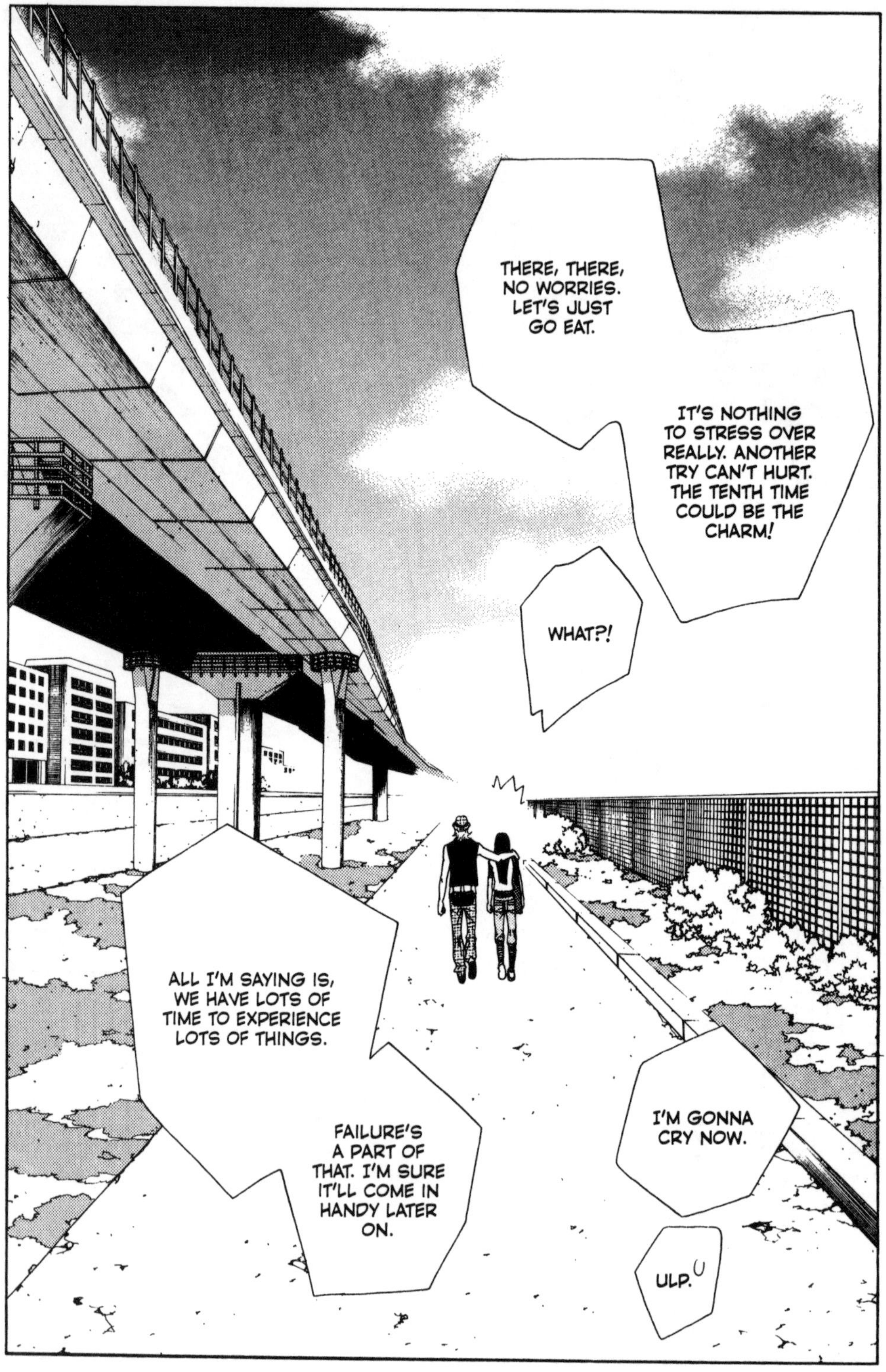
THERE, THERE, NO WORRIES. LET'S JUST GO EAT.
IT'S NOTHING TO STRESS OVER REALLY. ANOTHER TRY CAN'T HURT. THE TENTH TIME COULD BE THE CHARM!
WHAT?!
ALL I'M SAYING IS, WE HAVE LOTS OF TIME TO EXPERIENCE LOTS OF THINGS.
FAILURE'S A PART OF THAT. I'M SURE IT'LL COME IN HANDY LATER ON.
I'M GONNA CRY NOW.
ULP.

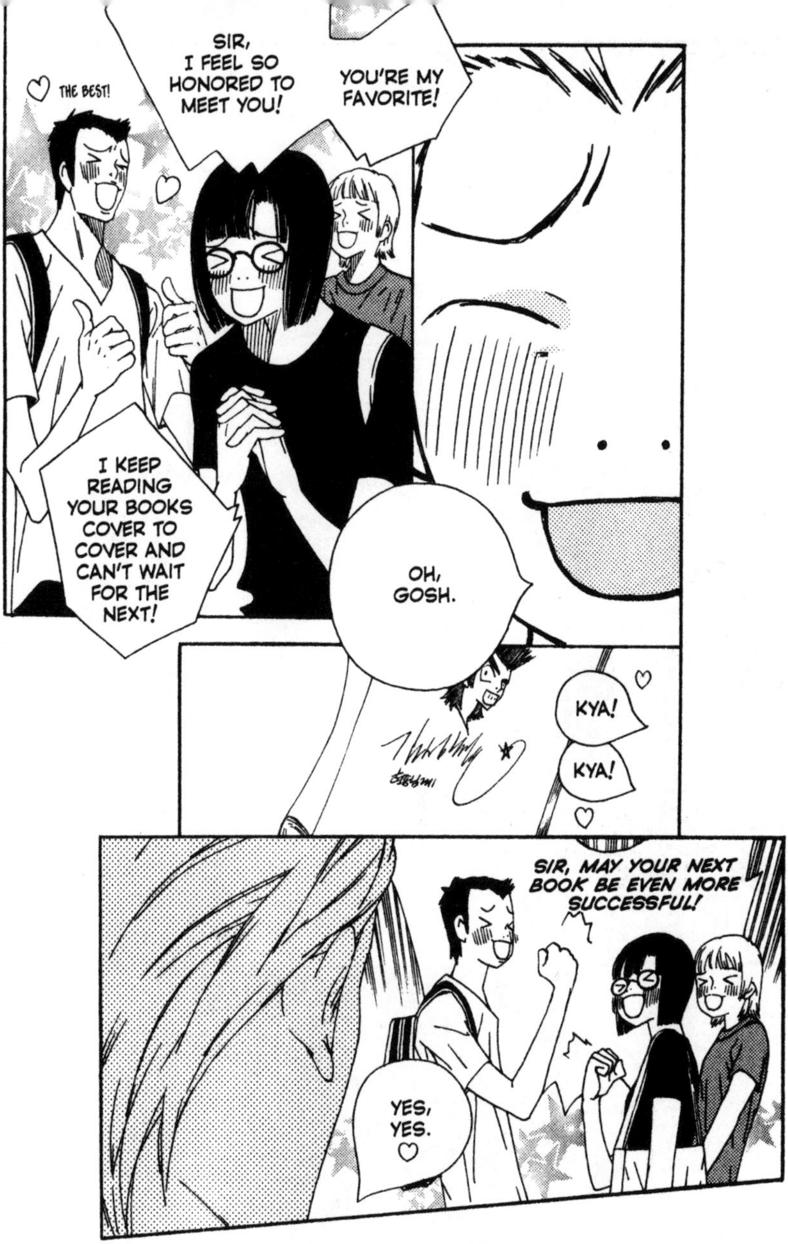
THE BEST!
SIR, I FEEL SO HONORED TO MEET YOU!
YOU'RE MY FAVORITE!
I KEEP READING YOUR BOOKS COVER TO COVER AND CAN'T WAIT FOR THE NEXT!
OH, GOSH.
KYA!
KYA!
SIR, MAY YOUR NEXT BOOK BE EVEN MORE SUCCESSFUL!
YES, YES. ♡

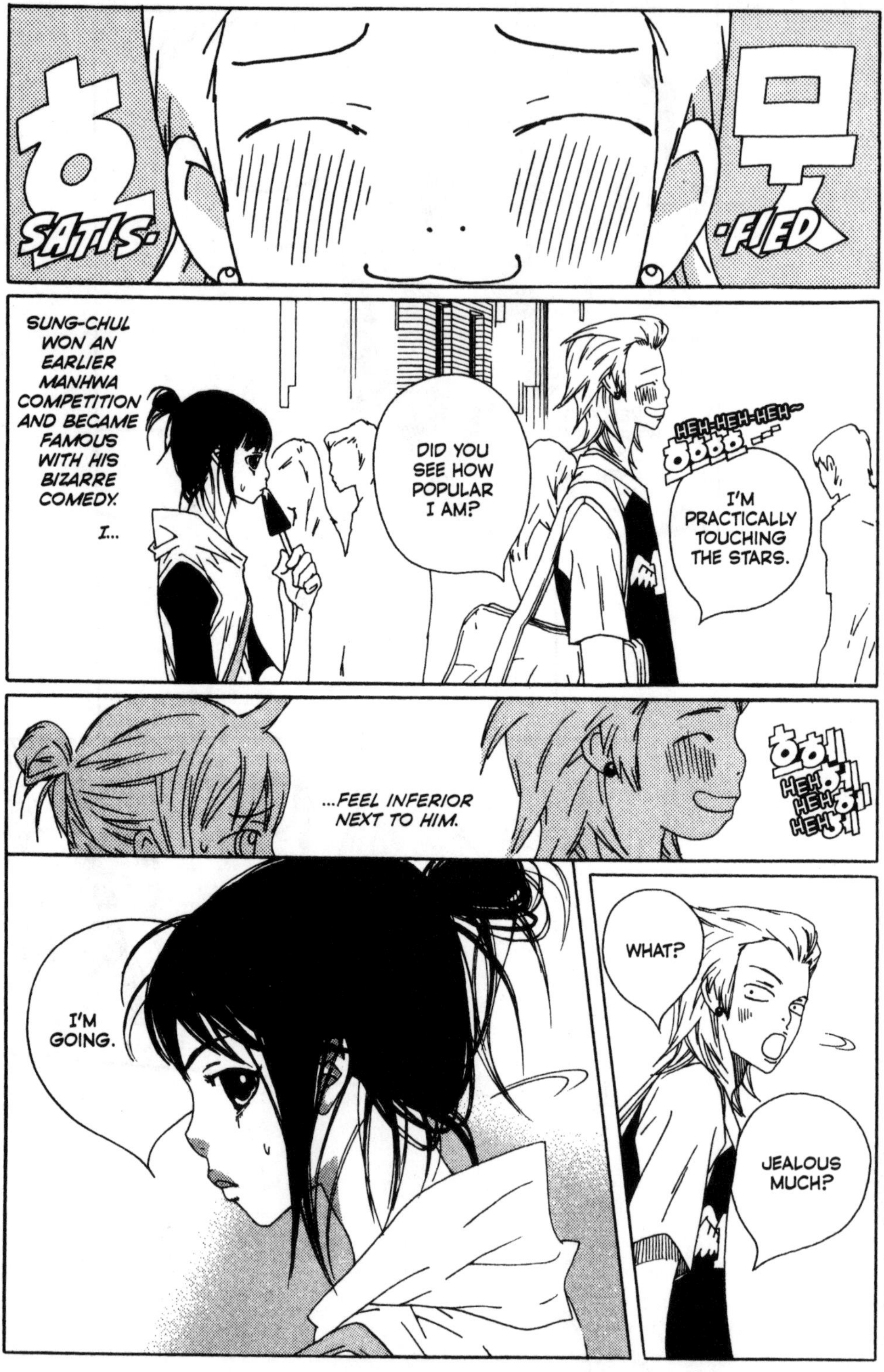
SATIS-
-FIED
SUNG-CHUL WON AN EARLIER MANHWA COMPETITION AND BECAME FAMOUS WITH HIS BIZARRE COMEDY.
I...
DID YOU SEE HOW POPULAR I AM?
HEH-HEH-HEH~
I'M PRACTICALLY TOUCHING THE STARS.
...FEEL INFERIOR NEXT TO HIM.
HEH HEH HEH
I'M GOING.
WHAT?
JEALOUS MUCH?

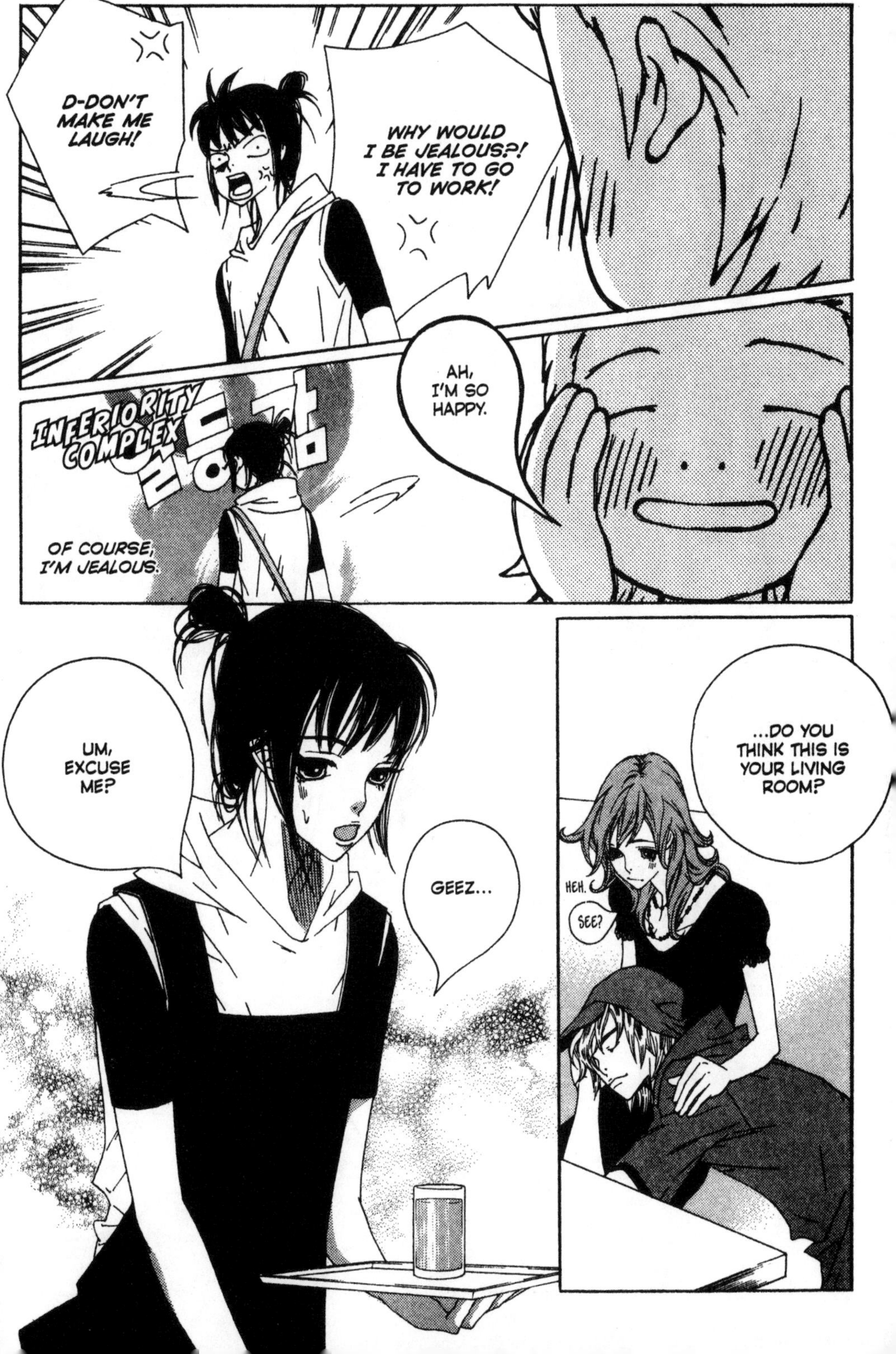

D-DON'T MAKE ME LAUGH!
WHY WOULD I BE JEALOUS?! I HAVE TO GO TO WORK!
INFERIORITY COMPLEX
OF COURSE, I'M JEALOUS.
AH, I'M SO HAPPY.
UM, EXCUSE ME?
GEEZ...
...DO YOU THINK THIS IS YOUR LIVING ROOM?
HEH.
SEE?

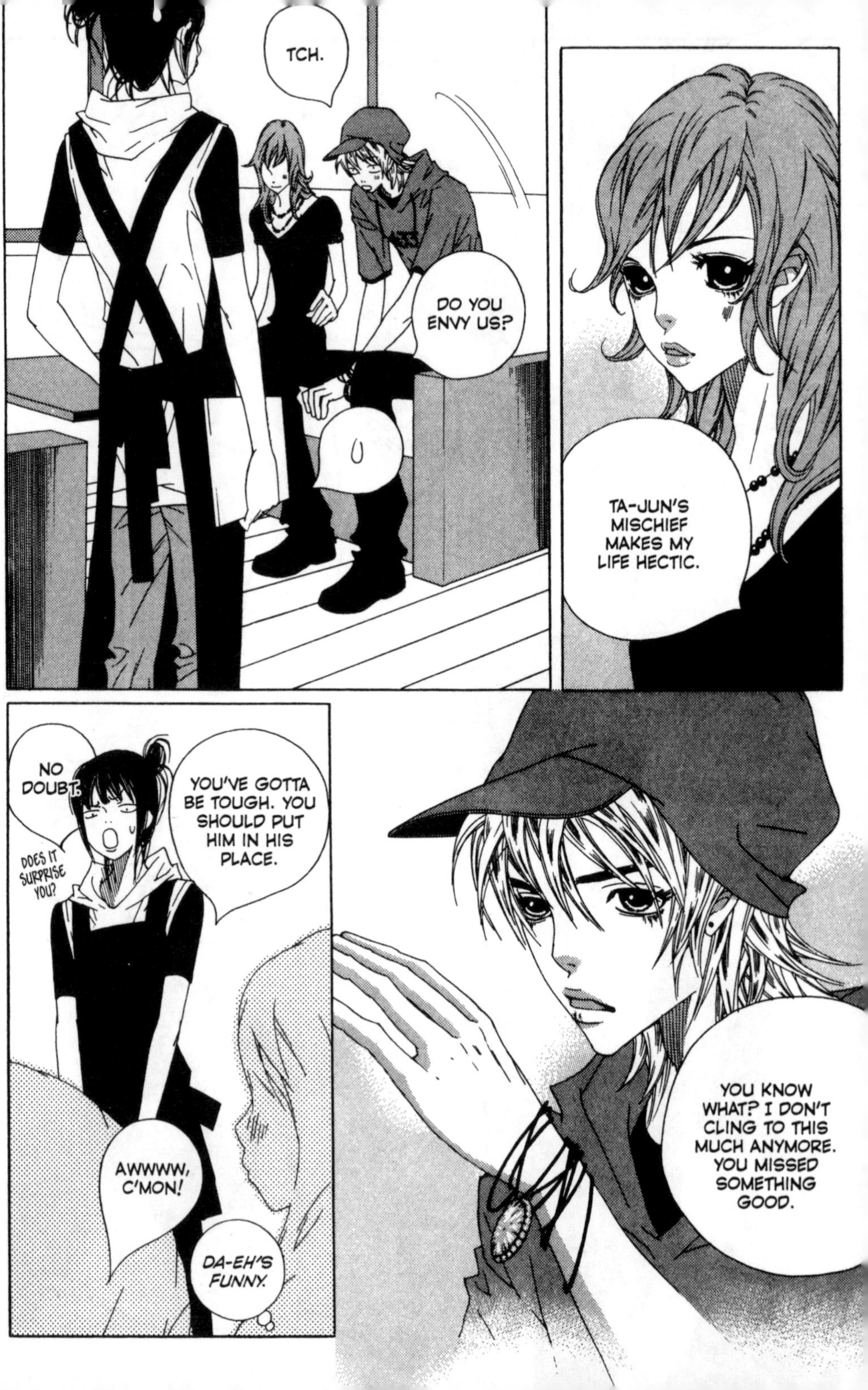
TCH.
DO YOU ENVY US?
TA-JUN'S MISCHIEF MAKES MY LIFE HECTIC.
NO DOUBT.
DOES IT SURPRISE YOU?
YOU'VE GOTTA BE TOUGH. YOU SHOULD PUT HIM IN HIS PLACE.
AWWWW, C'MON!
DA-EH'S FUNNY.
YOU KNOW WHAT? I DON'T CLING TO THIS MUCH ANYMORE. YOU MISSED SOMETHING GOOD.

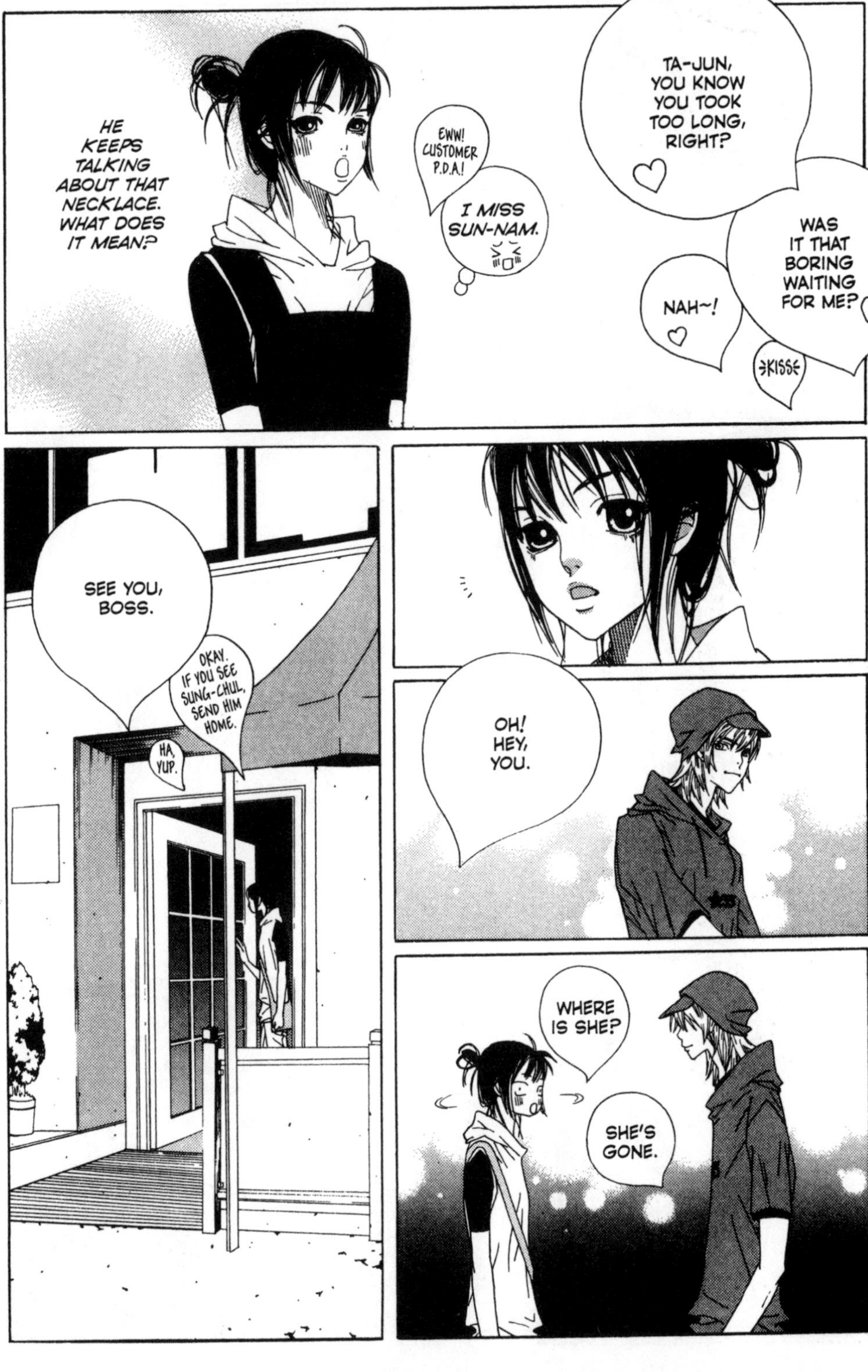

HE KEEPS TALKING ABOUT THAT NECKLACE. WHAT DOES IT MEAN?
EWW! CUSTOMER P.D.A.!
I MISS SUN-NAM.
TA-JUN, YOU KNOW YOU TOOK TOO LONG, RIGHT?
NAH~!
WAS IT THAT BORING WAITING FOR ME?
KISS
SEE YOU, BOSS.
HA, YUP.
OKAY. IF YOU SEE SUNG-CHUL, SEND HIM HOME.
OH! HEY, YOU.
WHERE IS SHE?
SHE'S GONE.

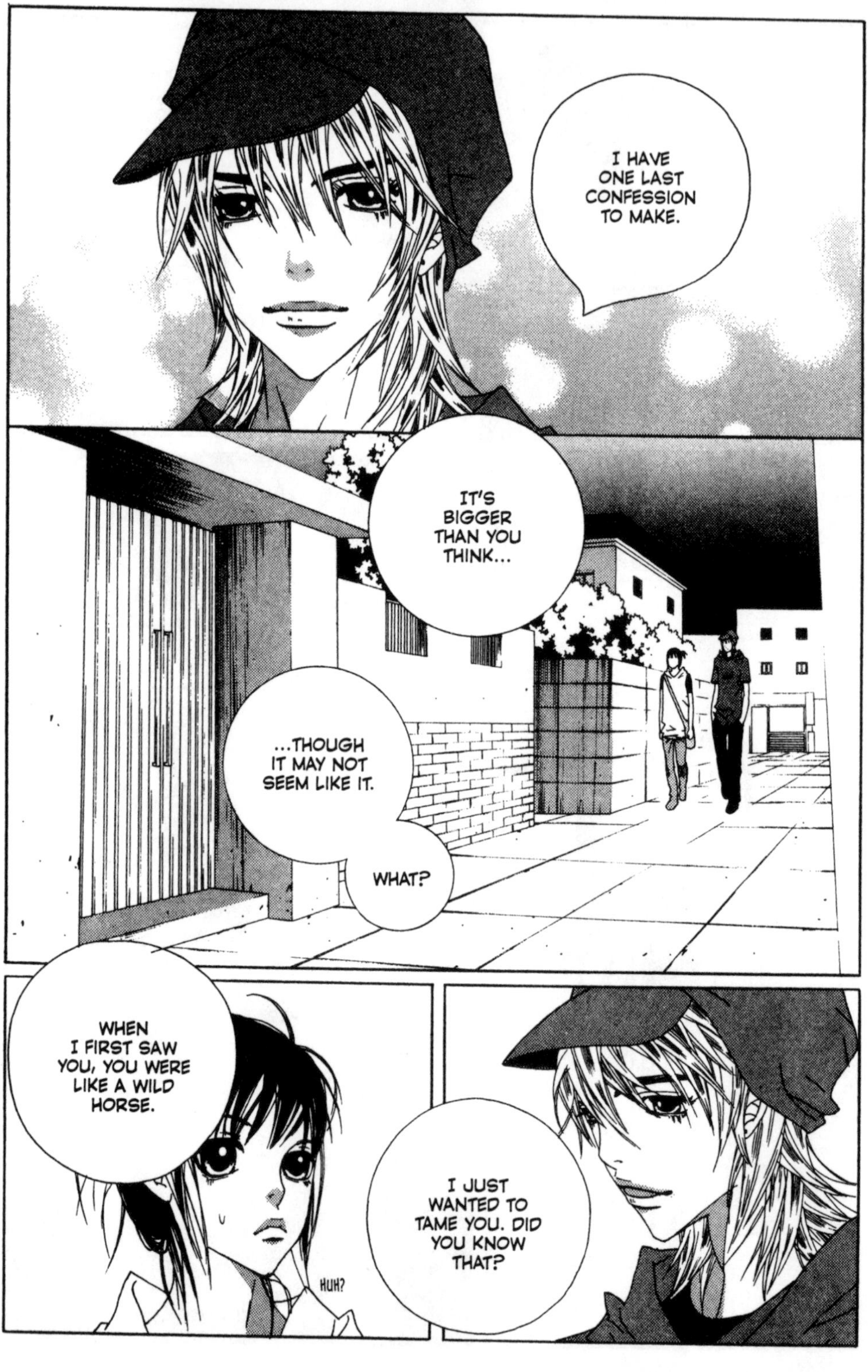
I HAVE ONE LAST CONFESSION TO MAKE.
IT'S BIGGER THAN YOU THINK...
...THOUGH IT MAY NOT SEEM LIKE IT.
WHAT?
WHEN I FIRST SAW YOU, YOU WERE LIKE A WILD HORSE.
HUH?
I JUST WANTED TO TAME YOU. DID YOU KNOW THAT?

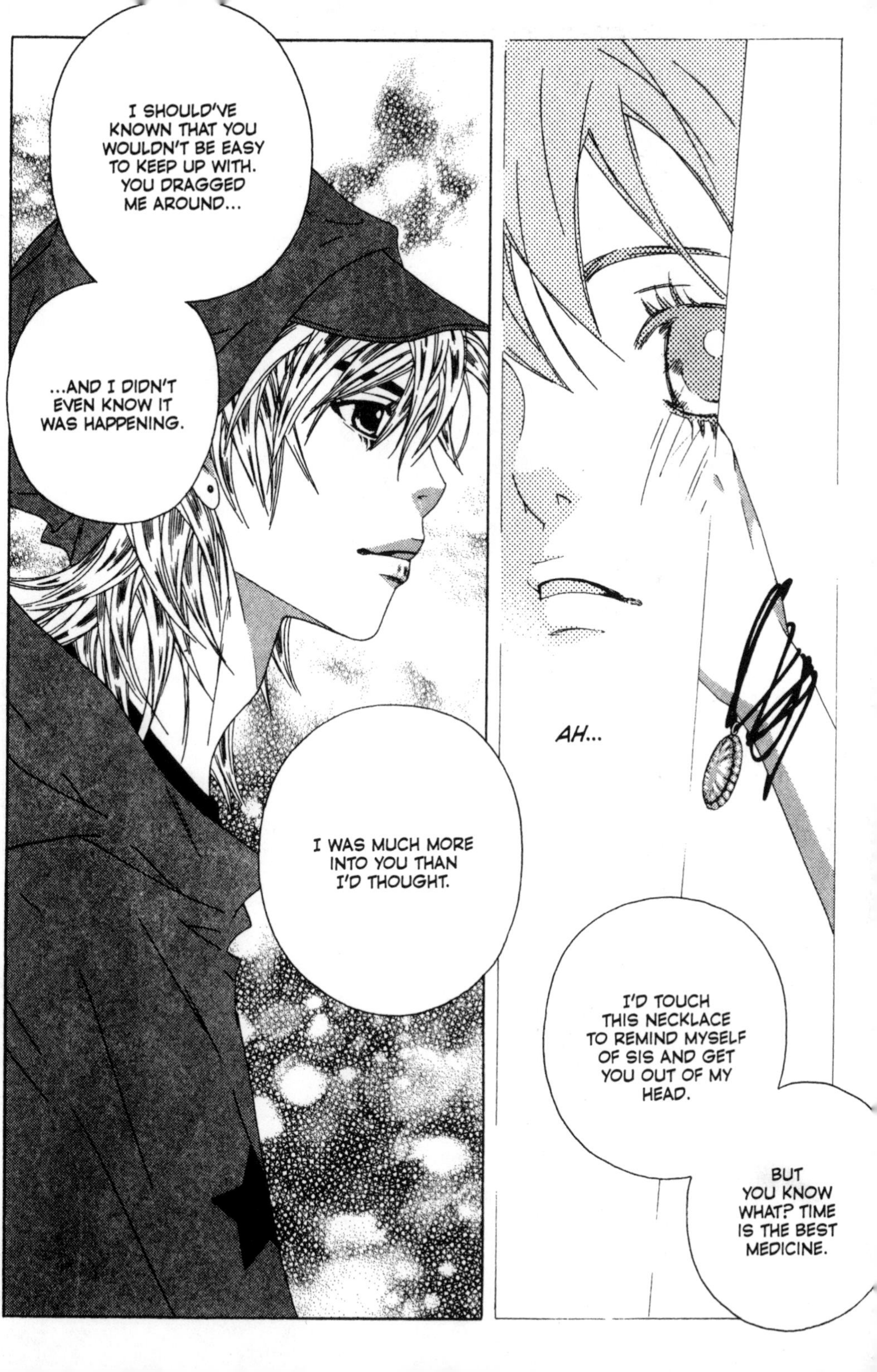
I SHOULD'VE KNOWN THAT YOU WOULDN'T BE EASY TO KEEP UP WITH. YOU DRAGGED ME AROUND...
...AND I DIDN'T EVEN KNOW IT WAS HAPPENING.
I WAS MUCH MORE INTO YOU THAN I'D THOUGHT.
AH...
I'D TOUCH THIS NECKLACE TO REMIND MYSELF OF SIS AND GET YOU OUT OF MY HEAD.
BUT YOU KNOW WHAT? TIME IS THE BEST MEDICINE.

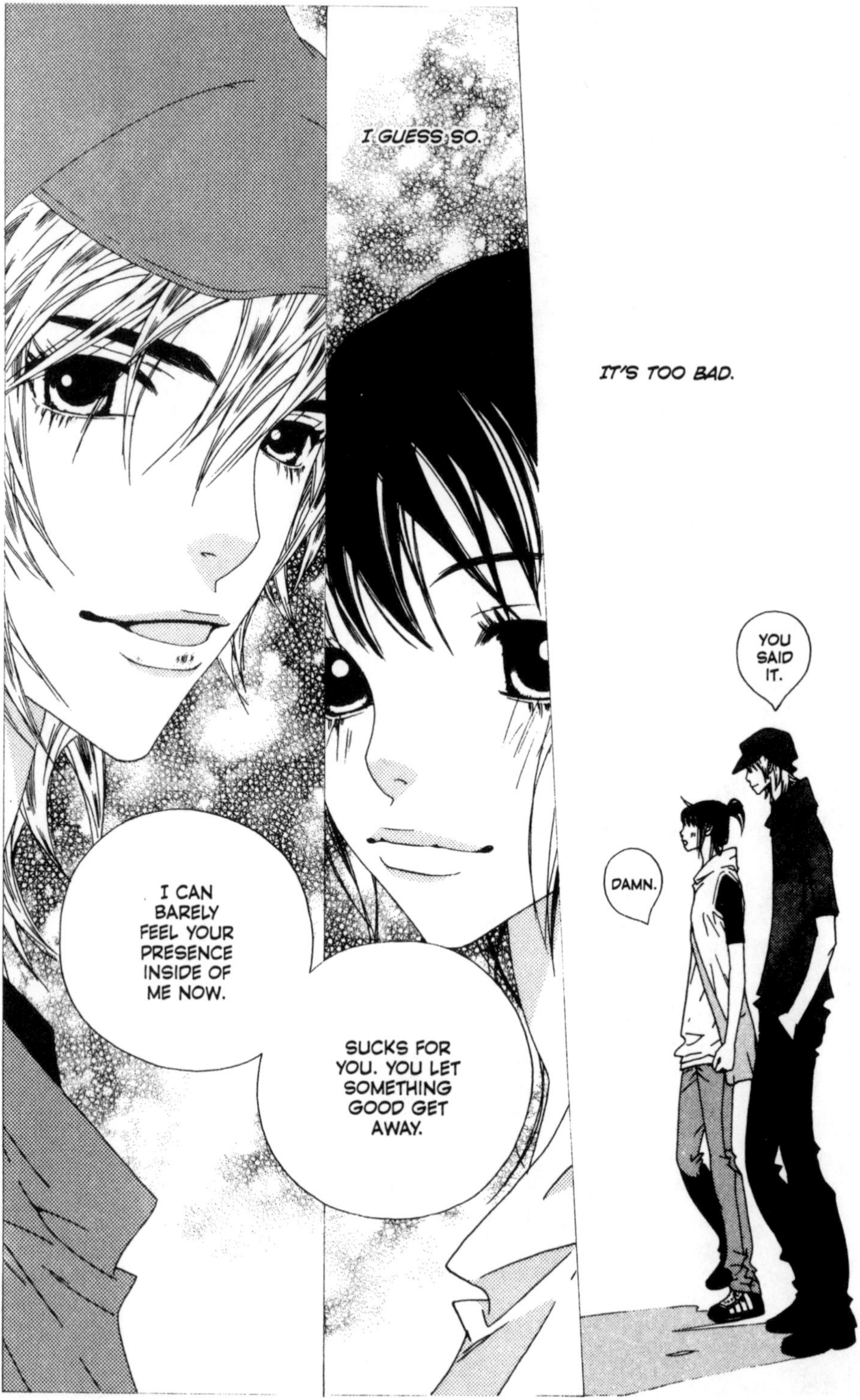
I CAN BARELY FEEL YOUR PRESENCE INSIDE OF ME NOW.
I GUESS SO.
SUCKS FOR YOU. YOU LET SOMETHING GOOD GET AWAY.
IT'S TOO BAD.
YOU SAID IT.
DAMN.

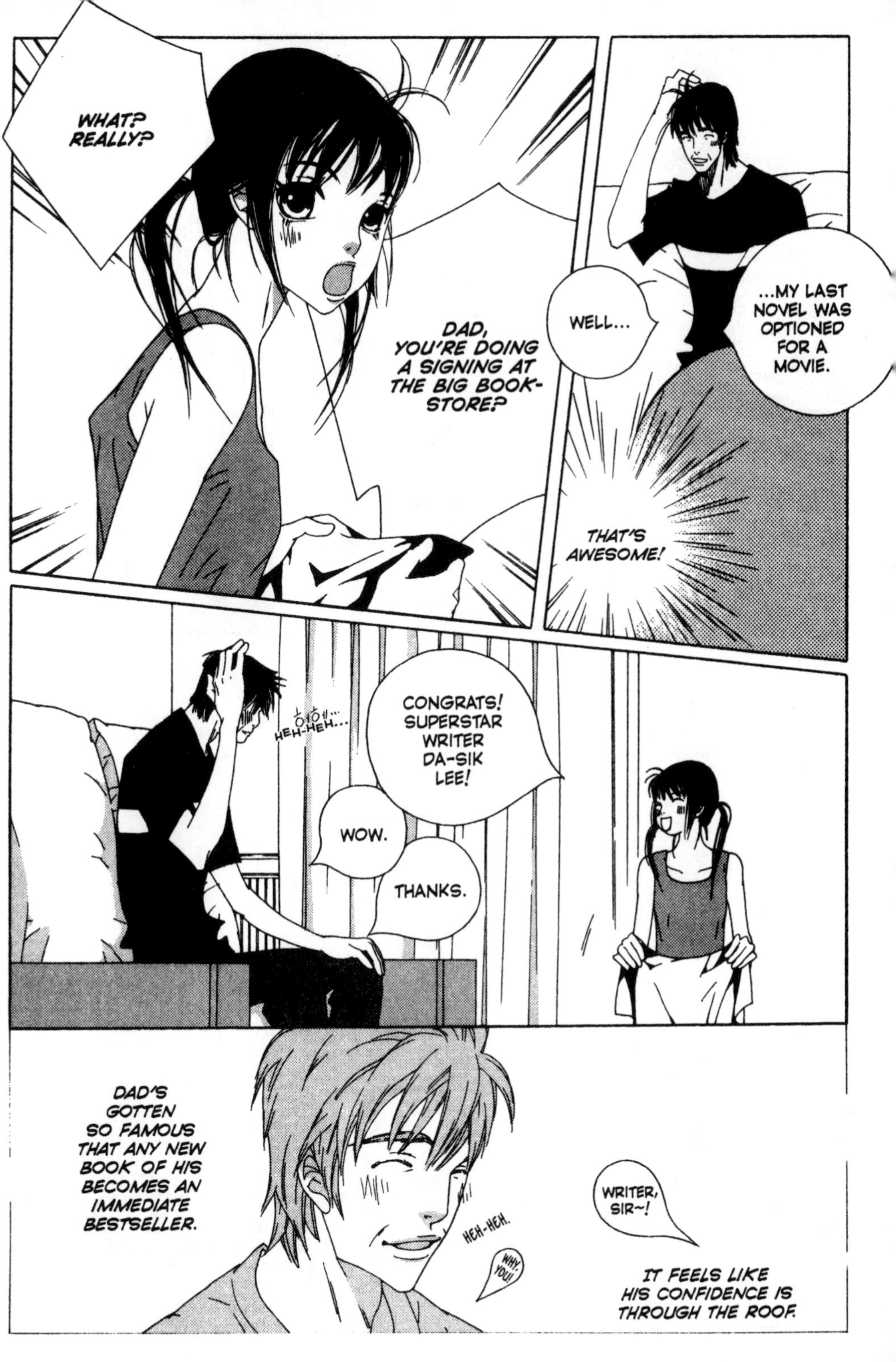
WHAT? REALLY?
DAD, YOU'RE DOING A SIGNING AT THE BIG BOOK-STORE?
WELL...
...MY LAST NOVEL WAS OPTIONED FOR A MOVIE.
THAT'S AWESOME!
흐헤...
HEH-HEH...
CONGRATS! SUPERSTAR WRITER DA-SIK LEE!
WOW.
THANKS.
DAD'S GOTTEN SO FAMOUS THAT ANY NEW BOOK OF HIS BECOMES AN IMMEDIATE BESTSELLER.
HEH-HEH.
WHY, YOU!
WRITER, SIR~!
IT FEELS LIKE HIS CONFIDENCE IS THROUGH THE ROOF.

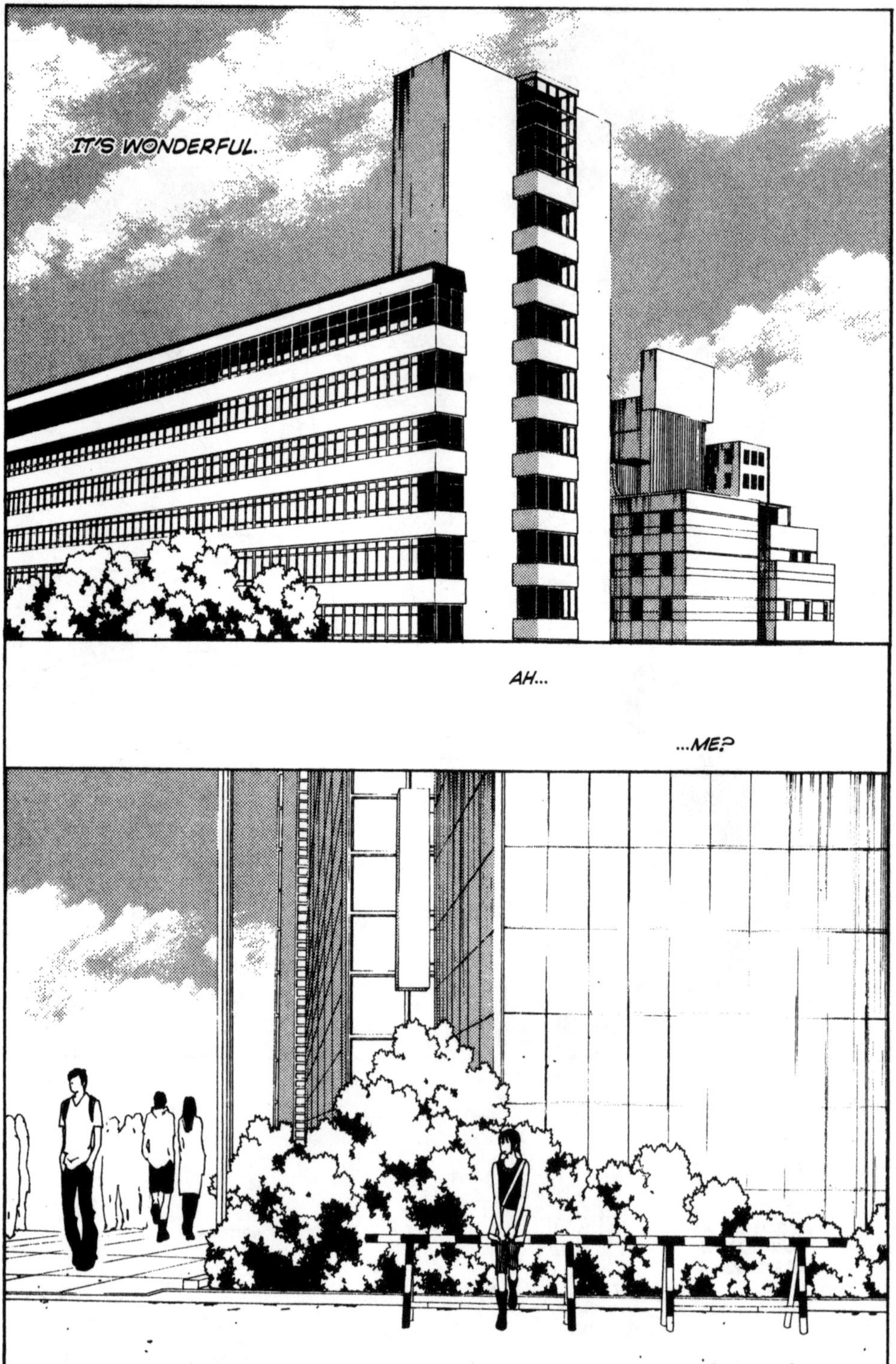
IT'S WONDERFUL.
AH...
...ME?

WHAT A GOOD-LOOKING GUY.

..I'M NOT MUCH OF ANYTHING YET.

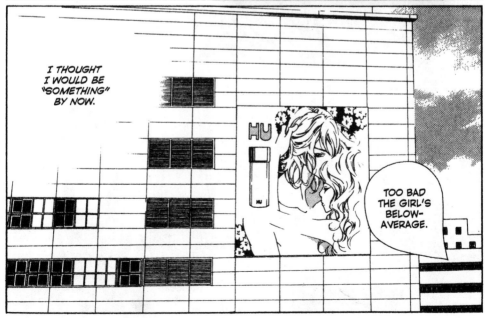

I THOUGHT I WOULD BE "SOMETHING" BY NOW.

TOO BAD THE GIRL'S BELOW-AVERAGE.

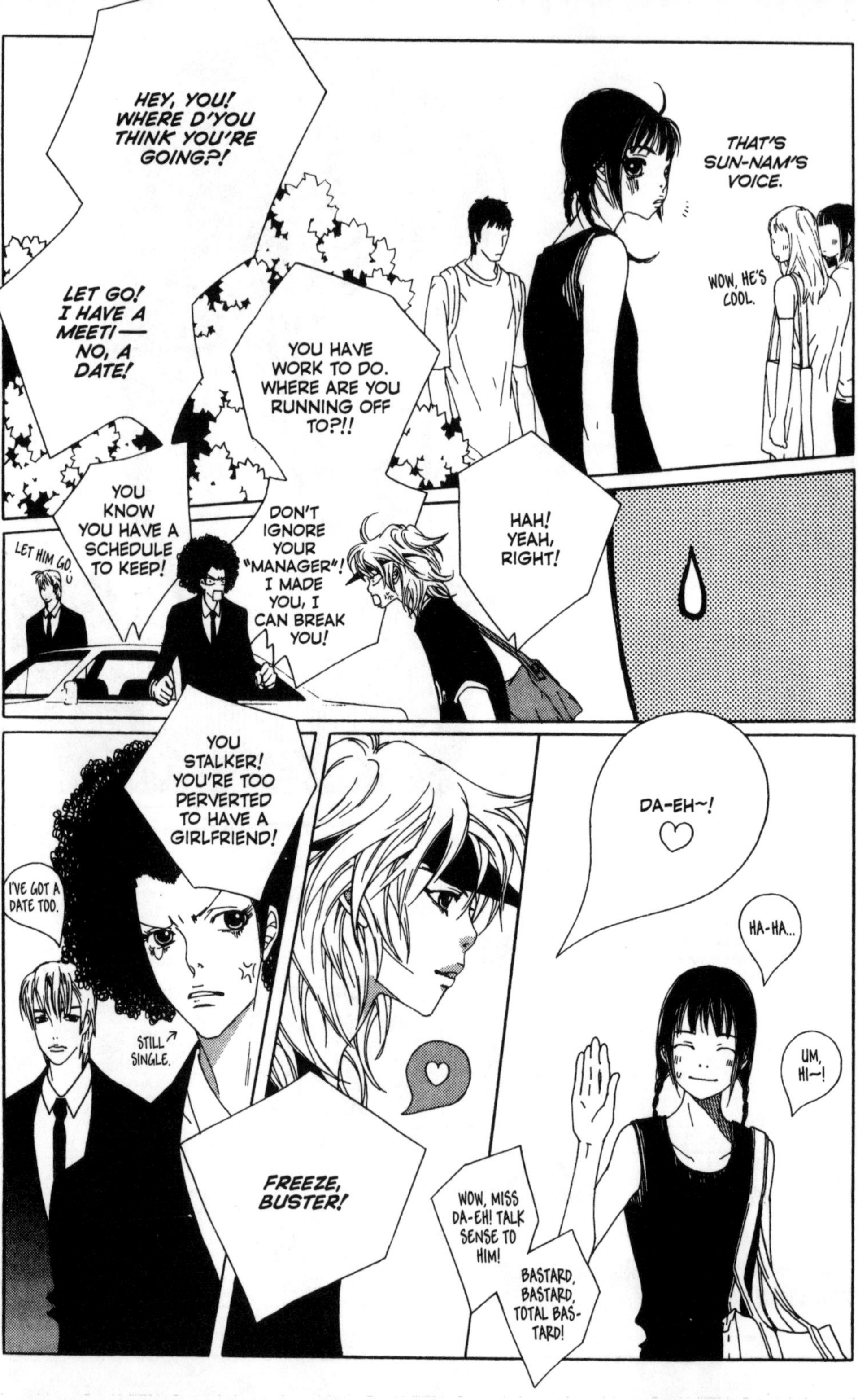
HEY, YOU! WHERE D'YOU THINK YOU'RE GOING?!
LET GO! I HAVE A MEETI— NO, A DATE!
YOU HAVE WORK TO DO. WHERE ARE YOU RUNNING OFF TO?!!
THAT'S SUN-NAM'S VOICE.
WOW, HE'S COOL.
LET HIM GO.
YOU KNOW YOU HAVE A SCHEDULE TO KEEP!
DON'T IGNORE YOUR "MANAGER"! I MADE YOU, I CAN BREAK YOU!
HAH! YEAH, RIGHT!
I'VE GOT A DATE TOO.
YOU STALKER! YOU'RE TOO PERVERTED TO HAVE A GIRLFRIEND!
STILL SINGLE.
FREEZE, BUSTER!
DA-EH~! ♡
HA-HA...
UM, HI~!
WOW, MISS DA-EH! TALK SENSE TO HIM!
BASTARD, BASTARD, TOTAL BAS-TARD!

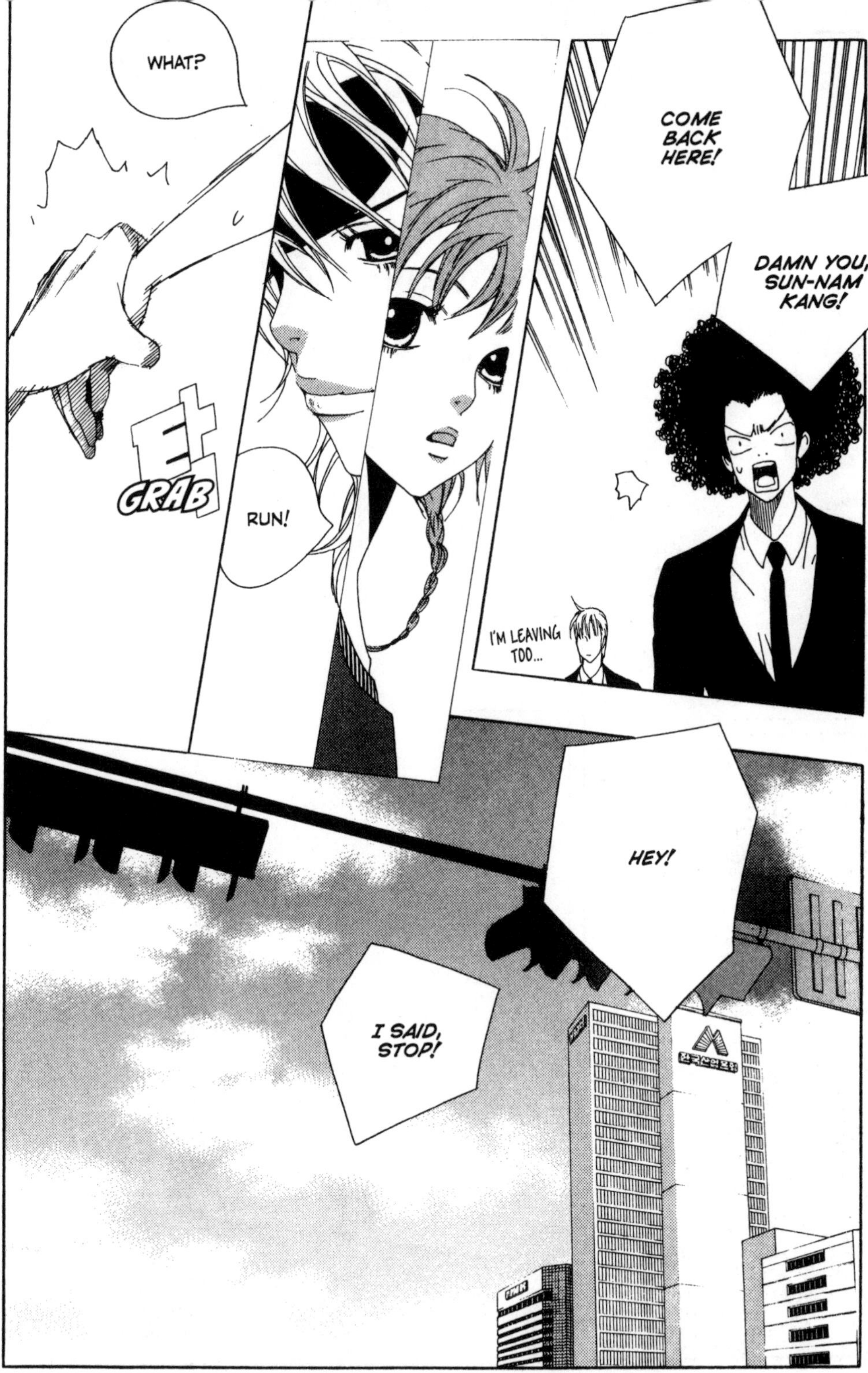
WHAT?
GRAB
RUN!
COME BACK HERE!
DAMN YOU, SUN-NAM KANG!
I'M LEAVING TOO...
HEY!
I SAID, STOP!

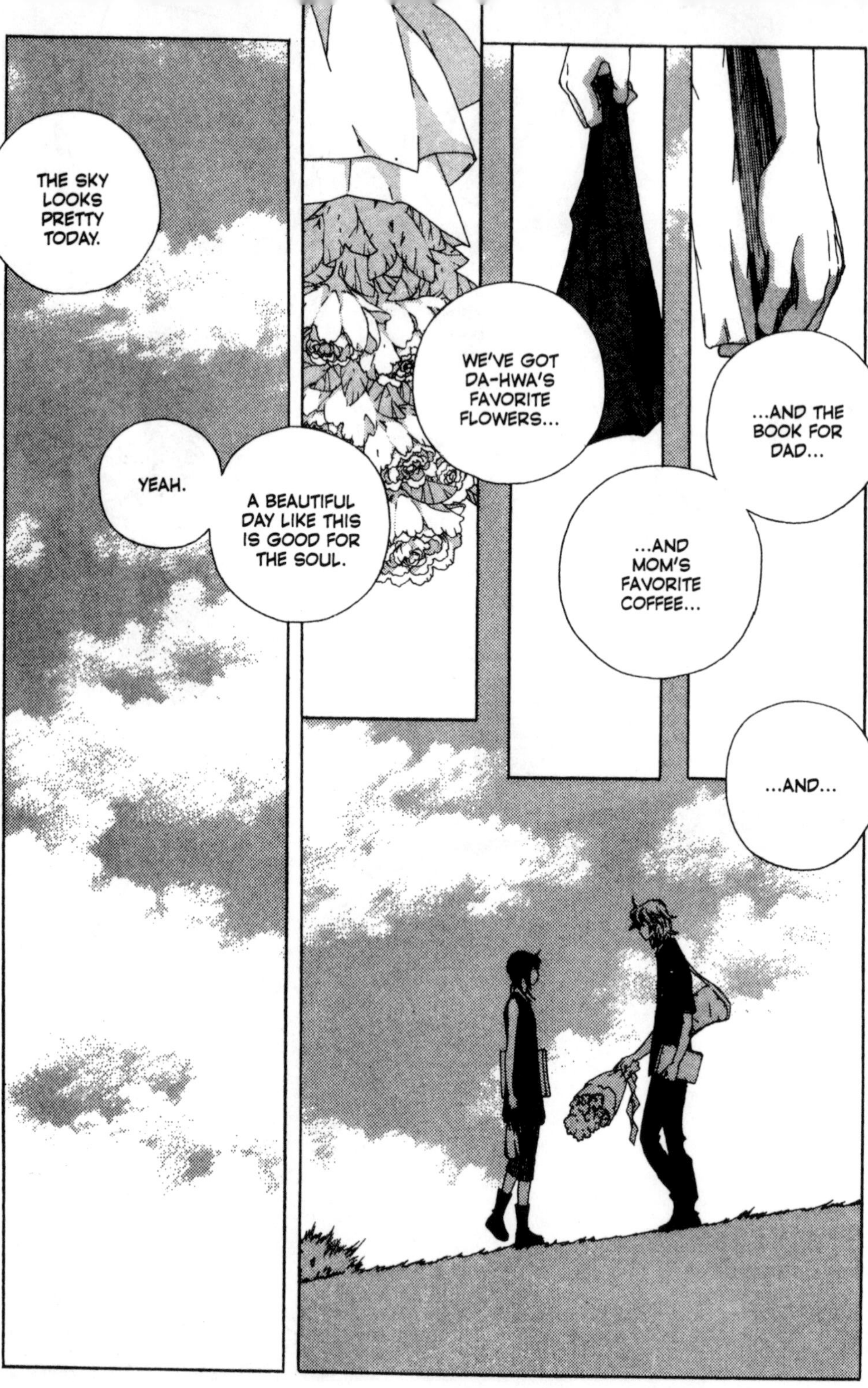
THE SKY LOOKS PRETTY TODAY.
YEAH.
A BEAUTIFUL DAY LIKE THIS IS GOOD FOR THE SOUL.
WE'VE GOT DA-HWA'S FAVORITE FLOWERS...
...AND MOM'S FAVORITE COFFEE...
...AND THE BOOK FOR DAD...
...AND...

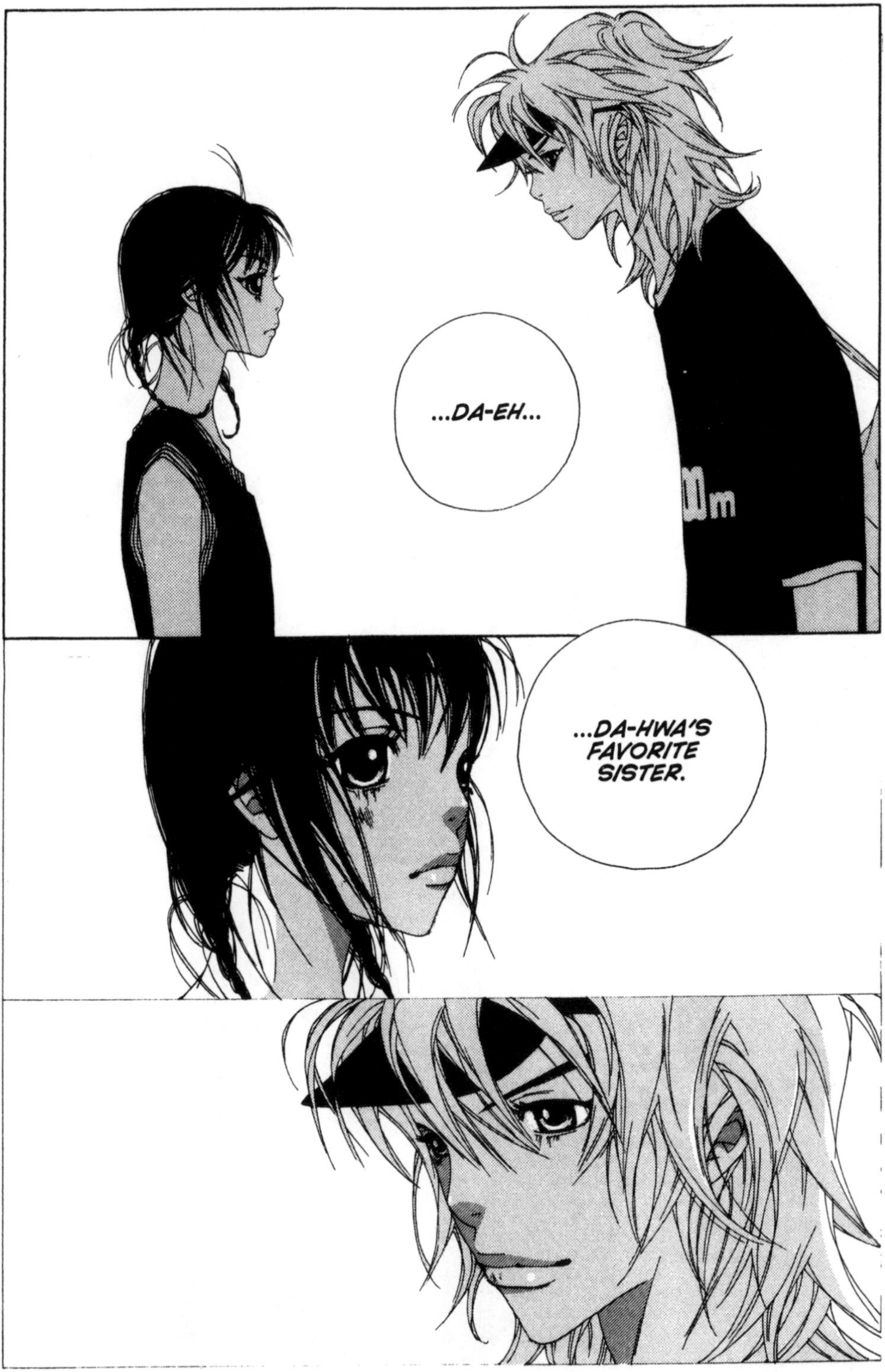
...DA-EH...
...DA-HWA'S FAVORITE SISTER.

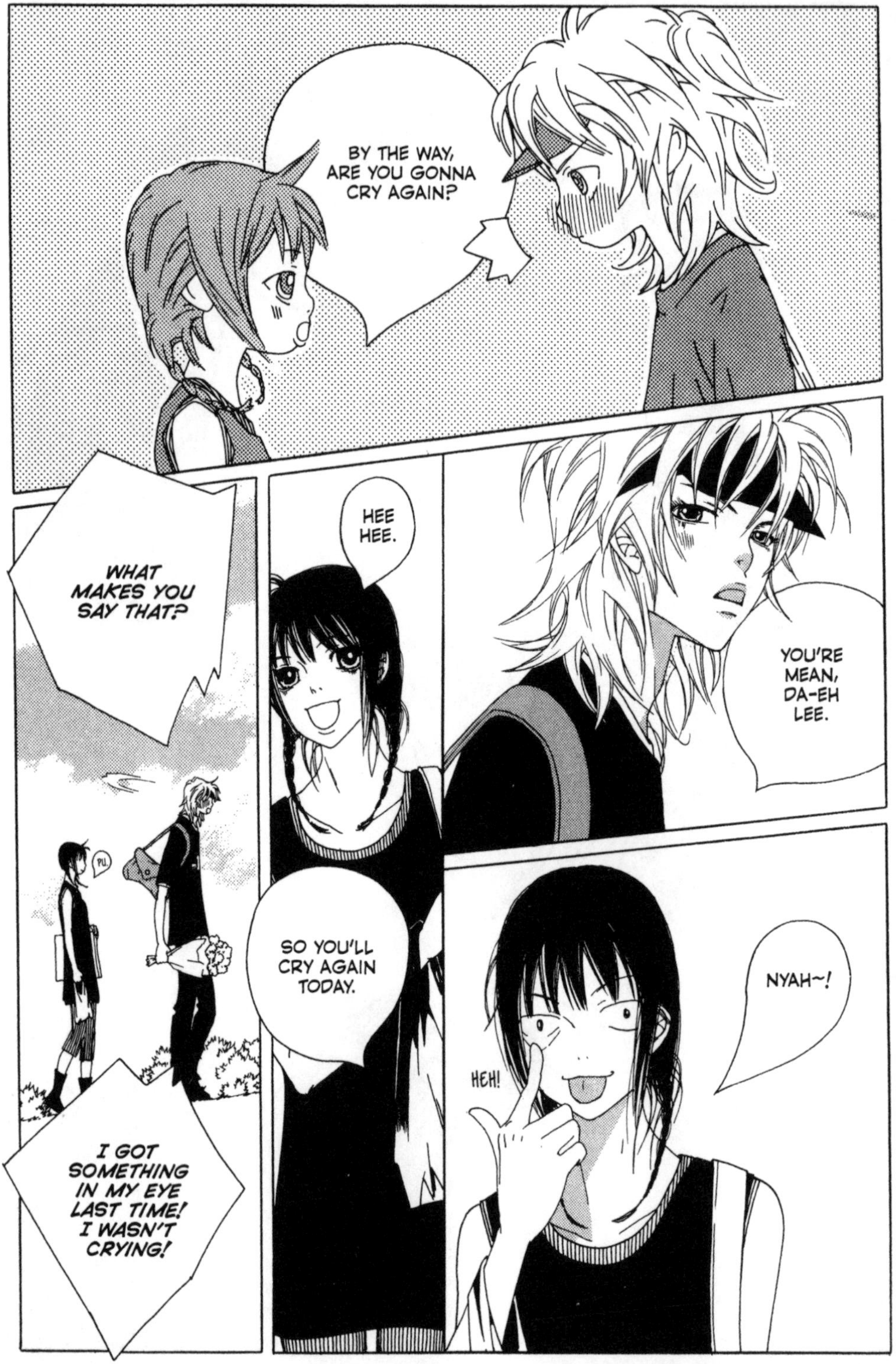
BY THE WAY, ARE YOU GONNA CRY AGAIN?
WHAT MAKES YOU SAY THAT?
PU.
I GOT SOMETHING IN MY EYE LAST TIME! I WASN'T CRYING!
HEE HEE.
SO YOU'LL CRY AGAIN TODAY.
YOU'RE MEAN, DA-EH LEE.
HEH!
NYAH~!

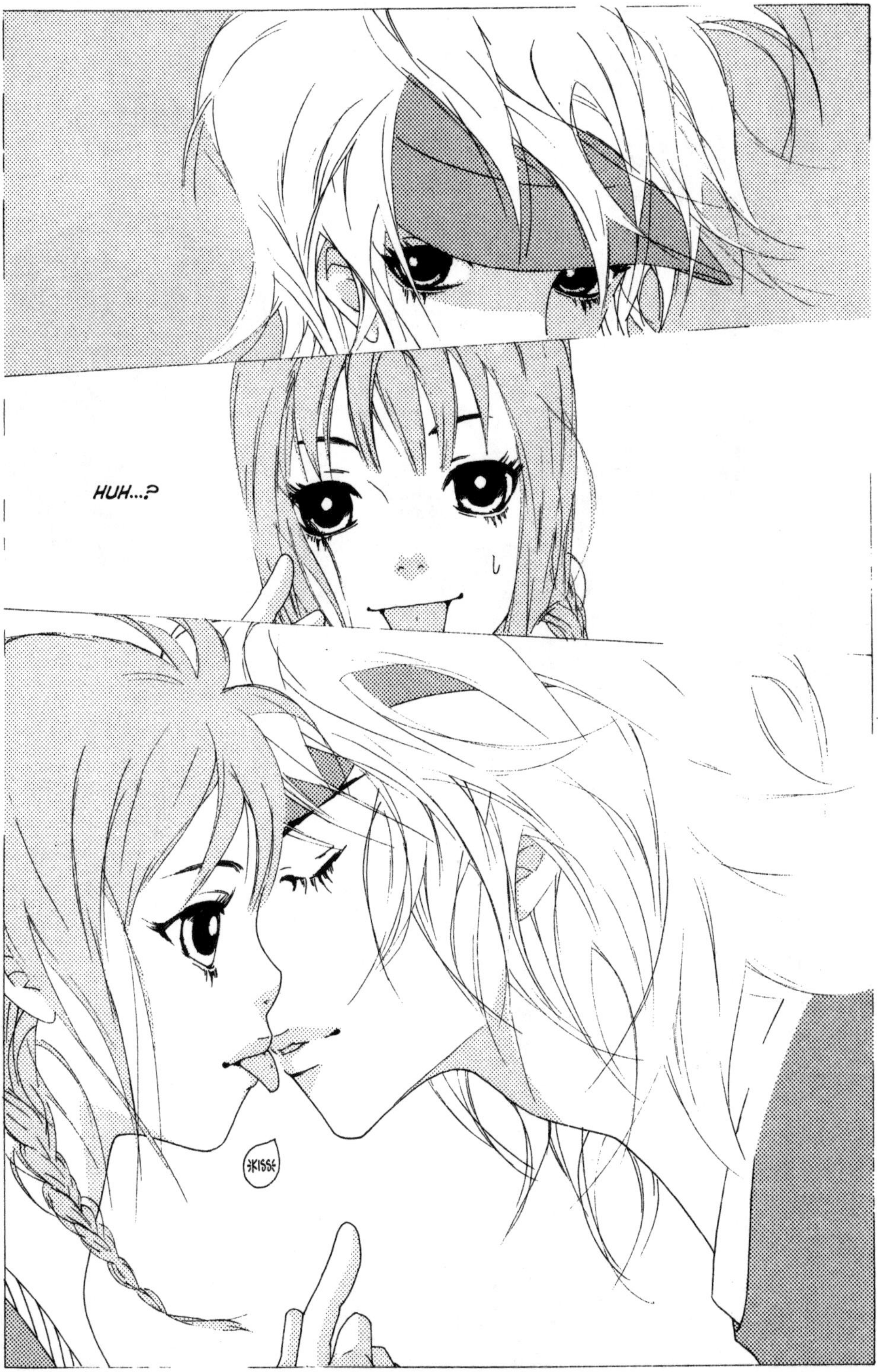
HUH...?
KISS

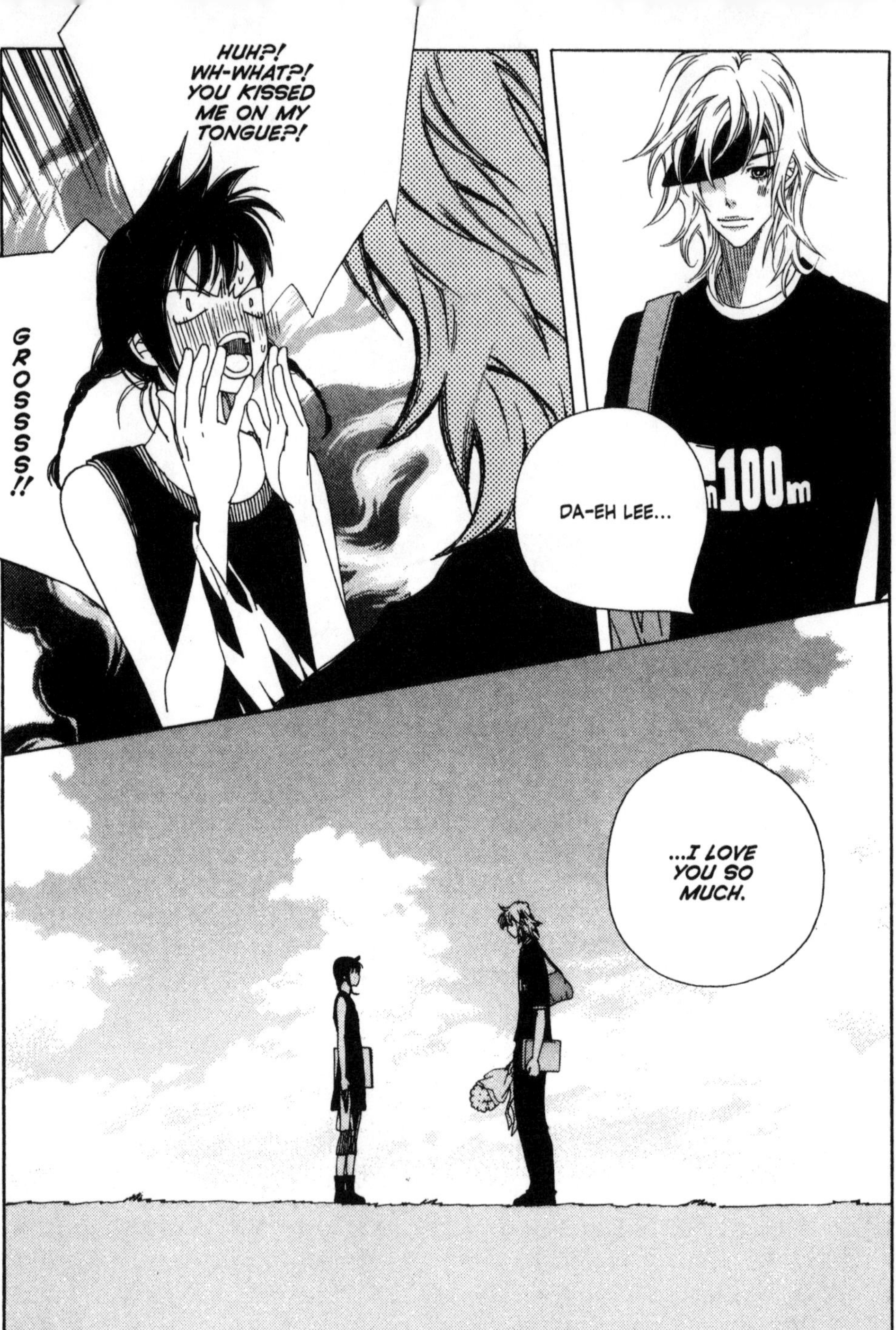
HUH?! WH-WHAT?! YOU KISSED ME ON MY TONGUE?!
GROSSSS!!
100m
DA-EH LEE...
...I LOVE YOU SO MUCH.

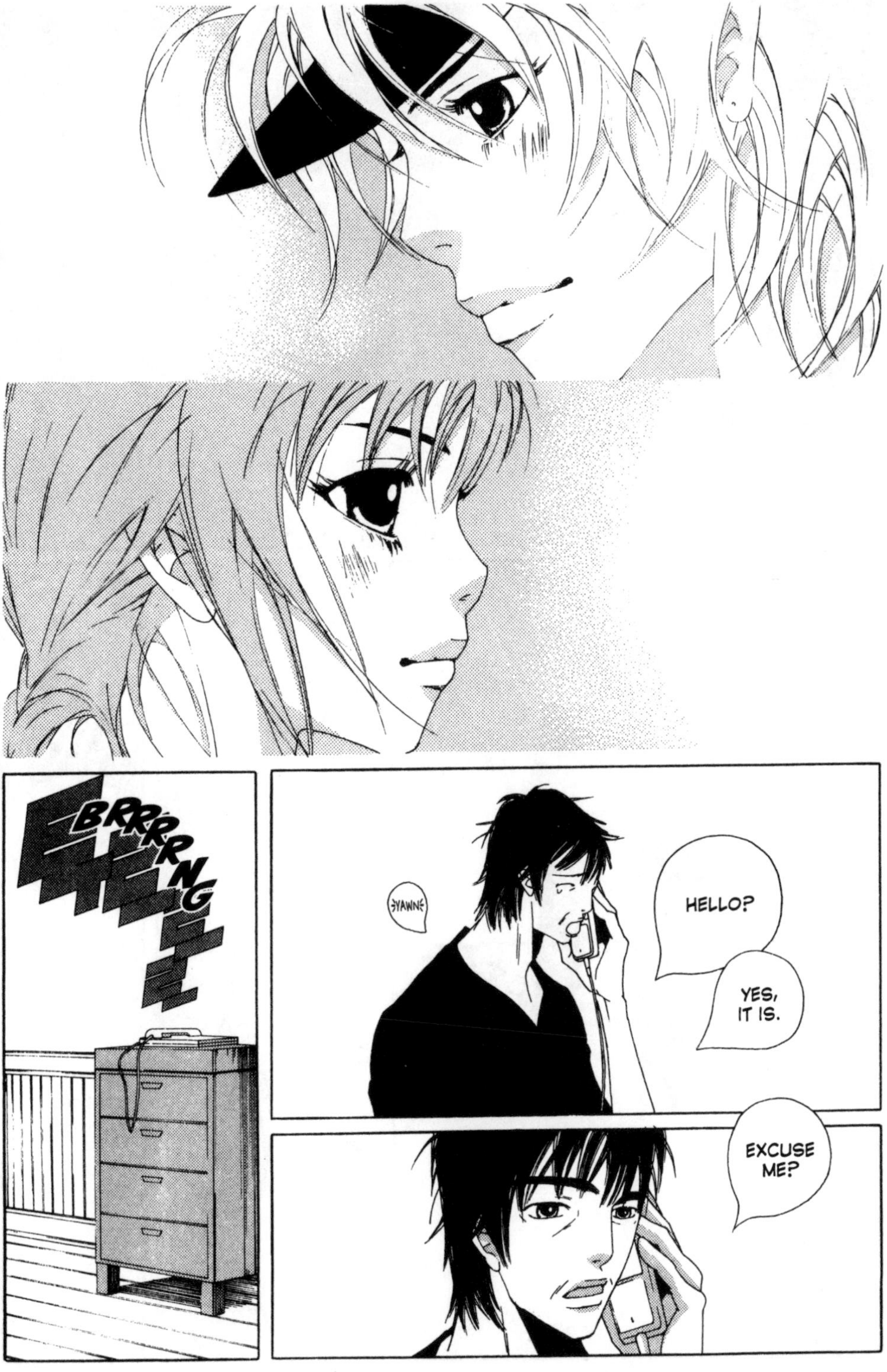
BRRRRNG
YAWN
HELLO?
YES, IT IS.
EXCUSE ME?

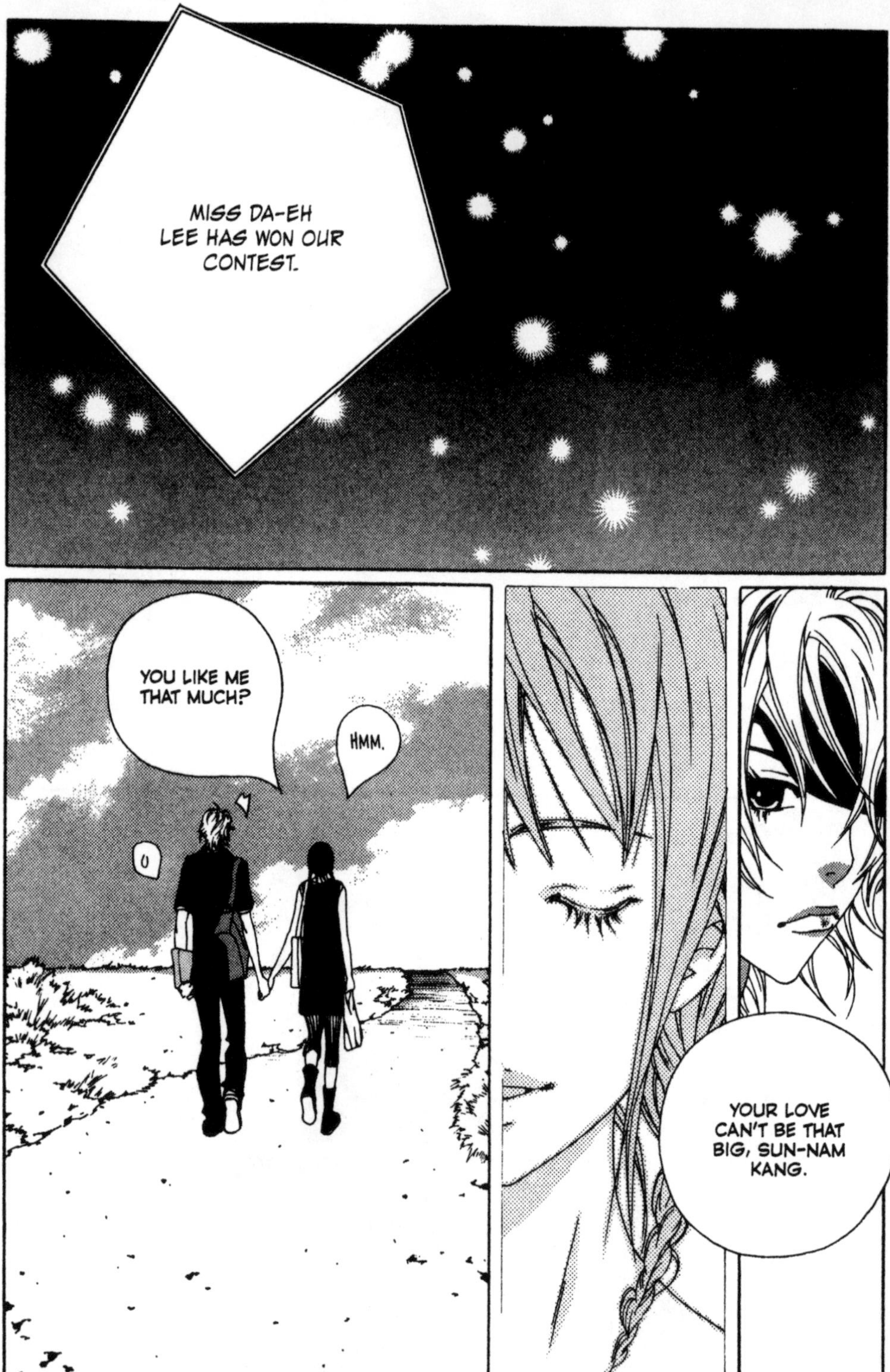
MISS DA-EH LEE HAS WON OUR CONTEST.
YOU LIKE ME THAT MUCH?
HMM.
YOUR LOVE CAN'T BE THAT BIG, SUN-NAM KANG.

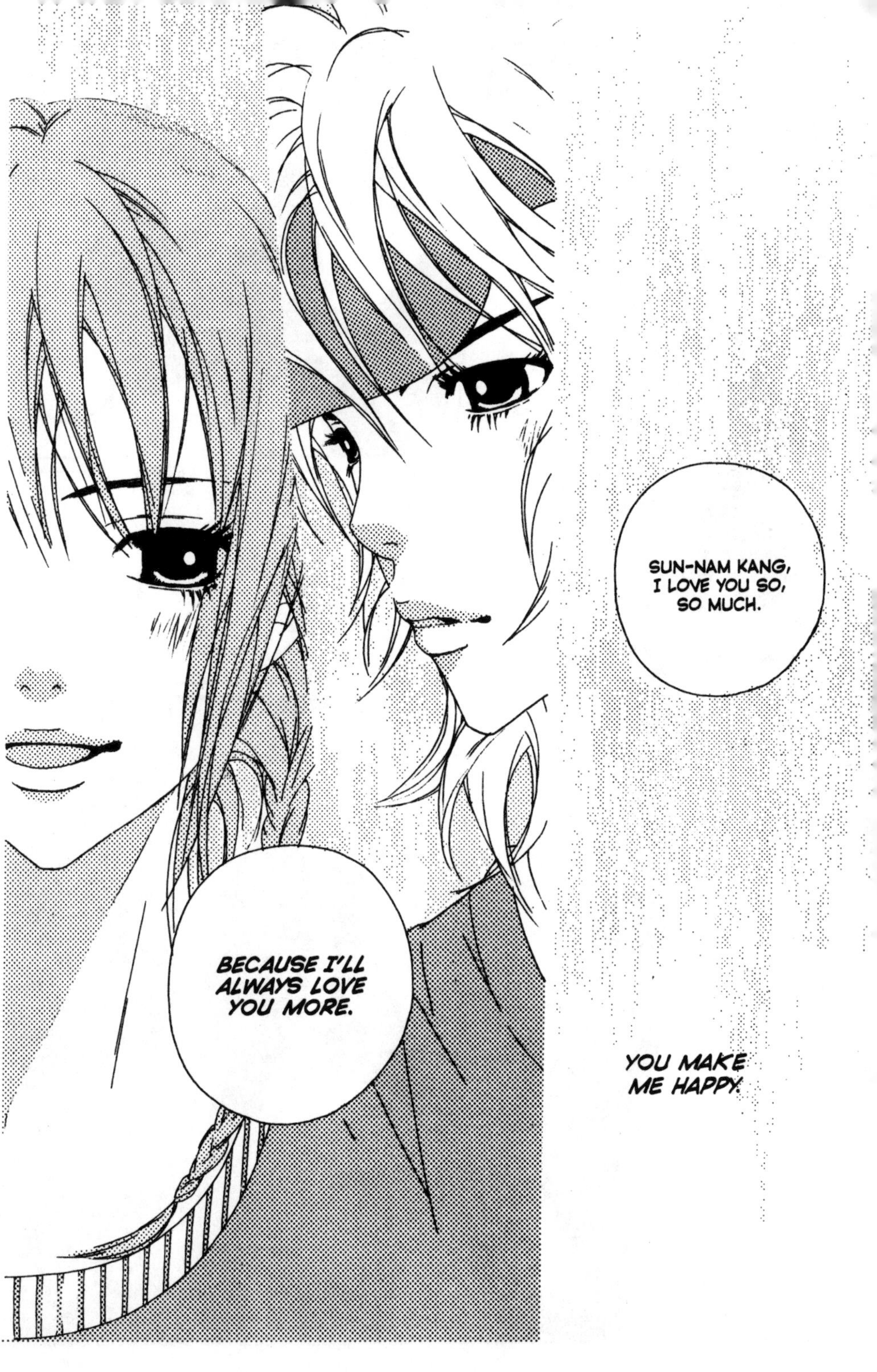
SUN-NAM KANG, I LOVE YOU SO, SO MUCH.
BECAUSE I'LL ALWAYS LOVE YOU MORE.
YOU MAKE ME HAPPY.

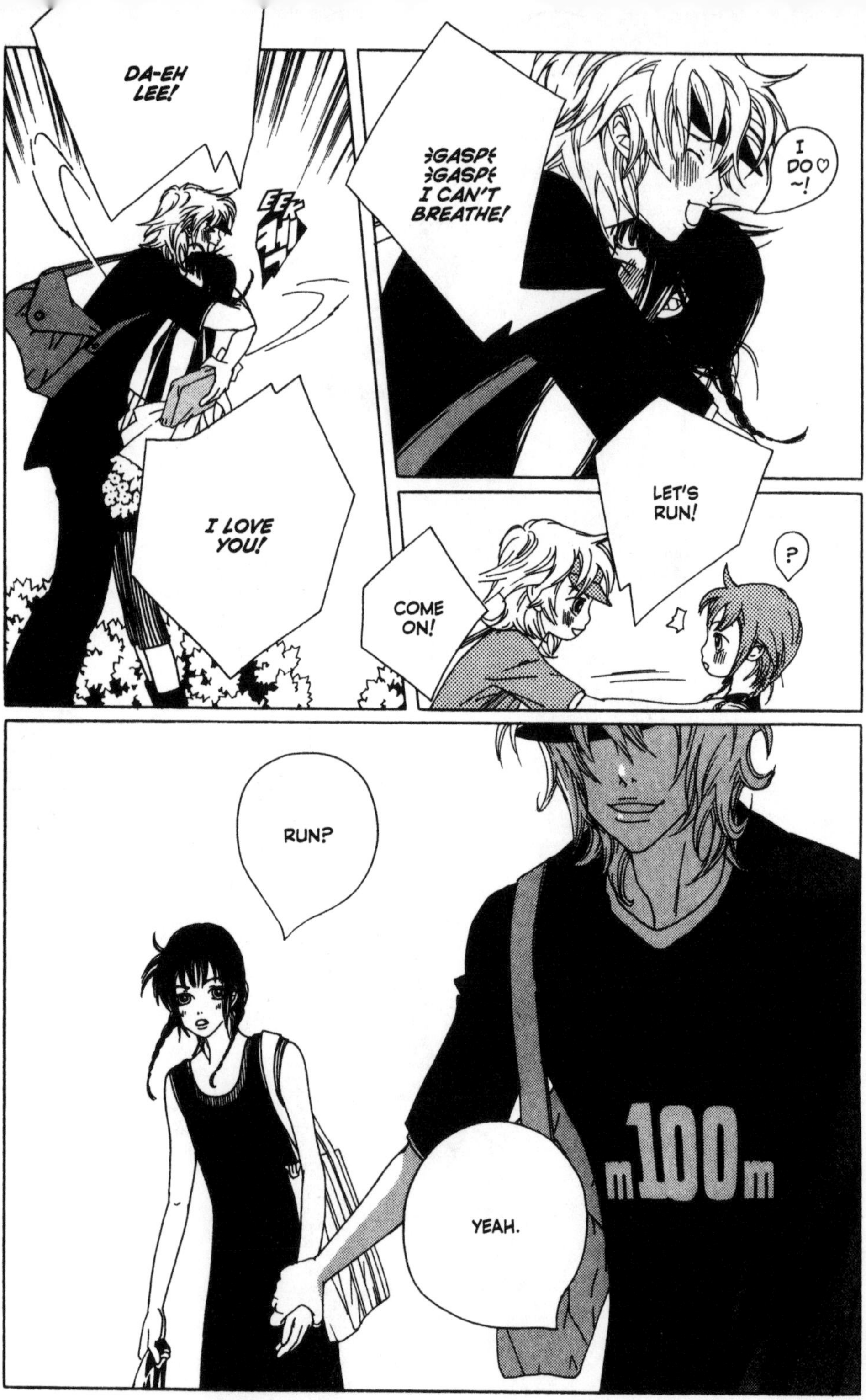
DA-EH LEE!
EEK
I LOVE YOU!
ꔮGASPꔮ ꔮGASPꔮ I CAN'T BREATHE!
I DO♡ ~!
COME ON!
LET'S RUN!
?
RUN?
YEAH.

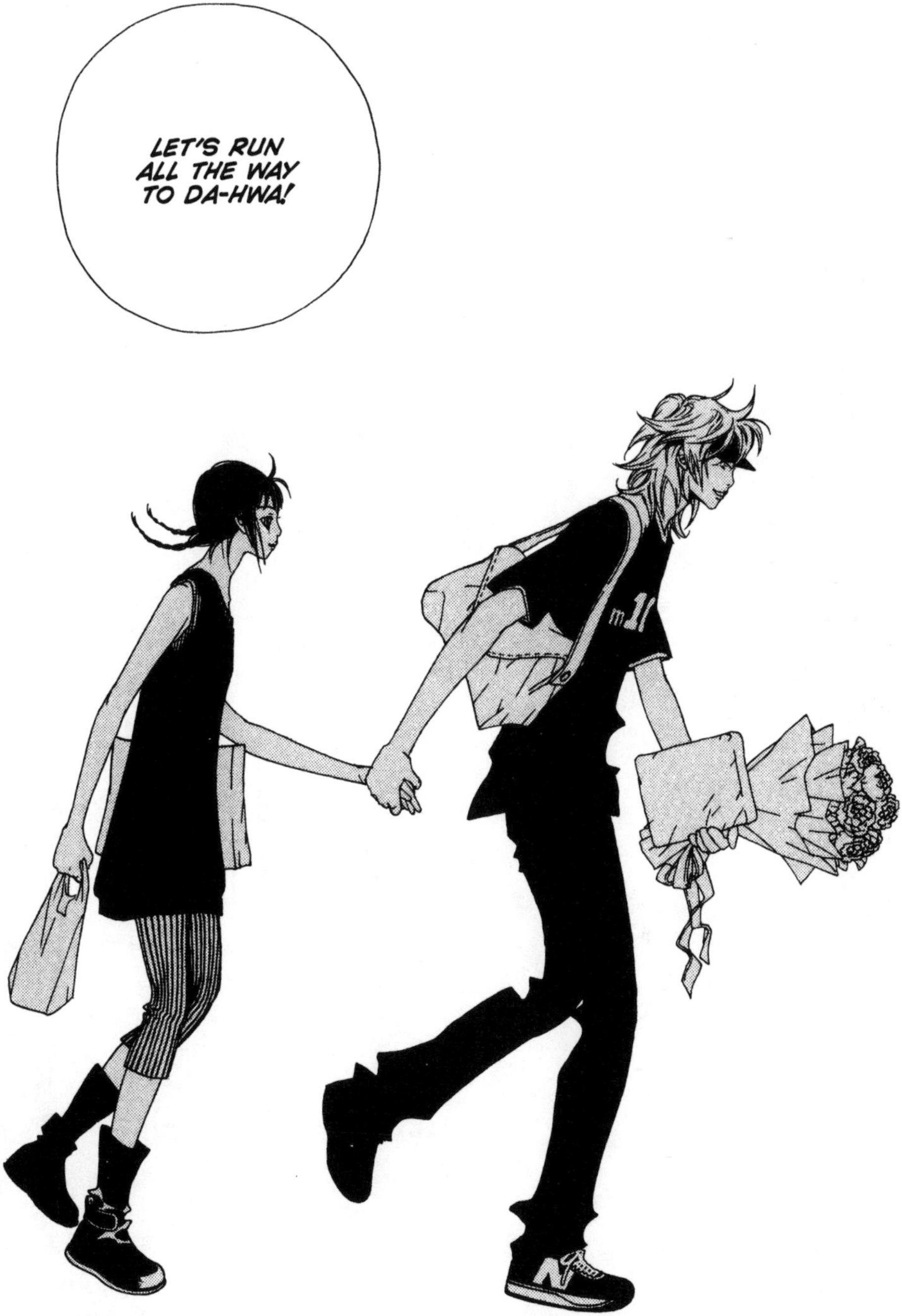
LET'S RUN ALL THE WAY TO DA-HWA!

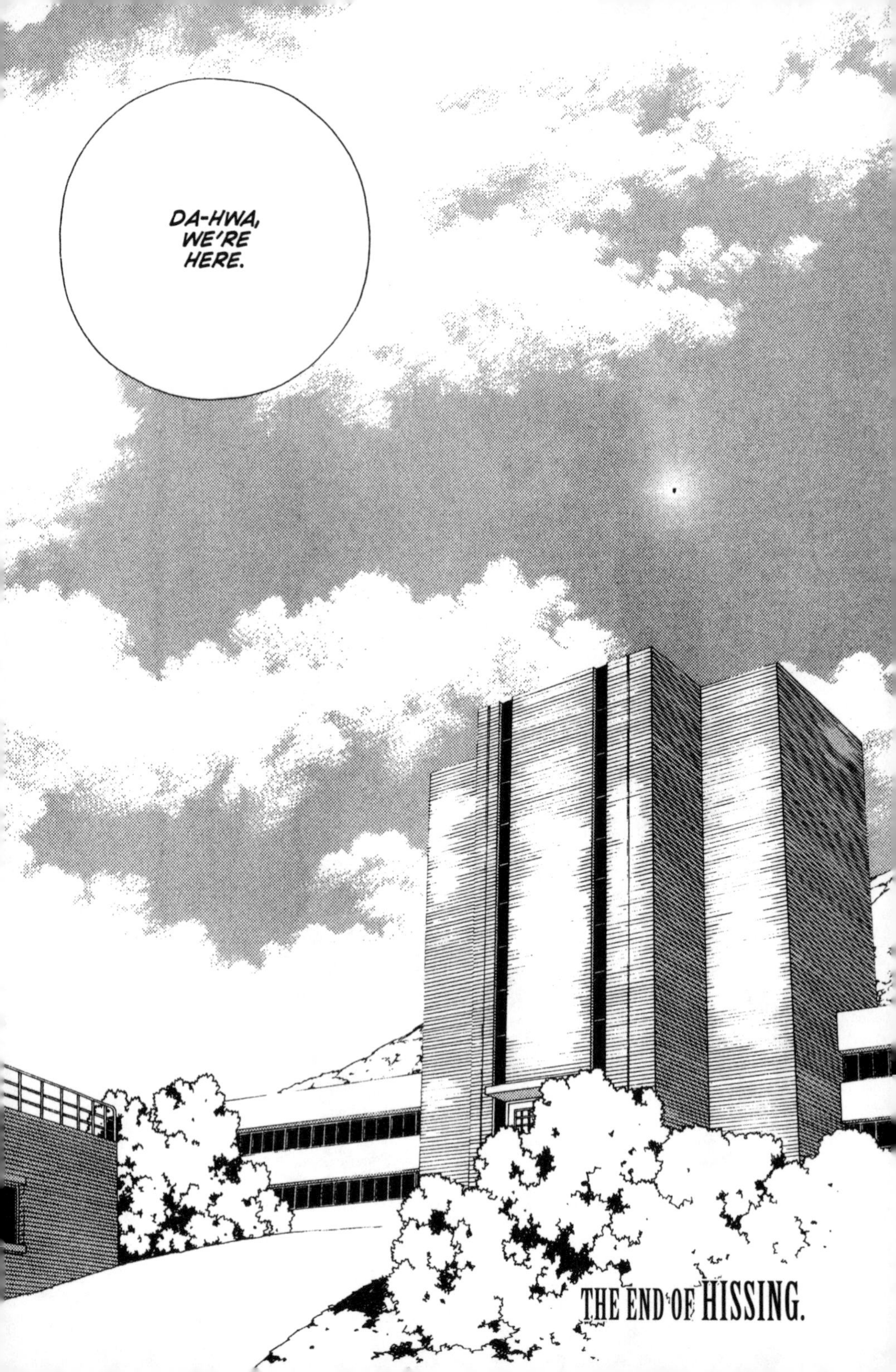
DA-HWA, WE'RE HERE.
THE END OF HISSING.

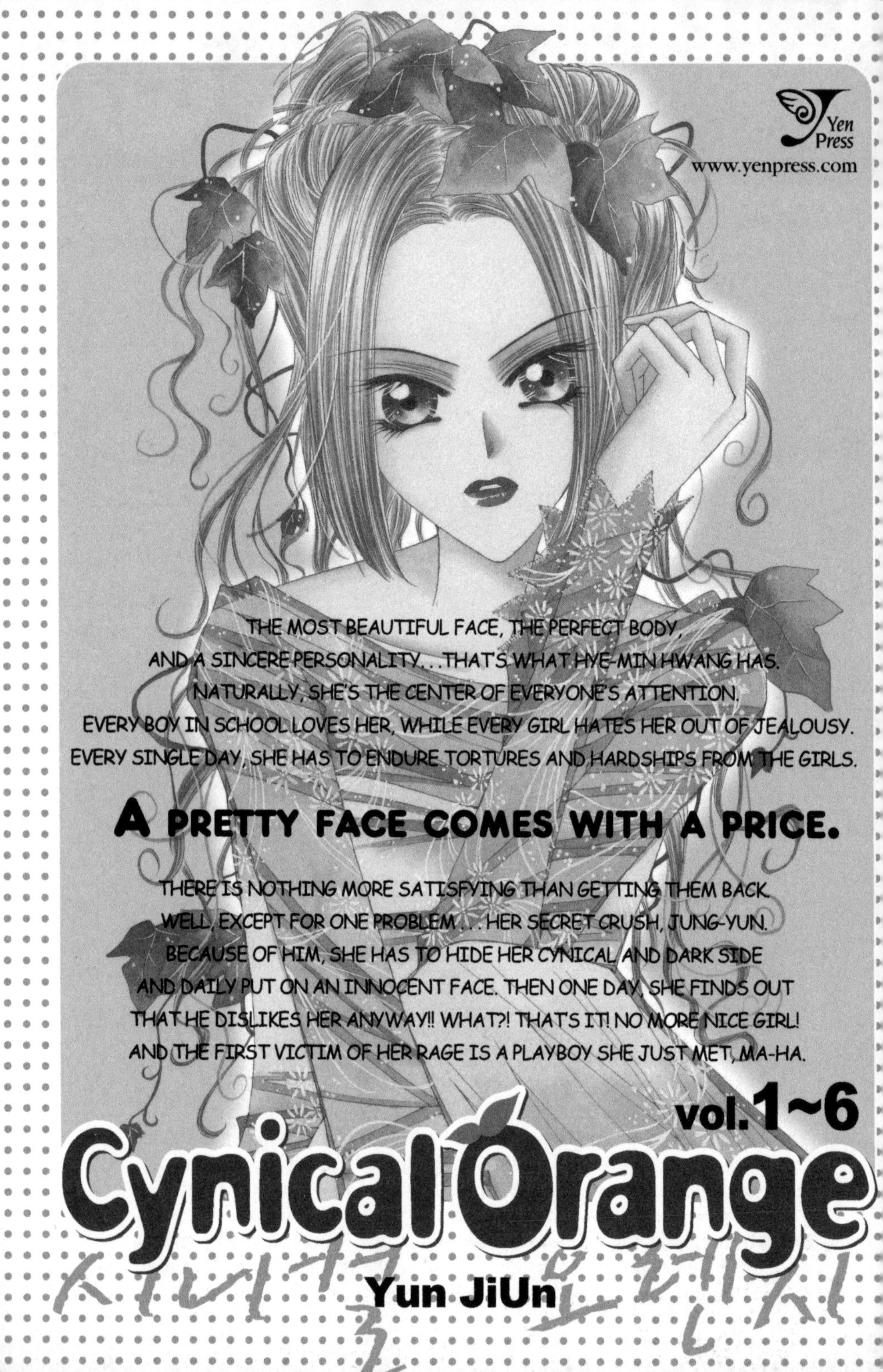
Yen Press
www.yenpress.com
THE MOST BEAUTIFUL FACE, THE PERFECT BODY,
AND A SINCERE PERSONALITY. . .THAT'S WHAT HYE-MIN HWANG HAS.
NATURALLY, SHE'S THE CENTER OF EVERYONE'S ATTENTION.
EVERY BOY IN SCHOOL LOVES HER, WHILE EVERY GIRL HATES HER OUT OF JEALOUSY.
EVERY SINGLE DAY, SHE HAS TO ENDURE TORTURES AND HARDSHIPS FROM THE GIRLS.
A PRETTY FACE COMES WITH A PRICE.
THERE IS NOTHING MORE SATISFYING THAN GETTING THEM BACK.
WELL, EXCEPT FOR ONE PROBLEM . . . HER SECRET CRUSH, JUNG-YUN.
BECAUSE OF HIM, SHE HAS TO HIDE HER CYNICAL AND DARK SIDE
AND DAILY PUT ON AN INNOCENT FACE. THEN ONE DAY, SHE FINDS OUT
THAT HE DISLIKES HER ANYWAY!! WHAT?! THAT'S IT! NO MORE NICE GIRL!
AND THE FIRST VICTIM OF HER RAGE IS A PLAYBOY SHE JUST MET, MA-HA.
vol.1~6
Cynical Orange
시니컬 오렌지
Yun JiUn

Hissing vol. 6

Story and art by EunYoung Kang

Translation: June Um
English Adaptation: Jamie S. Rich
Lettering: Terri Delgado

HISSING, Vol. 6 © 2005 EunYoung Kang. All rights reserved. First published in Korea in 2005 by Seoul Cultural Publishers, Inc. English translation rights arranged by Seoul Cultural Publishers, Inc.

English translation © 2009 Hachette Book Group, Inc.

Yen Press
Hachette Book Group
237 Park Avenue, New York, NY 10017

Visit our Web sites at www.HachetteBookGroup.com and www.YenPress.com.

Yen Press is an imprint of Hachette Book Group, Inc. The Yen Press name and logo are trademarks of Hachette Book Group, Inc.

First Yen Press Edition: March 2009

ISBN: 978-0-7595-2885-7

10 9 8 7 6 5 4 3 2 1

BVG

Printed in the United States of America